UNCTAD: Conflict and Compromise

UNCTAD
Conflict and
Compromise

The Third World's Quest for an Equitable World
Economic Order through the United Nations

by

BRANISLAV GOSOVIC

Ph. D., University of California, Berkeley

A.W. SIJTHOFF - LEIDEN 1972

338.9106
D69u
85868
Nov. 1973

ISBN 90 286 0091 4

Library of Congress Catalog Card Number: 79-157410
© A. W. Sijthoff International Publishing Company N.V. 1971

Printed in the Netherlands.

mami, tati, beki
i ljerki

ACKNOWLEDGEMENTS

This study represents the abridged and updated version of a doctoral thesis in political science, submitted in March 1970 at the University of California in Berkeley. It builds upon my monograph "UNCTAD: North-South Encounter," published in 1968 in *International Conciliation.*

My special thanks are due to Professor Ernst B. Haas, who guided my research, encouraged me to endure and showed great patience in reading the many drafts of the manuscript.

I owe my gratitude also to Professors Leo Mates, Paul Seabury and Jean Siotis.

A great number of international civil servants and delegates of various countries patiently withstood my many persistent and often naive queries and it is thanks to their kindness that I have managed to gain a better understanding of the issues involved.

Diego Cordovez, Christopher Eckenstein and W. R. Malinowski were extremely helpful and most stimulating with their criticisms and comments during the various stages of writing. Paul Berthoud, Bernard Chidzero, Eugene Chossudovsky, Sidney Dell, Said El-Naggar, Guy Erb, P. P. Kanthan, Alfred Maizels, David Millwood, S. Narasimhan, Ljubomir Sekulic, Johann Steinbacher, Karel Svec, B. N. Swarup, Glisa Tadic and Jorge Viteri de la Huerta gave me some valuable suggestions in connection with different sections and chapters of the manuscript. It goes without saying that they bear no responsibility whatsoever for my errors and omissions, faults of judgment, oversimplifications, insufficient and incomplete data, and plain inaccuracies.

Boyana Ristich, R. S. Arora, D. M. Kalhan, S.C., Ronald E. Williams and David Millwood helped in editing the manuscript, and S. S. Raman, Dorothy Thompson, Albertine de Barry and Maureen Henderson undertook the most thankless task of the typing of the text.

I am indebted to Kathryn D. Lewis, and to Olgivanna Lloyd Wright, Paul Sjeklocha and Slavko Komar. Ljerka Gosovic patiently stood by my side throughout the period, typed many drafts of various chapters, and did not complain excessively about my preoccupation with UNCTAD.

Belgrade, June 1971   *B. G.*

INTRODUCTION

The economic, social and political emancipation of a large number of Third World nations is one of the fundamental challenges to the contemporary international system. At the inter-nation level it would seem to recall certain domestic processes of the nineteenth and early twentieth centuries in Europe and North America; much as the working classes then felt that they were being exploited under capitalism, the developing countries today feel that they have for long been exploited in the world economy and prevented from obtaining their just share in the growth of world riches. They are fighting against the concepts and rules devised in the past, which help perpetuate their inferior status and which inordinately favor the industrialized capitalist nations. They strive for a new international division of labor which would allow them a more rapid industrial growth, and demand an international application of income redistribution policies. The expectations and aspirations of the developing countries are high, and they incessantly press for policy changes. However, their aims are hindered by the fact that they face a group of countries with superior economic power who molded the present international economic system and find it highly advantageous to preserve the *status quo*. Moreover, the international community which should come to their assistance is basically selfish and lacking in solidarity. Admittedly, the members of this community are becoming more and more closely linked. Modern means of warfare, communications and transport, technological progress, and the highly advanced economies of certain states have speeded up this process. However, those directly involved often find it difficult to grasp the dynamics of international relations,[1] and although most men and governments—willing or not—participate in this forward thrust of

1. "Again, reality is made up not just of the tangible facts which we have before us now, but also of the facts still to unfold. Realism is, moreover, the ability to discern what could happen when we do not know how, or do not wish, to take deliberate and timely action to shape the course of events." R. Prebisch, "Towards a New Trade Policy for Development," *Proceedings of the United Nations Conference on Trade and Development* (Geneva, 23 March-16 June 1964), Vol. II, p. 63. (Hereafter referred to as *Proceedings*.)

international community building, they continue to act within a familiar framework of concepts and institutions that lag behind the times and correspond to past situations. Seldom do they anticipate change through their actions. Furthermore since concepts, rules and institutions are imbedded in the perceived and/or true interests of those parties that find themselves in control at a given time in history, innovation becomes much more difficult.

History is made of conflicts between opposing interests, and indeed, such conflicts have been an essential source of progress for humanity since time immemorial. In recent years, the conflict between the more and less economically developed parts of the world has given rise to the United Nations Conference on Trade and Development (UNCTAD), the first international organization almost entirely devoted to the problems of the developing countries.[2] Even though the underlying causes which found their expression in UNCTAD call for revolutionary solutions, UNCTAD is in fact a forum for conciliation and reform. It proposes adjustments in the existing system, to make it equitable for all nations; it is an instrument to promote the economic development of the Third World.

Our study is conceived around the conflict/conciliation nexus between the developed nations of the West and the developing countries of the South. We have adopted a descriptive-analytical approach to determine how successful UNCTAD is as a forum for learning and consensus-building. In this study we shall discuss UNCTAD's origins, its substantive endeavors, its institutional traits and evolution, and its participants and their interaction.

---

2. The problem of labelling different groups of states involves a number of classifying, political and methodological difficulties, which we shall thoughtfully avoid and simply adhere to the usage of terms common in UNCTAD. Throughout the text *developed countries* refers to the countries that are members of the Organization for Economic Cooperation and Development (OECD), plus Australia, Finland and New Zealand. These countries are also referred to as "West", "western", "advanced", "developed market economies", "North", "rich", and the "B Group". The *socialist countries* refers to countries of Eastern Europe (except Yugoslavia). These countries are also spoken of as "centrally planned economies", "East", and the "D Group". The *developing countries* are all the members of the "Group of 77". We also refer to this group as the "South", "Third World", "poor", and "less-advanced". (The above groupings do not take into account those countries which were not members of UNCTAD at the time of this writing.)

TABLE OF CONTENTS

Acknowledgements   VII

Introduction   IX

Abbreviations   XIII

PART ONE   *The Origins of UNCTAD*   1

Chapter I   — The Historical Background of UNCTAD   3
Chapter II   — The 1964 Geneva Conference on Trade
                  and Development   28

PART TWO   *Substantive Policies in UNCTAD: The*
                Evolution of Consensus   61

Chapter III   — Manufactures   65
Chapter IV   — Commodities   93
Chapter V   — Financing   115
Chapter VI   — Shipping   138
Chapter VII   — Some Other Issue Areas   153
Part II   — Conclusion   171

PART THREE   *The Institutionalization of UNCTAD*   173

Chapter VIII   — UNCTAD Within the United Nations   177
Chapter IX   — Relations between GATT and UNCTAD   198
Chapter X   — UNCTAD—A Normative Forum or ...   218
Chapter XI   — Task Expansion   240
Part III   — Conclusion   263

PART FOUR   *Actors and Conflict Resolution in UNCTAD*   267

Chapter XII   — The Groups in UNCTAD   271
Chapter XIII   — The UNCTAD Secretariat   304
Chapter XIV   — Decision-Making in UNCTAD   316

Postscript   332

Bibliography   335

Index   340

XII

ABBREVIATIONS

ACABQ	Advisory Committee on Administrative and Budgetary Questions
ACAST	Advisory Committee on the Application of Science and Technology to Development
ACC	Administrative Committee on Coordination
BTN	Brussels Tariff Nomenclature
CECLA	Special Commission on Latin American Coordination
CENSA	Committee of the European National Shipowners' Association
CIAP	Committee on the Alliance for Progress
CICT	Commission on International Commodity Trade
CMEA	Council for Mutual Economic Assistance
CPC	Committee on Program and Coordination
DAC	Development Assistance Committee
ECA	Economic Commission for Africa
ECAFE	Economic Commission for Asia and the Far East
ECE	Economic Commission for Europe
ECLA	Economic Commission for Latin America
ECOSOC	Economic and Social Council
EEC	European Economic Community
EFTA	European Free Trade Association
EPTA	Expanded Program of Technical Assistance
ESA	Department of Economic and Social Affairs of the UN Secretariat
FAO	Food and Agriculture Organization
GA	General Assembly
GATT	General Agreement on Tariffs and Trade
GNP	Gross national product
GSP	General system (scheme) of preferences
IACB	Inter-Agency Consultative Board
IAEA	International Atomic Energy Agency
IATA	International Air Transport Association
IBRD	International Bank for Reconstruction and Development

ICC	International Coffee Council
ICCICA	Interim Coordinating Committee for International Commodity Agreements
ICITO	Interim Commission of the International Trade Organization
IDA	International Development Association
IFC	International Finance Corporation
ILO	International Labour Organisation
IMCO	International Maritime Consultative Organization
IMF	International Monetary Fund
ITC	International Trade Center
ITO	International Trade Organization
IWC	International Wheat Council
LAFTA	Latin American Free Trade Association
LDDCs	Least developed among developing countries
MFN	Most favored nation
OAU	Organization of African Unity
OECD	Organization for Economic Cooperation and Development
OEEC	Organization for European Economic Cooperation
OPEC	Organization of Petroleum Exporting Countries
OTC	Organization for Trade Cooperation
SDR	Special drawing rights
SITC	Standard International Trade Classification
SUNFED	Special United Nations Fund for Economic Development
TARS	Technical Assistance Recruitment Service
TDB	Trade and Development Board
TNC	Trade Negotiations Committee
UNCITRAL	United Nations Commission on International Trade Law
UNCTAD	United Nations Conference on Trade and Development
UNDP	United Nations Development Programme
UNESCO	United Nations Educational, Scientific and Cultural Organization
UNESOB	United Nations Economic and Social Office in Beirut
UNIDO	United Nations Industrial Development Organization

PART ONE

The Origins of UNCTAD

Chapter I

THE HISTORICAL BACKGROUND OF UNCTAD

International Organizations and the Problem of Economic Development: Some General Remarks

As planned during and after the Second World War under the leadership of the United States, the network of international organizations which was supposed to deal with economic problems was essentially geared for preventing recurrence of the disastrous events of the 1930's. The problems discussed by these bodies in the early years of their existence concerned mainly the economic interests of the developed countries and were "viewed and solved" in keeping with the concepts and theories of the West.[1] This was particularly so in the case of the General Agreement on Tariffs and Trade (GATT), the International Monetary Fund (IMF), and the International Bank for Reconstruction and Development (IBRD). Even "the United Nations economic functions were also originally conceived as an agent of Northern interests."[2] Since the composition of the UN membership did not make this organization fully suitable for the developed countries' purposes, all significant economic matters were shifted to GATT, to the international financial and monetary agencies, and to purely western institutions such as the Organization for European Economic Cooperation (OEEC) (later to become the Organization for Economic Cooperation and Development (OECD)). In these organizations, the developing countries did not participate on an equal footing with the developed nations, either in the management of policies or in decision-making.[3] At the same time, the West showed no particular inclination to approach trade and development problems through the UN, and failed to partici-

1. W. Kotschnig, "The United Nations as an Instrument of Economic and Social Development," in R. N. Gardner and M. F. Millikan, eds., *The Global Partnership* (New York: F. A. Praeger, 1968), p. 18.
2. J. Pincus, *Trade, Aid and Development* (New York, N.Y.: McGraw Hill, 1967), p. 373. Of course, this interpretation of UN economic functions differs from what is stated in Article 55 of the UN Charter.
3. *Proceedings*, Vol. I, p. 193.

pate constructively and at a high level in the Economic and Social Council (ECOSOC) and in the Second Committee of the General Assembly.[4] Consequently, although one of the main areas of concern envisaged by the UN Charter was economic and social development, it actually remained a marginal issue in this organization until the mid-1950's.

Economic development on a global scale, in fact, was hardly recognized as the task of the entire international community two decades ago, and it was much lower on the scale of international priorities than post-war reconstruction. The Cold War further obstructed multilateral action within the UN. The problems of developing countries were "taken care of" almost solely through bilateral aid, which anyway was given primarily for political and security reasons. While the bipolar situation acted as a spur for the major powers to aid developing countries, the former colonial metropolises were attempting to preserve their influence in the colonies which were gaining, or had already gained independence. The donor countries showed little sympathy toward multilateral aid efforts. Thus, the first major organized action of developing countries in the economic sphere—the proposal to create a Special UN Fund for Economic Development (SUNFED)—proved abortive.

In the mid-1950's, the problem of the economic development of developing countries was gradually on its way to becoming one of the principal areas of concern in international organizations, particularly the U.N. The developing countries, many of which were trying to create a material base to make the political independence they had gained through the United Nations meaningful, were facing unfavorable economic situations and had unhappy experiences. It was natural that they should turn for help to this same international organization. The membership explosion in the United Nations and the influx of newly independent states changed the voting strength of different groups, and this by definition meant that the UN system had to become more oriented to the problems of developing countries. A gradual shift of emphasis toward economic and social questions was taking place.

Originally, the developing countries—which were relatively few at that time—found that the central organs of the UN were not sufficiently responsive to their demands for the examination in depth of the trade and economic problems of development. They therefore took these problems to the UN regional economic commissions—for Asia and the

4. R. Gardner, "Trade and Development in the UN: A Challenge to U.S. Policy" (A background paper, Council on Foreign Relations, March 31, 1966), p. 9.

4

Far East (ECAFE) and for Latin America (ECLA)—where the majority was clearly on their side and where their views counted. Although their efforts were frequently obstructed, it was there that the developing countries began systematically gathering the material for presenting their case in other international forums. ECLA, in particular, under the leadership of its Executive Secretary, Dr. Raúl Prebisch, played a very important role in spreading knowledge and understanding of the developing countries' problems, and proposing new economic relations between the industrial North and the "peripheral" South. Also, the socialist countries in the UN, strengthened by four newly-admitted members in 1954, began to criticize the international trade system. These countries felt hurt and discriminated against by the prevailing commercial rules and practices, and by the economic boycott to which they were subjected. By combining their grievances with the ones crystallizing in the developing world, the socialist countries felt that they could break the hegemony of the West in international economic institutions.[5] While calling for international trade meetings and for the creation of a new trade organization, they always emphasized the needs of the developing countries. Partly as a result of the pressure exerted by the socialist countries, a number of reports and studies were produced by the UN Secretariat on the principles and mechanisms of international trade. They drew attention to the link between trade and development, the instability of commodity exports receipts and the developing countries' balance of payments difficulties.[6] It is these first moves of the socialist states—and the Soviet Union in particular—that were subsequently taken advantage of by the developing countries, which adapted them to their own purposes and used them to transform UN activities concerning trade and development.

The problems which led to the 1964 United Nations Conference on Trade and Development—popularly known as the Geneva Conference —fall into two categories: (1) the economic difficulties common to all developing countries encountered in the 1950's in their efforts to achieve a satisfactory level of economic development—difficulties which often arose through no fault of the countries concerned and which generally could not be eliminated without a concerted action by the international community; and (2) the lacunae in the institutional framework which was supposed to help cope with such difficulties.

5. R. Gardner, "The United Nations Conference on Trade and Development," in *The Global Partnership, op. cit.,* p. 103.

6. C. Robertson, "The Creation of UNCTAD" (paper presented to the 7th World Congress of IPSA, Brussels, 1967), p. 8. Reproduced in R. W. Cox, *International Organisation: World Politics* (London: Macmillan, 1969), pp. 258-274.

Difficulties Encountered by Developing Countries in the 1950's which Hampered Their Economic Growth.

Developing countries have many economic characteristics in common. *Inter alia*, their *per capita* incomes are below a certain cut-off point [7]; their rate of income growth *per capita* is relatively low among other reasons because of high population growth; only a small percentage of their gross domestic product is devoted to investment; generally more than 50 percent of their labor force is engaged in agriculture and there is a shortage of technical and managerial skills. Their *per capita* investment in public works and services is also low.[8] Under these conditions capital goods, skilled labor, and a modern technology are necessary requirements for economic growth.

In actual practice when the needs of developing countries to import capital goods and technical knowledge were increasing, their export earnings and capacity to import what they needed were inadequate. In other words, the growth of import requirements was not matched by the growth of export earnings—earnings which were further drained by increasing debt service payments. The gap which resulted between the needs and the available resources could not be bridged with gold and foreign currency reserves, so the developing countries had to rely on importing capital. This was by no means a permanent solution. To aggravate the situation further, the terms of trade for their exports, mainly primary commodities, were worsening, while the prices of imported manufactures, particularly the prices of capital goods, were consistently increasing.[9]

The developing countries failed to attain a high rate of export

7. The definition of a cut-off point seems to be arbitrary. It depends on which organization and for what purpose the definition is made and used. *The World Bank Atlas of Per Capita Product and Population* (IBRD, September 1966), giving the data for 1963 and 1964, indicates that the only countries which could be considered as "developing" and had a *per capita* income above $500 were: Greece - $510, Spain - $530, Cyprus - $530, Uruguay - $540, Trinidad and Tobago - $590, Argentina - $650, Venezuela - $780, Israel - $1070, and Kuwait - $3290. (Note that "$" throughout the text indicates U.S. dollars.)

8. Based on Pincus, *op. cit.*, p. 118. At this point, there is no commonly accepted set of indicators of under-development. G. M. Meier and R. E. Baldwin in *Economic Development - Theory, History, Policy* (New York: J. Wiley and Sons, 1957), p. 273, suggest several economic characteristics of an underdeveloped country: 1. it is a producer of primary products; 2. it faces population pressures; 3. it has underdeveloped natural resources; 4. it has an economically backward population; 5. it is capital deficient; and 6. it is foreign trade oriented.

9. See the *Final Act, Proceedings,* Vol. I, p. 4. According to Prebisch's estimate, between 1950 and 1961 the terms of trade for primary commodities fell by 26 percent in relation to those of manufactures, mainly owing to the rise in the prices of the latter (petroleum excluded). Prebisch, *op. cit.*, p. 13.

expansion: it was 8.4 percent *per annum* in the early 1950's and only 5 percent in the early 1960's. Although their exports increased by 50 percent in the period 1950-1962 (from $19.2 billion to $28.9 billion), their share in world exports declined from nearly $1/3$ in 1950 to slightly more than $1/5$ in 1962. The slower expansion of developing countries' exports and the worsening terms of trade [10] were due mainly to the fact that they exchanged primary goods for manufactures (commodities accounted for 90 percent of their exports). The primary product exports of developing countries expanded slowly because of the growing output of primary commodities in the developed countries,[11] which were insulated by agricultural protectionism; the use of synthetics and substitutes; the slow increase in demand for food from the developed countries; and the low elasticity of demand for some commodities with respect to price changes. Furthermore, prices of commodities declined following the Korean War. As a result, the developing countries' export surplus of the 1950's became by 1962 a deficit of $2.3 billion.[12]

During the 1950's most developing countries were oriented toward import substitution as the optimal way to achieve industrialization. The stress was placed on balanced growth rather than on specialization for export markets. They learned eventually that the small size of most domestic markets meant high costs and inefficiencies in industrialization. This, combined with the deteriorating terms of trade, led in the late 1950's to the realization that import substitution could be of limited assistance, and that it was necessary to increase exports to obtain sufficient foreign currency to pay for strategic imports. The export of manufactures and semi-manufactures could fulfil both needs: it could raise the export earnings of developing countries above what they could get through traditional exports, and it could bring about more efficient industrialization with their products exposed to competition in the world market.[13] Unfortunately, attempts by the develop-

10. This was partly due to the fact that the supply growth of developing countries' products outpaced the growth of demand for them. Some of the reasons for this were: immobility of resources leading to continued production of traditional crops, high prices during the Korean War bringing about the expansion of supply (minerals and tree crops), new countries seeking additional foreign trade sources and becoming significant producers of coffee, tea, petroleum, etc. Thus, the UN index of developing countries' export prices declined from the peak of 113 in 1951 to 84 in 1962. Pincus, *op. cit.*, pp. 233-234.

11. Note that the share of industrial countries in world exports of primary commodities rose from 47 percent in 1950 to 55 percent in 1961. In the same period the share of developing countries decreased from 41 percent to 29 percent (petroleum excluded). Prebisch, *op. cit.*, p. 13.

12. This paragraph is based on the *Final Act, Proceedings*, Vol. I, pp. 6-7, and Pincus, *ibid.*

13. I. Frank, "The Role of Trade in Economic Development," in *The Global Partnership*, pp. 45 and 56.

ing countries to export manufactures—especially those manufactures with which they could competitively enter the world markets—were thwarted by tariff and non-tariff barriers put up by the developed countries, e.g. differential tariffs, quantitative restrictions, administrative procedures, discriminatory practices, etc.

The developing countries, moreover, had to carry the heavy burden of payment of principal and interest on past loans, which began maturing in the mid-1950's, and tended to offset the benefits of foreign aid. The external debts of many developing countries accumulated, and the situation was aggravated by the shortness of the repayment periods, high interest rates, and the generally high profits of investors of capital from developed countries.[14] Other harmful effects on their balance of payments and their foreign exchange reserves were generated by the invisibles—i.e. shipping, insurance, and reinsurance. For example, in 1961 alone the deficit on their services account was $4,100 million, of which freight accounted for $1,900 million.[15]

The characteristics of the international trade patterns and their destabilizing and harmful effects on the potential economic and social development plans of developing countries were deemed *inter alia* to necessitate a change in the prevailing structure of international trade, so as to offer the developing countries a better chance to earn adequate and stable supplies of foreign exchange essential for the development process.[16]

The Lacunae in International Organizations with Respect to Problems of Developing Countries.

In 1963, just before the Geneva Conference, there were 43 international organizations and suborganizations dealing with commodity and other trade problems. The vacuum left by the non-ratification of the Havana Charter which provided for the creation of the International Trade Organization (ITO), was filled by a multitude of bodies. This proliferation of institutions was haphazard in nature, and it resulted in "duplication, dispersal of efforts, inadequate coordination, and lack of leadership." The United Nations could not offer a satisfactory forum

14. According to IBRD findings, the public and publicly-guaranteed debt of the developing world (excluding their debt to socialist countries) increased at an annual average rate of around 15 percent in the period 1955-1962 (from $8-10 billion to $24 billion). For all developing countries, servicing charges—i.e. interest and amortization—rose from $900 million in 1956 to $3,100 million in 1963, which meant that they grew at an average rate of 19 percent. Prebisch, *op. cit.*, p. 45.

15. *Proceedings*, Vol. I, p. 173.

16. *Ibid.*, p. 6.

for in-depth examination of the developing countries' difficulties. The two possible places for such discussions——the Second Committee of the General Assembly and the unrepresentative (17 seats) ECOSOC— had crowded and extensive agendas and met over relatively short periods of time. The specialized agencies were not considered suitable for the scrutiny of general trade policies because it was felt that their narrow organizational interests would not allow them to consider their own problems as subservient to a general aim. Moreover, many people in developing countries identified the IMF and the IBRD, for example, as mere extensions of Wall Street diplomacy, not truly concerned with the problems of the poor regions of the globe. In brief, there was no available forum that the developing countries considered capable of taking an overall view and devoting its entire attention to their trade and development problems.[17]

The main controversy centered around GATT. The developing countries concluded that the system of international trade as it had become institutionalized in GATT was biased in favor of the rich countries and was against them, and that it seriously hampered their efforts to achieve growth through trade.[18] They argued that it was un-real to assume that there was complete equality among members of GATT (in rights as well as in obligations), and they were unhappy that the developed countries refused to recognize the validity of this contention. Nor did the developed countries allow for the fact that economic development and world trade are closely inter-linked.[19] Furthermore, the developing countries had little influence and limited means of exerting pressure in GATT.

One of the four international agreements envisaged by the Dumbarton Oaks Conference aiming at the normalization of post-war international economy was embodied in the Havana Charter.[20] At that time, the concept of development and the obligations it imposed upon the international community were still in their infancy. Certain proposals regarding economic development which were made in the preparatory stages of the Havana Conference were turned down flatly—for example: industrial countries should undertake to facilitate the industrialization of backward areas by all means in their power; members should

17. "Commodity and Trade Problems of Developing Countries: Institutional Arrangements," report of the Group of Experts appointed under ECOSOC Resolution 919 (XXXIV), *Proceedings,* Vol. V, pp. 395-397, 414.

18. H. G. Johnson, *Economic Policies Toward Less Developed Countries* (Washington, D.C.: The Brookings Institution, 1967), p. 237.

19. Report of the Group of Experts, *op. cit.,* p. 409.

20. The other three were those negotiated in Bretton Woods, establishing the IBRD and the IMF, and in Hot Springs, establishing Food and Agriculture Organization (FAO).

9

supply one another with technical skills, production goods, and the necessary credits; when giving long and short term credits, recognition should be accorded to the fact that funds must be provided on a non-remunerative basis; industrialization and diversification should be accepted as sufficient justification for the application of restriction on imports by the developing countries; as a whole, countries that have not reached the advanced stage of industralization, as well as those in the early stages of economic development, should be free to employ import quotas for the sole purpose of protecting the growth of industries when other forms of protection are not satisfactory; an Economic Development Commission should be established within the ITO, which would be autonomous and could facilitate release from commitments as to commercial policy, etc.[21]

There were eight articles in the Havana Charter concerned with development questions. They allowed the developing countries with the consent of the ITO to withdraw tariff concessions, and to resort to quantitative restrictions, subsidies and preferential tariff arrangements. In addition, Chapter VI was devoted to international commodity agreements, while certain other provisions encouraged the developed countries to furnish capital assistance to developing countries. These provisions, however, were negotiated with the rather reluctant representatives of the West and were considered by the developing countries as onerous, inadequate, unjust and restrictive, or in the case of Chapter VI, simply innocuous, neither prohibiting nor promoting the conclusion of commodity agreements.[22] However, even these limited aims did not materialize; the Havana Charter was spurned by the United States, and ratified by only two countries, Liberia and Australia.

The Charter had envisaged the creation of the International Trade Organization, which would take place next to FAO, IBRD, IMF, and ILO as one of the specialized agencies of the United Nations. In 1947, when the creation of the ITO seemed reasonably possible, a group of 23 states decided to give a head start to the process of tariff reductions and began negotiating on tariff concessions outlined in Article XVII of the Havana Charter. In January 1948 the provisions of the General Agreement on Tariffs and Trade were put into effect, while the Final Act of the Havana Conference was signed by the plenipotentiaries of 53 countries somewhat later, in March 1948. The Agreement was based on reciprocal tariff concessions between the Contracting Parties, which agreed to adhere to the rules of non-discrimination and reciprocity in

21. See C. Wilcox, *A Charter for World Trade* (New York: MacMillan, 1949), pp. 142-143.
22. *Ibid.,* p. 152.

international trade. The Agreement did not provide for the creation of an institution; GATT was rather thought of as a contractual framework functioning within the ITO. However, since ITO never came into being, GATT actually continued as a permanent organization, although outside of the UN family. On the way toward a *de facto* institutionalization, it was decided that the Secretariat of the Interim Commission of the ITO (ICITO) should act as a secretariat for the Contracting Parties to GATT. Various other bodies were also established to operate between the periodic meetings of the Contracting Parties.

In 1954 it was agreed by the Contracting Parties to establish an Organization for Trade Cooperation (OTC) whose function would be to administer the General Agreement, to facilitate intergovernmental consultations on international trade, to sponsor international trade negotiations, and to study the related questions. The working party which drafted the agreement recognized the desirability of giving to the OTC the status of a specialized agency.[23] However, the OTC never came into being. As in the case of the ITO, the failure of the United States to ratify the agreement dealt it a fatal blow.[24]

It should be noted that only a few developing countries adhered to GATT at its inception.[25] The reason was that most of the Havana Charter provisions regarding development were not repeated in GATT, and all of Chapter VI, dealing with commodities, was omitted. Furthermore, the provisions for encouraging the study and solution of problems relating to the instability of world markets for raw material and basic foodstuffs were excluded.

Article XVIII of GATT recognized that the developing countries would need flexibility in their tariff structure in order to grant the necessary tariff protection for the establishment of particular industries; it therefore included rules for temporary and qualified releases from tariff bindings and from the prohibition against applying quotas in favor of economic development. But Article XVIII applied to all GATT

23. "The Developing Countries in GATT," a study prepared by the temporary secretariat of UNCTAD for the Geneva Conference. *Proceedings,* Vol. V, p. 443.

24. The OTC was to come into being after governments comprising 85 percent of total foreign trade of the Contracting Parties ratified it. Since the U.S. conducted more than 20 percent of this trade, the Congress' failure to authorize this international agreement represented an actual veto.

25. Of 17 Latin American countries that signed the Havana Charter, only three are among the original Contracting Parties to GATT. Other developing countries that adhered to GATT at its inception were Burma, Ceylon, India, Pakistan and China. The overseas territories of Belgium, France, the Netherlands, and the U.K. upon acquiring independence became Contracting Parties through the sponsorship of their metropolitan territories, without having to pay an entrance fee. "The Developing Countries in GATT," *op. cit.,* p. 434.

11

members, to developing countries as well as to those engaged in post-war reconstruction. Even if the authorization were granted, it could be appealed by any Contracting Party and could eventually be revoked. The only developing country that took advantage of Article XVIII was Ceylon: it was granted the right to impose quantitative restrictions. Even this, however, was achieved only after a very laborious procedure to determine whether the necessary criteria had been met.[26] The only pertinent provision in GATT referring to commodities was Article XX, which states that the Contracting Parties are not prevented from joining commodity agreements. This meant that there would be no constant pressure emanating from GATT for the negotiation of such agreements. Article XVIII thus remained the only legal commitment among the Contracting Parties with regard to the economic development of the Third World. The developing countries specifically objected that the procedures under Article XVIII were too cumbersome, the measures available insufficient to cope with their difficulties; and they objected that the concept of infant industry did not extend to the entire economy of a developing country. Why, they asked, should they invoke various provisions and exceptions to GATT simply in order to carry out their development policies, when the merits of these policies were obvious and should not, therefore, be treated as exceptions?

The underlying principle of GATT—reciprocity and bargaining in a *quid pro quo* situation—made its actions dependent on the big trading nations. For this reason, GATT produced results that on the whole were either injurious or not beneficial to the developing countries. Results were injurious, for example, when GATT allowed an increase in agricultural and other commodity protectionism requested by domestic interests in developed countries, and they were not beneficial when the reduction of industrial tariffs was concentrated on those products in which developed and not developing countries had comparative advantages.[27] Further, GATT was criticized for concentrating on industrial products and for its lenience on the agricultural and industrial protectionism practiced by developed countries. It was argued that its rules and methods had been distorted to serve protectionist ends.[28]

The developing countries hardly participated in GATT tariff con-

26. *Ibid.*, p. 439. Article XVIII was revised in 1955, and constraints on developing countries were loosened regarding the imposition of import restrictions which were necessary for a country's growth. Frank, *op. cit.*, p. 70. In addition, post-war reconstruction was eliminated as a reason to invoke Article XVIII. A new section was added providing for an easier escape for developing countries in balance of payments difficulties. (J. Evans, "The General Agreement on Tariffs and Trade," in *The Global Partnership, op. cit.*, p. 81.)

27. Johnson, *op. cit.*, p. 131.

28. *Ibid.*, pp. 239 and 241.

ferences for several reasons. Major raw materials that developing countries exported encountered no significant tariff obstacles, while barriers to commodities were usually hard—if not impossible—to negotiate, since they were imposed for balance of payments reasons, revenue purposes, or to protect domestic agricultural interests. The developing countries were seldom principal suppliers of manufactures, nor could they usually claim to have a substantial interest. Therefore, they could not initiate negotiations. Reciprocity in GATT required that a country have a good competitive position—that it have products which could compete on equal terms in the markets of industrial nations; then it could gain something from bargaining. On the other hand, in order to be able to offer something in return for concessions, it had to have a substantially protected market. In the developing countries, however, the volume of imports was determined mainly by the available foreign exchange, while tariffs were used primarily for fiscal and development purposes, not for protection. Moreover, benefits that could potentially accrue to them from the lowering of tariffs in the industrialized nations were generally nullified by the use of non-tariff devices in the developed markets—quantitative restrictions, revenue duties, internal charges, subsidies to domestic producers, etc. Consequently many developing countries stayed away from tariff negotiations, hoping that the developed countries would negotiate concessions among themselves which would also benefit them on the basis of the most-favored-nation clause.[29]

GATT only gradually became sensitized to the arguments and problems of developing countries. Its review in 1954 resulted merely in amendments of a secondary nature; in fact, the cardinal rules of the Agreement were reaffirmed.[30] Not until 1958 and the appearance of the so-called Harberler Report, was any serious consideration given to the problem of developing countries in GATT.[31] The report stressed that export growth in developing countries was not as rapid as in developed countries. It argued that this was largely so due to import tariffs and other barriers erected by developed countries against goods in which developing countries had particular exporting interests. This

29. *Ibid.*, p. 15; "The Developing Countries in GATT," *op. cit.*, pp. 446-448.

30. *GATT, International Trade 1954* (Geneva: GATT, 1955), p. 129. The developing countries, for instance, proposed the inclusion into GATT of Chapter VI of the Havana Charter, dealing with commodity agreements, but they were turned down. As an alternative, a working group was set up to consider proposals for intergovernmental action. Its suggestions were not accepted however, and the Contracting Parties decided instead to review trends and developments in international commodity trade at every session of GATT.

31. "Trends in International Trade, A Report by a Panel of Experts" (Geneva: GATT, 1958).

report persuaded the Contracting Parties to GATT to form a committee to study particular obstacles to the trade of developing countries, as well as measures necessary to increase the export potential of developing countries through improvements in production and marketing techniques. Finally, it was made less onerous for developing countries to join GATT.[32]

GATT, however, was waking up too slowly and too late to the realities of underdevelopment, and to the demands of developing countries that it ought to reflect the organic relationship between trade and development, and formally establish distinctions in treatment which are necessitated by the differences in economic structure and level of development.[33] As late as 1960, for example, it showed great apathy to trading arrangements among developing countries. When the Latin American Free Trade Association (LAFTA) came into being, the developed countries insisted on a strict application of Article XXIV (customs unions and free-trade areas), and this involved all sorts of problems. GATT's reputation was stained. It was stigmatized as the "rich men's club." Its legitimacy was under attack.

The mounting pressure by the developing countries, and their economic difficulties—analyzed and well-documented—somewhat softened the western governments' attitudes. Thus, in the late 1950's, the United Nations Special Fund, the International Finance Corporation (IFC), and the International Development Association (IDA) were created, partly to quell the continuing agitation of the developing countries for a UN capital development fund. The IMF began to study compensatory financing; the Interim Coordinating Committee for International Commodity Agreements (ICCICA) was more active than previously; and the UN Commission on International Commodity Trade (CICT) was joined by the developed countries when its terms of reference were changed in 1958. The UN regional economic commissions were also given more autonomy.[34] These marginal institutional changes did not satisfy the developing countries, nor did they help solve their economic problems. Thus, as the 1960's set in, the institutional controversy gained momentum within the United Nations.

32. "The Developing Countries in GATT," *op. cit.,* p. 461.
33. *Ibid.,* p. 442.
34. Robertson, *op. cit.,* p. 9.

Following its earlier initiatives,[35] in 1956 the USSR proposed the convocation of a world economic conference to consider *inter alia* the establishment of a world trade organization within the UN framework. This proposal, however, did not meet with adequate support.[36] Many developing countries that might have considered supporting a conference to deal solely with their own problems were not prepared to support one which would focus attention on East-West trade. In fact, at the same session of the Assembly, resolution 1027(XI) was adopted by an overwhelming vote which stressed that the existing international organizations and agreements already provided a satisfactory framework for the effective consideration of trade problems, payments arrangements, and related issues.[37] The resolution also indicated the need to avoid the waste of resources and the weakening of existing organizations in the field of trade by unnecessary duplication of their functions and activities. Yet, the socialist countries continued to press their point, and in 1958 the USSR again proposed in ECOSOC that a new UN Conference on Trade and Employment be convened to create an international trade organization based on the OTC model.[38] There was no likelihood of consensus on this matter among the ECOSOC members; many pointed out that the international situation made such a conference premature.

By 1961, however, the situation had changed. The question of East-West trade was relegated to the background, with the developing countries having assumed the initiative. In proposing a world trade

35. In 1954 the USSR called for an international conference of trade experts and started advocating an international trade organization with a universal membership. In 1955 the socialist countries introduced a draft resolution calling for the ratification of the Havana Charter which had been negotiated at the 1948 Conference for International Trade and Employment.

36. The USSR never brought its proposal (A/PV. 589) to a vote, but Yugoslavia and Poland submitted a draft resolution to the Second Committee of the General Assembly proposing that it consider the question of convening a world economic conference (A/C.2/L.319). (It did not call for such a conference to convene, as the USSR proposal had done). This proposal was rejected by a vote of 32 to 27, with 14 abstentions (A/3545). As summarized in D. Cordovez, "The Making of UNCTAD, Institutional Background and Legislative History," *Journal of World Trade Law* (May-June 1967), p. 255. What follows is based primarily on the Cordovez article, which gives an excellent and detailed overview of "the making of UNCTAD."

37. General Assembly resolution 1027 (XI) was adopted by a vote of 55 to 7, with 4 abstentions. The draft resolution was sponsored by Argentina, Australia, Belgium, Denmark, the Philippines, the United Kingdom and the United States.

38. Draft resolutions E/AC.6/L.216 and E/AC.6/L.217, summarized in *ibid.*, p. 256

conference and a possible institutional framework, they insisted that these be devoted to their problems. A number of factors which influenced the developing countries to ask for change in the institutional *status quo* have already been mentioned. Their expectations to achieve satisfactory economic development were not being fulfilled, and they were becoming increasingly unhappy and frustrated with their lot in world economy, especially with their international trading position as suppliers of primary commodities. Their growing disenchantment with international organizations because of their indifference to their pressing problems has also been noted. It may be added that many developing countries were worried about the establishment of regional economic groupings of developed countries and the discriminatory effects of such groupings.

The efforts of the developing countries were helped by the transformation of the UN membership (in 1960 alone 17 new states were admitted) which made it possible for them to form new and dominant majorities on economic and social questions, thus ending the control of the developed countries in this sphere. The newly independent states were vigorous and contributed to the political dynamism in the developing countries' movement. The developing countries, especially of the Asian and African groups, having forged a united front on the question of decolonialization, it was relatively easy for them to shift the focus to the problems of trade and development. The Belgrade Conference held in September 1961 was a definite sign of an organized common front of *all* developing countries on economic and social questions in the UN, even though the Latin American countries (unlike ECLA) were still on the sidelines, acting very cautiously on matters which might affront the United States. On the more general level, conceptual and theoretical advances were made in GATT and in the UN on trade problems. As a result, most people began firmly to link the commercial problems of developing countries with their development problems, and this provided a theoretical underpinning for their demands. Finally, the thaw in the Cold War softened the rigidities of a bipolar international system, making the situation within and without the United Nations more fluid and, consequently, more conducive to innovation.

In 1961 at the sixteenth session of the General Assembly the developing countries introduced two draft resolutions in the Second Committee, both calling for action in the field of international trade and both stressing the need to hold international meetings and conferences in order to seek solutions to their trade problems. One resolution was sponsored by the Latin American states,[39] the other by the African

39. Draft resolution A/C.2/L.550.

16

states and Indonesia.[40] After consultation, the African draft was withdrawn, while the Latin American draft was modified to take into account the content of the African one; it was then resubmitted in a revised form.[41]

What mattered most, however, was the amendment to this draft resolution sponsored by the African states and Indonesia, asking that a trade conference be convened. Its scope was eventually reduced; it asked only that the Secretary-General of the United Nations consult governments on the possibility of holding a world conference on international trade problems. The Second Committee approved the amendment by a roll-call vote of 45 to 36, with 10 abstentions.[42] It is this controversial decision that eventually led to the convening of the Geneva Conference. The results of the Secretary-General's survey showed that African, Asian, most Latin American, and socialist states, and the Holy See, were in favor of the conference, while the developed countries were opposed or uncommitted.[43]

An additional and very important push for holding a world trade meeting came from the Cairo Conference on the Problems of Developing Countries. Held in July 1962, just before the summer session of ECOSOC, it assembled representatives and observers from 36 developing countries.[44] The Cairo Declaration recommended that the develop-

40. Draft resolution A/C.2/L.556 and Add. 1.
41. Draft resolution A/C.2/L.550/Rev. 2 and Add. 1.
42. Those abstaining or voting against the amendment were the western countries and the Latin American countries (except for Cuba). At this point the Latin American countries were still divided and lukewarm toward the idea of a conference. Note also that Ethiopia, Iran, the Philippines, and Thailand abstained. For the exact vote see UN doc. A/5056. The revised text of the Latin American draft resolution was then adopted by a vote 81 to 0, with 11 abstentions. The abstentions came from Belgium, France, Ireland, Italy, Luxembourg, the Netherlands, New Zealand, South Africa, Spain, the UK, and the US. Unanimity was reached, however, after the request to the Secretary-General to prepare a provisional agenda for a possible conference was deleted. The resolution thus no longer prejudged the issue of whether or not the conference would be held, and was adopted unanimously by the General Assembly. Resolution 1707 (XVI), December 19, 1961.
43. Of 66 replies, 45 were favorable, 3 expressed no objection (Greece, Japan, Sweden), 18 were generally opposed (developed countries, Colombia, and Nicaragua). See E/3631 and addenda. Although the major traders still opposed the conference, their position no longer seemed inflexible. Cordovez, *op. cit.*, p. 258.
44. Afghanistan, Algeria, Bolivia, Brazil, Burma, Cambodia, Ceylon, Congo (L), Cuba, Cyprus, Ethiopia, the Federation of Malaya, Ghana, Guinea, India, Indonesia, Kuwait, Lebanon, Libya, Mali, Mexico, Morocco, Pakistan, Saudi Arabia, Somalia, Sudan, Tanganyika, Tunisia, the UAR, Yemen and Yugoslavia sent delegations; Chile, Ecuador, Singapore, Uruguay and Venezuela participated as observers. Dr. Raúl Prebisch, the Executive Secretary of ECLA, acted as the personal representative of UN Secretary-General. He volunteered for this assign-

ing countries should protect their common interests within GATT, as well as cooperate to strengthen the economic and social activities of the United Nations. The participants came out strongly in favor of holding an international economic conference under the aegis of the UN, preferably in 1963, to discuss "all vital questions relating to international trade, primary commodity trade, and economic relations between developed and developing countries." [45]

The political impact of the Cairo Declaration was of special importance: it indicated the forthcoming joint actions of developing countries on matters of trade and development within the UN. The United States and the other major western countries found it difficult to resist the pressure for holding such a conference any longer.[46] After a lengthy behind-the-scenes discussion, ECOSOC adopted a draft resolution sponsored by the developing countries, and the decision to convene the conference was at last formally taken.[47] Before this resolution was adopted, the United States, Japan, and Uruguay introduced a draft resolution asking the Secretary-General to appoint a group of experts to prepare a report on the activities in trade and related fields of the existing organizations—i.e., to report on problems of interest to the developing countries: assess the activities of the existing organizations, find overlaps and other lacunae, and propose the necessary changes and additional activities that could be warranted.[48] Although the U.S. representative allegedly had not intended it to be an alternative to the world conference,[49] most delegations saw the proposal as an attempt to further delay the conference and the creation of any possible new organization.[50] Once the resolution convening the conference was adopted, the proposal for a group of experts was less controversial, and the Council agreed to it after the sponsors gave assurances that the group would not deal with the substance of the problems, but would merely review the activities of the existing institutions.[51] The Group of

ment when the question was discussed with the executive secretaries of the regional commissions. By coming to Cairo, Prebisch for the first time confronted Asians and Africans, and projected his figure beyond Latin America.

45. Summarized in *ibid.,* p. 259. The full text is to be found in UN doc. A/5162.

46. The American policy makers, under the prodding of Adlai Stevenson, came to realize that by continued opposition they would only play into Russian hands and embitter the developing countries. Robertson, *op. cit.,* p. 14.

47. Draft resolution E/L.958/Rev.2 sponsored by Brazil, Ethiopia, India, Senegal and Yugoslavia and ECOSOC resolution 917 (XXXIV), August 3, 1962.

48. Draft resolution E/AC.6/L.278.

49. Summarized in Cordovez, *op. cit.,* p. 262. For records of the discussion see E/AC.6/SR.315-330.

50. Robertson, *op. cit.,* p. 15.

51. ECOSOC resolution 919 (XXXIV), August 3, 1962.

Experts eventually produced a document which was very significant for the consideration of the institutional issue at the Geneva Conference.

The adoption of the resolution in ECOSOC was just the beginning of the debate on the nature of the conference—particularly the contents of its agenda. The General Assembly considered this matter in the autumn of 1962. During the debate in the Second Committee, a joint draft resolution of 18 developing countries *inter alia* suggested that one of the basic points to be considered when preparing the draft agenda should be "methods and machinery to implement measures relating to the expansion of international trade." [52] Although the resolution was later amplified through amendments and subamendments, it did not explicitly state that the conference should discuss "the advisability of establishing a United Nations agency for international trade." [53] Representatives of the developing countries explained the lack of specific mention for a new trade agency simply to mean that no provisions should be made in the text of the resolution which would prejudge the issue before it was subjected to a thorough study. Actually at this point, there was as yet no agreement among the developing countries on the institutional issue. [54]

The developed countries of the West were surprised by the proposals to discuss institutional matters at the conference and they were not happy at the possibility of the conference considering questions of East-West trade. They felt that this was not in the spirit of the original ECOSOC resolution. Actually, when they agreed that the conference be held, the major western powers were informally assured by some cosponsors of this resolution that neither the institutional question nor the question of East-West trade would be discussed there. (In fact, it is on the basis of this private understanding that the United States agreed to vote for this resolution.) However, they were gradually outmaneuvered by the developing countries, which by then seemed to have grasped the tactic of step-by-step negotiation, a tool which was later, in the context of UNCTAD, to become their favorite manipulative device on institutional matters. In spite of the West's lack of enthusiasm then, the draft resolution was adopted by a roll-call vote in the Second Committee, and later, almost unanimously, by the General Assembly. The way was now open for preparations to be made for the conference to be held not later than the early part of 1964. [55]

52. Draft resolution A/C.2/L.648. It should also be noted that a draft resolution submitted by the USSR (A/C.2/L.645) proposed that the conference ought to consider the establishment of an International Trade Organization.

53. This is the wording of the subamendment by Burma (A/C.2/L.656) which was not incorporated into the draft resolution by its sponsors.

54. Cordovez, *op. cit.*, pp. 264-265.

55. The vote in the Second Committee was 73 to 10, with 23 abstentions.

The Preparatory Committee of the Conference met during 1963-1964 to agree on the agenda for the Conference, consider the administrative arrangements, and supervise the preparation and compiling of documentation.[56] Dr. Raúl Prebisch was appointed Secretary-General of the Conference early in 1963.[57] He headed the temporary secretariat which was composed principally of men from the UN Department of Economic and Social Affairs, and from regional economic commissions. With the help of outside experts, the secretariat prepared a number of studies and reports which provided the basis for the Conference's work.[58]

Subcommittee IV of the Preparatory Committee dealt with institutional questions and considered the report prepared by the Group of Experts: "Commodity and trade problems of developing countries: institutional arrangements." [59] The experts were divided in assessing the situation as well as in recommending the steps to be taken which would enable international organizations to deal more effectively with the problems of the developing countries' trade. Two basic trends of

---

Belgium, France, Ireland, Italy, Luxembourg, Rwanda, South Africa, Spain, the United Kingdom, and the United States were against, while Austria, Greece, Japan, the Netherlands, Portugal, Turkey, Taiwan, ten French-speaking African countries, and Iran abstained. *Ibid.,* p. 266. The result of the voting was mainly due to the bitter disagreement over timing. The developing countries insisted that the conference be held not later than September 1963. They had in mind the start of the Kennedy Round and the negotiations over the British entry into the Common Market, and wanted the conference to be held before these developments could bring in new political and economic considerations. Robertson, *op. cit.,* p. 16. The major Western powers, however, arguing that the Conference should be well prepared, were firm in their insistence that it be held in early 1964. Once the question of time was settled, the General Assembly resolution 1785 (XVII) of 8 December 1962, was adopted by 91 to 0, with 1 abstention.

56. The reports of the Preparatory Committee are to be found in *Proceedings,* Vol. VIII, pp. 3-59.

57. General Assembly resolution 1785 (XVII) provided that a Secretary-General of the Conference be appointed. This provision was intended by the developing countries to prevent the UN Under-Secretary for Economic and Social Affairs, Philippe de Seynes, and his department, which they considered western-oriented, from influencing the Conference. There were several candidates for the post; the most serious one, backed by the West was Sir John Crawford of Australia. However, developing countries, individually and collectively impressed U Thant to appoint Prebisch, who had made it known before the General Assembly resolution was adopted that, if invited, he would accept this post.

58. It should be noted that Prebisch's report to the Conference—"Towards a New Trade Policy for Development"—was of central importance. In a great mass of documents, studies and reports, it stood out as a relatively concise statement of the problem and a summary of developing countries' demands and proposals. (UN publication Sales No. 65.II.B.4).

59. *Proceedings,* Vol. V, pp. 374-423.

opinion were reflected, one for the preservation of the institutional *status quo* and the other for significant organizational changes. Some argued for the improvement and better use of the already existing machinery in GATT and for reorganizing the work of the ECOSOC and of the General Assembly. Others advocated a new specialized agency, a UN International Trade Organization. In between were those who suggested a permanent organ within the United Nations, backed by a standing committee and an executive body within the UN Secretariat. Such a forum could be provided by the UN Conference on Trade and Development itself. It was felt that this compromise solution would offer a structure similar to an international trade organization, while avoiding the political obstacles that the setting up of a fullfledged specialized agency would encounter in some western countries.

When the Preparatory Committee considered the report, it reached conclusions similar to those of the Group of Experts. Countries generally expounded the line of thinking which their own experts had advocated. In view of the disagreements, the Preparatory Committee did not make any suggestions to the Conference, using the rationale that the decision of the Conference on the institutional question would very much depend on what it decided on substantive issues. Although the Preparatory Committee was unable to arrive at a consensus on the institutional question, the majority of its members agreed that the new machinery should have wide authority in the field of international trade, that it should be able to supervise the implementation of decisions taken by the Conference, that it should be under the aegis of the UN, that it should be empowered to coordinate activities of the existing international bodies dealing with international trade, that it should be universal in membership, or as nearly so as possible, and that it should be acceptable to the majority of developing nations as well as the major trading nations.[60]

The Situation Prior to the Geneva Conference

Before discussing the Geneva Conference itself, let us briefly mention two other matters of importance: first, the changes in GATT; and, second, the UN Development Decade and the atmosphere in which it was initiated.

We have already spoken of the usual apathy of this contractual body toward the problems of developing countries, caused partly by the fact that they did not fit into the General Agreement's philosophy.[61] Al-

60. As summarized in Cordovez, *op. cit.*, pp. 276-278.
61. We have mentioned a study on the background and activities of GATT i.e., "The developing countries in GATT," prepared by the secretariat of the Geneva

though some individuals in the GATT secretariat did note the decline of developing countries' share in world trade in the early fifties, such theoretical "discoveries" were isolated and not pursued vigorously.[62] It was only much later that these problems received attention on the intergovernmental level in GATT. The western governments were still not prepared to think in terms of any remedial actions, while the GATT secretariat remained committed to the concept that its organization was devoted solely to the promotion of trade liberalization through negotiations of tariff concessions. The developing countries' problems appeared remote and difficult to deal with in a *quid pro quo* milieu.

The Haberler Report of 1958 marked the beginning of a changing orientation for GATT. However, the substantive and institutional modification was slow and perfunctory. The developed countries were generally reluctant to agree to significant innovations, even though GATT's Executive Secretary Sir Eric Wyndham White had been warning them for a number of years that reluctance would not help neutralize the drive to take matters away from his organization.[63] At the same time, the majority of developing countries did not press energetically for such modifications; they felt their efforts would either be futile because of western opposition or just result in some token action.

Upon considering the Haberler Report in 1958, the Contracting Parties established the Trade Expansion Program, setting up three committees. One of them, Committee III, was to be principally concerned with the removal of obstacles to the expansion of developing countries' exports into the developed marked economies. Based on the work of this committee, a set of principles, the "Declaration on the promotion of trade of the less-developed countries," was adopted in 1961 to serve as a base for the future work of GATT. In 1962 a Special Group on Tropical Products was established. During the same year, developing countries submitted a draft program of action which contained specific policy guidelines. It was adopted in the spring of 1963 as the Program of Action, but the EEC countries refused to

---

Conference. Note also "The significance of GATT for underdeveloped countries," by S. B. Linder, "The role of GATT in relation to trade and development," prepared by the GATT secretariat, and "A framework for trade between developed and less-developed countries," by I. Gal-Edd. All of these are contained in *Proceedings,* Vol. V.

62. To this effect see G. Curzon, "The GATT: Pressures and Strategies of Task Expansion" (paper presented to the 7th World Congress of IPSA, Brussels, 1967), p. 6. Reproduced in Cox, *International Organisation: World Politics, op. cit.,* pp. 248-257.

63. See Gardner, "The United Nations Conference on Trade and Development," *op. cit.,* p. 102.

endorse it on the grounds that more positive measures were required to increase the export earnings of developing countries; other developed countries, although accepting the objectives, placed reservations on many specific points. The Action Committee was set up to help implement the program, while Committee III continued to exist with its scope enlarged to cover systematic studies of trade and aid relationships in individual countries, to obtain a picture of export potential and market prospects, and to map out actions which would be required to overcome difficulties that such studies would reveal. Export promotion and the possibility of a trade information center within GATT were also considered. In 1963, the Working Party on Preferences was formed to discuss the preferences of developed countries toward developing ones, and of developing countries toward one another.

As the Geneva Conference approached, however, the developed countries were more willing to engage in a "patching operation" in GATT. They agreed that it would be much easier to defend this organization from the institutional onslaught of developing and socialist countries if it were to produce a "certain number of concrete results in the near future for developing nations." [64] Their strategy went along two complementary lines: first, firmly defend GATT's jurisdiction, and second, make it more acceptable and attractive to developing countries. At the ministerial meeting in 1963 it was decided that during the Kennedy Round "the developed countries cannot expect to receive reciprocity from the less-developed countries." [65] In the same year, the need was recognized for an adequate legal and institutional framework which would enable the Contracting Parties to discharge their responsibilities vis-à-vis the developing countries and a special committee was set up to consider this question. Notwithstanding pressure from the GATT secretariat and from western countries, this matter was held in abeyance pending the conclusion of the Geneva Conference and its decision on institutional matters. The developing countries did not want to prejudge the outcome of the Conference, nor to strengthen the hand of the West in its defense of GATT. At their XXI session in March-April 1964, the Contracting Parties decided that such a legal and institutional framework should be incorporated into the General Agreement. This decision eventually led to the adoption of the new Part IV, a matter to which we shall turn later. At the same session, it was decided to establish a trade information center within the framework of GATT, whose purpose it would be to supply developing countries

64. Report of the OECD Group (OECD doc. TC(64), 4 Feb. 1964), p. 28. Note that at this time developing countries in GATT outnumbered the developed ones by two to one.
65. See GATT doc. MIN(63)9, 21 May 1963, pp. 1-2.

with trade information and trade promotion advisory services.[66]

All these belated efforts to transform GATT, however, could not stem the institutional offensive mounted by the developing countries as we shall show later. But let us leave GATT now and turn our attention to the general situation in which the Geneva Conference was to take place.

As the 1960's set in, the concept of national economic development planning, which until the Kennedy Administration was considered as subversive by the United States, at last appeared to be generally accepted and legitimized in the United Nations. It was further agreed that national planning *per se* could not be fully successful and depended heavily on the nature of the international environment. In order, then, to advance the cause of the economic development of the Third World, it became necessary to think in terms of joint responsibilities and co-ordinated efforts through international organizations. In 1961 the General Assembly initiated the first UN Development Decade. The resolution adopted by the General Assembly proclaimed as a goal that the developing countries should attain a minimum annual growth rate in aggregate national income of 5 percent or more during the 1960's.[67] The General Assembly also reaffirmed the aim of increasing the annual flow of international assistance and capital to developing countries to 1 percent of the combined national incomes of the economically advanced nations,[68] and it recognized that international trade had a key role to play in effecting crucial changes in the economic structures of developing countries.

The basic problem was: what measures could be taken by the international community to enable the developing countries to remove themselves from the subsistence stages of economic development? Foreign aid alone, especially in its bilateral form, did not seem to be the only

66. With the traditional GATT efficiency, it was decided that this center would begin operation within a few weeks, in May 1964. This promptness did not characterize the previous actions of the Contracting Parties on this matter. They had discussed trade promotion as far back as 1961, and they had considered the Brazil proposal for the establishment of such a center in 1962. See GATT doc. COM/III/93, 26 Oct. 1962.

67. General Assembly resolution 1710(XVI), 19 Dec. 1961. The idea of the Development Decade was proposed by the United States. However, the growth rate concept and the figure of 5 % were suggested by a Nigerian delegate, after consulting R. Prebisch and H. Singer, in order to introduce an objective content into the entire exercise. This was controversial at the time, and the United States in particular objected. Apparently, with a quantified growth rate target, the Development Decade could no longer be treated only as a vague slogan.

68. General Assembly resolution 1711(XVI), 19 Dec. 1961. Note, however, that the 1 percent target had already been set in 1960; see General Assembly resolution 1522(XV), 15 Dec. 1960.

and proper solution, even if it were to reach the much higher levels that were proposed. It represented a "soft option" for donors as well as for recipients,[69] and it did not bring about adequate structural changes in the system of international trade. A more comprehensive set of measures had to be defined; this task was undertaken by the Geneva Conference. As the UN Development Decade started—and with the world trade conference approaching—one wondered whether a shift had occurred from narrowly national to more international motivations in the policies of states.[70] The launching of the Decade implied the multilateralization of action toward improving the conditions for development on the Asian, African and Latin American continents; however, the endorsement of its goals by the developed countries was of a very abstract and declaratory nature.

In the 1950's, the national motives of donors in helping developing countries were obvious: they needed friends for political and military purposes. As the Cold War began to lose intensity, the need to "court assiduously" every developing country appeared irrelevant. As a matter of fact, the disappearance of the "friendly South" in international forums, and the doubt that allegiance could be bought with money, led many to conclude that imposing ties of economic and political dependence was a more effective way of controlling the developing nations. Moral and humanitarian concerns hardly influenced the developed countries' policies vis-à-vis the developing world, and the contention that the West, and especially the imperial powers, should do their utmost to help because they had perpetrated centuries of exploitation and injustice in the southern hemisphere and were to a great extent responsible for the general backwardness of these regions, was generally ignored.[71] In fact, the developed countries had generally

69. The inflow of aid sometimes reduced the pressure on a developing country to develop competitive industries which would help it earn foreign exchange, while farm surpluses could dull the incentive to make the agricultural production more efficient. On the other hand, by giving aid, a developed country could feel relieved of moral responsibility and would have fewer qualms about adopting or maintaining commercial and other domestic policies which curtailed the chances for developing countries' exports to increase. Johnson, *op. cit.*, pp. 3-4.

70. M. F. Millikan, "An Introductory Essay," in *The Global Partnership, op. cit.*, p. 4.

71. Former colonial powers did assist individual developing nations, or groups of nations, although in most instances they were also inspired by the neocolonialist calculus. Thus, for example, for reciprocal concessions France extended to its former African colonies many of the policies that developing countries as a group were demanding from the industrial North—e.g. preferences, high relative and absolute volume of financial aid, extensive technical assistance programs, etc. For an enlightening statement of French motivations see the so-called "Jeanneney Report," "La politique de coopération avec les pays en voie de développement" (Paris: Ministère d'état chargé de la réforme administrative, juillet 1963).

25

concluded that action demanded of them—that they should greatly increase the flow of aid on more favorable terms and modify traditional commercial and financing policies for the benefit of developing countries—would not promote their own immediate interests. The cost of the proposed measures appeared considerable, while the structural alterations required, including the changes in the international division of labor, were often hardly tolerable. Furthermore, public opinion in the developed countries was never cultivated in favor of the developing countries' needs and demands, and strong opposition and hostility from these quarters was to be expected.

Although investing globally in the economic progress of the Third World meant a greater chance for peace and orderly growth in these areas, with all the beneficial consequences for the international system as a whole, the longterm dividends were outweighed by the immediate shortcomings as far as the developed countries were concerned. The mixture of self-serving political motivations, economic interests, and humanitarian, moral and internationalist incentives was insufficient to make them overcome their inertia and adopt radical new policies that would help the developing countries. In view of this general situation, it was unrealistic to expect that the Geneva Conference would produce adequate results. The words of the encyclical "Populorum Progressio", released in March 1964, on the eve of the Geneva Conference, represented yet another, perhaps somewhat pathetic appeal:

> ... advanced nations have a very heavy obligation to help the developing peoples. Their superfluous wealth should be placed in the service of poor nations, because the same duty of solidarity that exists for individuals exists also for nations. Otherwise, the continued greed of the rich nations will certainly call down upon them the judgment of God and the wrath of the poor.

The guidelines for the work of the United Nations Conference on Trade and Development were summed up in a joint declaration drafted by the developing countries in the General Assembly in the autumn of 1963. They maintained that "international trade could become a more powerful instrument and vehicle of economic development." They argued that "the existing principles and patterns of world trade still mainly favor the advanced parts of the world" and that present trends, instead of helping developing countries "to promote the development and diversification of their economies . . . frustrate their efforts to attain more rapid growth." To increase the resources available to these countries, the volume of their trade "should be increased and its composition diversified; the prices of their exports should be stabilized at fair and remunerative levels," and "international transfer of capital should be made more favourable." To achieve these broad objectives, "a dynamic international trade policy is required." [72] Such a policy should be based on the recognition that the less developed nations hold a special position in the world economy and need to be provided with special assistance. The removal of impediments to the trade of the developing countries would not be sufficient and should be supplemented by more positive measures directed toward achieving a new division of labor. More specifically, the developing countries expected that the Geneva Conference would lead, *inter alia,* toward the following outcomes:

(a) Progressive reduction and early elimination of all barriers and restrictions impeding the exports of the developing countries, without reciprocal concessions on their part;

(b) Increase in the volume of exports of the developing countries in primary products, both raw and processed, to the industrialized countries, and stabilization of prices at fair and remunerative levels;

(c) Expansion of the markets for exports of manufactured and semi-manufactured goods from the developing countries;

(d) Provision of more adequate financial resources at favourable terms so as to enable the developing countries to increase their imports of capital goods and industrial raw materials essential for their economic development, and better co-ordination of trade and aid policies;

(e) Improvement of the invisible trade of the developing countries, particularly by reducing their payments for freight and insurance and the burden of their debt charges;

(f) Improvement of institutional arrangements, including if necessary, the establishment of new machinery and methods for implementing the decisions of the Conference. [73]

---

72. Excerpts quoted from the "Joint Declaration of the Developing Countries," made at the Eighteenth Session of the General Assembly, General Assembly resolution 1897(XVIII), 11 Nov. 1963, Annex.

73. *Ibid.*

Chapter II

THE 1964 GENEVA CONFERENCE ON TRADE
AND DEVELOPMENT

"If all the peoples who live under precarious economic conditions and who depend on foreign Powers for some vital aspects of their economy and for their economic and social structure, are capable of resisting the temptation of offers made in cold blood although in the heat of the moment, and impose a new type of relationship here, mankind will have taken a step forward.

If, on the other hand, the groups of under-developed countries, lured by the siren song of the vested interests of the developed Powers which exploit their backwardness, contend futilely among themselves for the crumbs from the tables of the mighty of this world, and break the ranks of numerically superior forces; or if they are not capable of insisting on clear agreements, free from escape clauses open to capricious interpretations; or if they rest content with agreements that can simply be violated at will by the mighty, our efforts will have been of no avail and the lengthy deliberations at this Conference will result in nothing more than innocuous documents and files for international bureaucracy zealously to guard: tons of printed paper and kilometres of magnetic tape recording opinions expressed by participants. And the world will stay as it is."

> Ernesto Guevara Serna   (Che)
> in a speech to the first
> UN Conference on Trade
> and Development,
> 25 March 1964

The *Final Act* adopted by the Geneva Conference provided the basis for future action, a platform from which the developing countries could proceed to press their demands for radical changes in the world trade system and in international economic relationships.[1] It implied a shifting of emphasis from "stability to growth", and it underlined the international acknowledgement of the contention that the rules of international trade should take into account the differences in levels of economic development and bargaining ability, since all countries were not economically equal.[2] In a sense, the *Final Act* was a program or a manifesto of the developing countries, forcefully supported by the

---

1. For the *Final Act* see *Proceedings*, Vol. I, pp. 3-65.
2. Cordovez, *op. cit.*, p. 243.

socialist countries; it reflected primarily their views and objectives, and was adopted mainly because of their political unity and voting strength. Most developed countries did not fully subscribe to many of the *Final Act's* recommendations. In many cases the ambiguous wording concealed disagreements and different viewpoints.[3] The Conference thus could not reach definite conclusions on most of the substantive matters on its agenda, although its decisions, whether agreed by consensus or voted by majority, established a series of objectives that have dominated debates on development ever since. The principal specific achievement of the Geneva Conference was to establish the continuing machinery of UNCTAD, and even this came only after a very sharp confrontation over the nature of the institution to be created. Its main political outcome was the change in the traditional relationship between developed and developing countries. Previously, the developed countries, individually or collectively, were in a strong position vis-à-vis the developing countries because of the political fragmentation of the latter. At the Geneva Conference, conscious of their individual weaknesses, the developing countries acted and maneuvered together and pressed their demands as a tightly united group. This close unity of action gave them political weight, and helped them obtain concessions, especially in the institutional sphere.[4]

Substantive Results of the Conference

We do not intend to dwell at length on the work of the Geneva Conference in the substantive sphere. Points relevant to our discussion of events in the continuing machinery of UNCTAD will appear later in the text, and for the time being, it may be sufficient to list briefly some of the measures proposed in four major areas, i.e. commodities, manufactures, financing and shipping.[5]

3. Fifteen general and 13 special principles were recommended to govern international trade relations and create policies conducive to development. The votes of major western countries reflected their attitude toward the "new" philosophy. For example, the United States voted against, or abstained, on 11 general and 9 special principles; the United Kingdom on 10 and 6 respectively; France 8 and 5; F. R. Germany 10 and 5; Japan 8 and 5, and so on.
4. OECD doc. TC(64)14 (1 Jul. 1964), pp. 2-3.
5. A number of analyses on the work of the Geneva Conference have been published. See the cited works by Johnson, Pincus, Frank and Gardner. See also: "The Significance of the United Nations Conference on Trade and Development: Report to the Secretary-General," UN document E/CONF.46/140 (9 July 1964); G. de La Charrière, "La Conference des Nations Unies sur le Commerce et Développement: Bilans et Perspectives," *Revue du Marché Commun* (octobre 1964), No. 73, pp. 438-443; S. Weintraub, "After the UN Trade Conference: Lessons and Portents," *Foreign Affairs* (Oct. 1964), Vol. 143, No. 1, pp. 37-50; S. Dell,

Commodities. Since primary commodities account for approximately 85 to 90 percent of the developing countries' export earnings, this was the area in which action by the international community would have benefited them the most in the short run. The proposed solutions fell into three categories: (a) Measures for the removal of obstacles and discriminatory practices used to protect domestic agriculture and processing industries in the North; expansion of market opportunities for primary commodity exports, and increases in their consumption and import in industrialized countries. (b) Measures for the stabilization of primary commodity markets and the fixing of prices at equitable and remunerative levels, including commodity agreements. (c) International financial measures, including compensatory and supplementary financing for the stabilization of primary export earnings.

In an effort to secure better access for the South's primary commodity exports to the developed country markets, the Geneva Conference recommended *inter alia:* (1) A standstill provision whereby no new tariff or non-tariff barriers are created against such exports; (2) the removal of existing obstacles to developing countries' exports—tariff and internal fiscal charges (for example, the revenue duties imposed on tropical beverage products and bananas in Europe), and quantitative restrictions; (3) the discouragement in developed countries of domestic policies which stimulate the uneconomic production of those primary products which developing countries export; and, (4) the abolition of existing special preferential arrangements between some developed countries and some developing countries to take effect as soon as the international measures are applied, providing that the developing countries enjoying special preferences receive at least equivalent advantages.[6]

Improved access to the markets of developed countries would have greatly benefited the developing countries.[7] However, the participants at the Geneva Conference were aware that these proposals would face serious difficulties. Agriculture in the North is in a relatively weak competitive position because of the high costs of production. There-

---

"UNCTAD—Retrospect and Prospect," *Annual Review of UN Affairs* (1964/1965), pp. 52-85; G. L. Goodwin, "The United Nations Conference on Trade and Development—Beginning of a New Era?," *Yearbook of World Affairs* (1965), 19:1-25. For an extensive bibliography on the subject consult the appendix in *The Global Partnership, op. cit.*

6. "International Commodity Arrangements and Removal of Obstacles and Expansion of Trade," Annex A. II.1, *Proceedings,* Vol. I, pp. 26 ff.

7. Pincus estimates that the exports of the developing countries to the North could increase between $3-$5 billion annually as a result of free trade in commodities. The principal beneficiaries would be the exporters of petroleum, sugar, cotton, tobacco, lead, zinc and aluminum. *Op. cit.,* p. 292.

fore, any liberalization of commodity access would bring problems of adjustment, and most governments in the developed countries were not ready to undertake them. For this reason the developing countries in Geneva concentrated their pressure on international commodity agreements as a means to increase their primary commodity export earnings.[8]

Commodity agreements can be seen as an international counterpart of domestic agricultural interventionism, whose goal it is to maintain minimum prices for farm products and to influence the distribution of the national income in favor of farmers.[9] Experience with very wide fluctuations of commodity prices and their disastrous effect on the earnings of one- or two-crop countries made it obvious that the advantages of the free play of supply and demand in this sphere of international trade were rather limited. As we saw earlier, the ITO Charter had accepted the need for commodity control. Since the end of World War II, five commodity agreements had been concluded—for wheat, sugar, coffee, tin and olive oil.[10] It was felt in Geneva that the basic purpose for such commodity agreements was to stimulate a steady growth of primary exports, to maximize the export earnings of the developing countries by means of remunerative and equitable prices, and to stabilize the market.

Stabilization of prices is the recognized principle of commodity agreements. The Geneva Conference went beyond market stabilization and stressed the new principle of remunerating commodity producers in developing countries so as to maximize their income and provide them with expanding resources for economic development. The techniques that can be used in commodity agreements vary, depending on the nature of the commodity in question. *Inter alia,* they are: (1) floor and ceiling prices and price ranges; (2) quota arrangements; (3) minimum guarantee on import volumes; (4) long-term contracts and import targets, and purchase and sales arrangements; and (5) buffer stock schemes, fixing both a maximum and a minimum price for a given commodity, to be maintained by purchases for or sales from this stock. It was expected that a degree of predictability would result with regard to the export earnings of developing countries and that this, in turn, would help improve their economic and investment planning and allow the best possible use of available resources. It was also expected that

8. Johnson, *op. cit.,* p. 139.

9. For example, the Brasseur Plan as advocated by France at the Geneva Conference asked that higher prices be paid for southern commodities, and that this be financed by domestic levies in the industrial countries. See Pincus, *op. cit.,* p. 269.

10. For a description of the existing commodity agreements and their history, see Pincus, *op. cit.,* pp. 274-278; see also, "International Commodity Problems," UN Doc. E/CONF. 46/30 (10 Feb. 1964).

cycles of shortage and overproduction would be prevented and that developing countries would have steady resources, and their planning efforts would not be nullified by unpredictable market fluctuations.[11]

Supplementary financing is supposed to mitigate the difficulties that arise in developing countries from unexpected shortfalls in their export proceeds which are of such a nature or duration that they cannot be dealt with by short-term balance of payments support. In such a situation, developing countries would be entitled to transfers of international resources to help them through their balance of payments difficulties and to help them avoid disruption of their development programs. The scheme of supplementary financing would extend medium- and long-term credit and would be offered in addition to the compensatory financing facility of the IMF, which gives short-term balance of payments support.[12] The scheme was to be financed by contributions from participating countries, while only the developing countries were to be eligible for assistance.[13]

Manufactures. The Geneva Conference agreed in principle that developing countries should diversify and expand their exports of manufactures and semi-manufactures, and not be limited mainly to the export of commodities.[14] To achieve this end one of the proposals sought the establishment of a temporary preferential system for the access of such exports to the markets of developed countries. Simultaneously, it was proposed that products of developed countries would

11. One estimate is that commodity agreements on coffee, cocoa, tea, bananas and sugar could have increased the revenue of the developing countries by $600 million per year in 1961, and by $900 million per year by 1970. See J. Pincus, "What Policy for Commodities?," *Foreign Affairs* (January 1964).

12. Beginning in March 1963, and based on the decision of its Executive Board, the IMF introduced a system of drawings designed to compensate for the short-fall in export receipts of any country. When a country's export earnings fell below a recent average the IMF could, providing that it was satisfied that this fall was short-term and beyond the country's control, lend to it up to 25 percent of its IMF quota repayable in three to five years. This dit not represent an extension of a member's borrowing authority and could prejudice his access to ordinary Fund drawings. See E. M. Bernstein, "The International Monetary Fund," in *The Global Partnership, op. cit.,* pp. 140-141.

13. See "Supplementary Financial Measures," Annex A.IV.18, *Proceedings,* Vol. I, pp. 52-53. The scheme was proposed by Sweden and the United Kingdom.

14. In 1963 only about 10 percent of the developing countries' exports were manufactures and semi-manufactures. Their total share in the world export of manufactures and semi-manufactures was about 4 percent (while they bought almost 1/4 of the manufactured products entering world trade). The developing countries exporting manufactures and semi-manufactures concentrated on light manufactures with high labor content (textiles, footwear, clothing) or they processed local raw materials (metals, plywood, jute). Pincus, *op. cit.,* p. 181 quoting UN data.

continue to be duty-bound, while the developing countries would not be obliged to grant any reciprocal concessions. The Conference was divided over the preferences proposal, for its acceptance would have meant a general departure from the most-favored-nation (MFN) principle, and a clear recognition by the international community that inequality does exist among states in the economic sphere.[15]

In a sense, preferences could be seen as a form of "inverted protectionism", giving a better chance to southern goods in the markets of developed countries. Furthermore, northern protectionism was sufficiently high, and tariff reduction and elimination through preferences was deemed very important. As a result of preferences, the manufactured products of developing countries would be placed in a better competitive position—even when they originated from inefficient industrial processes. Basically advocated here was the establishment, in the optimal situation, of one-way free trade with a zero tariff applicable in the markets of developed countries for all industrial products originating in developing countries. This would create a price advantage for the exports of developing countries over their industrialized competitors; the newly created advantage would encourage, *inter alia,* a shift of processing industries closer to the sources of raw materials, increase domestic and foreign investment in their industrial output, and increase their export orientation which would result in improved domestic production and trading techniques.

The Transfer of Capital. At certain points during the Geneva Conference the argument could be heard in favor of "trade not aid". Although many developing countries had a political preference for more dignified forms of income transfer from the North—e.g., through the removal of the structural causes of their problems—the stress on financing and flow of aid resources could not be minimized. The participants in the Conference were quite aware of the fact that it was becoming increasingly difficult for developing countries to obtain either bilateral or multilateral aid in sufficient quantities. In absolute terms, the foreign aid flow was beginning to level off, and in relative terms it was declining, while the absorptive capacity of developing countries was increasing. Therefore, the Conference adopted the target that *each* individual economically advanced country supply financial resources to developing countries of a minimum net amount approaching as

15. The Conference took no action on the special Principle Three concerning preferences. Final Act, *Proceedings,* Vol. I, p. 22. See also the recommendation on preferences, Annex A.III,5, *ibid.,* p. 39. It states that "some developed countries are opposed to this principle, and support instead the application of the most-favored-nation principle in the extension of concessions by developed and developing countries."

nearly as possible 1 percent of its national income.[16] Regarding the terms of financing, "short periods of repayment, high rates of interest and limitations on the tying of credits to specific projects and to purchases from countries providing the capital" caused serious problems of debt servicing for many developing countries. The Conference therefore recommended a series of measures to ease this situation. *Inter alia,* it suggested that repayment be spread over considerably longer periods of time, that the aid be a blend of grants and loans, that interest rates should not exceed 3 percent and that loans not be tied to the purchase of capital equipment in the donor country.[17]

Shipping. In adopting a "Common Measure of Understanding on Shipping Questions", the Geneva Conference made only a first, modest step in this generally unexplored area, with a number of issues remaining unresolved and highly controversial. It was agreed in principle that there should be a close cooperation between users of shipping and liner conferences through consultation machinery to be established for that purpose. Among the matters that could be raised in such machinery were, *inter alia,* publication by conferences of their tariffs and regulations, increases in conference freight rates and a reasonable advance warning in this regard, the adequacy of shipping services, action to improve and promote the exports of developing countries, etc. The "common measure of understanding" suggested that international financing, aid, and technical assistance for the improvement of port operation and connected inland transport facilities in developing countries, should be made available on favorable terms and conditions. It also welcomed the development of merchant marines in developing countries ("on the basis of sound economic criteria"), and their participation in liner conferences as "full members on equitable terms".[18]

In summarizing, it can be said that in the short run the *Final Act* had three principal aims: (1) Increased access for developing countries' products, both by reducing northern agricultural protectionism, and, by introducing preferences on their manufactured and semi-manufactured products. (2) Regulation and stabilization of commodity markets, and offsetting the trend of deteriorating terms of trade by raising primary commodity prices to a remunerative level. (3) Adoption of measures to

16. "Growth and Aid," Annex A.IV.2, *ibid.,* p. 44. This represented a step forward as compared with the previous formulations of the target, which were less specific and spoke of the "1 percent of the combined national incomes of the economically advanced nations".

17. "Terms of Financing," Annex. A.IV.4, *ibid.,* p. 45.

18. See Annex A.IV.22, *ibid.,* pp. 54-55. For various reservations regarding the "common measure of understanding", as well as for the positions of developed and developing countries see the report of the Working Party on Shipping, *ibid.,* pp. 219-229.

increase the flow of financial resources to the South as well as to decrease the outflow of invisible payments from the South to the North.

The Institutional Problem at the Geneva Conference and the Birth of UNCTAD

No evaluation of the Geneva Conference would be satisfactory if it were confined to those provisions of the *Final Act* which deal with trade, financial measures and shipping. By themselves, these recommendations might have meant very little. By establishing the permanent organization, however, the Geneva Conference provided the base for a continuing debate and policy-making process in search of a consensus among the North and the South. This was a most important achievement.

Later we shall speak of the institutionalization and task expansion of UNCTAD and discuss additional points related to the 1964 Conference. We may now briefly turn our attention to the position of different groups of countries on the institutional issue when they arrived in Geneva, how the negotiations proceeded, and the crucial issues and how they were resolved.

The Setting. The initiative for the creation of the institutional framework had to come from the developing countries. There was already a detailed proposal for an ITO, submitted by the socialist states.[19] However, for two reasons it had to be of secondary importance: (1) the developed countries categorically declined to consider the establishment of a specialized agency, and (2) it was obvious that the Conference would be a confrontation between the West and the South, with the socialist countries and East-West trade playing only marginal roles.

The position of the developing countries as a group was not fully defined prior to the Conference. In their policy statements the three regional groups did stress the inadequacy of the existing institutional arrangements and the need for creating a new international organ.[20] The declarations submitted by regional groups of developing countries

19. A memorandum by the USSR (E/CONF.46/51), *ibid.*, Vol. V, pp. 428-429, and a draft resolution submitted by Czechoslovakia, Poland and the USSR (E/CONF.46/50), *ibid.*, Vol. I, pp. 244-268. These proposals had already been submitted to Session III of the Preparatory Committee, where due to lack of time they were not considered and were later referred to the Conference.

20. The three statements were: the Niamey resolution on UNCTAD adopted by the Economic and Social Commission of the Organization of African Unity (OAU) in December 1963, *ibid.*, Vol. VI, pp. 55-56; the Teheran resolution adopted by ECAFE (50 (XX)) in March 1964, *ibid.*, Vol. VII, p. 85; and the Charter of Alta Gracia adopted by the meeting of the Organization of American States (OAS) in March 1964, *ibid.*, Vol. VI, pp. 57-66.

indicated a general conviction that the creation of a specialized institution or agency would encounter insurmountable obstacles. More specifically, to establish such an organization, an international treaty would be needed, and many feared that as was the case with the Havana Charter, the United States Congress would fail to ratify the agreement. In this sense, the developing countries were more realistic than the socialist ones. The latter had suggested that the Conference create an International Trade Organization which would (1) be autonomous but act under UN auspices; (2) be open to all states regardless of their membership in the UN; (3) be empowered to deal with all questions of international trade; (4) have sufficient authority to ensure compliance with its own recommendations; and (5) be based on principles acceptable to all states.[21]

Of the developing countries' declarations, only the Charter of Alta Gracia contained a more detailed institutional proposal. The Latin American countries stressed the need for setting up an international organization within the UN system to deal with world trade problems, and with the problems of development in particular. Until such time, however, they proposed a transitional solution—i.e., the periodic conference with a standing committee, a permanent secretariat with its own budget, and *ad hoc* committees as required. This machinery was to work in close cooperation with ECOSOC. The proposal generally resembled the one that Secretary-General Raúl Prebisch made in his report to the Conference.[22]

On the institutional issue, the western countries held a tentative position, reached in the OECD before the confrontation in Geneva began.[23] There was a consensus among them on certain principles which were to serve as guidelines in the discussion of institutional questions. First of all the developed countries intended to allow the least possible disturbance of the institutional *status quo*. They only reluctantly agreed to attend the Conference, and their main aim was to block the establishment of any distinct new organization, be it an International Trade

21. It is interesting to note that the draft resolution of the socialist states (E/CONF.46/50, *op. cit.*) provided for equitable representation in all ITO organs for the three existing groups of states, with every country having one vote. Also, the deputy directors-general and the secretariat staff were to be selected with a view to ensuring equitable representation of the three groups.

22. For details see Prebisch, *op. cit.*, pp. 52-54.

23. Our discussion of the position of developed countries is based on the "Report on the Activities of the *Ad Hoc* Working Party of the Trade Committee," OECD doc. TC(64)4 (4 Febr. 1964). The OECD ministers established the Working Party in November 1963 to prepare the guidelines for a joint strategy that the member countries would pursue on trade and development subjects on the agenda of the Geneva Conference. Due to lack of time, the party's chairman made a personal report which, of course, did not commit member states.

Organization or any other similar specialized organization.

Their second objective was to protect the operation and competence of GATT. They recognized that this task was made more difficult by the fact that GATT had not as yet produced any beneficial results for the developing countries' trade. The developed countries felt that the UN should be informed about—and should discuss—trade and development problems, but in their view GATT was the appropriate instrument for the implementation of international trade policies. They also felt strongly that if some institutional solution were adopted in Geneva, particular care should be taken to ensure that the new body's functions did not overlap those of the existing international organizations, and that it should fit without difficulty into the UN structure. They generally agreed that GATT and other organizations both within and outside the UN, given the opportunity, were adequate for the effective consideration of trade and development issues.

The delegates to the OECD meetings acknowledged that the developing countries would have a dominant influence on the final outcome of the Conference. They also realized that pressure for establishing new institutional arrangements would intensify as the Conference progressed.[24] The participants, therefore, felt that it was premature to adopt an institutional plan, since the course of deliberations in Geneva would indicate the time when it would be necessary to take a stand—a stand which would then be firmly defended in order to achieve a compromise solution with other groups of countries. On the basis of the OECD guidelines the developed countries intended to take a bargaining position which would be at the minimal end of the continuum of possible institutional solutions.

At the same time it was true that some developed countries sensed that they could not assume a purely "static and negative" attitude in Geneva and that the developing countries could not leave the Conference completely empty handed. They, therefore, saw the possibility of accepting some degree of institutional innovation, even though as a group they arrived at such a conclusion only much later, during the final stages of the Conference. Some agreement, although incomplete, crystallized around a possible structure outlined within the OECD Working Group. There would be a periodic conference either specially called each time (presumably by ECOSOC, like the Geneva Conference) or adjourned; a standing committee would function in the interim

24. This conclusion was possibly based on the knowledge that few substantive concessions would be made in Geneva; as a result, the institutional sphere would remain the only hope for any concrete achievements. This would become clear to developing countries only in the later stages of the Conference, and they would then concentrate all their pressure on establishing a continuing machinery.

period, either as an offshoot of the Conference, or an existing committee reconstructed, like CICT. To avoid the "disguised creation" of a specialized institution, this standing committee would not be empowered to form any subordinate bodies. This machinery would be serviced by the Department of Economic and Social Affairs at the Headquarters Secretariat of the United Nations. Finally, in relation to this UN organ, GATT would maintain its activities in complete independence and with no interference whatever.

The Conference. During the initial stages of the Conference, the institutional question was generally in the background.[25] The relevant statements of delegates dealt with the assessment of existing international organizations and their activities—of GATT in particular.

Obviously, the arguments were both for and against GATT. Criticism against this organization was expressed succinctly by Prebisch. GATT with its 61 full members and 13 associate members was far from universal. Problems of trade were dealt with in a fragmentary fashion and not as part of the development problem. GATT had not demonstrated that it was an effective instrument for regulating trade between developed and developing countries; neither had it promoted trade among developing nations. Furthermore, the state-trading nations with the exception of Czechoslovakia had remained outside GATT, because at the time of its creation, trade between governments was considered an exception and a deviation. Agreements on primary commodities and their regulation were negotiated outside of GATT and were not subject to coordinated action.[26] On the pro-GATT side, the western representatives argued that GATT and other institutions had evolved sufficiently, and that there was no need to establish additional machinery until its purposes could be clearly ascertained and it was determined whether or not the existing international organizations could fulfil these purposes as well.

Originally, the views of the developing countries regarding the nature of an institutional solution varied. Some more radical delegations were ready to go along with the proposal of the socialist states for the creation of a new ITO; others were in favor of periodic conferences as a transitional means toward an ITO. Some talked about a periodic conference, without explicitly mentioning a new organization. Still others tended to support the view of the developed countries that adjustments in existing organizations and agencies would be sufficient to accomplish the purpose of the Conference. The situation was fluid

25. Note again that the most detailed discussion to be found on the institutional issue at the Geneva Conference is in Cordovez, *op. cit.*, pp. 281-328. We have relied extensively on his text.

26. Prebisch, *op. cit.*, p. 52.

38

when unexpectedly the first draft resolution on institutional machinery was submitted by Burma, Ghana, Indonesia, Nigeria, and Syria.[27] This draft led to negotiations on the nature of the institution and gradually shifted the focus to this question, making it the most important issue on the agenda during the closing weeks of the Conference. As there was no consensus on substantive issues, all the developing countries had by then agreed that an institution had to be created which would be capable of legitimizing and putting into effect their specific purposes and goals. They wanted an institutional tool which could be utilized to further pry open the tightly shut doors of traditional commercial and other economic policies of the West.

The draft resolution asked that the Conference be established as a permanent organ of the General Assembly (the ECOSOC being ignored intentionally), that it be the highest specialized forum in the UN competent to promote international cooperation in the field of trade and development, that it become the center for harmonizing the policies of governments and regional economic groupings, and that it have a permanent and independent secretariat and a separate budget. The Trade and Development Council would be a deliberating, executive and coordinating body of the Conference. GATT would be subjected to the changes considered necessary by the Geneva Conference, and would be brought under the purview of the new organization. As a matter of fact, GATT would *mutatis mutandis* become the Conference's commission on tariffs. The new body would be charged with the coordination and integration of the existing organizations.

As far as the West was concerned, this proposal represented a "disguised creation of a specialized agency" and as such was unacceptable. However, the sponsors of the resolution, after very close consultation with members of the temporary secretariat of the Conference, did not propose to make it acceptable to developed countries; rather, their chief aim was to agitate the group of developing countries which as yet was not cohesive and had no common platform on the institutional issue. Such a platform, of course, was a prerequisite for any kind of negotiations with the West. By being relatively "extreme", sponsors also hoped to gain a better bargaining position vis-à-vis the developed countries. In the former sense, the Burma draft was relatively successful: a week after its issue, the group of 19 Latin American countries presented their draft resolution, based on the Alta Gracia Charter.[28] It was more moderate in tone than the Burma resolution, as it did not contain any specific proposals on GATT, or on the independence of the

27. E/CONF.46/C.4/L.3 (20 Apr. 1964) *Proceedings,* Vol. I, pp. 244-269. The leading role in this group was played by Burma.
28. E/CONF.46/C.4/L.5 (28 Apr. 1964), *idem.*

secretariat, or on the executive role of the council. The group of developing countries could then begin consultations in an effort to reconcile the two draft resolutions and to produce a joint text.

Meanwhile, the western nations also had to show their hand. For the first time, and in accordance with their OECD deliberations, they reversed their previous policy stand and stated publicly that in principle they would not oppose the establishment of a periodic conference, a standing committee, or appropriate arrangements for a secretariat.[29] However, as to their nature, the draft resolution of the developed countries differed significantly from both the drafts of the developing countries. What were the differences? The western draft nowhere mentioned that the continuing machinery would serve as a transitional arrangement leading to ITO. The developing countries' drafts generally ignored ECOSOC, while the West emphasized that the new machinery should become part of ECOSOC. Also, the developed countries rejected the notion of a separate secretariat, and argued that any new secretariat should be an integral part of the UN Secretariat—i.e., the UN Secretary-General should make all necessary additional arrangements to assure that an adequate secretariat would be available for servicing the Conference and the Commission on International Trade. Another significant element in the western draft concerned the composition of the commission; it would be made up of 34 members with equal representation for developing and developed countries, including the principal trading nations.[30]

With the appearance of these draft resolutions, negotiations between the developed and the developing countries, as well as among the developing countries themselves, went behind the curtain. There are no records of what happened during those weeks, a fact which foreshadowed the typical negotiating pattern of the group system which was emerging. When these informal negotiations and the revised drafts surfaced, the developing countries acted as a group—"Group of 75"—with a joint draft resolution. There were two draft resolutions that counted now, the western and the southern.[31] These two were a bit closer to each other than the original ones. However, a number of controversial issues remained.[32]

29. E/CONF.46/C.4/L.9 (6 May 1964), *idem*.

30. Based on the summary provided by Cordovez, *op. cit.*, p. 294.

31. The revised draft resolutions of the developing, the western, and the socialist countries are presented in a comparative manner in *Proceedings*, Vol. I, pp. 268-287. The socialist draft now contained the idea of a periodic conference as a transitional arrangement toward the creation of an ITO; this brought it much closer to the position of the developing countries.

32. The "elements of deadlock" are summarized extensively in Cordovez, *op. cit.*, pp. 297-303.

The developing countries continued to insist on the eventual creation of an ITO, while the western countries would only concede "the continuing review of organizational arrangements in the light of experience of their work and activities." The developing states demanded that the Conference be an organ of the General Assembly based on Article 22 of the UN Charter, while the developed ones proposed that the new organization be established in accordance with Article 13 and Chapters IX and X of the Charter, which implied that it would be subject to the authority of both the Assembly and the Council. According to the western draft, the principal function of the Conference would be to: (1) promote international trade, and formulate principles and policies for such trade; (2) study the legal bases of multilateral trade relations only among countries with different systems of social and economic organization, and at different stages of development;[33] and, (3) on the basis of its study, recommend to the ECOSOC the establishment of special *ad hoc* machinery for the negotiation of legal instruments. On the other hand, the developing countries' draft gave overall responsibilities to the new institution which would: (1) develop policies for the expansion of trade between all countries; (2) establish principles and policies, plus means of action and instruments for putting them into effect; (3) establish negotiating machinery where appropriate for the adoption of multilateral agreements, and (4) review, evaluate, and coordinate the activities of other institutions in the field of trade and development.

The developing countries were also in favor of three specialized commissions (commodities, manufactures and financing cum invisibles); the developed countries were ready to accept only one (commodities), with the stipulation that additional commissions could be created later. In regard to the composition of the standing committee, the Group of 75 proposed 52 members, divided according to the equitable geographic distribution key which had been developed at the Conference;[34] the West, although it retreated from its earlier position on parity between developed and developing countries, maintained that the committee should be composed of 40 members, 12 of which would be the principal trading states.[35] Finally, the most crucial difference pertained to voting. The developing countries proposed that decisions on matters

33. Trade among countries at similar levels of development and with similar socio-economic systems—i.e., trade among developed countries—was to remain solely a function of GATT.

34. Thirty-two seats for the developing countries, 14 seats for the developed countries, and 6 seats for the socialist countries of Eastern Europe.

35. The sponsors of the draft indicated that they expected 14 out of 40 seats to go to the developed market economies, including 10 of the 12 permanent seats for major traders. *Ibid.*, p. 300. If the formula proposed by the developing coun-

of substance by the Conference be adopted by a two-thirds majority of those present and voting—by a simple majority in the standing committee—while those on the matters of procedure be adopted by a simple majority. The developed countries advocated that the Conference recommendations be adopted by a two-thirds majority—simple majority in the standing committee—including the simple majority of the 12 principal trading states present and voting.[36]

On the basis of the revised drafts, the parties engaged in further informal negotiations, but no consensus could be reached. The developing countries objected to the efforts of the other side to restrict the autonomy of the continuing machinery and to make it in any way subordinate to ECOSOC. They also disagreed with the contention that negotiating machinery could only be created in those areas where such machinery did not already exist; they pointed out that a great many countries, both developing and socialist, were members neither of GATT nor of similar institutions. As for the composition of the standing body, the developing countries felt that the formula worked out in Geneva—based on equitable geographic distribution—should be adhered to.[37] Finally, on the question of voting, the developing countries deemed the western proposal totally unacceptable, pointing out that it would give a virtual veto on matters of importance to 6 out of 12 major trading nations, in both the Conference and its standing organ. In his rebuttal, the spokesman for the developed countries argued that they accounted for over 80 percent of world trade, that the recommendations of the continuing machinery would ask of them to adopt certain policies which would affect their domestic situation, and that they therefore wished to ensure that their views would be taken into account. In other words, they feared that decisions could be imposed by a majority vote of the developing countries, so they wished to be placed on an equal footing through the special voting procedure.[38]

With time running out, no compromise solution in sight, and the Fourth Committee anxious to wind up its activities, the radical wing

---

tries were applied to a 40 member body, the developed countries would have received only 11 seats.

36. A section in this chapter will be devoted to discussion of the voting crisis at the Geneva Conference.

37. The spokesman for the developing countries rejected the concept of permanent, non-elective seats, but at the same time said that his group would have nothing against a gentlemen's agreement which would ensure the election of major trading nations to the standing body, in a manner similar to the election of some principal states to ECOSOC. Statement by Pakistan, E/CONF.46/C.4/L.18, *Proceedings,* Vol. I, pp. 237-239.

38. Statement by Norway on behalf of developed countries, E/CONF.46/C.4/L.19, *ibid.,* p. 239.

within the Group of 75 successfully pressed to have the draft resolution of the developing countries voted upon.[39] It was approved by 83 to 20, with 3 abstentions. The vote had a propaganda fallout in the sense that it demonstrated the determination and unity of the group of developing countries. And although it displeased the representatives of the developed countries, the vote and the pressure that it generated made them more willing to negotiate a compromise. On the other hand, the voting also represented a climax after which the tension and hostility generated by the institutional issue began to subside gradually, while those in the Group of 75 who were advocating conciliation slowly started to gain the upper hand.[40] All agreed that another attempt should be made to reach a compromise solution on the institutional issue.

The compromise was sought under Prebisch's leadership by a small circle of delegates who had been negotiating on this question all along.[41] Voting was the crucial issue, on which everything else depended. It was settled after the western countries dropped their insistence on having blocking power, and agreed that all substantive decisions should be adopted by a 2/3 majority in the Conference and a simple majority in the standing organ, while the developing countries accepted the additional procedure of conciliation, the general outline of which was hammered out during these same sessions.[42] There were other gaps between the opposing views that had to be bridged: primarily the size of the standing body, the functions of UNCTAD, and its relation to ECOSOC. Once these points were settled, the way was cleared for the adoption of a draft recommendation, which was presented by the small working group to the plenary. This recommendation was incorporated into the *Final Act*.[43] Eventually, its unchanged text, supplemented with the conciliation mechanism provisions worked out by the special com-

39. E/CONF.46/C.4/L.12/Rev.1, *ibid.*, pp. 241-243.
40. Consult later in this chapter our discussion of the group of developing countries at the Geneva Conference.
41. Among the participants were: Gardner (US), Unwin (UK), Viaud (France), Mates (Yugoslavia), Lacarte (Uruguay), Jolles (Switzerland), De Seynes (UN Under-Secretary for Economic and Social Affairs), etc. They reported on the progress of negotiations to their own groups. (It is interesting to note that by agreement with Prebisch, his close cooperator W. R. Malinowski was responsible in the acting secretariat for the institutional issue, from the earliest stage until voting on the draft resolution of the developing countries. Thereafter, Prebisch took over. The special role of these two men in the creation of UNCTAD is generally acknowledged.)
42. Since there was no time to work out the conciliation mechanism, the matter was referred to a special committee of governmental experts, to be convened after the Conference in order to work out a conciliation scheme which the General Assembly would consider later.
43. E/CONF.46/L.22, which became recommendation A.V.1, *ibid.*, pp. 58-62.

mittee,[44] was adopted as the General Assembly resolution 1995 (XIX). Thus the United Nations Conference on Trade and Development (UNCTAD) came into being as a permanent organ of the UN General Assembly on December 30, 1964.[45]

A Sketch of the Machinery that Emerged.[46] The Conference itself is the highest organ of the continuing machinery. It was to be convened at intervals not more than three years apart (so far, however, it has met at four year intervals). Its members are all countries that belong to the UN, specialized agencies, and the International Atomic Energy Agency. Thus, nine states that are not members of the UN are members of UNCTAD—F.R. Germany, the Holy See, the Republic of Korea, Liechtenstein, Monaco, San Marino, Switzerland, the Republic of Viet-Nam, and Western Samoa—making it larger than its parent organization. The Conference has not been brought into an organic relationship with the ECOSOC as the West desired; but the compromise calls for the Board to report to the General Assembly through the Economic and Social Council. Regarding the functions of the Conference, the resolution is somewhat ambiguous, as it reflects the strain between the view of the developed countries, which insisted on maintaining GATT's jurisdiction intact and preserving ECOSOC's primacy in the economic and social field in the UN, and the view of the developing and the socialist countries, which saw UNCTAD as the central UN organ for trade and development, and a transitional machinery leading toward a full-fledged International Trade Organization.

Hence, UNCTAD should "promote international trade"—particularly between countries at different stages of development, between developing countries, and also between countries with different economic and social systems—and when doing so, it should take into account "the functions performed by the existing international organizations." This clause aimed at protecting GATT's role in regulating trade among developed nations. UNCTAD is "to review and facilitate

44. "Proposals Designed to Establish a Process of Conciliation within the UNCTAD: Report of the Special Committee," UN doc. A/5749.

45. The resolution does not specify the Article of the UN Charter under which the General Assembly had set up UNCTAD. This is the result of a compromise between the developing countries and the developed countries, the latter continuing to adhere to their interpretation of the constitutional prerogatives of ECOSOC. However, it is considered that the establishment of UNCTAD falls under Article 22, as the only provision of the Charter which speaks of the General Assembly setting up its subsidiary organs. Cordovez, *op. cit.,* p. 309.

46. For a detailed description of the institutional framework of UNCTAD and its functioning, see *ibid.,* pp. 307-325. The acronym UNCTAD has caused some confusion because it is used to refer to both the permanent institution and its triennial conference.

44

BASIC ORGANIZATIONAL CHART of UNCTAD

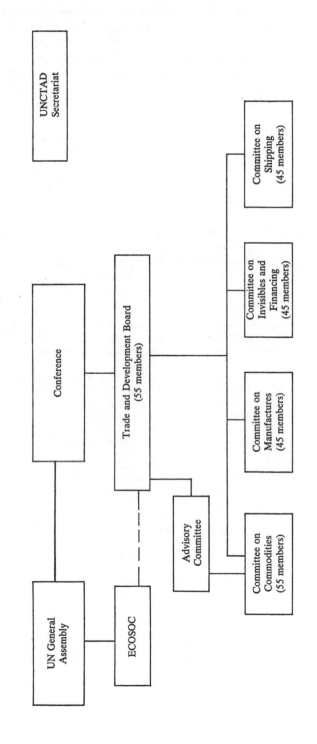

the co-ordination of activities of other institutions within the UN system," but when engaging in such pursuits, it should "co-operate with the General Assembly and the ECOSOC with respect to the performance of their responsibilities for coordination under the Charter of the UN." [47] Such equivocal wording accommodates two tendencies, one aimed at safeguarding the coordinating capacity of ECOSOC, the other wanting to see UNCTAD endowed with broad coordinating powers. Yet another confusing provision states that UNCTAD can initiate action for the negotiation and adoption of multilateral legal instruments in the field of trade, but with due regard for the adequacy of the existing organs for negotiations, and without duplicating their activities. There are two dubious points in this formulation: 1. Does "initiate" mean that UNCTAD itself is a competent organ for negotiation? and 2. What is the meaning of "adequacy" and "duplication"; how are they to be determined, and on what criteria? These original disagreements are not fully settled at the present day.

The Trade and Development Board, as the standing committee was named,[48] consists of 55 members, elected by the Conference for three years.[49] The Board attempts to ensure work continuity by acting on re-

47. The General Assembly was mentioned upon the request of the developing countries. Involved is the standing dispute of whether the General Assembly or the ECOSOC should be primarily responsible for coordinating functions of the United Nations. *Ibid.*, p. 311.

48. "Board" was acceptable to the developed countries, which objected to "Council" proposed by the developing countries, because this would imply an equal footing with the Economic and Social Council. While the developing countries objected to "Commission" proposed by the developed countries, because it suggested a functional commission of the ECOSOC, they agreed to "Board", because the Havana Charter provided for the standing body of the ITO to be called the "Executive Board." *Idem.*

49. The touchy problem of the Board's composition was resolved by paying attention both to equitable geographic distribution and the desirability of continuous representation of the principal trading states. Twenty-two members come from the Afro-Asian group of developing countries plus Yugoslavia (List A), 18 from the group of western countries (List B)—thus the "B Group", 9 from the Latin American group of developing countries, plus Trinidad and Tobago, and Jamaica (List C), and 6 from the socialist states of Eastern Europe (List D)—thus the "D Group". The Preparatory Committee of the Geneva Conference originally had established the above four lists of states for the purpose of dividing up the offices among them. (See Chapter XII for a discussion of groups in UNCTAD). Note that there are 29 states on the "B" list which comprises the "developed" countries. Seven of these are of minor importance—the Holy See, Iceland, Ireland, Liechtenstein, Luxembourg, Monaco, and San Marino, while Cyprus belongs to the Group of 77. Portugal is *de facto* excluded from membership on the Board because of African opposition. This leaves only 20 serious candidates from the B Group for the 18 seats to which it is entitled. For all practical purposes, all of them have a permanent seat on the Board. The United

commendations, declarations and resolutions that are passed by the Conference, in addition to adopting many of its own. It also serves as a preparatory committee for future sessions of the Conference. The Board is the main technical organ of the Conference, in the sense that all the other more specialized organs of UNCTAD report to it and are its subsidiary bodies. The Board is empowered to establish such subsidiary organs as may be necessary for its successful functioning. The General Assembly resolution directed the Board to establish committees on commodities, manufactures, and invisibles and financing related to trade. Since it was also directed to make a decision on institutional means for dealing with the problems of shipping, the Board at its first session added a Committee on Shipping. The Committee on Commodities consists of 55 members, while the other committees have 45 members each. All members are elected for three years.

As regards the rules of procedure in UNCTAD, those concerning the conduct of business are the same as in other organs of the United Nations, e.g. powers of the president, speeches, precedence, points of order, adjournment, closure and suspension of debate, etc. The Board is required to meet twice a year. One of the innovations as compared to other UN organs is the formal recognition of the existence of four groups of states; another innovation is the institution of a system of a geographic rotation, based on a seven-year cycle, for the offices of president and rapporteur for any given year in the work of the Board. Decisions by the Board and by the committees are taken by a simple majority of those present and voting, whereas in the Conference a 2/3 majority is required for substantive decisions and only a simple majority for the procedural ones. Before a vote is taken, however, a conciliation process may take place.[50] Appropriate for conciliation are those proposals before the Board or Conference or their subsidiary organs which substantially affect the economic and/or financial interests of particular countries, such as: economic plans; trade, monetary or tariff policies, or balance of payments; policies of economic assistance or transfer of resources; levels of employment, income, revenue or investment; and rights and obligations under international agreements and

---

States, Belgium, F.R. Germany, France, Italy, The Netherlands, Switzerland, the United Kingdom, Japan, Canada and Australia belong to the subgroup whose continuing representation on the Board is considered as desirable, according to an internal understanding reached by the developed countries at the end of the Geneva Conference.

50. For a detailed explanation and interpretation of conciliation process see R. Krishnamurti and D. Cordovez, "Conciliation Procedures in UNCTAD" in *Journal of World Trade Law,* Vol. 2, No. 4, July/August 1968, pp. 445-466.

treaties. Proposals which are not subject to conciliation are procedural matters; studies or investigations; establishment of subsidiary bodies by the Board, within its competence; recommendations of a general nature which do not require any specific action; and proposals involving action in pursuance of recommendations which have been unanimously adopted by the Conference. The conciliation procedure is quasi-automatic, since it is set into motion by a request from a small number of states—ten in the case of the Conference, five in the case of the Board, and three in committees. When a request for conciliation is submitted after the conclusion of a debate on any proposal, the voting is suspended, and the conciliation mechanism begins to operate. The contested proposal is referred to a conciliation committee; this is an *ad hoc* body, which should be small in size and composed of those countries interested in or affected by the matter under consideration, while keeping in mind the equitable geographic distribution. This committee does not vote. It reports to the next session of the Board, which, if it finds it necessary, can extend the committee's mandate until its next session. Depending upon the success of conciliation, the Board can adopt a resolution, either unanimously or by a majority vote. It is interesting to note that the conciliation procedure should apply also to matters which involve changes in the fundamental provisions of General Assembly resolution 1995 (XIX), but which provisions are to be considered "fundamental" for the purposes of conciliation is determined by a simple majority of the Conference or the Board.

For the servicing of the new UNCTAD machinery, an "adequate permanent and full-time secretariat within the United Nations Secretariat" was established. Its head—appointed by the UN Secretary-General and confirmed by the General Assembly—holds the rank of Under-Secretary of the United Nations, and has the title of Secretary-General of UNCTAD. Dr. Raúl Prebisch was appointed to this post in February 1965. The staff of the UNCTAD secretariat is part of the UN Secretariat staff, and it is therefore subject to the same rules and regulations. Appointments are made by the Secretary-General of the UN upon the recommendation of the Secretary-General of UNCTAD.

The Developing Countries at the Geneva Conference

The emergence of a united group of developing countries and the voting controversy were among the highlights of the Geneva Conference. This background will assist us in our discussion of actors and the decision-making process in UNCTAD. The Joint Declaration of the Developing Countries at the 1963 session of the General Assembly led to the appearance of the Group of 77—a new phenomenon in international

48

organizations.[51] On the basis of this declaration the three regional groups tried to precoordinate their respective positions and elaborated the regional declarations—Alta Gracia, Niamey, and Teheran. However, to advance from the agreement on a generally worded resolution to group action in an organized and disciplined manner was a step which required a great deal of time and effort.

This process was clearly noticeable in the Fourth Committee of the Conference which dealt with institutional problems. Its agenda included a highly political issue. Thus, it was there that the political differences in the developing countries' coalition were most visible. Yet, at the same time all developing countries had a vested interest in the establishment of a suitable machinery. Moreover, this was a matter which everybody quite clearly understood and could get excited about, without the technicalities and complexities of economics and financing that were beyond the reach of many delegates. In other words, it offered suitable raw material for political mobilization, especially so because of the very negative attitude adopted by the West, and by the United States in particular, on institutional matters.

When the draft resolution containing the institutional proposal was submitted by Burma, Ghana, Indonesia, Nigeria and Syria, only a degree of incipient solidarity existed in the Group of 75. The draft was prepared and tabled without consulting other developing countries. Burma and Ghana were rather sympathetic to the socialist proposal for an ITO and this was reflected in many places in their draft resolution, which basically expressed the views of the more radical developing countries. As such, it had little chance of winning the endorsement of the Group of 75 as a whole. However, its primary purpose was different. The draft resolution was intended to spark off negotiations among the developing countries themselves and to spur them into adopting a forceful negotiating platform.[52] The temporary secretariat members who played a crucial role in the formulation of the five-power draft were striving to unite the developing countries, a condition which they felt was a prerequisite to confrontation with the West. Many delegates were made to realize that if they remained divided, the developing countries would continue to be "a bunch of beggars" and the "clientele of the rich", while united they would be a "political force".

The differences between the Burmese and Latin American draft resolutions could not be easily reduced. There was no agreement on the

---

51. General Assembly resolution 1897 (XVIII), Annex (11 November, 1963). It was signed by 75 countries, hence the original name "Group of 75".

52. For example, the Latin Americans were inspired to redraft certain "mild" provisions of their text before it was tabled, and to make them more demanding.

request of the more radical members of the group that the maximum institutional demands be incorporated in the joint draft. The radical wing was not a solid coalition. The position of some delegations very much reflected the personalities of their leaders. But to characterize the consistent members of this constellation—for example, Burma, Indonesia or Dahomey—one could say that they based their actions on the concept of class-struggle against the rich nations. This was in sharp contrast to the approach of the moderates—as typified by India—who saw the Geneva Conference as an effort at international cooperation, of developed and developing countries alike, in the search for compromise solutions to the economic development problems of the Third World.

The long process of drafting the joint resolution was speeded up when six western nations introduced their draft on institutional matters. The provision for parity between the West and the South on the proposed 34-member standing committee caused a very negative and emotional reaction among the developing countries and contributed to their feeling that a joint and firm stand must urgently be taken. When adopted, their joint draft resolution did not represent a full consensus. The radical wing was generally displeased with the conciliatory nature of certain provisions. Yet, once the draft was made public, all the developing countries stood firmly behind it. Furthermore, the western proposal for the special voting procedure galvanized the solidarity of the Group of 75. In the early stages of the Conference, the developed countries had faced the institutional issue in a somewhat conciliatory mood. But, as their group position hardened, the developing countries found it easier to gather around the common denominator of their grievances, and to disregard the minor differences that separated them.[53]

The bitter clash over the institutional issue in the public meetings was not quite duplicated on the level of informal negotiations between developed and developing countries; there the goal of reaching a compromise was never out of sight. However, the informal negotiations could not produce consensus on two basic questions: the nature of voting and the composition of the standing committee. As the time allotted for deliberations on the committee level was to end soon, the radical members of the Group of 75 grew impatient and argued that

53. The West's new stand coincided with the realization that the creation of extensive machinery could not be avoided, and the arrival of a new US negotiator on the institutional issue. The hard line promoted by Richard Gardner to many delegates from developing countries personified the aloof and insensitive North. Note, however, that some sort of a balance was established with the arrival of Edward Heath of the United Kingdom, who gathered the support and confidence of many developing countries with his generally positive approach to the institutional matter. In fact, the outcome of the institutional controversy was significantly affected by the role Heath played.

50

efforts should not be wasted on attempting to negotiate with the West. Instead, they proposed that the institutional machinery be put into motion by a vote; they further objected to any weakening of the joint draft resolution for the sake of a compromise. As their pressure could not be resisted and to satisfy them and to preserve the unity of the group, other developing countries agreed to have a vote.

Once the vote was taken and the matter was out of the Fourth Committee, the developed countries approached Prebisch and asked him to help find a base for a compromise. On the basis of the "Prebisch paper" last minute negotiations took place. In the Group of 75, the radical wing expressed angry dissatisfaction with the way negotiations were being handled by those delegated in the name of the group, and by Prebisch. They apparently had expected that the resolution voted through in the Fourth Committee would be adhered to in its entirety, in contrast to the negotiators who saw it as a flexible negotiating platform.[54] Some ministers at the meeting of the "75" bitterly attacked the compromise proposals, the negotiators, and even Prebisch—who had come to the group in order to speak in favor of some flexibility in this matter. At this point, the vociferous and uncompromising delegations among the developing countries appeared to have a majority, and many feared that the nascent Group of 75 was splitting up under the strain, and also jeopardizing creation of the new machinery. These delegations disavowed the negotiators and refused to support them in their search for a compromise with the developed countries.[55] Exposed to violent criticism, the delegates on the original negotiating group withdrew and asked the representatives from the radical wing to substitute for them. The idea was to have the "radicals" talk directly with the developed countries. In these meetings it appears that the new representatives of the Group of 75 behaved as if on a rostrum, and failed to establish a dialogue with the other side. Having realized that such an approach

54. Robertson, *op. cit.,* p. 20.
55. Particularly vociferous were Tanzania, Guinea, Dahomey, Burma, Ethiopia and the Philippines. Part of the problem lay in the fact that the ministers of some developing countries returned near the end of the Conference, and being uninformed about what went on, they acted like "a bull in a china shop." They were especially emotional on the voting issue, and showed lack of understanding for the intricacies of negotiations. Also, during the Conference, the press noted the presence of a group of Chinese diplomats in Geneva, who on several occasions held meetings with certain Asian and African delegations. It has been alleged that they inspired the actions of the radical wing and kept encouraging them to assume positions which would break up the Conference, thus demonstrating that it is useless to try to cooperate with the capitalist world. Further, it has been suggested that the militancy of some delegates was encouraged by certain developed countries which thus hoped to prevent the emergence of a compromise and the establishment of a new machinery.

did not lead to a solution, they allowed matters to return to the hands of the original negotiators. The conciliatory line was fully reinstated, and it became apparent that opposition to a compromise did not command the support of a sufficient number of developing states. Things further calmed down when the tentative compromise was reached on the voting issue.

Later we shall speak in greater detail about the Group of 77. For the time being, let it suffice to conclude that in spite of internal disagreements and political differences, the group of developing countries emerged from the Geneva Conference as organizationally unified, an instrument for collective negotiations. There was no doubt that it would continue to act within the machinery that was to be created. The joint declaration by the seventy-seven developing countries sounded relatively optimistic in its appraisal of the Conference.[56] Those who drafted the text partly covered their ill-feelings about the lack of concrete achievements. Too much criticism, they reasoned, would disturb the delicate balance achieved near the end and would hurt the chances for the continuing machinery to come into being, since the recommendation still had to be finalized and approved by the General Assembly. Also, it could possibly have adverse psychological effects on the developing countries, whose mobilization might slacken were the Conference to be declared a "total failure". In fact, they were protecting the two most important outcomes of the Conference, the emergence of the Group of 77 and the continuing institutional framework.

The Voting Controversy at the Geneva Conference. It seems that the delegates generally paid no serious attention beforehand to the possible ways of making decisions in the organization which was to be created. Many never engaged in such speculation, because they simply figured that the creation of new machinery could somehow be avoided. Others, on the assumption that the new body would be a part of the United Nations, deduced that the decisions should be made in the same manner as they are made in the General Assembly. The developing countries were taken rather by surprise when the first western draft asked for a parity between the two groups on the standing committee, and they were astonished when its revised version provided that a simple majority vote of 12 major trading nations would be necessary to reach any decisions on substance. The surprise was somewhat misplaced and such a move should have been anticipated. There was the

56. "Joint Declaration of the Seventy-Seven Developing Countries," *Proceedings, op. cit.,* Vol. I, pp. 67-68. Beginning with this declaration, the group acquired its present name, "the Group of 77." Of the original "75", New Zealand was excluded, while Kenya, South Korea and South Vietnam came in, making the new total of "77".

precedent of the ITO and later of the OTC, where major developed countries attempted to secure a privileged position for themselves, either through weighted voting or by providing for a special composition of the main bodies.[57]

Also, there were various pronouncements by the American decision-makers in the early 1960's on the subject of majority voting in the United Nations. At that time, the developed countries began to feel irritated by the developing countries' majorities, especially when the latter voted through a number of resolutions which were not to the liking of their more powerful colleagues. The United States in particular did not sympathize with the "unruly" and "uncompromising" majority of the developing countries which no longer could be effectively held under control. When President Kennedy came into office, the issue of creating a more "reasonable" decision-making system for the UN was raised—a system which would involve neither a veto, nor the principle of "one state, one vote".

What were some of the proposals to adjust voting procedures in the UN organs to the "power realities" in this organization, which were considered in Washington? The U.S. State Department did not take "weighted voting" into serious consideration for several reasons. To introduce such a procedure would mean amending the UN Charter; this, in turn required a 2/3 majority in the General Assembly and approval by the Security Council, and both measures were deemed impossible to obtain. Furthermore, it was felt that no system of weighted voting could overlook the population factor; the United States would

57. It is interesting that in the United States one of the criticisms of the Havana Charter was directed also at the fact that it contained no provision for weighted voting. In fact, it has been argued that the major trading nations turned their backs to the ITO because they failed to get voting rights for themselves they had got at Bretton Woods. [R. Townley, *The United Nations, A View from Within* (New York: Ch. Scribner's Sons, 1968), p. 229]. The advocates of the ITO claimed that it really made no difference whether the rule "one state, one vote" prevailed in this organization. Regarding the escape clauses and the balance-of-payments clause, in particular, the ITO would be guided by whatever the IMF said, and the United States could protect its interests in the IMF through the weighted voting procedure. Regarding the economic development clause, the United States and other industrial powers would control the majority on the Executive Board (composed of 18 members, 8 of which were to be states of chief economic importance). If the matters were sent to the Conference of the ITO, the possibility existed that the developing countries could muster a majority and outvote the industrial states. But, continued the argument, the economic differences among the developing countries were sharp, and their voting was not likely to be monolithic. There would be no single sharp cleavage of interests, and the voting pattern would constantly change, from issue to issue and from time to time, while a majority of countries would not seek to form—and would not succeed in forming—a cohesive voting bloc. See Wilcox, *op. cit.*, pp. 184-185, 197.

then be at a disadvantage since it has only 7 percent of the world's inhabitants. Also, a study was conducted about key votes that had taken place in the General Assembly in the past (the study was based on various voting formulae which were devised according to population and budget contributions by all countries). The results showed that weighted voting would have reduced the number of resolutions passed in spite of the American opposition, but at the same time to a much greater extent, it would have reduced the number of resolutions supported by the United States and approved by the UN.

Since weighted voting did not seem to be in the interest of the United States, some other solution had to be sought. One alternative was "dual voting", or a system of double majorities. For example, decisions of substance in the General Assembly would be made by a 2/3 majority of those present and voting, including therein a 2/3 vote of Security Council members. This method would "preserve" the principle "one state, one vote", while not requiring the sensitive and complicated exercise of assigning different weights to votes of countries. Still another proposal involved committees with selective representation, a method which, it was thought, would introduce "greater responsibility" into the decision-making process through provisions for election to permanent seats for those members that have special interests and responsibility in a given matter.[58]

Negotiations over the possible creation of a continuing machinery offered convenient testing grounds for the U.S. policy-makers in their efforts to implement a "more responsible" system of decision-making in the United Nations. Weaker stress probably would have been placed on this matter had not the developing countries at the Conference coalesced into an organizationally unified group that caucused together, relied on common spokesmen, and voted through a number of resolutions over the opposition of the West.

The voting issue was raised by the developed countries with two purposes in mind: first, to restrain the voting power of the emerging bloc of developing nations, and second, to improve the bargaining power of the West on other institutional questions. The first western proposal—aimed at counteracting the large numbers that the 77 had in their favor—called for equal representation of the two sides in the standing committee. However, the committee could not affect the decisions taken by the Conference itself, unless it were to be conceived as a directorate with the Conference acting only as a consultative body. This, of course, was unlikely, in view of the general consensus that the

58. For a discussion of the US policy see R. Gardner, "Adapting U.N. Procedures to Reflect Power Realities," in his *In Pursuit of World Order* (New York: Praeger, 1966), pp. 267-273.

Conference should be the supreme organ of the new machinery. Comprehension of this fact and the realization that it would be impossible to limit the size of the standing committee led to the withdrawal of the equal representation proposal. The special voting procedure, which was then advanced, aimed at both the Conference and the standing committee.

The West tried to present this second proposal as a concession to the developing countries who had raised such an uproar over the earlier one on equal representation. In effect, this was just a more sophisticated means to achieve the same aim. The developing countries understood this, and put up an even stronger resistance. At this time, it became obvious to many that the developed countries would not accept the decision-making procedure used in the General Assembly. Also, it was clear to everybody, including the U.S. delegation, that the developing countries would never accept the "12 major traders" formula, and that particularly for newly independent nations, the question of "one country, one vote" was an issue of far-reaching political implications.

The United States delegation was the main, if not the only, exponent among the developed countries of the hard-line on the decision-making issue.[59] There were several reasons for this. The general position of the United States at the Geneva Conference could be characterized as "unselective negativism".[60] More specifically, the voting question was used as a bargaining tool on several different levels. In relation to the entire institutional problem, it could play the central role in a package deal. In regard to decision-making, it could be used to obtain some sort of a modified majority voting procedure. As a matter of fact, the US delegation was trying to achieve a version of "dual-voting", whereby

59. Many western delegates felt that this matter was not important, since only recommendations can be adopted by the UN organs. They considered that the US pressure was misplaced. France, for example, disagreed with the special voting formula. Although the idea of permanent seats in the standing organ—the EEC would have got 5 out of 12—seemed appealing initially, the French delegation had second thoughts. A special voting procedure might be more binding than a simple majority vote. In other words, a decision adopted by a majority of 12 trading nations would exert a much stronger pressure on a country that finds itself outvoted than would a decision adopted only by a simple or 2/3 majority of the Conference, or the standing committee. One could safely ignore the latter.

60. According to one member of the US delegation, they had received instructions based on a decision made in the highest echelons of their government, to offer nothing to the developing countries, to make them understand that the entire idea of UNCTAD is worthless, and to make it clear that the United States would do nothing to help. They were also instructed to vote negatively on any recommendation where they disagreed even slightly. The consequences of these instructions could be best seen in the substantive issue areas, but they were also quite evident in the negotiations on the institutional issue.

all decisions calling for action on key questions must be adopted by a majority which would include a majority of the western nations, as well as a majority of the developing nations. And in the ultimate analysis, the voting issue could be used, if necessary, as a wrecking tool, because a rigid position on this subject could effectively prevent any consensus with the developing countries and would torpedo the creation of a continuing machinery. Finally, it is worth noting that at least part of the US rigidity in the later stages of the Conference was caused by the commitment to the position which became known to the public. Domestic politics and the approaching election also entered into the picture as additional causes of the unyielding attitude.[61]

To those involved in the small group of negotiators it was clear that most matters within UNCTAD competence could hardly be subject to majority decisions, and that the developed countries could not be forced to undertake an action or accept a policy against their own will. Of course, majority resolutions in the area of general principles might cause some political fallout, but they would yield very few practical results in the field of trade and development. They could even have a deleterious effect and interrupt dialogue on any given issue. This, for instance, was the case with the ECOSOC resolution recommending the establishment of SUNFED. Until the resolution was passed in 1957, the developing countries could maintain a constant pressure and keep a discussion going. Once the resolution was passed, the developed countries had only to sit back and refuse to implement it. They did not even care to justify their position.

During the last minute negotiations, the question was raised how the decision-making process in the proposed machinery could be adjusted without affecting majority voting and other politically sensitive issues. More specifically, how could the developed countries avoid being outvoted from day to day, and from issue to issue? One delegate suggested that some method of postponing the vote could offer a way out of the impasse. This thought led to the conciliation mechanism, which is essentially a formalization of practices prevailing in UN diplomacy anyway—i.e., long and arduous negotiations by small groups of delegates "representing" larger groups, formal caucuses, or *ad hoc* voting align-

61. The developing countries voted increases for the UNESCO budget in 1964, without the approval of "those countries who pay the largest share." This was attacked in the American Congress which is sensitive to "taxation without representation," and complaints were voiced about the great disproportion of voting power in UN organs and the real power of states. Thus, the United States made it clear that the successful resolution of the decision-making question was a precondition for its participation in any continuing machinery of UNCTAD. See Gardner, "Trade and Development in the UN; A Challenge to U.S. Policy," *op. cit.,* pp. 23, 27-28.

56

ments, until a compromise is reached. The conciliation procedure provided for a "cooling-off" period during which accord could be sought through quiet diplomacy.

The solution adopted in the end—that is, first conciliation, then voting—is in the final analysis logically inconsistent in an international forum which does not possess the decision-making powers of national legislatures. After the process of conciliation is over, and if there is still serious opposition from those countries whose consent is necessary for effective action, the logical step in view of the nature of the present international system, is to continue conciliation and not to vote. However, those who negotiated on this matter disregarded the logical inconsistency and were more aware of the element of political pressure. The option of voting had to be left open. A vote used indiscriminately loses value, but a vote used sparingly and judiciously is a weapon that hangs like "the sword of Damocles" over the heads of the developed countries.

GATT After the Geneva Conference

Before we end this chapter, let us discuss briefly the changes which occurred in GATT soon after the Geneva Conference. We noted that in the spring of 1964 the Contracting Parties had formally decided that a legal and institutional framework should be incorporated into the General Agreement to handle their activities related to the expansion of developing countries' trade. This led to the adoption of Part IV in February 1965; it was immediately applied *de facto*, pending its ratification. Having been ratified by a sufficient number of Contracting Parties, Part IV became an integral component of the General Agreement in June 1966.[62]

Essentially Part IV reflected the new trade philosophy of the *Final Act*. In applying the General Agreement it was explicitly recognized that the diversity of economic development among the Contracting Parties should be taken into account; it was further recognized that in the case of developing countries, the notion of equality and equal treatment cannot always apply. Part IV contains general principles and objectives relating to the trade of developing countries, and the agreement of developed countries not to ask reciprocity for concessions that they make to developing countries. More specifically, Part IV, like the *Final Act*, provides for the standstill of tariff and non-tariff barriers on products of special interest to developing countries, gives high priority

62. For the provisions of Part IV see General Agreement on Tariffs Trade, *Basic Instruments and Selected Documents*, Thirteenth Supplement (Geneva: GATT, July 1965).

to the reduction and elimination of the existing barriers, fiscal charges and revenue duties, and provides for the elaboration of measures to stabilize commodity markets and secure equitable and remunerative prices for primary goods. On the institutional side, the Committee on Trade and Development was established to supervise the implementation of Part IV.[63]

Opinion is divided on the causal relationship between the Geneva Conference and Part IV of GATT. Supporters of GATT maintain that it discussed these questions long before the Geneva Conference, and that the Conference was not the cause of Part IV. Supporters of UNCTAD hold that had not the decision been taken in 1962 to convene the world trade conference, GATT would have been much slower to wake up to the demands of developing countries. In other words, what happened in GATT before 1964 was in anticipation of the Geneva Conference. Both opponents and proponents agree that the Conference itself and its outcome, especially in the institutional sphere, introduced an element of expedience in GATT and speeded up the adoption and ratification of Part IV. This meant the broadening of its competence and attention to problems of the Third World. It also meant that GATT would be better prepared to face the institutional challenge of UNCTAD.

GATT is a contractual agreement and Part IV has been incorporated into it with the same treaty status and binding force as the rest of its provisions.[64] However, one should be aware of the appended reservation which states that commitments should be applied:

> to the fullest extent possible—that is, except when compelling reasons, including legal reasons, make it impossible.[65]

The Contracting Parties are thus provided with an escape clause. It also means that Part IV is similar to the *Final Act* in yet another sense— i.e., it is *de facto* unenforceable. The danger of non-implementation is caused by the absence of reciprocity, the glue which holds together the rest of the General Agreement and makes it operational. Moreover, Part IV has not been ratified by all developed countries, France being the most notable abstainer.

---

63. Note also that the "Executive Secretary" of GATT was renamed the "Director General", a title which is usually given to heads of full-fledged specialized agencies. This upgrading of the title, which came in the spring of 1965, was necessary to keep up with the rival UNCTAD, headed by a "Secretary-General".

64. E. Wyndham White, "Whither GATT?" press release, GATT/1006 (Oct. 1967).

65. Art. XXXVII, para. 1, Part ᵀᵛ.

Conclusion

The 1964 Geneva Conference on Trade and Development ended in an acrimonious atmosphere of polarization between the developed and the developing countries, but fortunately this was neither its only nor its permanent legacy. In addition to the *Final Act*, the continuing machinery of UNCTAD was established. Although it was only reluctantly accepted by the developed countries and weakened due to lack of consensus on its powers and functions, it was to provide the policymaking forum where a permanent dialogue could be established, *inter alia*, in the search of a consensus on various substantive matters raised during the Conference but not settled due to wide disagreements between national representatives. The way was also left open for strengthening and improving UNCTAD. The provision for reviewing institutional arrangements and recommending necessary changes and improvements reflected the view of the developing and socialist states that UNCTAD represented only a transitional arrangement toward a more comprehensive international organization. Finally, the Geneva Conference saw the organizational birth of the Group of 77, a new factor in the life of international organizations.

These legacies of the Geneva Conference provide us with the main themes for the discussion of UNCTAD in the period following 1964— i.e. the crystallization of substantive consensus, institutionalization and task expansion, and actors and conflict resolution.

Substantive Policies in UNCTAD:
The Evolution of Consensus

PART TWO

Essentially, **UNCTAD** aims at reshaping the pattern of international economic relations, though its contribution to this global task cannot be judged without the benefit of a historical perspective. Less ambitiously, one could ask what changes in the environment can be attributed directly or indirectly to this organization, and whether it has benefited the developing countries and helped improve their position in the world economic system. It is indeed difficult to be categorical in answering such questions. Due to policy disagreements, concrete actions so far have been few and isolated. As we have already pointed out, the Geneva Conference only initiated the process of the evolution and maturing of policy on the basis of newly articulated norms, the majority of which were not subscribed to by developed countries anyway and were rather high considering the current reality. Also, **UNCTAD** is only one of the sources shaping the environment and its influences are generally diffuse (partly because of its limited institutional prerogatives) and not amenable to establishing a firm cause-effect relationship. Consequently, one may find it hard to prove, for example, that it was **UNCTAD** that speeded up the maturing of views in a given developed country, or that it was **UNCTAD**'s existence and its activities which have been the cause of changes in other international organizations.

Since the Geneva Conference, the fruits of **UNCTAD**'s labors in the substantive sphere have been primarily reflected in the upgrading and expansion of the already existing limited consensus, and in the emergence of new consensus on the previously controversial issues on its agenda.[1] Therefore, in depicting **UNCTAD**'s performance and the

1. *Consensus,* of course, is not an unambiguous concept, and to be assessed truly it has to be linked to action, in the final analysis. Also, consensus cannot be viewed mechanically and in the abstract, divorced from a reference point. In terms of consensus attainment, UNCTAD may appear successful because its members have agreed to a given measure and have come to terms on its implementation. But if the content of the agreed package is compared with the nature of the task involved, or with the *ideal* solution, and it is found to be at a very low common denominator indeed, this can be hardly termed a success. In fact, such consensus may contribute to the perpetuation of the *status quo* and

progress made thus far, our basic frame of reference is the evolution of consensus and the gradual change in trade, financing and invisibles concepts and policies taking place as a result of deliberations in this international forum.

For analytical and heuristic purposes, the policy-making process in UNCTAD can be viewed as consisting of progressive stages. We have classified them as follows:

(1) *Problem recognition.* This stage begins with a confrontation and eventually progresses to a point where all the parties admit the existence of a problem, and agree that it would be desirable to enter into a constructive dialogue aimed at a new solution.

(2) *Recommendation.* During this phase a rapprochement of viewpoints occurs via studies, debates, persuasion. A breakthrough is achieved when agreement crystallizes on the new principles involved. Only after the attainment of this basically political agreement on a once controversial proposal, are conditions created for its implementation, either through the unilateral action of states putting into effect UNCTAD's recommendations, or on the basis of a multilateral agreement.

(3) *Rule-making.* This is a complex and time-consuming effort where a balance is reached between varying national interests, and specific features of a multilateral understanding or agreement are negotiated upon.

(4) *Implementation.* This is a final stage when recommendations, new principles, or negotiated multilateral instruments are put into effect by the states. It represents the linkage between the newly crystallized consensus and practice.

The extensive and multifaceted agenda of UNCTAD compels us to be very selective regarding the issues on which we focus attention. Moreover, due to the very limited scope of our endeavor, the great number of issues, and the peculiar content and history of each, most of them may not get the treatment that they deserve. Our discussion reflects the principal fields of UNCTAD's activities: manufactures, commodities, financing and shipping, and also deals briefly with the socialist countries in UNCTAD, the problem of the least advanced developing countries, and trade expansion and cooperation among the developing countries.

---

thus be contrary to UNCTAD's ultimate goals. Furthermore, various resolutions and recommendations unanimously agreed to, as the primary outputs of UNCTAD, in many instances are not a very reliable indicator of consensus. They may be implicitly contradictory, or so vague as to conceal the absence of agreement on basic policy matters, or at a much higher (verbal) denominator than would have been the case had such a resolution contained a commitment to act.

Chapter III

MANUFACTURES

In the field of manufactures and semi-manufactures we have focused exclusively on general preferences, overlooking such important matters as restrictive business practices, liberalization of non-tariff barriers, tariff reclassification, etc. This is the item on UNCTAD's agenda that has undergone a prolonged and sustained negotiating process, and which perhaps has attracted most attention. In fact, general non-reciprocal preferences for manufactured products of developing countries are a symbol of success for the entire organization—a heretical idea finally approaching fruition and implementation, a proof that policies of states evolve, consensus results, and action is eventually undertaken.

Preferences

The concept of preferences is not of recent origin; commercial policies which discriminate in favor of one country or a group of countries have always existed, and the most-favored-nation (MFN) clause has not been altogether sacrosanct.[1] The Havana Charter provided for exceptions in order to make possible the continuation of existing preferential agreements, and did not preclude the possible creation of free trade areas and customs unions. Furthermore, its Article XV, although hard to invoke, permitted the introduction of new preferential arrangements if these were intended to promote economic development. Only the first two exceptions were incorporated into GATT, while Article XV shared the fate of the Havana Charter. Subsequent attempts to include this article into GATT failed, giving rise to the criticism that exceptions to the MFN clause were permitted only in those circumstances which were of interest to developed countries.

Preferences at the Geneva Conference. The Geneva Conference had before it several proposals for the establishment of general preferences

1. See "Trade in Manufactures and Semi-Manufactures," *Proceedings,* Vol. IV, pp. 3-42.

for developing countries' exports of manufactures and semi-manufactures.[2] The debate showed a wide divergence of views, and laid bare some of the main problems which the negotiation and implementation of such a scheme would pose.

The United States, starting from the premise that developing countries export both a small volume and a narrow range of manufactures and that there are only a few of them exporting such products, argued that preferences would have little effect and would not bring about any significant expansion of their earnings; consequently, it was not worth tampering with the MFN system. After the Kennedy Round, furthermore, tariffs would fall so low that the establishment of preferential margins would be irrelevant. It was also argued that general preferences would create new discriminatory practices, encourage uneconomic production, hamper efforts toward general tariff reductions by creating vested interests among developing countries in the continuation of the preferential *status quo*, etc.[3] The view of the United States, however, was not shared by all developed countries and some major western trading nations were overtly more or less sympathetic to the preferences proposal.[4]

Yet, the divergence of views among those developed countries which in principle agreed with preferences was significant. The United Kingdom, supported by F.R. Germany, Holland and Denmark, felt it desirable that there should be a single preferential scheme applied to all developing countries by all industrial nations.[5] In contrast, France and Belgium advocated selective preferences: terms of preference—the preferential margin, duration, type and quantity of imports to which preferences are to apply, etc.—would be negotiated either bilaterally by

2. The matter had already been considered in GATT's Working Party on Preferences and in UNCTAD's Preparatory Committee. See GATT doc. L/2073 (Oct. 1963), and *Proceedings*, Vol. VIII, p. 29. The most elaborate statement on preferences at the Geneva Conference is by Prebisch in his "Towards a New Trade Policy for Development," *op. cit.*, pp. 35-40.

3. For a summary and a discussion of the US argument, see Johnson *op. cit.*, pp. 165-170, and Pincus, *op. cit.*, pp. 205 ff. For a comprehensive treatment of the American policy see S. Weintraub, *Trade Preferences for Less Developed Countries* (New York: Praeger, 1966).

4. It has been argued that some developed countries made "grand gestures and offers" knowing that the United States would block them. Robertson, *op. cit.*, p. 4.

5. The United Kingdom viewed this as the application of the Commonwealth preferences on a worldwide basis, which would sufficiently compensate those developing countries that enjoy special tariff treatment in its markets. Therefore, the abolition of Commonwealth preferences on manufactures and semi-manufactures was made conditional upon the participation of all major trading nations in the general scheme.

an industrial country and a developing country of its choice, or by a joint committee of exporting and importing countries.[6] Aimed at preserving intact the EEC links with the associated African states, the selective approach, moreover, could enable a developed country to maintain discretion and maneuverability and, if necessary, use preferences for the promotion of its own economic and political goals. The critics of selective preferences asserted that such an approach would divide the developing world into vertical preferential compartments, pose a threat of economic and political subjugation of developing countries, discriminate toward some of them, and so on.[7]

In presenting the case for preferences the developing countries pointed to the substantial tariff and non-tariff barriers in the developed countries directed against those manufactures in which they enjoyed actual or potential comparative advantages. Also, they criticized the discrimination against processing built into the existing tariff structures of the developed countries, which constituted a serious obstacle to the export of processed raw materials from the South. It was argued that general preferences would bring the manufactured products of the developing countries closer to real equality of treatment, in contrast to the MFN principle which could not do this for several reasons. For instance, unless the tariff is zero, there is no equality with the domestic producers, nor even with the producers within the regional groupings of developed countries. Also, as we have discussed in Chapter I, tariff negotiations which were conducted on the basis of reciprocity did not significantly affect the manufactures and semi-manufactures from the developing areas, which to begin with were subject to higher nominal and effective tariffs [8] than the typical exports from industrial countries.

6. This is the well-known Brasseur Plan, first advocated by Belgium in GATT in 1963, essentially repeated in the "Memorandum Concerning Certain Items on the Agenda of UNCTAD," submitted to the Geneva Conference by France. *Proceedings,* Vol. VI, pp. 23-25.

7. See UNCTAD document TD/B/AC.1/1 (23 Mar. 1965), pp. 21-22, for the various objections that were raised. (Hereafter UNCTAD documents will be referred to by their symbols only—i.e. TD/... See the bibliography for an explanation of their meaning. Only in certain instances will the titles be given.)

8. For a study on the structure of protection in the developed countries and its effects on the exports of processed goods from developing countries see TD/B/C.2/36 (25 May 1967). The nominal tariff is the duty as it is charged on a given product when it is imported. From this, one distinguishes the effective tariff which corresponds to the protection granted to the manufacturing process carried out inside the country. The effective protective incidence of a given tariff on a transformed product depends among other things on the value added by the transformation process, and on the duty at which raw materials and other inputs are imported. The lower the value added in a transformation process, the higher —everything else being equal—the protective effect of a particular nominal duty

Finally, the developing countries stressed that the export of manufactures was of great importance for their economic growth.

In working out their joint proposal on preferences,[9] the developing countries ran into some internal disagreements which were caused by their varying levels of economic development and their different situations in the world economy. Those developing countries already producing and exporting manufactures felt that no distinction should be made among beneficiaries, while the less developed ones wanted part of the market reserved for them alone, either by a system of quotas or by higher preference margins for their products.[10] A second problem revolved around the existing special preferences that some newly independent states enjoyed in the markets of the former colonial powers. Would special preferences for manufactures and semi-manufactures be sacrificed for the general scheme, and if so, how would these countries be compensated for losses they would incur once they gave up their preferential status? After some considerable disputation, general formulae applying to these controversial issues were agreed to. The principle of non-discrimination among developing countries was affirmed, but it was simultaneously admitted that special treatment may be granted to the less developed ones, in accordance with the criteria that would be determined in a special body to be established by UNCTAD. As regards the existing special preferences for manufactures, they were to be abolished *pari passu* with the effective application of the general scheme, provided that the countries enjoying them would get at least "equivalent advantages".[11] Evidently, the consensus had not crystallized on these issues. What mattered at that time, however, was that the Group of 77 had a joint negotiating position.

---

on the transformed product. For example, if a raw material is imported duty free, and if the transformed product—with a value added through processing of 20 % —faces a nominal tariff of 5 %, the effective tariff is equal to 25 %. On the other hand, a nominal tariff of 10 % on a manufactured product with a 50 % value added, yields a 20 % effective tariff.

9. E/CONF.46/C.2/L.40 in *Proceedings,* Vol. I, pp. 154-156.

10. As a precedent for this type of differentiation, they could point to the Montevideo Treaty establishing LAFTA. Among the tariff reductions negotiated within this framework there were a number of concessions which were only applicable to the products coming from the least advanced members. For a summary of proposals on how to relate preferences to disparities in development see TD/B/AC.1/1 (23 Mar. 1965), p. 39.

11. It was not spelt out what the term "equivalent advantages" meant—possible compensation in the newly accessible markets or financial payments? Furthermore, would this criteria be based on the established trade flows or on the potential ones also? For the various proposals on compensation see *ibid.,* pp. 29-30.

The long debate on preferences had just begun during the Geneva Conference. Though not directly related to general preferences, there was an implicit recognition of the need for new rules when it was agreed that the developing countries should be allowed in principle to grant tariff concessions to each other, without being obliged to extend the same to industrial nations.[12] This was not within the scope of exceptions provided by the GATT rules. However, there was a deadlock over the main proposal for non-reciprocal preferences to be extended to the manufactures of the developing countries in the western markets. As we have already seen, some developed countries were firm in insisting that the MFN principle should continue as the sole basis for extending tariff concessions to developing nations.[13] Therefore, the primary task facing the new machinery of UNCTAD was to arrive at a unanimous decision on a principle that preferences for the manufactures and semi-manufactures of developing countries are desirable and should be established. Only then could the member states tackle seriously the specific problems generated by the developing countries' proposal which, in brief, provided that: (1) all developed countries should give preferential access to their markets to all manufactures and semi-manufactures originating in the Third World, without any limitations as to volume; (2) the duration of the scheme should be limited in time; (3) under clearly specified conditions the importing nations should be allowed to exclude certain products and to apply safeguard measures; (4) provisions should be made for the special position and needs of the least developed of the developing countries; (5) at least equivalent advantages should accrue from the general scheme to those countries previously enjoying special preferences, so that they could renounce them; and (6) there should be a provision for international supervision of the scheme.[14]

Between Geneva and New Delhi. In 1966 the Group of Preferences in UNCTAD launched the scrutiny of the technical aspects of a scheme based on a working hypothesis that general non-reciprocal and non-discriminatory preferences would be granted.[15] Likewise, early in 1966,

12. Recommendation A.III,8, *Proceedings,* Vol. I, pp. 41-42. Note that it remained ambiguous whether such preferences could also be established between different regions and continents, and not be limited to regional and subregional levels.

13. Recommendation A.II.5, *ibid.,* p. 39. Their consolidated draft resolution which developing countries voted through on the committee level was withdrawn at the plenary, and the Conference noted the absence of consensus. The real decision of the Conference was that the consideration of preferences should be continued.

14. TD/B/C.2/AC.1/7 (31 May, 1967), p. 10.

15. TD/B/84 (8 Aug. 1966), p. 3.

the United States, the United Kingdom, France, and F.R. Germany—the so-called "Group of Four"—began to explore in the OECD the issues involved. In the initial period, American scepticism about the general scheme of preferences (GSP) and the reservations that the US held on principle were shared by Canada, Switzerland, Japan, and, to a certain extent, by Sweden and Norway. In spite of wide methodological differences—France, for example, continued to advocate the selective approach—other developed countries accepted the desirability of the GSP.[16] The developing countries meanwhile remained united on their position, although there was still controversy between the Latin American and African states over special preferences; moreover, the less advanced countries continued to fear that the GSP would exclusively benefit the more developed nations in their group.[17]

However, no significant progress could be recorded until 1967, when the US President announced his country's revised policy on the subject:

> We are ready to explore with other industrialized countries—and with our own people—the possibility of temporary preferential tariff advantages for all developing countries in the markets of all the industrialized countries.[18]

Those developed countries which exhibited some misgivings vis-à-vis preferences had little choice but to fall in line. A meaningful dialogue in search of practical solutions could now be expected.

Why did the American decision-makers change their strategy against the traditional policy, and in spite of fear of "low-wage" products in the US market and the related opposition to such tariff liberalization? In its negative stance toward the GSP, the United States became increasingly isolated politically from the developing and developed countries, while its influence on the content of the scheme was diminished. The tendency toward proliferation and solidification of the Yaoundé Convention based EEC preferential arrangements on the African continent was viewed with alarm in Washington. At the same time, the Latin American countries were getting more restless. The GSP was not taking shape and the special preferences were becoming more extensive; so, their clamor

16. See OECD doc. TC(66)29 and "Octroi de préférences aux pays en voie de développement," (Genève: Communautés Européennes, Bureau de Presse et d'Information, 1967).

17. This was evident, for example, during the discussion in GATT on Australia's request for a waiver to grant unilaterally preferences to selected industrial products originating from developing countries.

18. From the speech by President Johnson to the American Chiefs of State at Punta del Este on April 14, 1967. Department of State *Bulletin*, Vol. 56, No. 1454 (8 May, 1967), p. 709. See also J. Reston, "Punta del Este: Least-Favored Nation Doctrine," *The New York Times*, International Edition (April 15-16, 1967).

for vertical preferences in the US—as "defensive measures" against the "Afro-European bloc"—began to intensify.[19] Of course, any such move would have had a negative impact on US relations with the developing countries of Asia and Africa, and would have added to the trend which divided the developing world into tighter spheres of influence.

With the aid of new strategy, the United States could alleviate some of the above mentioned challenges. For example, Latin American countries could be mollified by showing that the US was, after all, doing something active to secure better access for them to European markets, and especially to the EEC. Also, Washington could state that it would extend preferential treatment to all developing countries, excepting those that discriminate against its products and give reverse preferences to some industrialized nations.[20] In this manner, a wrench of sorts could be thrown into the EEC's, mainly French-promoted, policy of consolidating the preferential links with a substantial part of Africa. Furthermore, the GSP could have a dampening effect on the further proliferation of special preferential arrangements, while the significance of the existing ones would be reduced. All of these elements called for a reassessment of the situation and played a role in convincing President Johnson of the need to change the policy stand of his country.[21] Officially, however, the United States was committed only to the exploration of the preference proposal, to see whether consensus could be reached.

Another boost to the GSP was provided by the generally unsatisfactory results of the Kennedy Round for the developing world. One of the principal arguments against preferences at the Geneva Conference was the claim that after these tariff negotiations, duties on industrial products would be so low that they would no longer represent a real obstacle to manufactures exported by developing nations. In reality, effective protection of the processing stages of production remained one of the principal obstacles to the developing countries' exports. Products of special interest to them received significantly smaller tariff

19. The Inter-American Committee on the Alliance of Progress (CIAP) recommended "a policy of transitory, defensive measures", arguing that it is inequitable for the products of some developing countries "to enjoy preferences outside the hemisphere plus non-discriminatory access to the United States." As quoted in TD/B/82/Add.2 (20 Jul. 1966), p. 29. Note that the Latin American countries were upset mostly with the possible effect of special preferences on their primary commodities exports to the EEC.

20. This suggestion was first made by Denmark. Quoted by Weintraub, *op. cit.*, p. 136.

21. See the statement by A. M. Solomon, Assistant Secretary of State for Economic Affairs, to the Subcommittee on Foreign Economic Policy of the Joint Economic Committee, Hearings, 90th Congress, Vol. I, pp. 79-83.

reductions than other items—particularly those items characterized either by advanced technology or capital intensity, of which the developed countries were the major suppliers. Some categories of products especially important for developing countries received smaller cuts than the average, although they were already subjected to higher tariffs and various non-tariff barriers. Among these were foodstuffs, beverages, textile products and clothing.[22]

Once the general principle of granting preferences to developing countries was tentatively conceded by all concerned, the aim was to design a scheme which would command the consensus, and balance and safeguard the interests of developing and developed countries alike. The work proceeded on two levels. Within the OECD, the Group of Four was elaborating a collective position for member countries. In UNCTAD the Group on Preferences was examining different aspects of the scheme, although the developed countries made it clear that this did not involve any commitment on their part to grant preferences.[23]

A. *The Main Issues.* Of greatest concern to the developing countries were product coverage, the relationship between vertical preferential arrangements and the GSP, and the status of the least developed among them. The developed countries were mainly concerned with safeguard procedures designed to protect their markets from the possible harmful effects of preferences.

(1) *Product Coverage.* Most developing countries possessed only the rudiments of industries, and many of them produced essentially a limited range of semi-processed items.[24] In order to make the GSP of value to all developing countries, the Group of 77 argued that processed and semi-processed agricultural goods and raw materials should be treated as manufactures or semi-manufactures, and therefore be granted preferences. This was a very controversial proposal. First, there was no internationally accepted definition of manufactures and semi-manufactures. The definition given by the UNCTAD secretariat, which reflected the thinking of the 77, also included semi-processed and processed agricultural products in this category.[25] However, the B

22. TD/6 (4 Sep. 1967), pp. 3-4.
23. TD/B/134/Rev.1 (25 Jul. 1967), p. 23.
24. In 1965, for example, processed agricultural products accounted for 100 % of the manufactured exports of Somalia, El Salvador, Togo, and Yemen, and for more than 50 % in Cuba, Algeria, Paraguay, Senegal, Iraq, Morocco, Nicaragua, Ethiopia, Argentina, Uruguay, and the Dominican Republic. See tables 7, 8 and 9 in TD/12/Supp.2 (13 Oct. 1967).
25. According to this definition, primary commodities are products of the farm, the forest, fishing, hunting or any mineral to whose value manufacturing has added only a minor contribution. Semi-manufactures are those products which require further processing or incorporation into other goods before they become

Group declined to accept this; it held that products falling into Chapters 1-24 of the Brussels Tariff Nomenclature (BTN) were to be treated as agricultural products.[26] Secondly, processed and semi-processed agricultural products were highly sensitive and for the most part received a high degree of tariff and non-tariff protection in developed countries. The issue was especially delicate because in many instances the protection of processing industries was so closely related to agricultural protection. Processing industries often had no other choice than to use high-priced domestic agricultural raw materials. Thus, the high tariffs on such products protected both the agricultural input and the industrial transformation process.

The Group of 77 argued that limited product coverage would considerably curtail the effect of the GSP and decrease its immediate value for many developing countries.[27] The majority of developed countries proposed that this matter required further study on a product-by-product basis.[28]

(2) *Safeguards for Developed Countries.* The "escape clause" and the "tariff quota" were the two most widely mentioned safeguards.[29] The "escape clause" system provided that a developed country could limit the volume of imports and scope of tariff reductions when serious injury threatened or affected a sector of its economy.[30] The advantage of this system was that it placed no limitations on the volume of exports on those products enjoying preferences, and that remedial action would be taken only by some donors against the most competitive products (and according to one proposal only against the most competitive exporters,

a capital or consumer good. Manufactures are manufactured goods for consumption of households (including processed food), capital goods for households, and capital goods for industry. TD/B/C.2/3 (2 Jul. 1965). (The most important processed agricultural goods are: prepared meats, fish, vegetables, fruit, juices, wine, alcoholic beverages and tobacco manufactures.)

26. During the Kennedy Round it was left to a country's discretion to draw a line between agricultural and non-agricultural products. There was no unanimity, but, in general, products considered as agricultural fell into chapters 1-24 of the BTN. TD/B/C.2/AC.1/7 (31 May, 1967), p. 32.

27. See TD/12/Supp. 2 (13 Oct. 1967), pp. 1-9. In 1965, for example, processed agricultural goods accounted for 19.0 %, or $751.7 million, of manufactures and semi-manufactures imported into major developed countries from the developing countries (petroleum, unwrought non-ferrous metals, and ships and boats not included).

28. TD/B/134/Rev.1 (25 Jul. 1967), p. 25.

29. For a detailed discussion of safeguards see TD/B/C.2/AC.1/7 (31 May, 1967), pp. 18-25.

30. One version of this system would have duties eliminated on all products from developing countries, with no *ab initio* limitations on the volume of imports and no exclusion of certain products. Another proposal would have an *ab initio* negative list, with the escape clause applying to other products.

thus not affecting the majority of developing countries). However, there was a danger of indiscriminate unilateral recourse to the escape clause, which could seriously subvert the purpose of the GSP. Therefore, the Group of 77 stressed the need to determine internationally objective economic criteria as a basis for invoking the escape clause. It was also hoped that any recourse to this safeguard would be preceded by consultations and agreement in an international body including all countries concerned.[31]

The "tariff quota" system applied to particular tariff headings. Beyond the ceiling provided by a quota, further imports would be subject to MFN rates. This method made it less likely that preferences would be suddenly eliminated by a developed country because of market disruption. Also, it could provide for differentiation among countries according to their levels of economic development. Conceivably, "tariff quotas" would help persuade legislators in developed countries to favor preferences, since the competition from "cheap labor" would be limited to only a share of the market in a given product. On the debit side: there is the possibility that quotas would not be large enough; their cellings and allocations might prove hard to negotiate; decisions on quotas would be subject to pressure by interest groups; a GSP based on tariff quotas might not easily absorb the existing special preferences; and it would be difficult to avoid discriminating among developing countries.

Still another method of safeguards was proposed: products included under the GSP would be granted a duty reduction, rather than a zero tariff treatment. This was more likely to be accepted by various domestic interests; however, developing countries would still be left at a disadvantage in the regional groupings, and a mere reduction of tariffs would not be sufficient to stimulate a significant inflow of exports as the total elimination would.

(3) *Vertical Preferences*.[32] Two problems faced UNCTAD: (a) how

31. TD/B/134/Rev.1 (25 Jul. 1967), p. 24. International practice gave little encouragement to developing countries' demands. Such a procedure exists in EEC. In GATT, EFTA, and LAFTA, the escape clause is invoked unilaterally, although it is subject to consultations. In these groupings a country acting unilaterally is exposed to retaliatory measures, something difficult to envisage in UNCTAD's GSP. Furthermore, the experience with the Long Term Arrangement on Cotton Textiles demonstrated that "market disruption", of which the importing country is the sole judge, has been used not to allow any significant increase in the import of specific items. TD/5/Add.1 (31 Aug. 1967), p. 38.

32. Historically speaking, special preferences originated in the 1930's as an attempt by colonial powers to consolidate ties with their overseas territories. They maintained the free import of industrial raw materials and foodstuffs from the colonies, and the free export of industrial products to them, while goods of other nations were subjected to high protectionist barriers. After gaining independence,

would special preferences for manufactures and semi-manufactures relate to the GSP, and (b) if they were to be abolished or phased out, how would the "equivalent advantages" be determined for the countries concerned? It is evident, of course, that special preferences for commodities, which constitute a much more controversial issue, are not really at stake here.

The developing members of the Commonwealth—mainly from Asia, and particularly India, Pakistan (and Hong Kong)—had established significant trade flows of manufactures (especially textiles) into the British market.[33] In general, they seemed ready to forego their special status in return for a satisfactory GSP, and they did not appear very insistent on equivalent advantages and compensations. The great majority of African countries—associated with either the EEC or the Commonwealth—had no significant preferential exports of manufactures into those markets, although for some of them this flow was important if the wider scope of product coverage is assumed. Yet, the EEC associates in particular were insistent on equivalent advantages and compensations, even though the trade flows in most cases were only potential.[34] This was understandable in view of their non-competitiveness: losing a protected market where they enjoyed an exclusive preferential status and did not have to compete on equal terms with industrially more advanced developing countries could be harmful. Moreover, their position was related to the bargaining process over the nature of the GSP.

Attempts to determine the "equivalent advantages" depended upon many factors—*inter alia*, the number of developed countries participating in the GSP, the number of products included, the extent of preferential margin, the duration of the scheme, the supply capacity of

the former colonies were not eager to sever these ties, since they thus had significant commercial advantages over countries which conducted their trade under the MFN regime. The appearance of the EEC brought a territorial spread of French vertical preferential arrangements, causing alarm among those developing countries which faced increasing discrimination in the lucrative European markets. In fact, inspired by the Yaoundé Convention of June 1964, Nigeria was the first "outsider" to gain the associate status in the EEC which was formalized in the Lagos Convention of July 1966. For an extensive discussion of the problem see TD/16 and Supp. 1 (11 Jan. 1968). (We devote additional space to special preferences in the chapter on commodities.)

33. The share of preferential suppliers in the United Kingdom's total import of manufactures from all developing countries amounted to approximately 70 % in the mid-1960's. TD/16 (12 Jan. 1968), p. 4.

34. In 1965, for example, less than 6 % of their total exports to the EEC were manufactured goods. This accounted for 2.5 % of total EEC imports of manufactures from all developing countries. *Idem.*

a given developing country, and so on.[35] In view of this, many felt that the relationship between special and general preferences could be discussed meaningfully only after the main elements of the GSP were agreed to. Some countries felt that the two could coexist for a short period of time, while others—mainly the Latin American nations—argued that special preferences should be abolished immediately upon the advent of the GSP.[36]

Also important to the outcome of the GSP debate were the reverse preferences which some developing countries gave to some developed nations as a reciprocal concession for the special privileges they enjoyed. Reverse preferences caused some developing countries to discriminate heavily against the "outside" trading partners, and the United States administration posed their abolition as a precondition for submitting the GSP to Congress for approval, arguing that it could not convince the Congress to extend preferences to those developing countries, unless they gave equal treatment to all developed countries.[37] The developing countries giving reverse preferences, and particularly the EEC associates, were reluctant to discuss this matter, because of fear that by not granting any type of reciprocity to the developed countries in question they would lose their special tariff status, and/or considerable financial and technical support.[38]

(4) *The Least Developed among Developing Countries.* In 1966, for example, 79 developing countries accounted for only 6% of the total Third World exports of manufactures to developed market economies.[39]

35. For a discussion of the relationship between special preferences and the GSP, see TD/B/C.2/AC.1/7 (31 May, 1967), pp. 51-57.

36. TD/12 (1 Nov. 1967), pp. 9-10. For the discussion in the Group on Preferences see TD/B/C.2/AC.1/SR.1-21, and TD/B/134/Rev.1 (25 Jul. 1967), p. 28.

37. Among the issues involved was also the contest between the United States and France over the latter's sphere of influence on the African continent.

38. Through the web of dependence which they had woven, the developed countries enjoying reverse preferences were in a good position to influence the developing countries involved and their attitude in UNCTAD. Note also that reverse preferences cause custom revenue losses, tend to direct the imports to economically less favorable sources, and can impede domestic industrial development if the developing countries are not completely free to raise trade barriers against all industrially advanced countries.

39. See table 2 in TD/10/Supp.1 (31 Oct. 1967) and Table 7 in TD/12/Supp.2 (13 Oct. 1967). In 1969, five developing countries plus Hong Kong, accounted for approximately 60 % of developing world's exports of manufactures and semi-manufactures into developed countries (Hong Kong - 23.0 %, Taiwan - 8.8 %, India - 8.5 %, Yugoslavia - 8.0 %, Mexico - 5.9 % and South Korea - 5.7 %). Brazil, Argentina, Pakistan, Israel, Philippines, Iran, Malaysia, Algeria and Ghana accounted for another 22 % approximately. See TD/B/C.2/102 (24 Dec. 1970), pp. 33-34.

This did not mean that the GSP would be of no use to them in the near future: many of these countries had either the capacity, or a speedily mobilized potential to exploit the advantages that the GSP would offer them in relation to processing raw materials and agricultural products.[40] Still, the question had to be raised as to whether the GSP should differentiate in favor of the least developed developing countries (LDDCs).[41] It was suggested, for example, that safeguard measures should not apply to their products, that a given percentage of the tariff quota be reserved for their exports, and that more advanced developing countries should grant them preferences.[42]

(5) *Some Additional Problems.* There was the issue of which countries would receive preferences. Here, economic and political difficulties arose. There was no internationally accepted definition of a developing country, and there was no commonly accepted cut-off point to separate developed from developing countries. In fact, many countries fell into the borderline category. Thus the dilemma: if treated as beneficiaries, they may excessively utilize their advantages over other developing countries; if excluded they may suffer considerably. The political problem was related to the group system in UNCTAD. Certain countries that did not belong to the Group of 77—for example, Greece, Israel, Portugal, Spain, and Turkey—were considered by the West either as developing or as falling into the borderline category. On the other hand, some developing countries in the Group of 77 were also borderline cases: Argentina, Mexico, Venezuela, Yugoslavia, to mention a few. Thus the question: how should the list of beneficiaries be established?

There were also the questions of how to achieve equitable distribution of the burden among donors, in what form should the less advanced B Group members take part in the GSP, how would the socialist countries contribute in view of the fact that customs play only a marginal role in their system of planned foreign trade, who would supervise and administer the GSP once it came into being, and how long would preferences last.

B. *The Charter of Algiers and the OECD Platform.* As the New

40. For example: oil, seeds, timber, ores, food, fish, etc. TD/17 (24 Nov. 1967), p. 7.

41. We shall deal with the overall problem of LDDCs in a later section. For a discussion of LDDCs and preferences, see TD/B/C.2/AC.1/7 (31 May 1967), pp. 40-48; also, TD/B/134/Rev.1 (25 Jul. 1967), p. 27.

42. It was argued that since the more advanced developing countries would gain more from the GSP, they should open up their markets to LDDCs. Of course, the latter would have a better chance of placing their products here than in the highly competitive western markets. (See Chapter VII for the discussion of LDDC problem.)

Delhi Conference was approaching, the Group of 77 and the B Group had to evolve their negotiating positions on preferences.

Although the OECD consultations did not yield an operational GSP as some may have hoped, they did narrow down some differences that separated the developed countries. The selective approach was no longer advocated by its proponents. The consensus announced in November 1967 stated that:

> ... temporary advantages in the form of generalized arrangements for special tariff treatment for developing countries in the markets of developed countries can assist the developing countries to increase their export earnings and so contribute to an acceleration in their rates of economic growth.[43]

This represented a significant philosophical amendment and a departure from the traditional process of trade liberalization according to the most-favored-nation principle.

A number of specific issues, however, could not be settled. They were of two kinds: (a) those caused by the cleavage primarily between the United States and France,[44] on the question of special and reverse preferences; and (b) those resulting from different economic structures and levels of development of B Group members, and differing ways in which they would be affected by the GSP. Thus, there was no agreement on the phasing out of special and reverse preferences. Neither could consensus be reached on the nature of safeguards—namely, whether "the escape clause" or "the tariff quota" system were to be adopted, and whether all countries would adopt similar arrangements, or each country would adopt a solution suited to its peculiar conditions. Nevertheless, the accent was put on the equitable sharing of the burden caused by improved access for the products of developing countries. It was generally agreed that the interests of "third developed countries" —those developed countries whose export trade might be affected adversely by general preferences—would be taken into account when designing the GSP.[45] Yet there was no agreement on how this could be done.

43. See "The Report of the Special Group of the OECD on the Trade with Developing Countries," OECD doc. TC(67)16, reproduced in TD/56 (29 Jan. 1968). It is interesting that the B Group could not form any quantitative judgement on the effects of GSP on export earnings of developing countries. In the absence of this guideline, they allegedly based their judgment on political and psychological elements—i.e., a strong feeling among the developing countries that preferences would help them and should therefore be granted. *Ibid.*, p. 9.

44. We purposely do not say the EEC, since some of its members, particularly the Netherlands and F. R. Germany, leaned in favor of phasing out the special preferential arrangements.

45. Note the case of Japan and significant competition between its light industry products—which in 1964 accounted for 42 % of its exports—and the

The Algiers Charter adopted by the ministerial meeting of the Group of 77 in October 1967, spelled out what the developing countries expected from the GSP. Some headway was made on the controversial problem of suspension of special preferences, although this was not reflected in the wording of the relevant provision.[46] Informally, the Latin American countries soft-pedalled their demands for the immediate abolition of the vertical preferences, while the African countries, and especially the EEC associates, agreed tentatively to their suspension. They looked for compensation through wider product coverage, and through special measures for the less developed members of the group —most African countries felt that by definition they belonged to this category. Hence, the demand for inclusion of processed and semi-processed agricultural and raw materials into the preferential scheme was affirmed, and agreement in principle was reached on special measures for LDDCs within the GSP. However, no solution was found to the overall problem of LDDCs, and various measures that were proposed failed to encounter unanimous support. The African countries, therefore, hinted that they would go back on their concession on special preferences if a satisfactory solution were not found to this problem.

A brief comparison of the Algiers Charter and the OECD report indicated several important differences; in essence, they were due to the dilemma of how to make the GSP meaningful to all developing countries while simultaneously taking account and protecting the needs and interests of developed nations.[47] Regarding the product coverage, the Group of 77 asked that processed and semi-processed primary products be included in the scheme, as a matter of principle, while the majority

exports of developing countries. Japan was also worried about the move of US capital to Taiwan, South Korea and Hong Kong, which would intensify if the industries of developing countries were to enjoy preferences in all industrial markets.

46. In this sense, the Algiers Charter did not differ from the joint draft resolution of the 77 at the Geneva Conference in 1964. It spoke of "at least equivalent advantages" ... "to enable them to suspend their existing preferences on manufactures and semi-manufactures." The Algiers Charter, TD/38 (3 Nov. 1967), p. 9. Note however, that the spokesman of the 77 said in the General Assembly that the developing countries had reached full agreement in Algiers on the suspension of special preferences for manufactures and semi-manufactures. UN doc. A/C.2/L.980 (24 Nov. 1967). The norm which guided the 77 was that a country that had previously enjoyed special preferences should in no case suffer a decrease of exports to its traditional markets, without a corresponding increase in the new markets, meant that only through practical application of the GSP could the difficulties surrounding special preferences and their abolition be resolved.

47. See the Algiers Charter (TD/38), the OECD Report (TD/57), and the comparison of their main elements contained in TD/II/C.2/L.3 (7 Feb. 1968).

of developed countries felt that this could be done only on a case-by-case basis. The developing countries asked for unrestricted and duty-free access, while the OECD members felt that improved access may take the form of duty-free treatment or substantial reductions below MFN rates. Regarding safeguards, the Group of 77 stated that any such procedure must be agreed upon internationally, while action would be temporary and subject to consultation, approval and review. The B Group felt that the nature of safeguards should be examined and agreed upon among developed countries. Also, each of them should be able to exclude some products *ab initio* from preferential treatment—products in which the developing countries were already competitive—although the developed countries should consult within the OECD in order to keep lists of exceptions as short as possible. The developing countries specified duration of the GSP for 20 years, while the developed nations argued that special tariff treatment should be for a period of 10 years, and that margins of preference should not be guaranteed.[48] The developing countries asked that all members of the Group of 77 be entitled to benefit from the GSP, while the B Group opted for a self-election method, where special tariff treatment would be extended to those claiming developing status. Individual developed countries might deny this claim from any applicant for compelling reasons, not based on competitive criteria.[49] Finally, the 77 argued that negotiations at the New Delhi Conference should lead to an agreement on the GSP; the B Group conceded only that the views of the developing nations should be taken into account in the formulation of the GSP, since it could not be put into effect without their support.

The New Delhi Conference. We continue to focus attention on the area of expanding consensus on preferences. Before considering the confrontation of the B Group and the Group of 77, we should note the further crystallization of the position of the developing countries; it occurred in the initial stages of the Conference, which met in February and March of 1968. The broad outline of principles presented in the Algiers Charter was not complete, nor could it serve as a very useful negotiating document. A more detailed position for the Group of 77

48. In this manner, they wanted to leave the door open for further international negotiations for the reduction of tariffs on the MFN basis before the ten year period elapsed.

49. This provision for the *ab initio* exclusion of a country was given a nick-name—the "Cuba clause". It could be used to discriminate against developing countries politically obnoxious to a donor. The self-election method also would ensure that the less-developed members of the B Group benefit from the preferential scheme. Their case could not be left to the decision of the 77, as they might try to shorten the list from the top so as to maximimize the value of the GSP for themselves, it was argued. See TD/56 (29 Jan. 1968), pp. 10-13.

had to be drafted in New Delhi.[50] The outcome of this process can be viewed from two perspectives: what new elements it introduced into matters which were controversial within the group, and how did it relate to the position of developed countries—that is, did it follow a conciliatory line or was a bargaining position the maximum common denominator of demands?

Perhaps the most important advance made within the Group of 77 related to vertical preferential arrangements for manufactures. It was explicitly agreed that these would coexist with the GSP during a transitional period which would last at least five years after the general preferences went into effect; only then would the situation come up for review, with the goal of speeding up the merger of general and special systems. Although there was resort to postponement and no explicit solution was envisaged, an important step forward was taken when the Latin American countries in particular refrained from asking for the immediate abolition of special preferences and agreed to a transitional period.[51] Unlike the Algiers Charter, the draft resolution also contained a paragraph on reverse preferences; it provided that these should be phased out during the same transitional period. A provision was also included to the effect that developed countries losing this status should refrain from taking retaliatory measures or from demanding other advantages which would have the same effect as reverse preferences. The problem of the less advanced members of the Group of 77 was taken into account by firmly asking for a broad product coverage, plus the non-application to LDDCs of limitations and exceptions instituted by developed countries.

Vis-à-vis the West, the Group of 77 could opt for one of two alternatives: (1) to move toward compromise in the areas of safeguard clauses, *ab initio* exceptions, duration of the scheme, depth of cuts, and especially product coverage, and thus possibly achieve in Delhi an agreement on the main provisions and principles of the GSP, or (2) to shun compromise, elaborate the group's stand at the highest common denominator of demands, without compromising on any of the major principles. The second view prevailed. There were several reasons for

50. Drafting took quite a while, and the position paper of the 77 was not ready until 11 March, 1968, two weeks before the scheduled end of the Conference. TD/II/C.2/L.5, *Proceedings of the United Nations Conference on Trade and Development*, Second Session (New Delhi, 1 February—29 March 1968), Vol. I, pp. 275-278. (United Nations publication Sales Number E.68.II.D.14). Hereafter referred to as *Proceedings, New Delhi*.

51. Some Latin American countries continued to object to this solution until the last minute. Within the Group of 77 they were accused of stalling the agreement on GSP in order to strengthen their demands for special treatment in the US market.

this, most important of which was the unity of the 77. By assuming a maximalist position, and taking all interests and views into account, a common front could be preserved and cleavages within the group patched over.[52] It also gradually became clear that during the New Delhi Conference the developed countries were not likely to make any substantial concessions beyond the OECD Report. In view of this, tactically it made little sense for the 77 to dilute their demands, and their stand was to be maintained with a view to negotiations in the future.

When the position of the developing countries was made known, the B Group spokesman labelled it as too extreme and argued that it did not offer a common meeting ground for further useful discussions in the formal bodies of the Conference. The main differences centered on product coverage, as well as on exceptions and the nature of safeguards.[53]

Preferences were one of the most important topics during the last minute high-level negotiations at the New Delhi Conference. The crucial issue was product coverage and its impact on the scope and effect of the GSP. An informal paper negotiated by a small contact group of representatives of developed and developing countries, but not adopted by the Conference, reflected some slight progress.[54] Although the B Group adhered to the definition of manufactures and semi-manufactures as expressed in BTN chapters 25-99 as the basis for granting general preferences, its members were "prepared to examine, in the context of their agricultural policies and the principle of all developed countries making substantially equivalent contributions, the possibility of including processed and semi-processed products classified in chapters 1-24 BTN." The deletion of the "case-by-case approach" clause made some hope that processed and semi-processed agricultural products would still be included in the GSP as a matter of principle, with the understanding that the developed countries could then proceed to exclude certain items from the expanded basic list.[55] The group of delegates which negotiated the informal paper could scarcely deal with

52. The less advanced members of the 77 were suspicious that their more industrialized peers were prepared to settle for limited product coverage (BTN chapters 25-99) proposed by the B Group. They generally considered any attempts at compromise on this issue as defeatist and threatening their interests.

53. See OECD report (TD/56), the draft resolution of the 77 (TD/II/C.2/L.5) and the report of the Second Committee of the Conference in *Proceedings, New Delhi,* Vol. I, pp. 261-281.

54. "Preferences," 23 March, 1968 (mimeo).

55. This was especially so as the United States mooted the possibility of its accepting the broad product coverage (BTN chapters 1-99), with safeguards and exceptions.

and reach agreement on other aspects of the problem—depth of cuts, *ab initio* exceptions, safeguard mechanisms, "equivalent advantages", which countries should be beneficiaries, etc. Furthermore, the developed countries were lukewarm to the suggestion that they should make specific commitments to increase technical, financial and commercial assistance to the LDDCs.

Yet, the compromise draft was a step forward, in that it pinned down certain areas of limited consensus on the principles of the scheme. However, the African countries felt that it was very weak and it needlessly compromised the position of the 77. They especially objected to the provision on product coverage, and also argued that the status of LDDCs was not defined clearly. Consequently, as a group they refused to endorse the negotiated draft resolution.[56]

The New Delhi Conference thus could do no more than recognize the unanimous agreement that general preferences should be established. It stated that the objective of the general non-reciprocal, non-discriminatory system of preferences in favor of developing countries—including special measures for LDDCs—should be to increase their export earnings, promote their industrialization, and accelerate their rates of economic growth. It provided that a Special Committee on Preferences be established to continue consultations on the matter, with the general aim of settling the details of the arrangements in the course of 1969 with a view to seeking legislative authority and the required waiver in GATT.[57] It was perhaps too optimistic to expect the Conference to make visible progress in the definition of the GSP, and its relationship to existing special and reverse preference systems. Yet the commitment of the West to a general preference scheme was established, a detailed position of the 77 formulated, and the existing differences made clearer. This provided a starting point for gradual progress toward consensus on the specific components of a preference system.

The Aftermath of New Delhi. Contrary to expectations, the GSP did not come into being in 1969 and the period following the New Delhi Conference was characterized by repeated delays in the timetable

56. Note also that the beneficiaries of special preferences were reluctant to go on record as being prepared to relinquish special preferences for generalized preferences, which at the end of the Delhi Conference still seemed vague and not easily attainable. Moreover, in view of the forthcoming renegotiations of the Yaoundé Convention, the African states associated with the EEC, may have preferred not to have their hands tied by a specific agreement in UNCTAD.

57. Resolution 21 (II), *Proceedings, New Delhi,* Vol. I, p. 38. The first meeting of the Special Committee on Preferences was to be held in November 1968, while the second meeting was envisaged for the first half of 1969 so that the committee could draw up its final report to the Board.

adopted.[58] While consultations in the capitals of potential preference giving countries were in progress, UNCTAD's Special Committee on Preferences did not have much to do.[59] However, by July 1969 all developed countries intending to grant preferences had submitted their illustrative lists to OECD, i.e. each donor put forward a negative list specifying products from chapters 25-99 of the BTN on which it was not prepared to grant preferences, and a positive list giving those items from chapters 1-24 of the BTN on which it was willing to grant preferential treatment. Each list was accompanied by a statement of assumptions, qualifications and conditions on which a country—or a group of countries—based its policy. By November 1969 this documentation was forwarded to UNCTAD and to the developing countries. The submissions were provisional, and were intended to serve as the basis for consultations with the developing countries, while work went on in the OECD toward an early elaboration of a mutually acceptable GSP. The eighteen members of OECD which decided to participate in granting preferences to developing countries included: the EEC (Belgium, France, F.R. Germany, Italy, Luxembourg, the Netherlands), the Nordic countries (Denmark, Finland, Norway and Sweden) which put forward a joint submission, Austria, Canada, Ireland, Japan, New Zealand, Switzerland, the United Kingdom and the United States.[60]

Although "as concerted an approach as possible" was followed, a number of significant differences appeared. On the other hand, characteristics of individual submissions were "carefully weighed as parts of balanced unities", and it was often misleading to compare certain features of different schemes in isolation. Among the major points, the following should be singled out: [61]

(1) *Product coverage.* Regarding processed and semi-processed agricultural products falling in the BTN chapters 1-24, in general, limited positive lists were presented. The Nordic countries, were the more liberal donors in this instance, the United Kingdom and the United

58. Most notably, the new administration in Washington did not meet the revised deadline of March 1, 1969 for submitting its offer to OECD because it was reviewing the entire matter. It faced a growing pressure, however, primarily because the EEC was among those who tabled their lists on time.

59. See reports of the Special Committee on Preferences: TD/B/243 (19 May, 1969) and TD/B/256 (3 Jul. 1969); also, TD/B/262 (14 Jul. 1969).

60. Australia was the absentee. But this country had taken the lead by establishing preferences under tariff quotas on selected goods from developing countries as far back as 1965. Many have characterized this as a token gesture. See Pincus, *op. cit.,* p. 232. Others have argued that the Australian preferential scheme actually protected this country from excessive imports of textiles and toys from developing countries. "The Preference Game," *Far Eastern Economic Review* (8 Apr. 1968).

61. What follows is based on the OECD documentation (OECD doc. C(69)142) forwarded to UNCTAD. TD/B/AC.5/24 (14 Nov. 1969).

84

States' offers not being as satisfactory, while the EEC and Japan, presented very short lists of items on which they were prepared to grant preferences. As regards BTN chapters 25-99, Japan, the United Kingdom (with a proviso that it would make a final decision on primary products in the light of action to be taken by other major donor countries), the Nordic countries and Switzerland were prepared to grant preferences on all products. Canada and the United States offered preferences for certain primary products in BTN chapters 25-99, while the EEC was prepared to do so only for manufactures and semi-manufactures falling into these chapters.

(2) *Depth of tariff cut.* (a) Regarding chapters 25-99 of the BTN, the EEC, the Nordic countries, the United Kingdom and the United States envisaged duty-free entry. Japan, in principle, adhered to zero duty, although it offered only a 50% reduction on certain products, such as "textile sundries", leather and shoes. Other donors resorted to linear tariff reductions, mainly falling short of duty-free entry. (b) Regarding chapters 1-24 of the BTN, the Nordic countries, the United Kingdom (with few exceptions) and the United States contemplated tariff-free entry for those products included in their positive lists. Other donors opted for variable tariff reductions, according to the products. The EEC and Japan, for example, offered only minor reductions on a few selected items.

(3) *Exceptions.* The EEC and the Nordic countries envisaged no exceptions regarding chapters 25-99 of the BTN. However, their position was subject to change depending on the offers made by other developed countries. The United Kingdom tabled a list of exceptions, including *inter alia* cotton and silk textiles, as well as those products on which revenue duties were levied. Among the products on the US exception list were cotton textiles, footwear, petroleum and petroleum products. Japan excluded hydrocarbons because of the fiscal character of tariffs in this instance.

(4) *Safeguards.* All the donors provided for safeguards so as to retain some degree of control over the trade which might be generated by the new tariff preferences. They reserved the right to limit or withdraw, entirely or partly, certain advantages granted to developing countries (either for domestic reasons or in order not to injure the interests of third countries). Such measures would be exceptional, and would be put into effect only after the aims of the GSP and interests of the developing countries were taken into account. (a) Austria, the EEC and Japan, envisaged the application of *a priori* limitations formulae with quantitative ceilings.[62] (b) All other preference-giving countries

62. These countries provided that should the prescribed ceiling for a given product be exceeded, tariff preference could be suspended and the MFN tariff

opted for escape-clause type measures without *a priori* limitations.[63]

A number of standing reservations and conditions voiced at the New Delhi Conference and elsewhere were reiterated.[64] What was most important, the United States made its offer conditional on the elimination of special preferences on products covered by the scheme, the immediate abrogation of the reverse preferences, and the adoption of a common scheme by all developed countries.[65] Regarding the last point, the EEC was of a different opinion; it argued that if the idea of preferences was to be implemented rapidly, countries granting preferences should use "mechanisms best suited to their specific positions".

With the provisional offers on the table, consensus building had entered a qualitatively new stage. Consultations over specific and practical problems were ushered in. It became possible for the 77, for regional groups, and for each developing country to assess the potential advantages of the offers, and to present specific demands in relation to each submission.

At the session of the Special Committee, held in the spring of 1970, the developing countries presented their reactions to the offers made. They asked for improvements in product coverage, reduction of exception lists, special measures for LDDCs, flexible and liberal use of ceilings and escape clauses, etc. The developed countries thereupon returned to the OECD, to finalize their submissions. The matter was back in UNCTAD in autumn 1970, when agreement was reached on mutually acceptable arrangements for a generalized system of preferences to be introduced in 1971.[66] In an important follow-up action, agreed texts for rules of origin were adopted in December 1970. The

---

would begin to apply. Regarding those products falling into BTN chapters 1-24, the EEC and Japan proposed to use the escape clause procedure without limitation of preferential imports.

63. In their submission, the Nordic countries provided that consultations should be held with the exporting country(ies) when an imported product disturbs or threatens to disturb the market. However, in case of urgent necessity the donor could introduce limitations on imports unilaterally. As a rule, imports should not be reduced to a level below the one prevailing before the disturbance, safeguard action should be confined to those developing countries causing injury and should be temporary, and consultations should be held in the organization in charge of examining the functioning of the GSP.

64. See TD/B/309/Add.1 (16 Jul. 1970), pp. 43-45.

65. The United States argued that duty-free entry, without quantitative ceilings and with a bare minimum of exceptions would, if adopted by all countries, satisfy the criterion of equivalent advantages for those countries giving up their special preferences.

66. For the reports of the Special Committee on Preferences see TD/B/300 and addenda (27 Apr. 1970) and TD/B/329 and addenda (12 Oct. 1970). The final submissions by developed market economies are contained in TD/B/AC.5/34 and addenda.

objective of the rules of origin, of course, is to confine the benefits of GSP to developing nations and to exclude goods which are essentially produced by third countries. An agreement on this was essential if delays in introducing preferences were to be avoided.[67]

In the process leading to the agreement, three elements were of importance. First, perfection was not sought and the system of preferences was placed in a dynamic context. In other words, by proceeding with implementation as rapidly as possible, many unresolved problems and unsatisfactory solutions could be tackled in a pragmatic manner, on the basis of experience. The developing countries, especially, realized that their demands for more extensive product coverage would not be met immediately;[68] also, they concluded that seeking greater harmonization of offers could result in the lowering of benefits, and that a single system was more likely to emerge through a gradual coordination of various operating schemes. Secondly, many countries on both sides were prepared to compromise their previously rigid positions. And thirdly, the agreement was in a sense hustled through, so as to make it a part of the second Development Decade strategy launched by the UN General Assembly at its 25th anniversary session in the fall of 1970. Also, the 77 had in mind the 1972 presidential elections in the United States, and hoped that the Congress would approve preferences before the election fever took hold.

Several developments made the consensus possible. The United States assumed a more flexible attitude following the adoption of a compromise package proposal at the OECD ministerial meeting held in May 1970. It no longer insisted that a single common scheme be adopted by all donors. Instead, it placed emphasis on the harmonization of offers and their yielding of comparable results, as well as on equitable sharing of burden.[69] Although the question of reverse preferences remained to be resolved through consultations between the parties directly concerned, with a view to finding solutions before the imple-

---

67. See the reports of the Working Group on Rules of Origin: TD/B/AC.5/20 (13 Jun. 1969), TD/B/AC.5/31 (8 Jul. 1970), and TD/B/AC.5/38 (21 Dec. 1970).

68. There was an implicit "take-it-or-leave-it" element in the terms of the OECD countries. The developing countries concluded that there was no other choice but to settle for the best that they could get at the time.

69. During the consultations it became evident that the EEC would not change its position and agree to non-restricted preferential access. The 77 and others argued that preferences should not be scuttled by insisting on a common scheme, especially as the US and EEC offers were comparable in terms of potential effect despite many technical differences. Their argument was strengthened when the spokesman for the EEC attested that great flexibility would be exercised in administering ceilings and quotas, and that in the majority of cases the ceilings will be more or less disregarded.

mentation of various schemes, the United States was prepared from the outset to treat the developing countries which extend reverse preferences as beneficiaries. In return, it expected that these countries would give assurances that such preferences will be phased-out over a reasonable period of time.[70] Finally, it withdrew its demand that special preferences be fully eliminated over a 5-year period, and it agreed to treat the developing countries enjoying such privileges as beneficiaries.[71]

Those developing countries receiving special preferences, agreed to share their existing advantages in return for new export opportunities they expect to obtain in other developed countries.[72] The premise came to be accepted that there would be a reasonable *a priori* assurance that these developing countries would obtain equivalent advantages provided that the offers of major donors were "broadly comparable". How the beneficiaries of special preferences were affected by generalized preferences would be kept under close and constant review.

The least advanced members of the Group of 77, and in particular the African countries, accepted the OECD offers, although their demands for more extensive product coverage and special measures were not generally met, and they did not expect significant immediate advantages from the GSP. In spite of the rhetoric,[73] when the cards were on the table these countries were not prepared to stall the agree-

70. Although the US softened its stand and accepted a declaration of intent, its basic position remained unchanged and was an integral part of its offer. Informally, it mentioned 1975 as a deadline for the abolition of reverse preferences. It had to climb down on reverse preferences, because it was not possible to resolve this very complicated issue in a hurry. (It is interesting that the United States could not obtain from the developed countries in question a declaration that they are prepared to see reverse preferences phased out without penalty to the developing countries concerned.)

71. Yet, the United States reserved its right to extend special preferences. Also, if trade under special preferences on items covered by the scheme increased and assumed significant proportions, it reserved the right to declare as ineligible for its concessions those developing countries benefitting from special preferences.

72. The beneficiaries of special preferences generally understood that their privileges often contributed to the freezing of their economic structures and meant an excessive dependence on certain developed countries. Moreover, the associates of the EEC could expect that their interests be protected to a degree by the ceilings established on various products.

73. In view of their general dissatisfaction, the African countries and the EEC associates in particular, insisted that serious negotiations could begin only after the final submissions of the OECD members were brought to light. This implied a further delay and the loss of a politically favorable moment to pin down the consensus. (Note that a considerable amount of good will had been generated during the 1970 spring meeting of UNCTAD's Special Committee on Preferences, possibly because the 77 were pleasantly surprised by the concrete offers and cooperative attitude of the developed countries, something they were not used to in the UNCTAD context.)

ment. They had apparently concluded that their demands and wishes would fare better once the system began to operate. Keeping an eye on the unity of their group, as well as on other issues on UNCTAD's agenda, they shifted the emphasis from "equality of benefits" to "effective beneficial participation".

The final offers of the developed countries differed somewhat from the original ones, the changes reflecting partly the wishes of the developing countries and partly the effects of the "equitable burden sharing" principle. Generally, most submissions were improved.[74] On the other hand, the United Kingdom and the Nordic countries were not able to fully maintain their relatively liberal initial proposals, in view of the fact that other donors did not follow their example.[75]

In all their basic aspects, however, the offers remained unchanged. The safeguards were to be exceptional, and applied only after taking into account the aims of GSP and the interests of LDDCs. However, although consultations could be held where and when possible, the donors could act without consulting the beneficiaries. Moreover, the donors would review the functioning of safeguard measures unilaterally. Preferences were to last ten years, they would be temporary and not binding, and there was nothing to forestall a subsequent withdrawal in whole or in part of the advantages granted to developing countries. Likewise, GSP could not prevent further reductions of tariffs either unilaterally or through MFN negotiations in GATT. Self-election criteria for claiming beneficiary status was retained.[76]

Regarding the rules of origin, agreement could not be attained on a comprehensive system with uniform rules. Rather, two broad categories were adopted: i.e. rules of origin based on the process criterion, to be applied by most donors with variations, and rules based on the value-

74. For the summary of changes in various offers consult TD/B/329/Add.1 (9 Oct. 1970). For example, the United States added 57 items to its positive list (BTN chapters 1-24). The EEC, on the other hand, added only a few processed and semi-processed agricultural products, arguing that high surpluses of agricultural products and special preferences extended to the associated African states prevented it from being more generous in this area.

75. The United Kingdom added to its list of exceptions man-made fibers and woollen textiles. It also deleted a number of products which were on its original positive list (BTN chapters 1-24). The Nordic countries tabled a list of products sensitive to market disruption (e.g. jute fabrics, cotton textiles, footwear) which could be subjected to special treatment, including initial exceptions in some countries. This they did because the major trading nations exempted a variety of products or substantially restricted imports.

76. In addition to the members of the Group of 77, Cuba, Turkey, Bulgaria, Romania, Mongolia, Spain, Malta, Israel and Greece declared themselves as developing countries. One of the key unsolved problems related to the status of Hong Kong, the greatest potential beneficiary of preferences.

added criterion, to be used by the United States, Canada, and New Zealand. Yet, the aim remained to harmonize the different rules of origin under the GSP at a later stage.[77]

No concrete measures in favor of less advanced developing countries could be agreed to,[78] and their problems were to be taken care of in the dynamic context, on the basis of general guidelines. Among the adopted provisions were: (1) Donors would consider on a case-by-case basis the inclusion of products which are of interest mainly to LDDCs, as well as greater tariff reductions on such products, and in applying safeguards they would pay particular attention to the interests of LDDCs. (2) During the annual review of GSP, special attention would be given to its effects on the exports and export earnings of LDDCs, and further measures in their favor would be considered. (3) In other areas of UNCTAD's competence, attention would be given to measures related or complementary to GSP, especially those which would enable LDDCs to benefit more fully from preferences. (4) The attention of other international organizations was called to the possibility of taking related measures to enable LDDCs to export products which are included in GSP, e.g. financial and technical assistance for the establishment and development of industries.[79]

The socialist countries—USSR, Poland, Hungary, Czechoslovakia and Bulgaria—in announcing their contribution to the aims of the generalized preferences undertook among other things to implement the following: the inclusion of special provisions into their economic plans which would help expand their imports from developing countries; preferential treatment for developing countries' products in their procurement policies; granting technical assistance for the construction of industrial undertakings in developing areas; the acceptance in partial repayment of credits granted for the construction of such plants of

77. See TD/B/AC.5/38 (21 Dec. 1970).

78. Among the specific measures proposed but not agreed to, were that safeguards should not apply to their least competitive products, and that there should be a free import of their processed agricultural goods, handicrafts, footwear, etc. TD/B/300 (27 Apr. 1970), pp. 95-96.

79. The Latin American countries proposed a number of related measures, *inter alia:* that UNIDO's ability to carry out studies and to provide technical assistance for the establishment of such industries be reinforced; that within the UNDP special funds be established for the execution of related pre-investment studies; that within the IBRD family special funds for long-term financing of such industries at low rates of interest be formed; that the developed countries make additional contributions to the regional development banks for financing the export of products included in GSP, as well as imports of capital goods necessary for the establishment or expansion of industries manufacturing such products. *Ibid.*, pp. 102-103.

goods produced by them; etc.[80] The proposed measures were to apply to industrial products, as well as to raw materials, and processed and semi-processed agricultural goods, and no time limit was suggested as to the duration of the preferential treatment.[81]

As for the review and implementation mechanism, it was agreed that appropriate institutional arrangements would be established within UNCTAD.[82] Also, the B Group envisaged within the OECD a machinery to consider equitable burden sharing, the use of safeguards, and the effect of ceilings and quotas.

UNCTAD would review the effects of preferences on exports, export earnings, and economic growth and industrialization of developing countries. It would also consider the specific aspects of the system, including rules of origin, the effects of GSP on the earnings of those developing countries sharing their special preferences, the complementary efforts made by the developing countries to utilize the advantages offered by general preferences, the measures undertaken by the socialist countries, etc.[83]

A compromise solution on preferences has emerged in spite of a number of standing differences among the developed countries, and among developed and developing ones. Admittedly, it is far removed from a contractual, zero duty, no escape, full coverage, uniform preferential scheme which was envisaged originally. Thus the system is in fact a variety of schemes offered by various countries, or groups of countries; it contains no built-in guarantees and the donor(s) can

80. For their joint communique see TD/B/329/Add.3 (9 Oct. 1970). Note that Romania was not among donors, and that Bulgaria—although it would give preferential status to products of developing countries—expected to be treated as a beneficiary of GSP in the western markets.

81. The decision of the socialist countries was organically linked with the New Delhi Conference resolution 15(II). See Chapter VII for our discussion of the subject. The measures socialist countries propose to undertake were welcomed by the 77. This was important for the socialist countries in view of the long-standing stricture especially by the B Group spokesmen, arguing that a simple removal of tariffs in the centrally-planned economies would mean little for the expansion of developing countries' exports.

82. There was no consensus regarding the machinery to fulfil the role. The B Group favored the Committee on Manufactures, while the 77 and the D Group asked that the mandate of the Special Committee on Preferences be extended. (See Chapter X for additional comments on this subject.)

83. TD/B/329 (12 Oct. 1970), pp. 13-14. An annual review to assess and analyze the functioning of the system is provided for. A triennial review is to assess the benefits of the system, and consider the possibilities for its improvement and modification. A comprehensive review near the end of the ten-year period will consider whether the system is to be extended. *Ad hoc* consultations on matters which may require urgent consideration are envisaged. They may take place with the assistance of the UNCTAD Secretary-General.

shut-off the carefully built export drive of a developing country. Exceptions took in precisely those products, or categories of products where developing countries enjoy comparative advantages, and can compete effectively in the markets of developed countries.[84] Product coverage is not broad enough to meet the interests of all developing countries, and especially of the less advanced ones. Ceilings and quotas to be applied by certain donors, carry in themselves the inherent danger of being utilized in a discriminatory manner.

Yet, in spite of everything, the agreement represents a milestone for UNCTAD and international economic relations. Provided that various offers survive the scrutiny of the ratifying authorities—the greatest obstacle being the protectionist mood of the US Congress—generalized preferences will be the first major item on UNCTAD's agenda brought to maturation and based on the underlying premise that something very special has to be done for the developing countries in the international trade system. It is an important precedent, likely to help advancement in other issue areas, provided that those involved have approached this undertaking unfeignedly. The sincerity of commitment of preference-giving countries to new principles and actions will be tested ultimately through their use of safeguards and non-tariff barriers, as well as their willingness to allow for the improvements of the system as it takes shape.

84. Note, for example, that of total exports of manufactures from developing countries to developed market economies in 1969, textiles and clothing accounted for 32.8 %, and food products for another 12.8 %. TD/B/C.2/102 (24 Dec. 1970), pp. 33-34.

Chapter IV

COMMODITIES

Among the principal fields that UNCTAD is taking on, commodities
are of the greatest interest and of central importance to the majority of
developing countries. As much as 85% of developing countries' export
earnings continue to be generated by primary commodities, and three
out of four among them earn more than 60% of their foreign exchange
by exporting just one, two or three primary products.[1] At the Geneva
Conference the developing countries argued that the promotion of their
economic development should be the central aim of an internationally
planned, coordinated and continuous intervention with the "free play"
of commodity market forces. We have touched briefly in Chapter II
upon various measures proposed to improve their position in the
commodity trade. However, the fact that the relevant recommendations
were adopted unanimously in 1964 did not mean that consensus prevailed; rather, the uncertain and sometimes contradictory wording of
agreed statements often masked important conceptual disagreements
and differences of view. Many western countries were not fully convinced that a regulation of commodity markets is required. Also, they
showed little enthusiasm for the proposed trade liberalization measures
aimed at enabling the developing countries to augment their commodity
exports. To admit the development needs of the Third World as one of
the basic criteria for the commercial and tariff policies in the field of
commodity trade would have represented too sharp a break with the
traditional practices, and implied a disturbance of powerful vested
interests and of the prevailing international division of labor.

Before we embark on our discussion of UNCTAD's labors, it may
be useful to recall that among the major problems associated with
commodities are price fluctuations and their effect on the foreign exchange earnings of developing countries, agricultural protectionism and
revenue taxation in the North, as well as the competition natural

1. Report of the Commission on International Development, *Partners in
Development* (New York: Praeger, 1969), p. 81. For the developing countries
with the highest concentration of export earnings in a single product see TD/B/309
(7 Aug. 1970), p. 44.

products face from synthetics and substitutes. Stockpiling and surplus disposal by major industrial countries are also significant. Among the problems in the camp of commodity-exporting developing countries, we find the lack of coordination of their production and marketing policies, and above all the long-range structural requirement for diversification of production as a means of avoiding the dependence on the export of one or several commodities.

Primary products are many. Not all of them are problematical, while those that are, face diverse vicissitudes. The classical dichotomies between agricultural and non-agricultural commodities, raw materials and foodstuffs, tropical and temperate zone commodities, are supplemented in UNCTAD by a classification of commodities exported by developing countries (petroleum excluded) based on their market characteristics, i.e. the existence of substitutes in consumption and trade barriers. Thus, there are those commodities which are produced wholly or mainly in the developing countries—e.g. tin and non-competing tropical foodstuffs and beverages like coffee, cocoa, tea, bananas. They suffer from the vagaries of the commodity markets; they are often subjected to fiscal levies and taxes which tend to depress the growth of their consumption; in certain markets they face the discriminatory special preferences. There are also those commodities which are produced wholly or mainly in the developing countries, but which are confronted with the competition of synthetics and various substitutes manufactured in industrial nations—e.g. natural rubber, jute, hard fibers. The producers of these commodities find themselves in a special quandary, because in addition to the typical problems they also have to worry about higher productivity, quality and diversification of end uses if they aspire to hold their own against substitutes. Among the commodities produced in substantial amounts in developed and developing countries alike are various mineral ores and metals, as well as agricultural produce—e.g. sugar, grains, fats, oils, cotton, tobacco, citrus fruit, etc. In the case of the latter, the developing countries encounter the agricultural protectionism which is strongly entrenched in most developed countries and is manifested through tariffs, variable duties, quantitative restrictions, procurement policies, etc. Moreover, developed countries usually give subsidies and price support to commodities they produce uneconomically, so as to make a competitive thrust into foreign markets.[2]

In the pages that follow we shall discuss commodity agreements and

2. See TD/B/109 (5 Oct. 1966), p. 4, and TD/8/Supp.1 (14 Nov. 1967), Chapter I. The classification also speaks of those commodities produced mainly in developed countries, viz., meat, dairy products, vegetables. The trade barriers these products face could act as a deterrent to the creation of an export potential of developing countries in this area.

the related problem of buffer stock financing, trade liberalization, and synthetics and substitutes.

International Commodity Agreements

Following the Geneva Conference, the developing countries continued to argue that there is a need for a general agreement on commodity arrangements. By codifying general guidelines they expected that it would be easier to relate new principles to practical action, that consistency and uniformity of methods would result, and that clashes on questions of principle and philosophical issues would be reduced. However, most developed countries preferred an atomistic and incremental approach to a comprehensive redefinition of rules; they felt that differences in trade philosophy were hard to bridge, and refused to consider the possibility of concluding a general agreement on commodity arrangements.[3] Realizing that for the time being efforts to adopt an overarching instrument were likely to divert attention from and to retard the solution of specific commodity problems, the 77 had to fall back on the commodity-by-commodity strategy common in the past. On the other hand, a set of generally adopted guidelines may yet evolve through practical action, negotiation of agreements on individual commodities, and debates on specific policy proposals.[4] Thus, for example, the Board has managed to agree on a set of general principles on pricing policy which would serve as guidelines for intergovernmental consultations and concrete action intended to stabilize markets for individual commodities.[5]

International commodity agreements aim at stabilizing the price of a given product within a certain prescribed range, remunerative to the producers and equitable to the consumers, and at regulating the quantities traded commercially. They can also coordinate national production and consumption policies, give guarantees on terms of

3. A secretariat study on a general agreement (TD/30 (19 Dec. 1967)) was briefly discussed at the New Delhi Conference and then passed to governments for their comments. At the fourth session of the Committee on Commodities the developed countries generally felt that it would be useless to continue the consideration of this matter. TD/B/248 (16 Jun. 1969), also, TD/B/C.1/49 (8 Oct. 1968), TD/B/C.1/64 (10 Mar. 1969) and TD/B/C.1/65 (10 Mar. 1969).

4. The New Delhi Conference referred to the Board eleven draft resolutions on commodities on which it had been unable to agree or which it had not had sufficient time to consider. These were belabored in the continuing machinery and consensus gradually emerged on the majority of controversial issues. See TD/B/309/Add.1 (16 Jul. 1970), pp. 36-37.

5. Board resolution 73 (X) in TD/B/327 (30 Sep. 1970), Annex I. The operational value of this policy agreement appears questionable, however, in view of the fact that it is interspersed with qualifiers such as "when possible" etc.

access to the markets of consuming countries, and secure a reasonable share of market growth. At the time of the Geneva Conference, coffee, tin and olive oil agreements were in operation; sugar and wheat agreements continued but were inoperative. No new commodity agreement was added to this group since UNCTAD came into being. Basically unaltered, olive oil and tin agreements have been renewed under UNCTAD's auspices twice already. The sugar agreement was also renegotiated in UNCTAD, in 1968. Coffee (1968) and wheat (1967) were renegotiated elsewhere. During the entire period, vain attempts were made to conclude a cocoa agreement. We shall speak of cocoa and sugar, as the two major commodities on UNCTAD's agenda; action on wheat and coffee as well as on other commodities, will be also mentioned.

Cocoa. Inherently, cocoa is a commodity for which it should not be very difficult to negotiate an agreement. For example, it does not face the competition of producers from major developed countries; there is no threat of substitution by artificial products; at present there is no grave tendency to overproduce; it is easily storable and thus suitable for a buffer stock scheme; overproduction can be mitigated by converting cocoa into oleo-margarine; etc. But, a cocoa agreement has eluded the international organizations for a number of years.[6]

A serious drop in cocoa prices began in 1965, as UNCTAD initiated steps for a cocoa conference. Held under its auspices, the 1966 Cocoa Conference made some progress; it agreed on the maximum size of the buffer stock, determination of quotas, and channelling of excess cocoa into non-traditional uses. However, there was no consensus on the floor price, and on the operative features of the buffer stock and its pre-financing.[7] The cocoa producers expressed their disappointment and criticized some developed nations for non-compliance with the *Final Act* recommendation of securing a minimum remunerative price for commodity producers. They argued that the agreement should follow the *Final Act* guidelines and provide for stable and remunerative prices, an effective buffer stock, favorable pre-financing on the first buffer stock by international monetary institutions or governments of industrial countries, effective means of control, and measures to reduce barriers to cocoa trade and its consumption.[8]

Consultations continued, however, and by October 1967 it appeared

6. The FAO Cocoa Study Group began its work in 1957. The 1963 UN Cocoa Conference failed because of disagreements over the price range. In 1964, the Alliance of Cocoa Producing Countries (Ghana, Nigeria, Ivory Coast, Brazil, and Togo) was unsuccessful in an attempt to introduce a coordinated sales policy.

7. For details see TD/B/81 (11 Aug. 1966).

8. TD/B/106 (16 Sep. 1966).

that the major problems were solved. The memorandum of agreement provided for a price range (20-29c per pound); a combination of export quotas and a buffer stock (maximum capacity 250,000 tons); financing of the buffer stock to be paid by the producers with a levy of 1c per pound on cocoa entering international trade; etc.[9] Only the secondary problems such as the status of non-member countries, special preferences in the EEC, the voting procedure in the future cocoa council, etc., remained in limbo.[10] The time was ripe to convene another cocoa conference, it seemed.

There were some bad omens, however. The memorandum was met by an angry outcry from cocoa traders—who earn their living through price variations—particularly in the United States and in the United Kingdom. The powerful lobby of the cocoa merchants and the processing industry could mount an effective opposition in the US Senate, where the cocoa agreement would have come up for ratification simultaneously with the coffee agreement. To many, it appeared tactically unwise to have two commodity agreements on the Senate floor at the same time; also, with the presidential election year at the doorstep, it was wise to avoid a battle with powerful domestic interests. These factors led many observers to conclude that Washington had rejected the possibility of a cocoa agreement *a priori* and that the 1967 Cocoa Conference was doomed even before it started.[11]

9. For the memorandum see TD/COCOA.1/11 (25 Oct. 1967). It was adopted by a working party made of principal producing countries (Ghana, Nigeria, the Ivory Coast, Cameroun, Brazil, Mexico and Ecuador), and of principal consuming countries (the United States, F.R. Germany, France, the Netherlands, the United Kingdom, Switzerland and the USSR).

10. The memorandum did not fulfil the expectations of the producers. They had asked for a minimum price of 26c per pound; the 20c that was agreed to was rather low in view of the fact that only on one occasion in the past twenty years had the price of cocoa fallen below this figure. It was hoped that the buffer stock would be the primary instrument to deal with price fluctuations and to intervene in the market whenever necessary, while export quotas and controls would be used only in exceptional situations; the memorandum provided that the quota system be put into effect first, while the buffer stock would act as a reserve, buying the temporary surplus at the end of the year. It was hoped that the consuming countries would contribute to the financing of the buffer stock; in the end, the producing countries agreed to shoulder the 1c levy themselves. (Speech by Prebisch to the Second Committee of the General Assembly on 9 December 1967. Mimeo).

11. Note the conspicuous absence of Prebisch during the conference proceedings, even though he had previously taken an extremely active part in the consultations. It has been speculated that he had been forewarned of the US unwillingness to join a cocoa agreement at that point in time, and consequently chose not to be present. According to another interpretation, Prebisch felt he had become a liability to the negotiations because he was disliked by certain consumer countries. Moreover, the African states associated with the EEC, resented his very

One day before the end of the conference, the delegations were close to an agreement. However, a compromise solution proposed by the chairman and which appeared acceptable to all participants, could not be considered; the United States withdrew from negotiations because of the "lack of instructions" regarding this proposal. In explaining this move, the US delegate argued that the conference was too short and that there remained a number of unsolved problems such as the treatment of fine flavor cocoa, the establishment of control machinery, duration of the agreement, the transfer of quotas, obstacles to consumption, special preferences, processed cocoa, and the size of the cocoa council to be created and its location. The critics of the US position pointed to the long preparatory work and the fact that all articles of the agreement had been revised; they argued that the remaining problems could be resolved in the machinery which would be created. The producing countries felt that genuine problems, like pricing and quotas over which the previous conferences had foundered, were not the cause of the failure this time.[12]

Yet efforts had to continue, and the New Delhi Conference—in one of its more important decisions in the field of commodities—recommended that the cocoa conference be convened no later than the end of June 1968 with the aim of concluding a cocoa agreement.[13] It proved impossible, however, to comply with this recommendation. Some producing countries engaged in stalling tactics by reserving their position on certain technical points. The slackening of desire on their part to have an immediate agreement could be easily explained by the high prices that cocoa began to enjoy (from the low point of 11c per pound in 1965, the price of one type of cocoa skyrocketed to about 50c per pound in late 1968). Also, the producing countries could not always see eye to eye, and a considerable amount of disputation occurred in their ranks, especially between Brazilians and Africans, e.g., over special preferences.[14] But, the main difficulties continued between

strong statements on vertical preferential arrangements, which were to be one of the issues raised in the negotiations. As a result, he concluded that the proceedings would fare better if he were absent.

12. For the various statements at the closing session of the conference see TD/COCOA.2/EX/SR.13 (21 Dec. 1967). Note that during the final stages of the conference additional complications appeared because of the linkage with the coffee negotiations held in London. Under the heading of fine flavor and processed cocoa, the US and Brazil delegations actually fought their battle over Brazil's instant coffee exports.

13. Resolution 16(II), *Proceedings, New Delhi*, Vol. I, p. 34.

14. One of the important disputes during the 1967 conference was generated by the special preferences for cocoa extended by the EEC to its African associates. Brazil made their abolition a precondition for its taking part in the cocoa agree-

producing and consuming countries. And although during the various preparatory meetings a number of technical problems were resolved, including the administrative provisions for the proposed international cocoa organization, when the June 1970 consultations collapsed *inter alia* over the producer-consumer discord on the price range, the cocoa pact seemed as remote as ever.[15] One of the underlying, although unreported causes of the failure lay in the opposition of the chocolate industry, especially in the United States, to an agreement. The hard line position, or stalling tactics of certain consumer countries reflected this state of affairs.

Sugar. The economic provisions of the 1958 sugar agreement became inoperative in January 1962: the United States at that time refused to buy Cuban sugar, while Cuba on account of this was not prepared to accept that its overall quota be reduced. Violent price fluctuations ensued in the sugar market.[16] The first attempt at renegotiating the agreement was made in 1965 under UNCTAD's auspices. The draft agreement contained some novel features, for example, stronger measures to protect the price range, certain preferences for sugar exporters from developing countries, prices at reasonably remunerative levels, commitments by developed countries to liberalize access to their markets, etc.[17] However, the 1965 conference ended in failure.

When the 1968 Sugar Conference was convened after a period of overproduction and low prices, the chances of concluding an agreement were much brighter. The groundwork was carefully laid by Prebisch, in cooperation with the International Sugar Council and the Sugar Consultative Committee. Cuba, as the largest exporter, appeared ready to enter into an agreement.[18] Finally, there was a good deal of flexibility,

---

ment, even though its difficulties with cocoa in the EEC were not directly attributable to special preferences. This was part of the negotiating stand of the Latin American countries, which wanted for coffee and cocoa a proportional access guarantee to the EEC in the short run, and the extension of preferences to all developing countries in the long run.

15. Producers asked for a 25-34c range in view of the new market situation and inflationary tendencies; consumers adhered to the 20-29c formula agreed to in 1967.

16. In 1963 the price of sugar had reached a peak of 107 pounds sterling per ton. This incentive increased sugar production and supply, and prices went tumbling down to 12 pounds sterling per ton, which represented barely one-third of the production cost per ton of cane sugar incurred by an efficient producer. *The London Times*, September 11, 1967.

17. TD/5/Add.1 (31 Aug. 1967), p. 20. For the draft agreement see TD/SUGAR.6/4 (1 Oct. 1965).

18. Cuba's goal was to double its sugar output, produce 10 million tons by 1970, and then enter into an agreement, with its quota being determined on the basis of this larger production figure. Another element that acted as an obstacle

with no ambition to reach a perfect solution, and a willingness to conclude an agreement without the participation of the United States and the EEC.

In concluding the agreement, the 1968 conference resolved several outstanding problems such as the price range, the system of export quotas through which the agreement would handle persistent over-production and bring about short-term price stabilization, the access to markets of those industrial countries producing beet sugar,[19] and the problem of the re-exporting of Cuban sugar from socialist countries that acquire it through barter trade.[20]

Several new provisions in the agreement were the result of UNCTAD's deliberations. The developing countries exporting sugar, in contrast to the developed ones, were entitled to special measures. For example, under certain conditions they would be required to hold less stock, and they would have priority on quota increases whenever a distribution of shortfalls in export quotas takes place. In fixing quotas, the developed countries exporting sugar accepted quotas lower than their exports in previous years, thus making it possible for developing countries to increase their exports. A hardship fund of 150,000 tons was established to meet the special needs of those developing countries that have sugar available over their quotas; priority would be given to small countries whose export earnings depend on sugar and to those burdened with excessive stocks.[21] A special provision on landlocked countries was adopted, whereby they would be exempted from supply commitments and penalties for failing to supply their quota.[22] And finally, the importing developed countries undertook specific commitments regarding the curtailment of their sugar production and market access guarantees to imported sugar; the first instance ever that such a provision was included in a commodity agreement. It needs to be

was that Japan and Canada were not tied to long-term contracts and enjoyed the low prices that prevailed in the market; therefore, they tended to stall. "The Great Sugar Triumph," *The Economist*, October 26, 1968.

19. Although the production cost of cane sugar in developing countries is one-fourth the production cost of beet sugar in industrial countries, the governments concerned regard the arguments in favor of reducing beet sugar output as academic. Large investments have been made in the processing industry, while sugar beet is of importance to farmers as a high-value break crop which best prepares land for wheat.

20. The text of the agreement is to be found in TD/SUGAR.7/10 (24 Oct. 1968).

21. The decisions on the allocation of this hardship fund are made by a committee made up of an independent chairman and six other members serving in their personal capacity.

22. Other countries may incur cancellation of their basic tonnage if they do not meet their basic quota obligations.

100

emphasized that one of the important reasons for the failure of the 1965 Sugar Conference was the inability of the negotiators to come to an agreement precisely on this point.

The agreement came into force on January 1, 1969, thus meeting the deadline set by the New Delhi Conference.[23] The average daily price of sugar in September 1968 stood at 1.33c per pound; in March 1969 it reached 3.57c, which was above the floor price of 3.25c provided for in the agreement.[24] For the first time since 1962, the International Sugar Council had re-established control of that segment of the world sugar market which is not subject to various preferential trade arrangements, i.e. less than one-half of the total annual sugar trade. In connection with this, and for a better understanding of the problem, it should be kept in mind that a very large part of the sugar produced in the world today receives considerable support from governments, either through subsidies or strongly protected homemarkets. In fact, many countries aim at self-sufficiency. Consequently, the scope for an increase in sugar exports from developing countries where it is produced economically is very limited. This fundamental problem is not dealt with effectively on the international level, and this will continue so long as sugar production and export is highly subsidized in developed countries.[25]

Coffee and Wheat. Although the 1968 coffee agreement and the 1967 wheat agreement were not renegotiated under UNCTAD's auspices, a brief mention of these agreements is necessary because of their relation to the *Final Act* and to the problems encountered in this organization.

The slow recovery from wartime production cutbacks and the upsurge of demand raised coffee prices in the 1950's. This created an incentive for new planting which a few years later resulted in overproduction and caused coffee prices to fall drastically. Since coffee was a crucial commodity for many Latin American countries, the Kennedy administration, as a part of the new policy initiated under the Alliance for Progress, decided in this instance to overlook the traditional opposition of the United States to commodity market regulation. This made the international coffee agreement feasible in 1962. Its operation showed that it was possible to maintain a stable and, more or less, remunerative level of earnings for a commodity tending toward chronic overpro-

---

23. Resolution 16 (II), *Proceedings, New Delhi,* Vol. I, p. 35.
24. TD/B/C.1/61 (1 Apr. 1969), pp. 15-16.
25. For example, the EEC, which is not among the members of the 1968 sugar agreement, aims to produce 105% of its sugar requirements. The 5% is an insurance margin, exported with the help of large subsidies when necessary. *The Economic Times* (Bombay), January 29, 1971, p. 3.

duction, and to promote the long-term balance of production and consumption.[26]

The 1967-68 renegotiation of the coffee agreement was very protracted and difficult; yet, all parties concerned desired to have an agreement (in contrast to cocoa), and the negotiators were able to resolve some knotty technical, economic and political problems. Sharp disputes occurred among the producing countries over the changes in basic export quotas to take new planting into account, as well as over the differing price movements for various types of coffee and the temporary adjustment of quotas separately for each of the main types of coffee. Yet, they managed to iron out their differences in the end. The disagreement between the United States and Brazil over the latter's fast growing exports of soluble coffee also endangered the renewal of the pact. Brazil's newly founded coffee industry bought coffee beans from surplus stockpiles on preferential terms and after processing, exported instant coffee. It managed very quickly to capture a significant slice of the US market for this type of coffee, thus giving rise to vociferous objections from coffee merchants and the coffee industry in that country.[27] As a compromise, the 1968 agreement provided that no member shall apply measures which amount to discriminatory treatment in favor of processed coffee and against green coffee. If this occurs anyway, after a certain procedure is satisfied and the exporter does not rectify the situation, the importing countries can apply countermeasures. In doing so, they shall have due regard for the needs of developing countries that are striving to broaden their economies through industrialization and the export of manufactured products.[28] This uneasy compromise reflected both the problem of infant industries in developing nations and the underlying theme of UNCTAD's efforts to effect changes in the international division of labor.

Certain features of the agreement were related to its long-run aim to reduce the production of coffee to the level of consumption through diversification of the economies of exporting countries. Thus a diversification fund of at least $150 million was established for the first time, in order to finance projects that would cut down coffee surplus and divert resources to other uses in coffee producing countries. Yet, the

26. TD/B/C.1/46 (16 Jan. 1968), p. 71. The prices under the agreement added $550 million to the exporters' income and in 1964 their earnings were 30% above those in 1962.

27. In 1967, Brazil exported $23,346,000 worth of instant coffee to the United States, as compared to $685,000 in 1965. TD/B/C.1/50/Add.1 (16 Sep. 1968), p. 17.

28. Article 44 of the 1968 coffee agreement, reproduced as the Senate Executive Document, 90th Congress, 2nd Session, D. (Washington, D.C.: US Government Printing Office, 1968).

consuming countries were not obliged to contribute to this fund.[29] (Note however, that following the 1969 decisions of the IBRD's Board of Executive Directors on the IBRD's role in the field of commodities, a favorable attitude toward diversification funds and projects became possible in the World Bank Group).[30] A more effective production control was envisaged also. Thus, for example, a country would not be entitled to any increases in its April 1969 quotas until its production plans for 1972-73 were approved by the Executive Board of the International Coffee Council with a distributed simple majority vote.

Turning our attention to wheat, we see that this is a primary commodity of export interest almost exclusive to developed countries. In the case of the 1967 wheat agreement, a higher price range for wheat was decided upon, and the terms of the agreement were finalized and made an essential part of the Kennedy Round package before all interested governments were given a chance to express their opinion. Developing countries, whose imports accounted for approximately 46% of the total wheat trade in 1966-67, were not present when the higher price range was determined.[31] The superior bargaining power of the developed countries that export wheat, made it easy for them to obtain prices which they considered remunerative for their producers. In fact, they warned that only a higher guaranteed price of wheat could generate the volume of production necessary to feed the world population adequately, and they secured a floor price which was higher than the maximum price then prevailing in the world market.[32] On that

29. Each country having an export quota of 100,000 bags or more must participate in the financing of this fund according to the formula: 0.60c times the number of bags over 100,000. A country may incur the suspension of its voting rights and be ineligible for quota increases, if it does not comply with the formula.

30. In future the IBRD will consider requests that it should give technical assistance to commodity diversification funds, or act as executive agent for such funds. It will also give special consideration to diversification projects which provide alternative employment to factors employed in the production of surplus commodities, and to the projects which aim to improve the competitiveness of primary products in world markets. TD/B/309/Add.1 (16 Jul. 1970), pp. 35-36.

31. The developed countries that took part in these negotiations, together with Argentina as the only developing country that participated, accounted for 94% of total wheat exports, but only for 23% of total wheat imports. TD/B/157 (4 Sep. 1967), p. 4. The Memorandum of Agreement on Cereals which was negotiated during the Kennedy Round was later incorporated into the International Grains Arrangement, which consisted of the Wheat Convention and the Food Aid Convention. The latter provided that the developed countries send 4.5 million tons of grains each year, for a period of three years, to developing countries in the form of aid. It was adopted mainly as a result of American pressure asking other industrial countries to contribute more to the total burden of aid. Originally, the US had asked that 10 million tons be earmarked for this purpose; of the 4.5 million tons agreed to, the American share was set at 42%.

32. The "collective contract" technique utilized in the case of wheat, is an

occasion, the UNCTAD secretariat expressed the hope that the developed countries would exhibit the same positive attitude toward "remunerative prices" when negotiating agreements on commodities which they import from the developing countries.[33]

Other commodities. The New Delhi Conference adopted a program for international action on commodity market stabilization, setting target dates for studies, consultations and negotiations on nineteen commodities.[34] This program was intended as a supplement to the more general recommendations of the Geneva Conference, an effort to establish precise guidelines and priorities for action. In addition to recommending the conclusion of agreements on cocoa and sugar, a joint UNCTAD/FAO consultative committee on oilseeds, oils and fats was proposed to work out short- and long-term measures in this field; the establishment of a buffer stock for jute, and the possibility of concluding formal agreements on certain hard fibers where informal agreements already existed (sisal, henequen and abaca) were advanced. Regarding a number of other commodities, including rubber, bananas, tea, and iron ore, the Conference recommended studies, intergovernmental consultations, and remedial action to cope with the problems that these products face.

In the period following the New Delhi Conference, the program for international action on commodity market stabilization has been generally confined to the realm of consultations, review and studies.[35] And although progress has been made in identifying problems relating to a number of commodities of current concern, the next and much more difficult step remains, viz., adopting practical measures for their solution. In the meanwhile, only about 20% of total primary commodity exports (excluding fuels) from developing countries are covered by commodity agreements.[36] And if the process of negotiating commodity

---

understanding between the producers who concur not to sell at prices above an agreed ceiling, and the consumers who agree not to buy below an agreed minimum price. The record high production in 1968, and the 20% increase of output in developing countries which reduced their import requirements, caused a strong downward pressure on the prevailing prices and threatened the agreement.

33. TD/B/157 (4 Sep. 1967), p. 4. Note that during the 1971 renegotiations of the wheat agreement, the major exporting countries failed to agree on the choice of a reference wheat and a new price range. They maintained the International Wheat Council as a forum for consultation and as a center for the collection of information on prices, sales and freight rates of wheat, and also agreed on the extension of the Food Aid Convention.

34. Resolution 16(II), *Proceedings, New Delhi*, Vol. I, pp. 34-36.

35. See TD/B/309/Add.1 (16 Jul. 1970), pp. 22-29, and TD/B/312 (29 Jun. 1970).

36. In the period 1965-67, coffee accounted for 10.4% of developing coun-

agreements proceeds at its usual pace, a number of years are likely to pass before a significantly larger share of commodity markets is brought under international regulation.

Buffer Stock Financing. One method of price stabilization that can be employed in commodity agreements is the buffer stock. Exporters of primary goods have an obvious preference for this technique because it allows them to sell their product without necessarily having to curtail exports or be subjected to quota limitations even when the indicator price approaches the agreed minimum; it is the buffer stock that absorbs the surplus to decrease the supply and maintain the price above the floor level. The critical element in a buffer stock scheme is the pre-financing and regular financing of its capital and operating costs until it becomes self-sustaining. In 1964 the tin buffer stock was the only one in existence. It was financed entirely by the producing countries. Consuming countries did not contribute voluntarily to the tin buffer stock, although they took part in directing its operation, while terms of reference of international financial institutions prevented them from extending assistance to schemes for commodity market stabilization.

At the Geneva Conference, the developing countries wanted both producers and consumers to participate in the financing of buffer stocks; in fact, some felt that the developed countries should provide the major part of the financing. They also proposed the creation of a central fund to assist in the financing of short-term market stabilization schemes, including buffer stocks.[37] No consensus was reached regarding these proposals, and the producing countries continued to shoulder the entire burden of financing the tin buffer stock when the agreement was renegotiated in 1965.[38] The 1967 draft agreement on cocoa also provided for exporting countries to finance the buffer stock.

The Algiers Charter had demanded that the developed countries and international financial institutions participate in the pre-financing of buffer stocks.[39] At the New Delhi Conference there was no agreement on this issue. The developed countries argued against the creation of a central fund, because it would immobilize the already scarce resources. Some accepted the possibility of joint producer/consumer participation

---

tries' primary commodity exports (excluding fuels), sugar - 6.7%, tin - 2.5%, wheat - 1.6%, and olive oil - 0.2%. Commodities listed in resolution 16(II) of the New Delhi Conference (excluding sugar) account for another 35% of these exports. TD/B/C.1/61 (1 Apr. 1969), Annex.

37. TD/B/120 (5 Jun. 1967), pp. 13, 18-19.

38. The size of the tin buffer stock was set at 20,000 tons, or the equivalent in cash. The ceiling price of 1,605 pounds sterling per long ton of tin was established by the third International Tin Agreement. TD/B/309/Add.1 (16 Jul. 1970), p. 21.

39. TD/38 (3 Nov. 1967), p. 6.

in pre-financing, with case-by-case determination of costs, while others insisted that the first call be made on private capital. An impasse occurred when the Group of 77 proposed that international financing institutions be enabled to make sufficient resources available whenever the need arises to pre-finance a buffer stock. Actually, the developing countries wanted these institutions as the main source of pre-financing. The B Group opposed any decision on this matter before the completion of the joint IMF/IBRD study on the stabilization of primary commodity prices, and the issue had to be remitted to the continuing machinery.[40]

Consensus was finally attained at the third session of the Committee on Commodities.[41] It was agreed that a buffer stock should be equipped with adequate funds through a regular income until it became self-sustaining. This income should be secured in an equitable manner from all parties concerned, without imposing an undue burden on developing countries. In regard to pre-financing, all possibilities should be considered, particularly the resources that could be made available from international financial institutions. Other sources of pre-financing would be private capital and loans or other voluntary contributions from governments of both developed and developing countries.

This consensus on the level of principle was tested quickly thereafter, when the fourth International Tin Agreement was negotiated in April-May 1970; the compulsory contributions to the buffer stock continue to be made by producing countries only. Voluntary contributions can be made by any country, of course, but, only the Netherlands has availed itself of this opportunity thus far.[42] As far as assistance from international financial institutions is concerned, the 1969 decision of the IMF is important. At that time, its Executive Board established a facility for assistance to members in connection with the financing of international buffer stocks of primary products. The IMF can provide finance directly only to its members and not to an international commodity body, and only to those members who, taking into account their transactions with a buffer stock, have a need to draw because of balance of payments difficulties.[43]

40. *Proceedings, New Delhi*, Vol. I, p. 235. A verbal compromise proposal that IBRD and IMF examine in the framework of their study the possibility of finding resources for pre-financing buffer stocks, proved unacceptable too. TD/86 (18 Mar. 1968), p. 9.

41. TD/B/202 (14 Nov. 1968), Annex I.

42. TD/B/312 (29 Jun. 1970). In refusing to contribute to the buffer stock, the consuming countries reasoned that since the producers benefit from it, they should also bear the cost. The fact that the Committee on Commodities had passed a unanimous resolution on this matter, they obviously did not view in any way as a binding obligation.

43. TD/B/309/Add.1 (16 Jul. 1970), pp. 34-35. See also "The Problems of Stabilization of Prices of Primary Products," a Staff Study, Part II (Washington,

Improved access to the markets of developed countries is of special importance for agricultural commodities. GATT's work, and in particular the Programme of Action adopted in 1963,[44] antedated the Geneva Conference recommendations on trade liberalization for primary products of interest to developing countries. It should be recalled that the *Final Act* called for a standstill on trade barriers, and a substantial reduction and possible elimination of customs charges, internal charges and revenue duties. It also suggested that quantitative restrictions be eliminated, insofar as possible, within the first Development Decade; if maintained for compelling reasons, they should be non-discriminatory and should be revised periodically so as to allow the developing countries to share in the market growth.[45] The reservations voiced by developed countries, however, were a forewarning of the difficulties that implementation of these provisions would face. They acknowledged the need to adjust their trade policies so as to foster commercial exchange with the South, but they objected to time limits which did not take into account their existing commitments and national legislation, spoke of internal social and economic disequilibria caused by such trade liberalization measures and of the need for any changes to be compatible with their economic and administrative systems, and repeatedly stressed the fact that the recommendations of the *Final Act* could be considered only as general directives, not as binding obligations.[46]

It was not surprising, therefore, that in the period following the Geneva Conference, the standstill was not being observed, much higher tariffs continued to apply when commodities were exported in packed or processed rather than bulk form, there was no visible progress in eliminating revenue duties and heavy internal fiscal charges on tropical and other products, etc.[47] The reasons for the inaction or negative

---

July 1969). Drawings under this facility are in addition to member's existing access to the IMF's resources, and can be made up to a limit of 50% of quota without any restriction. However, a joint upper limit of 75% of quota is imposed on total drawings outstanding under this facility and under that of compensatory financing. (See Chapter V for a discussion of compensatory financing.)

44. For the Programme of Action see *Proceedings*, Vol. V, pp. 482-483. The developed countries qualified their stand with a number of reservations. For example, regarding the standstill provision, they would conform except "where special and compelling circumstances rendered departure from it unavoidable."

45. Recommendation A.II.1, *ibid.*, Vol. I, pp. 29-30.

46. *Ibid.*, pp. 121-122.

47. TD/B/120 (5 Jun. 1967), pp. 25-32. For a detailed account of the situation before the New Delhi Conference, see TD/5/Add.1 (31 Aug. 1967), pp. 26-31.

action were obvious. High-cost agricultural producers in the North did not look kindly upon any measures which would make them more vulnerable to products from the developing countries. From their own governments they sought stronger protection to keep imports out, and special support measures which in some cases could even allow them to penetrate into foreign markets. As for those commodities not produced by their farmers, governments in developed countries were not eager to deprive themselves of considerable revenue brought in by fiscal charges and customs duties.

The Algiers Charter called for the elimination, by the end of 1968, of restrictions introduced since 1964 in spite of the standstill. It proposed the introduction of a partial refund to developing exporters from various internal duties and revenue charges. Regarding those primary products which compete with domestic producers in the North, it suggested that a percentage of domestic consumption be allocated to developing exporters, particularly a share in any prospective growth, to be determined on a country-by-country and commodity-by-commodity basis through multilateral negotiations.[48]

These demands were reiterated in New Delhi, but the majority of the developed countries held that they could not accept additional commitments not to introduce new barriers or to eliminate the existing ones. Their attitude was either negative, or vague and calculated to foster delay.[49] As a result, the New Delhi Conference could not adopt a resolution on trade liberalization.[50] The proposal of the 77 that negotiations begin before the end of 1968 for the removal of barriers to the primary commodities originating in developing countries, and that these negotiations be based on the principle of non-reciprocity, the recommendations of the *Final Act* and the program elaborated in the Algiers Charter, fell on deaf ears. All developed countries were willing to concede was that action to increase access should be undertaken as an international cooperative endeavor "whenever possible".

When they were told that the interests of domestic primary producers in developed countries should be reconciled with those of external suppliers, the 77 in New Delhi no longer insisted on the outright abolition of agricultural protectionism but asked that they be allocated a share of any increase in domestic demand for primary commodities in the developed countries. They expected that the New Delhi Conference

48. TD/38 (3 Nov. 1967), pp. 7-8.
49. Note, for example, the wording proposed by a group of developed countries: "Governments should consider the possibility of envisaging the reduction of levies which may in effect have hampered the growth of consumption of a given commodity." *Proceedings, New Delhi*, Vol. I, p. 397.
50. See *ibid.*, pp. 241, 248-254. Also, TD/L.29 (25 Mar. 1968), pp. 25-31.

108

would take the first step by approving the principle of allowing market access within these limits, but this proved too optimistic.[51] A slight verbal dent in the fortress of agricultural protectionism was made in one of the working groups of the Conference, which dealt, *inter alia*, with the world food problem and its relationship to international trade. The Declaration on the World Food Problem—in the form adopted by the Conference—urged that the developed countries "carry out, to the extent practicable, measures providing more favourable conditions of access to their markets for primary products exporting countries, particularly bearing in mind the interests of developing countries, and permitting primary products exporting countries, to participate in the growth of the markets of industrial nations."[52] On this issue both developed and developing countries that are exporters of primary products found themselves aligned, although not overtly, against agricultural protectionism in general and against EEC policies in particular. Although vaguely worded and inoperative, this provision was nonetheless the first instance where the principle of market sharing was internationally agreed upon. The specific access commitments included in the 1968 sugar agreement represented the first modest practical development along these lines.

What the New Delhi Conference could not do was accomplished by the Tenth Board in September 1970; it adopted a resolution on the liberalization of trade and access to markets for primary commodities.[53] This highly-negotiated text is essentially a rehash of what had already been stated in the *Final Act* and elsewhere, except that, due to the efforts at accommodating the views of all developed countries, it has been weakened and diluted with various qualifying clauses and reservations. Yet, this time the guidelines appear to have been accepted by all parties concerned, and hence may inaugurate a more positive policy of trade liberalization. On the other hand, one cannot escape the impression that the resolution adopted by the Tenth Board is more of a plea for a standstill, than for any distinct improvements in the present situation.[54] It is also interesting to note that whereas previously pricing

51. The B Group did not agree that the UNCTAD secretariat be asked to study individual commodities and the possibilities of increasing the share of developing countries' exports in the growth of consumption in the industrial countries.

52. Resolution 9 (II), *ibid.*, p. 30.

53. Board resolution 73 (X) in TD/B/327 (30 Sep. 1970), Annex I, p. 9. Compare this with the draft resolution of the Group of 77 presented to the New Delhi Conference. TD/II/C.1/L.10, in *Proceedings, New Delhi*, Vol. I, pp. 248-249.

54. Thus, for example, "developed countries should, to the fullest extent possible, not create new tariff or non-tariff barriers or increase existing barri-

policy and the liberalization of trade were treated as two separate propositions, they were linked together in this resolution. This was done in order to obtain the support of the EEC, and of France in particular, which continues to advocate a comprehensive organization of commodity markets.

Special preferences (tariff concessions, quota restrictions applied preferentially, price concessions) enjoyed by the primary products of certain developing countries in the markets of certain developed countries, act as one of the barriers to efforts toward the liberalization of commodity trade.[55] The *Final Act* recommended that such preferential arrangements which discriminate against other developing countries be transitional and subject to progressive reduction, and that they should be abolished *pari passu* with the effective application of international measures providing at least equivalent advantages for those countries enjoying them and finding them essential for the maintenance and growth of their export earnings.[56] In view of this recommendation, UNCTAD's task was, first, to assess and quantify the effect of special preferences for primary products on the trade of those countries enjoying them,[57] and secondly, to determine and negotiate national and international measures which would offer "equivalent advantages".

Some progress has been recorded in this direction in the Group of 77. After protracted polemics between the Latin American and African countries, at the Algiers Ministerial Meeting the African group agreed in principle that the UNCTAD secretariat and the regional groups should undertake studies, commodity by commodity and country by country, to determine the effect of the abolition of special preferences.[58] If conducted, such studies could impart more precision to intergovernmental deliberations, which are now bedevilled by conflicting assumptions.[59] Provided that the estimates thus arrived at satisfy all

---

ers . . ."; or "as far as possible, developed countries should refrain from introducing new fiscal measures affecting primary products wholly or mainly produced in developing countries . . ." *Idem.*

55. For the discussion on the extent and effect of special preferences consult TD/16 (12 Jan. 1968) and T/D16/Supp.1 (11 Jan. 1968).

56. Recommendation A.II.1, *Proceedings*, Vol. I, p. 30.

57. This would be a complicated exercise, especially in the case of the Yaoundé Convention package deal. For example, in addition to determining the advantages of special preferences, it would be also necessary to determine the costs of reverse preferences and to what extent such costs outweight the former advantages.

58. TD/38 (3 Nov. 1967), p. 7. This was considered as a significant concession by the African countries.

59. Inconclusive attempts have been made to determine in quantitative terms the value of such variable factors as preferences. In the case of the EEC special preferences on commodities, of the actors concerned, Latin American countries

concerned, the next question would ask what international actions could satisfy the criterion of equivalent advantages. For some commodities, the opening of new markets through trade liberalization could outweigh the advantages gained through special preferences provided that a developing country is competitive and it can reorient its exports, build up new trade links and adjust to differences in markets. For other commodities, the equivalent advantages could be attained if a commodity agreement were negotiated that would offer stable and remunerative prices.[60] Special financial measures for those countries enjoying special preferences—particularly the weak and non-competitive ones—may be necessary in order to help them diversify their exports, improve their productivity and adjust production so that they can compete in the world markets. However, each one of these possible spheres of action presents peculiar difficulties and is not susceptible to rapid and effective solutions.

A developing country may not be afraid to give up its special preferences, provided that it can compete efficiently with other producers from developing countries, and provided that commodities in which it specializes have a good outlook for the future. But if it is highly dependent on the assured outlet, and especially if it relies heavily for its export earnings on one or two primary products, it will have serious reservations about any proposals for abolishing special preferences on commodities. This attitude will persist until such time when internationally negotiated measures are put into effect which would offer these countries greater benefits, and allow them to diversify their trade beyond the few developed nations on which they depend at the present.

Synthetics and Substitutes

The recommendation on synthetics and substitutes adopted by the Geneva Conference called on the developed nations not to encourage additional investment in the production of synthetic materials that compete with the natural products exported by the developing countries and not to give special encouragement to new synthetics that may displace other natural products. Whenever a departure from this

---

believe that they are hurt; Africans believe that they are benefited; the EEC alleges that nobody is hurt and nobody is benefited; while the United States argues that these preferences have no serious effect on the Latin American countries' exports, with the exception of a very few commodities like bananas. Weintraub, *op. cit.*, pp. 84-86.

60. Note, for example, that the preferred suppliers in the Commonwealth get a significantly higher price for sugar than is provided in the 1968 sugar agreement.

principle should be envisaged, international consultations were to be held to determine measures which would mitigate the adverse effects that some developing countries would be exposed to. The Conference also recommended that there should be improved access to the markets of developed countries for those products facing the competition of synthetics, that research should be promoted to determine additional uses for the natural products thus threatened, and that synthetic products should not be represented as though they were natural ones.[61]

No visible progress on this matter was recorded between the Geneva and New Delhi Conferences, although a number of commodities were considered. Developing countries realized that they could do very little to either affect or slow down the technological expansion of the industrial North, so they concentrated their demands primarily on improved access to developed markets for those natural products threatened by synthetics, as well as on financial, technical and marketing assistance in this field.[62]

The New Delhi Conference could not adopt a resolution on synthetics and substitutes, because several points remained controversial.[63] The participants could not agree on the financing of research to improve the competitiveness of natural products threatened by synthetics; also, a proposal to set up a special fund under UNCTAD auspices for research on the improvement of market conditions, cost efficiency, and diversification of end uses of these products failed to win the endorsement of industrial nations—western or socialist. Again, there was no agreement on the restriction of synthetics that compete with natural products, nor was consensus reached on improving access to markets of developed countries for such products through progressive removal of tariff and non-tariff barriers, and elimination of differential tariffs on their processed and semi-processed forms. The developed countries agreed to consider such measures "as far as possible", but only for products facing "excessive" competition from synthetics. They were also prepared to give "sympathetic consideration" to requests for financial and technical assistance from the developing countries plagued by this problem, while they are trying to diversify into other areas of production.[64]

One year later, in May 1969, the Committee on Commodities worked out a compromise text which commanded the approval of all participants. It recommended that the developed countries should progressive-

61. Recommendation A.II.7, *Proceedings*, Vol. I, pp. 32-33.
62. TD/B/120 (5 Jun. 1967), p. 16, and *Proceedings, New Delhi*, Vol. I, pp. 237-239.
63. *Ibid.*, p. 390.
64. TD/L.29 (25 Mar. 1968), pp. 12-15.

ly reduce trade barriers hampering access of those natural products which faced serious competition from synthetics and substitutes, with a view to the eventual elimination of such barriers. When decisions were taken on the creation and use of synthetics, developed countries would take account of the supply and demand for both natural and synthetic products that were affected. Furthermore, no special encouragement would be given to the creation and utilization of new production when natural commodities could satisfy current and future world market demands. Finally, the UNCTAD Permanent Group on Synthetics and Substitutes was to study the means of promoting scientific research on commodities threatened by synthetics, and to examine possibilities for the financing of such research.[65]

However, qualifying clauses like "urged to bear in mind", and the fact that both the developed and socialist states reserved their position in regard to financing the research, speak for the vagueness of the text and the absence of commitment to act. Yet, the resolution could be used to offer general guidelines in the consideration and recommendation of remedial action on specific commodities. In effect, its substantive provisions have found their way into the strategy for the second Development Decade. In the meantime, UNCTAD's Permanent Group on Synthetics and Substitutes, on the basis of studies and deliberations, has recommended action on specific commodities and has also begun a factual survey of the current research efforts, and of the need for an expanded research program for the main natural products facing competition from synthetics.[66] Elsewhere, the United States and some other developed countries have adopted, or are in the process of adopting, measures to remove tariff barriers to trade on new and improved forms of natural rubber,[67] while the IBRD, as we have already seen, has agreed to participate in financing research aimed at reducing production costs and development of new uses for primary products.

In terms of consensus evolution UNCTAD has done moderately well in the field of commodities. Conceptual advances have been

65. TD/B/248 (16 Jun. 1969), pp. 1-2, Annex I.
66. Among the commodities which are receiving attention are rubber, cotton, hard fibers, jute and allied fibers, vegetable oilseeds and oils, and mica and shellac. See TD/B/287 (10 Nov. 1969).
67. Note the decision of the US government to ban for medical reasons the use of cyclamates for human consumption. Many other countries followed suit, including the United Kingdom, Japan and Canada. Estimates as to the amount of sugar displaced by artificial sweeteners vary between 500,000 and 700,000 tons per year. For 1970 it had been estimated that the prohibition of cyclamates in Japan would result in a 200,000 ton greater net import demand for sugar. TD/B/309/Add.1 (16 Jul. 1970), p. 31.

113

recorded and agreement has emerged in a number of cases, even though most of the time the common denominator was considerably lower than the developing countries' expectations. However, the developed countries were generally reluctant to declare their unequivocal acceptance of recommendations flowing from UNCTAD, and insisted on escape clauses and reservations.[68] Indeed, it has been difficult to translate the policy consensus into action in the field of commodities, and the implementation of scores of solutions advocated and agreed upon in this forum has been sorely lacking. Trade liberalization measures have remained largely unexecuted, while the few limited practical moves aimed at commodity market regulation reflected only to a degree the guidelines enunciated in 1964, and were a far cry from the decisive and systematic international action envisaged at the time of UNCTAD's birth. In fact, no new commodity agreement on primary products of interest to developing countries has been concluded, and the "law of the jungle" continues to dominate most commodity markets, with the merchant speculators and monetary nerve centers, especially in the United Kingdom and the United States, often determining the fate of a commodity.[69] The developed countries have spoken recurrently of the need to diversify production in developing countries. Yet, it was usually difficult to obtain the necessary international support for such actions. And once a developing country began to diversify successfully, it collided head-on with the pattern of the present international division of labor and its built-in defenses, and with steps taken by governments in many developed countries to safeguard the position and interests of their constituents.

The developed countries generally do not find it in their short-term interest to engage in a concerted and meaningful implementation of commodity policies moved in UNCTAD, and if there is no political will or some compelling reason to overcome this initial barrier, then actions along prescribed lines are very hard to attain. In view of this, UNCTAD's role in the field of commodities should not be belittled. Its main task so far, and its principal achievement, has been that of gradual consensus building, keeping the issues alive, establishing multiple points of pressure,[70] and opening up new areas for consideration.

68. The developing countries have tried to get around this by inserting time targets into the recommendations. Thus, for example, 31 December 1972 is mentioned in the strategy for the second Development Decade as a date by when the commodity market regulation and trade liberalization measures agreed to in UNCTAD should be implemented.

69. S. Narasimhan, "International Commodity Problems," *Foreign Trade Review* (New Delhi), Oct.-Dec. 1970, p. 290.

70. In fact, it is the pressures from UNCTAD that have led to the decisions of the IBRD and the IMF to assist in solving problems of price stabilization and other problems affecting primary products.

Chapter V

FINANCING

Financing was one of the less controversial items on the agenda of the Geneva Conference. The transfer of capital did not raise such fundamental problems as did the proposed changes in the international division of labor and in the rules of international commerce. Financial aid to developing countries dated back to the early post-war years, and many of the proposals made in 1964 were not new. In fact, many of the goals advanced in Geneva were, in one form or another, already considered in the OECD's Development Assistance Committee (DAC).[1] Difficulties arose from the reluctance of the majority of developed countries to assume a firm commitment on aid outlays, their unwillingness being reinforced by the uncertainties of the international monetary situation. They were also reluctant to substantially soften the prevailing terms and conditions of official lending, which had roots in commercial and profit-making operations and generally were not in harmony with development financing, which required concessional or no-interest lending. Moreover, the major donors continued to think of foreign aid as a useful policy instrument, and were averse to divert a significant portion of the allocated funds to multilateral institutions, because this would curtail their ability to control such resources and to use them for the promotion of national goals.[2] On the domestic front in many developed countries difficulties arose due to the balance of payments problems, the general shortage of resources, the reluctance of parliaments to approve the expansion of aid, and the strength of public

1. In addition to its basic fact-binding function and elaboration of common policy positions, DAC attempts to influence policies of its members through moral suasion and evaluation of countries' performances against the adopted criteria. See S. J. Rubin, *The Conscience of Rich Nations* (New York: Harper & Row, 1966). DAC members are: Australia, Austria, Belgium, Canada, Denmark, F.R. Germany, France, Italy, Japan, Netherlands, Norway, Portugal, Sweden, Switzerland, United Kingdom, United States and the Commission of the EEC.
2. In the case of one major donor, the United States, aid to developing countries serves as a multi-purpose instrument. See J. M. Nelson, *Aid, Influence, and Foreign Policy* (New York: The Macmillan Co., 1968), pp. 1-30; also E. B. Haas, *Tangle of Hopes* (Englewood Cliffs, N.J.: Prentice-Hall, 1969), pp. 144-151.

opinion that aiding the developing countries was futile and did not bring about any worthwhile results.

In the following pages we shall briefly consider: the volume of aid; terms of aid and aid tying; supplementary financing; and the international monetary reform.

The Volume of Aid

As we have seen, the 1964 Geneva Conference recommended that each economically advanced country should endeavor to supply financial resources annually amounting to a minimum of 1% of its national income to the Third World. In the summer of 1967, UNCTAD's Committee on Invisibles and Financing unanimously agreed that the objective for developed countries should be to increase the net flow of their development assistance in order to attain the 1% target.[3] A few months later, however, the B Group made it clear that it did not consider this agreement as a basis for action, thus dampening the hopes of those who felt that developed countries had accepted the obligation to increase the flow of financial assistance.

For an uninformed observer it was slightly confusing to listen to UNCTAD debates prior to the New Delhi Conference and hear about the non-implementation of the target, then to read the DAC figures which showed that in 1965, for example, its members as a group had met the target.[4] The discrepancy was partly due to the fact that DAC's data also included the flow of assistance to Southern Europe, while UNCTAD's did not. More important, however, was the different interpretation of the 1% target. As the basis for determining the target, DAC had been using "national income", measured as net national product at factor cost; this gave a denominator approximately 20-25% lower than the "gross national product at market prices", the figure used by the UN organs as the basis for calculations.[5]

3. See "Agreed Statement of the Problems of Development," TD/B/119 (5 Jun. 1967). The attitude of the socialist countries toward the volume of aid target is discussed in Chapter VII.

4. See *Development Assistance Efforts and Policies of the Members of the Development Assistance Committee* (hereafter referred to as *DAC Review*), 1967 Review (Paris: OECD, 1967), p. 105. According to these figures, many developed countries had met the target. For example, France at 1.87%, the United Kingdom — 1.26%, the United States — 0.98%, etc.

5. *United Nations Yearbook of National Accounts Statistics*, 1965, UN Publication Sales No. 66.XVII.2, p. XI, offers the following definition: "*Gross national product at market prices* is the market value of the product, before deduction of provisions for the consumption of fixed capital, attributable to the factors of production supplied by normal residents of the given country. It is identically equal to the sum of consumption expenditure and gross domestic

The targets specified by the General Assembly and by the Geneva Conference, spoke also of "national income". However, in 1961, while formulating the target for the first Development Decade, the General Assembly used a report which compared financial outflows to the combined gross domestic products of developed countries.[6] Consequently, the developing countries and members of the UN Secretariat argued that the General Assembly intended the term "national income" to be interpreted in the gross rather than the net sense. This was especially because the achievement of the target in terms of net national income at factor cost would have required no great effort on the part of donors; in 1962, for example, the net flow stood at 1.02%.[7] Accordingly, the UN documents referred to the 1% target in terms of the GNP concept. On the other hand, although some early issues of *DAC Review* appear to have used the GNP, after the Geneva Conference the DAC data was presented on the basis of net national product at factor cost.

The controversy over the meaning of the 1% target is an outstanding example of the ambiguities and disagreements concealed in the resolutions and recommendations of international bodies, even when enunciated in quantitative terms. As a matter of fact, the New Delhi Conference was stymied on this very point for as many as eight weeks. The B Group used it as a device to stretch out the talks and divert attention from other financing topics, a tactic that was probably agreed before the Conference began.[8] In the end, the donors gave in and accepted the redefined target: "each economically advanced country should endeavor to provide annually to developing countries financial resource transfers of a minimum net amount of 1% of its GNP at market prices in terms of actual disbursements."[9] They presented this

capital formation, private and public, and the net exports of goods and services plus the net factor incomes received from abroad. *Net national product at factor cost* is the value at factor cost of the product, after deduction of provisions for the consumption of fixed capital, attributable to the factors of production supplied by normal residents of the given country. It is identically equal to the national income ... *National income* is the sum of the incomes accruing to factors of production supplied by normal residents of the given country before deduction of direct taxes."

6. "International Flow of Long-Term Capital and Official Donations, 1951-59" (A/4906), pp. 19-20. The information in this paragraph is based on TD/7/ Supp. 1 (17 Oct. 1968), pp. 31-33.

7. *DAC Review, 1967*, p. 105. Note also that professional opinion favored the GNP version of the 1% target. See "Measurement of the Flow of Resources to Developing Countries," UN Publication Sales No. 67.II.D.17.

8. Throughout the deliberations the developed countries adhered firmly to the definition of the target as being 1% of the "net national income at factor cost". See TD/II/C.3/CG/Misc. 2 (5 Mar. 1968).

9. Resolution 27(II), *Proceedings, New Delhi*, Vol. I, p. 39. Note that following

as a major concession to the 77 and all that could be expected from the Conference in the field of financing. Granted, the redefined target in terms of GNP at market prices represented an approximate increase of about 20% in the possible transfer of resources to developing countries.[10] However, most developed countries, and some major donors in particular, refused to commit themselves to a timetable for attaining the 1% GNP transfer. The developing countries and some donors felt that the target date should be set for 1972. In fact, Sweden, the Netherlands, France and Canada were prepared to accept a specific target date: 1972 or 1975. The others, however, were noncommital.

The efforts in New Delhi to establish also a sub-target for official aid failed, though it was agreed in principle that such flows should represent a substantial part of the total aid.[11] It might be recalled that when the 1% target was first mooted by a non-governmental organization in 1958, it referred only to grants and concessional loans. As adopted by the various UN organs, the target emerged as a compromise between donors and recipients, in the sense that it did not differentiate between commercial transactions and concessional aid for development purposes. And so, the 1% target encompasses also the private capital flows, to wit, direct private investment, portfolio investment, guaranteed export credits, etc. The private capital flow, of course, is seldom conceived as development assistance and it is incidental to normal commerce and finance. It does not respond directly to government policies, it concentrates in certain geographic areas and activities, it gives rise to fears of foreign domination of a country's economy, its behavior is volatile, the terms of private export credits are onerous, the repatriation of profits and other incomes in most cases exceeds by far the private investment flow, etc.[12]

These two themes, namely, making the target into an operational

---

the New Delhi Conference the *DAC Review* offers figures on the fulfilment of the 1% target, both in terms of national income and gross national product.

10. The relationship of net national product at factor cost (or national income) to GNP at market prices varies from country to country. For example, national income is 81% of GNP at market prices in the United Kingdom and the United States, 82% in the Netherlands, 80% in Japan, 76% in F.R. Germany, 75% in France, 84% in Switzerland, etc. See "Measurement of the Flow of Resources to Developing Countries," *op. cit.*, pp. 106-107.

11. Resolution 27(II), *Proceedings, New Delhi*, Vol. I, p. 39. During the debate on the committee level, some developed countries stated their readiness to provide a minimum of 0.75% of their GNP by way of net official financial transfers. *Ibid.*, p. 283.

12. TD/7 (11 Oct. 1967), pp. 8-9. Observe that in the period 1960-68 the net private flows to developing nations averaged around 36% of the total net flows. TD/B/C.3/71 (20 Feb. 1970), p. 17.

commitment by establishing a unanimously agreed date for the implementation of the 1% GNP transfer, and improving upon its content by adopting a sub-target for the minimum level of official aid, were central in UNCTAD's debates on the volume of development assistance following the New Delhi Conference. Due to the discord among the developed countries, it proved impossible to attain consensus on these issues.[13] However, a step forward was taken eventually, when the implementation and official development assistance targets—though hedged by reservations of certain donors—found their place in the strategy for the second Development Decade. Thus: a) by the year 1972 each developed country should fulfil the 1% target, while those failing to do so should endeavor to comply not later than 1975; and b) each developed country should make an effort to transfer by the middle of the 1970's a minimum net amount of 0.70% of its GNP at market prices in the form of official development assistance.[14]

The aid flows and the implementation of the development assistance target are continuously scrutinized in UNCTAD, as well as in DAC.[15] In this regard, the following major points should be made: a) Many developed countries have shown themselves responsive to UNCTAD recommendations on the volume of aid, especially so after the New Delhi Conference. Australia, Canada, Denmark, the Netherlands, Norway and Sweden have introduced legislation or taken administrative steps to achieve the 1% target, and have increased the flow of their official assistance. The target has also had a marked effect on the aid performance of F.R. Germany and Japan. However, since these countries are mainly small or medium-sized donors, this means that their improved performance will have a limited impact on the ratio of development assistance to the combined GNP of developed nations.

13. See reports of the UNCTAD's Committee on Invisibles and Financing on its third and fourth sessions, TD/B/236 (13 Mar. 1969) and TD/B/318 (1 Aug. 1970).

14. The identical target recommended by the Pearson Commission is to be attained by 1975, but in no case later than 1980. Report of the Commission on International Development, *Partners in Development, op. cit.*, p. 149. Note that "official development assistance" refers to bilateral grants and loans on concessional terms, and official contributions to multilateral agencies. Together with "other official flows", i.e. export credits extended by independent governmental institutions, purchases of bonds of multilateral agencies, etc., it constitutes "official financial transfers". 0.70% of GNP by way of official development assistance, is broadly equivalent to 0.75% of GNP by way of official financial transfers which was proposed at the New Delhi Conference. TD/B/C.3/71 (20 Feb. 1970), p. 12.

15. We base ourselves on UNCTAD documents TD/B/C.3/71 (20 Feb. 1970) and TD/B/309 (7 Aug. 1970). Note that UNCTAD figures refer to net flows of financial resources to the developing countries of Africa, Asia and Latin America.

b) The gradually deteriorating performance of the traditional major donors, especially of the United States (which alone accounted for 45% of total DAC flows in 1968) and the United Kingdom, as well as of France (which however has been over the target all along), has been largely responsible for the real flow of financial assistance to the South tending to decline in relation to the growth of the aggregate GNP of the donor countries. c) As a group, the DAC members have not been moving toward the achievement of the development assistance target, the net flow fluctuating a few points above or below 0.70% of GNP at market prices. In 1969, for example, when the net flow of official and private financial resources from developed countries and multilateral agencies to the developing countries of Africa, Asia and Latin America amounted to $12.4 billion, the estimated DAC average was 0.67%, which was not much different from 0.70% in 1963, or 0.66% in 1966, or 0.73% in 1968, although markedly lower than 0.86% recorded at the beginning of the first Development Decade in 1961. d) Regarding the total official flows, which are controlled by governments and should gauge their concern with problems of development and their attitude toward internationally accepted goals, these were virtually stagnant in absolute terms while showing a pronounced tendency to decrease as the proportion of the developed countries' aggregate GNP at market prices. Total official flows stood at 0.40% in 1968 (only 0.38% if the net official development assistance is taken into account), as compared to 0.60% in 1963, 0.45% in 1965, and 0.43% in 1967.

The debate on the implementation and up-grading of the development assistance target promises to be a protracted and ever-widening one. On the agenda we find the demand for a larger transfer of official development funds to multilateral institutions and financing agencies. The Pearson Commission has already proposed that a minimum of 20% of the total flow of official development assistance should be diverted as grants and capital subscriptions for multilateral development aid.[16] There is also the problem of inequities in aid distribution and a more equitable allocation of funds. Another issue of growing importance in this debate concerns the outflow of capital from the developing countries—estimated at $8 billion in 1968, a figure which includes

16. *Partners in Development, op. cit.*, p. 25. Such flow was only 9.5% in 1968. TD/B/C.3/71 (20 Feb. 1970), p. 16. It is the major donors that are responsible for this situation because of their apparent lack of enthusiasm to channel a greater portion of funds through multilateral agencies. For example, in the 1966-68 period, the multilateral contributions of the United States were on the average 6.4% of its total aid expenditures, France — 4.5%, the United Kingdom — 10.6%. The Scandinavian countries, at the other extreme, contributed more than 50% of their development assistance to multilateral institutions. *Partners in Development, op. cit.*, p. 391.

payments for investment income and amortization,[17] but not the movement of indigenous capital for which no reliable data exists.[18]

Although the development assistance target has had little or no operational impact on the decision-makers in some developed countries, many DAC members are making efforts to reach, or have already surpassed the 1% GNP mark, and the target has become an accepted standard against which to measure the performance of donors. Moreover, it is opening up new avenues for discussing international development assistance, its improvement and multilateralization, and further clarification of the concept of aid.

Terms of Aid and Aid Tying

In June 1968, the outstanding public and publicly guaranteed external debt of the developing countries amounted to $ 47.5 billion, with debt service payments estimated at $ 4.7 billion. The rapid build-up of public debt service imposed a serious strain on many developing countries, and resulted in a situation where the combined total of interest and amortization payments absorbed on the average 40% of official bilateral loan disbursements, and was competing with imports and other needs for available foreign exchange. In many developing countries, the ratio of public debt service to export earnings exceeded 15%.[19]

Following the Geneva Conference, which failed to pass unanimously the recommendation on terms of financing,[20] both DAC in 1965 and the General Assembly in 1966, adopted broadly similar specific targets urging the developed countries to make external resources available to developing countries on easier terms and conditions. The General Assembly asked that by no later than 1968, at least 80% of assistance

17. See TD/B/C.3/73 (20 Feb. 1970).
18. Not even a rough estimate of this outflow could be worked out. Note however that in 1967 the reported inflow into the United States from developing countries amounted to $543 million ($200 million in 1966). *Ibid.*, p. 19. Also, according to an estimate, in 1962 the unrecorded capital flows from developing countries amounted to $2.5 billion. I. M. D. Little and J. M. Clifford, *International Aid* (London: Allen and Unwin, 1965), p. 219.
19. See *Partners in Development, op. cit.*, pp. 72-73, 152ff., 373. Difficulties of debt servicing are compounded because the developing countries have to repay loans in hard currencies. The expansion of their economies does not always result in a comparable expansion of their exports, which are often hampered by the protectionism in the developed countries. Moreover, grants are seldom in a convertible currency, while loans are usually tied and cannot be used to service past debts. (Note that government credits from socialist countries are usually repayable with commodities from debtor countries or in their national currencies.)
20. Recommendation A.IV.4. The roll call vote was 91:9:25. *Proceedings*, Vol. I, p. 44.

should be provided at interest rates of 3% or less, with repayment periods of 25 years or more.[21] The DAC 1965 target on financial terms and conditions of development assistance called for compliance within three years. The so-called "DAC average terms" would be satisfied if a donor were to extend 70% or more of its official commitments in grants, or if the following three conditions were fulfilled: 1) at least 81% of official commitments to be given as grants or loans at 3% interest charge or less; 2) at least 82% of total commitments to be given as grants or loans with a maturity of 25 years or more; 3) there should be a weighted average grace period of 7 years or more.[22]

Positive action by certain donors to meet the 1965 DAC terms could not offset the negative trend caused by the decline in the proportion of grants related to gross official disbursements (80% in 1960, 65% in 1964, 56% in 1967, 51% in 1968),[23] increases of official lending by hard donors, and the stagnation or decline of flow from the principal soft donors. Commitments at an interest rate of 3% or less declined from 84% to 78% in the period 1964-67, loans with a maturity of 25 years or more declined from 84% to 75%. In 1967 the weighted average interest rate was 3.8% on official bilateral commitments; the weighted average grace period 5.3 years.[24]

Yet, efforts to upgrade the terms target continued. The Algiers Charter called upon the New Delhi Conference to agree that by the end of 1968 the norms of lending as specified in the 1965 DAC recommendation and General Assembly resolution 2170 (XXI) be attained. Also, it asked that after a date to be agreed upon, all development lending be on IDA terms (50 years maturity, 0.75% interest). Pending the implementation of this goal, there should be a considerable lowering of interest rates and an increase in grace periods and maturities. The Charter also reiterated the proposal for the establishment of a multilateral interest equalization fund to subsidize the interest margin between loans obtained in capital markets and multilateral concessional development loans.[25] It might be recalled that at the Geneva Conference, it was suggested that the IBRD should borrow at normal terms from private investors, then relend the capital to developing countries on concessional terms through IDA. The developed countries would subsidize the difference by contributing regularly to an interest equalization fund.[26]

21. General Assembly resolution 2170 (XXI) (6 Dec. 1966).
22. *DAC Review 1965*, Annex B.
23. TD/B/C.3/72 (20 Feb. 1970), Annex III, p. 5.
24. For the extent of compliance with the 1965 DAC terms see *ibid.*, pp. 25 ff.
25. TD/38 (3 Nov. 1967), pp. 4-5, 15.
26. This was the so-called "Horowitz proposal". Recommendation A.IV.11, *Proceedings*, Vol. I, p. 48. See also TD/7/Supp. 11 (6 Dec. 1967).

The New Delhi gathering, however, could not reach a consensus on specific guidelines regarding softening of terms, or on a multilateral interest equalization fund. The Group of 77, supported by Sweden and the Netherlands among the donors, advanced alternative norms which went beyond DAC and General Assembly specifications. They proposed that by the end of 1970 either a country should provide 80% or more of its official aid in the form of grants (DAC target 70%); or it should provide 90% of its official aid commitments as grants or loans (DAC target 81%) at 2.5% or less (DAC target 3%), with a repayment period of 30 years or more (DAC target 25 years), and attain a minimum grace period of 8 years (DAC target 7 years). The B Group countries took note of these suggestions with the intention of considering them in the evolution of their assistance policies. The Conference also called upon the developed countries to improve the norms set in the 1965 DAC recommendation.[27]

After a long negotiation within the DAC, in February 1969 DAC members agreed to supplement their 1965 target on terms and conditions of aid.[28] Many considered this as a deferred achievement of the New Delhi Conference. The 1969 recommendation applied to countries that extend less than 70% of their total official development assistance in the form of grants or grant-like contributions. They should either provide at least 85% of their official development assistance commitments so that each transaction has a minimum concessional element of 61%, or ensure that 85% of their official development assistance commitments contain an average concessional element of at least 85%.[29] It was also agreed that in judging the compliance with the new target, both terms and the volume of aid will be taken into account. Namely, a country meeting the norms on financial terms and conditions, but which is considerably below the DAC average of volume of official assistance as a percentage of GNP, will not be considered as having met the terms target. This was the first instance where the donors as a group went on record, although indirectly, regarding the need for an agreed minimum volume of official development assistance. On the other hand, note that unlike the 1965 norms which apply to total

27. Conference resolution 29 (II), *Proceedings, New Delhi*, Vol. I, pp. 40-41.
28. "Supplement to the 1965 Recommendation of Financial Terms and Conditions of Development Assistance," TD/B/C.3/L.61 (21 Feb. 1969).
29. "Concessional element" is defined as the face value of a financial commitment, less the discounted present value of the required amortization, plus interest payments, using a 10% discount rate. For a discussion of the concessional element of loans, see G. Ohlin, *Foreign Aid Policies Reconsidered* (Paris: OECD, 1966), p. 4. Also see TD/B/C.3/72 (20 Feb. 1970), Annex I. Expressing a loan in terms of its concessional element makes it possible to express each set of loan terms as one value. This permits comparing loans whose terms differ.

official commitments, the 1969 supplement refers only to official development assistance. In other words, it does not encompass official export credits, which represent a significant portion of total official flows in many countries, and carry hard terms and short maturities.[30]

Although the new target is not directly comparable to the 1965 norms, and in theory could result in the application of terms harder than those permitted under the 1965 recommendation, it is generally agreed that if implemented it would have the effect of improving the terms of lending.[31] Yet, as in the case of volume of aid target, the problem of implementation remains. And although by 1968 some donors had met the 1965 terms in the sense that their grants and grant-like contributions represented more than 70% of their total official commitments, the overall terms did not improve.[32] Neither were the developed countries willing to consider the establishment of a multi-lateral interest equalization fund; in fact, they even objected to the convening of an intergovernmental group to consider this question.[33] Also, they looked with a jaundiced eye at the persisting demand of the 77 that the norms as spelled out in New Delhi be accepted and implemented.[34] Whether the strategy for the second Development Decade will speed up the implementation of the terms targets remains to be seen; nonetheless, one of its guidelines calls on developed coun-

30. See "Export Credits and Development Finance: National Export Credit System" (UN publication Sales No. E.69.II.D.7). In the absence of foreign exchange and because of insufficient long-term development finance, developing countries resort more and more to these sources in search for financing of their capital goods acquisitions. Governments that extend or guarantee export credits justify the hard terms by pointing to the autonomy of the institutions extending such credits, or to the need to obtain the capital at market rates which are not guided by development needs and rationales.

31. For the comparison of the 1965 and the 1969 DAC norms and their potential effects see TD/B/C.3/72 (20 Feb. 1970), pp. 9-24.

32. TD/B/309/Add.1 (16 Jul. 1970), p. 84.

33. See the comments of governments on convening such a group in TD/B/270 (24 Jul. 1969). Also TD/B/C.3/76 (23 Feb. 1970). Note that the Pearson Commission has recommended that at least one-half of the interest payments received by the developed countries on official bilateral lending should be used to subsidize the interest rates on some World Bank lending. *Partners in Development, op. cit.*, p. 222. (In 1969 the interest rate charged by the IBRD was 7%, as compared to 4.25% in late 1940's).

34. These debates are not purely academic, as it may appear. For example, projections show that if the New Delhi norms were adopted and implemented, the cumulative debt of developing countries after 20 years would be about $ 10 billion less than under the second alternative of the 1969 DAC supplement (assuming grants to be 46.8% of total official commitments). TD/B/C.3/72 (20 Feb. 1970), p. 6. The Pearson Commission has also recommended a target: interest of no more than 2%, a maturity of between 25 and 40 years, and a grace period of 7 to 10 years. *Partners in Development, op. cit.*, p. 167.

124

tries to reach the norms set out in the 1969 DAC recommendation before the end of 1971, and to undertake by the end of the 1970's measures to bring about practical results in line with the recommendation of the New Delhi Conference.

The dominant motive for aid tying varies from one donor country to another; among the important reasons are balance of payments considerations, promotion of exports and efforts to gain a foothold in new markets, bids to get support from legislators for foreign assistance, etc. It has been said that "aid tying is essentially a weapon in the war for the reserves of the developed world, and the developing countries (are the) civilian casualties." [35] Due to adverse balance of payments effects resulting from the recipients' using aid funds to buy goods in third countries, the United States initiated the aid tying practice in the early 1960's. For various reasons, other donors generally followed suit, and by 1967 only 16% of official flows remained untied.[36] Tied aid, of course, contributes to the difficulties of developing countries by limiting a recipient's discretion to choose the optimal and least costly source of supply (especially true of double tying, i.e. tying of a loan not only to a given market but also to a given product, or to a narrow range of products so designated as to attempt to ensure that they be "additional" to what the recipient would have imported from the donor under normal conditions). It has been argued that the direct cost of aid tying, i.e., the difference between the cost of importing the same goods from the tied source and the cheapest source, amounted to about $ 1 billion in 1965.[37] Elsewhere, it has been stated that the practice of tying reduces the real value of aid by at least 20%, not to mention the indirect costs of tied shipping and insurance.[38]

With regard to tied aid, the Geneva Conference recommended that part of the repayment for such loans should be accepted in the national currencies of the debtors; that development loans should as far as possible not be tied to specific projects; that loans for the purchase of

35. *DAC Review 1968*, p. 67.
36. *Partners in Development, op. cit.*, p. 77. Note that one of the central issues in renegotiating the replenishment of IDA in 1966 and later, was the balance of payments safeguard related to the procurement policy. The United States had committed by then $ 424 million to IDA; $ 295 million of this amount was spent elsewhere, imposing a drain on the US balance of payments. (The United Kingdom, on the other hand, contributed $ 125 million and it received $ 125 million in contracts.) *Financial Times* (London), 29 December, 1966. The IDA negotiations ended with the principle of international bidding maintained, but with an agreement that until June 1970 the United States' contribution will be called upon only for financing purchases in that country. *DAC Review 1968*, p. 77.
37. TD/7 (11 Oct. 1967), p. 20. See also TD/7/Supp.4 (1 Nov. 1967).
38. *Partners in Development, op. cit.*, p. 77.

125

capital equipment should not be tied to purchase in donor countries; and that if the recipient is able to show that he can get better rates and terms elsewhere, the donor should either intervene to lower the prices or release the funds for purchases elsewhere.[39]

In 1965 DAC recommended that donors should endeavor jointly and individually to remove procurement restrictions. Within the process of aid tying, it asked that they try to ensure that tied purchases are made under best conditions, i.e. to ensure competition between domestic producers, make the widest range of goods and services available, allow purchases to be made in other developing countries, etc.[40] In 1966, the General Assembly called for the progressive untying of loans with respect to the sources of supply. Where loans were tied to a source, the donor should allow a percentage for utilization in other developing countries and/or developed countries belonging to the same zone as the creditor country. It also called for an international advisory body which would provide information to recipients regarding sources of supply and the costs and quality of equipment.[41]

The New Delhi Conference urged the developed countries, though in a vague and qualified language, to take what practical measures they could to reduce aid tying and to mitigate its harmful effects. Among the practical measures proposed were: greater provision for the use of aid funds to cover local costs; allowing procurement in developing countries; the establishment of pooling systems where contracts might be decided by international competitive bidding within a group of donor countries, etc.[42] The demand of the 77 that donors subsidize the excess costs of procurement which resulted from tying practices, was not accepted.

One of the second Development Decade strategy guidelines contains the principle of untied aid; the main practical measure that it envisages is the utilization of tied loans by recipients for purchases in other developing countries. In fact, a move in this direction has already been made by F.R. Germany and the United States, which adopted a policy of allowing procurement in developing countries under otherwise tied aid contracts.[43] It is also important to note that the Tokyo meeting of

39. Recommendation A.IV.4, *Proceedings*, Vol. I, p. 45.
40. *DAC Review 1965*, Annex B.
41. General Assembly resolution 2170 (XXI) (6 Dec. 1966). The proposed body would be important in view of the fact many developing countries do not apply the competitive procurement technique, even if no tying restrictions exist.
42. Resolution 29 (II), *Proceedings, New Delhi*, Vol. I, p. 41.
43. Pending agreement on complete untying, the United States will permit foreign aid procurement in most lower income countries. This represented the expansion of the step previously taken with respect to Latin American countries. See AID press release, September 22, 1970.

DAC, held in the fall of 1970, agreed in principle that contributions to multilateral institutions should not be tied, and that such untied contributions should be increased. Regarding the bilateral development assistance, for the first time a large majority of DAC members declared that they were prepared to adhere to an agreement on aid untying. To this end, they agreed to enter into discussions on an urgent basis in order to elaborate a scheme for governmental consideration. It was also agreed that measures to untie should be devised in such a manner as to minimize the risk of reducing the volume of assistance, and that the scheme should be based on the principle of reciprocity.[44]

Compensatory and Supplementary Financing

Partly in response to the recommendation of the Geneva Conference, IMF liberalized and enlarged its compensatory financing facility in 1966. *Inter alia*, it raised the limit for outstanding compensatory drawings from 25% to 50% of a member country's quota, with the limitation, however, that drawings in any 12-month period should not exceed 25% of the quota (except in the case of shortfalls caused by disasters and major emergencies), and that any drawings beyond 25% of the quota would be granted only if the member had fulfilled the specific requirements of the facility, and had cooperated with the IMF, where required, in the search for appropriate solutions to its balance-of-payments difficulties.[45] The developing countries argued, however, that the new facility did not fully meet the objectives of the Geneva Conference recommendation, and among other things asked that drawings up to 50% of a country's quota should be immediately available and not subject to any conditions. Moreover, they argued that even further liberalization of IMF's compensatory financing facility— which was a short-term measure, with a standard IMF period of

44. TD/B/AC.10(1)/CRP.1 (2 Nov. 1970). Some donors were not prepared to commit themselves regarding the urgency of such a scheme. France, for example, who is over the target of 1%, argues that the real issue is not untying, but the volume of aid. See also the Pearson Commission proposals on aid untying, *Partners in Development, op. cit.*, pp. 189-193.

45. See recommendation A.IV.17, *Proceedings*, Vol. I, p. 52. For the analysis of the extent to which amending of the compensatory financing facility met the objectives of the above recommendation see TD/5/Add.1 (31 Aug. 1967), p. 53. The Geneva Conference had also asked that the drawing of credits through the compensatory financing facility should not directly or indirectly prejudice a member country's ability to make an ordinary drawing. The 1966 decision separated the compensatory financing facility from the other drawing facilities of the Fund, in the sense that compensatory drawings are ignored "not only from the standpoint of the total drawing facilities of a member but also from the standpoint of tranche policies to be applied to the member."

repayment of 3-5 years, aimed only to give breathing space to a country while it adjusts to a new external situation—could not substitute for the proposed supplementary financing scheme—a long-term instrumentality, seeking to prevent reductions and disturbances in the investment and development plans of developing countries stricken by unexpected shortfalls of their primary export earnings.[46]

The Geneva Conference called upon the IBRD staff to examine the feasibility of a supplementary financing scheme. In 1966, the study on supplementary financial measures prepared by the Bank was presented for the scrutiny of governments in UNCTAD.[47] Thereupon, the Board established the Intergovernmental Group on Supplementary Financing to consider this matter. The basic feature of the IBRD proposal was the close and continuing relationship between the administering agency and the country in question, i.e., a country would have to enter into an agreement with the administering agency regarding the reasonable expectations of its export earnings over a specified period of time, as well as on the policies it should follow in carrying out its development plans. As long as a developing country follows its commitments and its exports fail to yield the anticipated foreign exchange (that is, where a deficiency in exports occurs as compared to reasonable expectations specified in the policy package) for reasons beyond its control, the agency is supposed to provide adequate supplementary financing.

On the eve of the New Delhi Conference, a number of questions were still pending: the cost of the scheme (estimated between $ 300-400 million per annum, according to IBRD); its administration, and the relationship between the administering agency and other international financial institutions; the content of the policy package, i.e., the prior agreement of a country and the agency on export projections, development programs and policies, and feasible domestic adjustments to offset export shortfalls; how financial commitments would be linked to export projection utilized in development plans; form and terms of assistance (whether the terms should be concessional and flexible); etc. Moreover, there was an alternative scheme of supplementary financing, submitted by F.R. Germany.[48]

Before the New Delhi Conference met, however, many potential

46. See the Algiers Charter TD/38 (3 Nov. 1967), p. 16, and resolution 31(II) of the New Delhi Conference in *Proceedings, New Delhi*, Vol. I, p. 43. For a comparison between compensatory and supplementary financing see TD/B/C.3/ 41 (6 Feb. 1967), Annex D. See also our Chapter II for a brief reference to supplementary financing proposal at the Geneva Conference.

47. For the IBRD study see TD/B/43 (17 Jan. 1966).

48. For an account of the initial considerations of the IBRD study in the inter-governmental group see TD/B/C.3/44 (8 Mar. 1967). For the situation immediately preceding the New Delhi Conference see TD/33 (16 Nov. 1967).

donors indicated that no resources would be immediately available for commitment to the supplementary financing scheme. Among the reasons mentioned were the unfavorable international monetary situation, the balance of payments difficulties of various developed countries, as well as the replenishment of IDA. In spite of this, the developing countries expected that the Conference would agree on the basic principles of the scheme, and pointed out that the agreement in principle did not entail financial obligations for a considerable time to come.[49]

Although many developed countries in principle had given their support to the supplementary financing scheme, France was its leading and outspoken opponent. It argued that this was only a palliative addressed to symptoms and not to the true causes of difficulties experienced by the primary commodities' exporters from the Third World. Instead, France continued to advocate the organization of commodity markets as a way to solve the basic problems of instability and inadequacy of the developing countries' export proceeds.[50] Also, the United States was beginning to manifest openly a degree of scepticism toward supplementary financing, the scepticism which it actually harbored from the very start. Its attitude was motivated partly by the complexity of the scheme, and partly by the mood of the Congress, which even made it difficult to get through the replenishment of IDA funds. These reservations had an impact on the proceedings in New Delhi. The Conference could do no more than state formally the principle that developing countries are entitled to a transfer of additional international resources to help them avoid disruption of their development programs by unexpected export shortfalls. The participants could not agree on the definition and assessment of "reasonable expectations", the scope and nature of the understanding between the administering agency and an individual country, the measures to be undertaken by those applying for assistance, the relationship between the supplementary and compensatory financing, etc., and the matter was tossed back to the expanded Intergovernmental Group on Supplementary Financing.[51]

As the New Delhi Conference adjourned, it was not quite clear whether the IBRD scheme had been superseded, or whether it would continue as the basis for further discussions. An alternative, simplified type of scheme had been advanced by F.R. Germany as early as 1967. It omitted export projections and any prior understanding on policy matters. Rather, on a case-by-case basis, the responsible agency would

49. TD/41 (16 Feb. 1967), p. 4.
50. TD/B/C.3/44 (8 Mar. 1967), p. 4.
51. Conference resolution 30(II), *Proceedings, New Delhi*, Vol. I, p. 42, and the report of the Third Committee, *ibid.*, pp. 288-290.

establish retrospectively whether the decline in export receipts was a shortfall from reasonable expectations.[52] The simplified version of the scheme did not appeal to the 77 and to several developed countries. They primarily objected to its discretionary character, as well as to the fact that recipient countries would be highly uncertain both regarding the amount of assistance they would receive, and the criteria by which such determinations would be made.

At the session of the intergovernmental group in July 1969, developed countries—including the United Kingdom which had sponsored the original suplementary financing proposal in 1964—rejected the IBRD scheme and expressed preference for a discretionary arrangement.[53] In fact, most donors were not prepared to accept what they regarded as a possible open-ended commitment to provide resources for the Bank staff scheme. When the developing countries decided not to press for its adoption, the IBRD proposal on supplementary financing was in fact tacitly shelved. The Group of 77 played a flexible gambit in this instance; by agreeing to discuss the second best alternative, the developing countries shunned the maximum demand and made possible a compromise with the B Group.

The Ninth Board held in September 1969, asked the IBRD "to consider working out arrangements for supplementary finance and, if appropriate, to consider introducing them." The Bank was instructed to elaborate the scheme on the basis of the conclusions adopted in UNCTAD's Intergovernmental Group on Supplementary Financing.[54] These conclusions provided, *inter alia*, that the discretionary supplementary financial measures would be administered within the World Bank Group, in consultation with IMF. The administering agency should at its discretion adapt the measures to the merits and needs of each case, with the possibility left open for establishing objective criteria on the basis of experience, so as to "provide reasonable assurance of help to protect a country's development plan" against the detrimental effects of export shortfalls. It is interesting to note that any understanding between the agency and the country receiving aid from the scheme should "be no different in character" from those which arise in the relationships between the Bank and its members. This was previously a controversial point, because the IBRD scheme envisaged considerable internal policy commitments by developing countries. Many developing countries objected to this, and the Algiers Charter stated that scheme should not involve internal policy commitments

52. TD/33 (16 Nov. 1967), p. 27.
53. UNCTAD press release TAD/401 (7 Jul. 1969).
54. Board resolution 60(IX) in TD/B/(IX)/Misc. 9 (24 Sep. 1969), Annex I. For the report of the intergovernmental group see TD/B/260 (7 Jul. 1969).

"which prejudice the sovereignty of any member country as defined by that country." [55] Furthermore, potential recipients were not eager to see an explicit link established between their domestic performance and external multilateral assistance. However, fully aware of the reciprocity element involved, i.e. their commitment to consult and perform in return for the scheme, the developing countries had assumed a very flexible position on this matter all along, so as not to give the B Group an excuse to scuttle the IBRD proposal.

In spite of the apparent consensus that was reached, the basic problem remained: most developed countries were not prepared to foot another multilateral development assistance bill in addition to replenishing the IDA coffers. This was reflected in the vagueness of the Board resolution, which contained qualifiers such as "consider" and "if appropriate".

The original recommendation on supplementary financing adopted by the Geneva Conference in 1964 was consistently interpreted by the 77 to mean that resources for the scheme should be additional to total aid levels, that is, they should not be diverted from the normal flow of basic development finance.[56] However, not until the summer of 1969 did the donor countries agree that it would be of little value to divert resources from basic development finance for the purpose of supplementary financing measures. It is in the light of this conclusion of UNCTAD's intergovernmental group, and due to the lack of any reasonable prospect to obtain the additional funds for supplementary financing, that in August 1970 the President and the management of IBRD deferred further detailed consideration of the discretionary scheme. The decision was based on the fact that having contributed $ 800 million per year to the third replenishment of IDA (fiscal years 1972-74), the majority of developed countries were not predisposed to consider contributing additional funds for the purpose of supplementary financing.[57] The Group of 77, and some B Group delegations as well— especially Scandinavians who expressed concern at the manner in which the subject had been handled—were taken aback by this decision. The developing countries argued that although the implementation of

55. TD/38 (3 Nov. 1967), p. 16. The Latin American countries were especially insistent on this point, and refused to agree on the possibility of having continuous consultations with the Bank on their economic performance. This was partly due to their already having confronted the Fund and the Bank in similar situations, as well as the United States within the framework of the Alliance for Progress.

56. TD/33 (16 Nov. 1967), p. 3. Many suspected that funds for supplementary financing would result from transfers and cutbacks, rather than through an increase of commitments.

57. The President of IBRD informed the Tenth Board of this through the Secretary-General of UNCTAD. TD/B/327 (30 Sep. 1970), pp. 45-48, and Annex IV.

supplementary financing was dependent on additional resources, the IBRD should have nonetheless drafted a scheme and made an estimate of its cost.

The Board tried to give the appearance of keeping the issue alive by adopting a long declaration on the subject, calling for an effort to work out the details of a discretionary scheme and to assess the possible cost, and inviting the IBRD to report to its next session. However, it appears that, temporarily at least, the supplementary financing has been placed in cold storage by the Bank.

With the competing claims for scarce resources—difficulties are experienced in attaining the replenishment of IDA at the previously agreed level—the donor countries apparently assign secondary importance to supplementary financing. As for the developing countries, they have shown some ambivalence regarding the entire matter. Although in UNCTAD they push strongly in favor of the scheme, in the World Bank, where the proposal is lodged now, they have not exhibited a similar determination. As a consequence, and in spite of what is said in UNCTAD, the developed countries are perhaps getting the impression that for the time being this is not a matter of top priority as far as the developing countries are concerned. Part of the reason for the developing countries' behavior in the Bank is possibly linked to the absence of organized action by the Group of 77 in this institution, and the preference of each developing country to seek advantages on its own, leaving political pressure to a forum like UNCTAD. Part of the reason may be linked to the fact that export trends have been relatively favorable during recent years, and that only a few developing countries would have found it necessary to resort to supplementary financing had it been in existence.[58]

In the meantime, the compensatory financing facility of the IMF remains as the only mechanism in international organizations to deal with the effects of unexpected shortfalls of export earnings of countries heavily dependent on primary commodity trade. As for the IBRD, and while supplementary financing is under review, its Executive Directors have authorized the President to give assurances "that, should a developing member of the Bank, for reasons outside its control, experience an unexpected shortfall in its export earnings which threatens to disrupt the implementation of its development program, the Bank Group would examine the case on its merits with a view to determining whether and how it could shape or modify its lending and other operations for that

58. On trends in export instability see G. F. Erb and S. Schiavo-Campo, "Export Instability, Level of Development, and Economic Size of Less Developed Countries" in *Bulletin* (Oxford University Institute of Economics and Statistics), Vol. 31, No. 4, 1969, pp. 263-283.

country in such a way as to help the country to overcome the difficulties." [59]

International Monetary Reform

The Geneva Conference asked that "any arrangements for the solution of currency problems of the major trading countries should take fully into account the needs of the developing nations" and that studies of the international monetary system should not be isolated from the examination of new trade policies. The developed countries either abstained or voted against this recommendation. [60]

The Group of Experts on International Monetary Issues which met in response to this recommendation concluded that a reform of the international monetary system ought to make it more responsive to the needs of economic growth in both the developed and the developing countries. The experts held that the developing countries have a legitimate need for additional liquidity, to be provided in part through the expansion of reserves and in part by increasing the credit facilities. They concluded that a link should be established between the creation of international liquidity and the provision for development finance. Finally, they argued that the monetary reform should be truly international, and that the developing countries should be represented both in the discussions leading to it and in the operation of new liquidity arrangements. [61] At that time, negotiations on the international monetary reform were held in the exclusive circle of the Group of Ten (i.e. the ten IMF members who signed the General Arrangements to Borrow—Belgium, Canada, F.R. Germany, France, Italy, Japan, the Netherlands, Sweden, the United Kingdom and the United States—plus Switzerland, which although not a member of IMF is associated with the Group of Ten), while suggestions could be heard that the distribution of new reserves should be limited to a small group of developed countries.

The B Group strongly opposed any discussion of international monetary reform in UNCTAD. [62] The Group of 77, on the other hand,

59. Letter from the President of the World Bank to the Secretary-General of UNCTAD, dated 4 May, 1971. TD/B/353 (21 May, 1971), p. 3.
60. Recommendation A.IV.19 in *Proceedings*, Vol. I, p. 53. The vote was 87:11, with 17 abstentions. For a useful discussion of international monetary reform and the developing countries see Johnson, *op. cit.*, pp. 212-236.
61. TD/B/32 (1 Nov. 1965).
62. It is worth noting that DAC members took a dim view of the Geneva Conference recommendation on international monetary issues and of the related proposal to convene the expert group. Suggestions were even made that they should refrain from participating in the selection of experts, and from submitting

argued that UNCTAD is fully competent to discuss international monetary issues. In their draft resolution, which was tabled when the report of the group of experts was presented to UNCTAD's Committee on Invisibles and Financing Related to Trade, the developing countries asserted UNCTAD's competence, asked that they be represented in the discussions leading to any reform of the international monetary system, including international liquidity, and proposed that the report of the group of experts be forwarded to the international monetary institutions. The developed countries objected to sending the report of the group of experts to IMF, were against a simultaneous discussion of the matter in more than one international forum, and felt that only after a given point should it be envisaged to broaden the discussions beyond the Group of Ten. The 77 were insistent however, and the draft resolution was adopted by a vote.[63]

All along, the developing countries contended that a truly international approach should be undertaken with regard to international monetary reform, and supported the idea that this matter should be dealt with in the IMF. Their pressure and actions strengthened the hand of IMF, prevented the discussion and implementation of the monetary reform from being restricted to the Group of Ten, and helped broaden these discussions by initiating joint meetings with the Executive Directors of the IMF, thus making it possible for the developing countries to take part.[64]

This partial and delayed penetration by developing countries into the sphere of decision-making dominated by and reserved for rich nations, was of more than symbolic value because it helped bring about the agreement that they should have a share in the distribution of the new liquidity. The developing countries, however, feared that direct benefits to themselves from the Special Drawing Rights (SDRs) would be limited because of the high percentage of votes required to activate the scheme.[65] They were also dissatisfied with the fact that a link was not

---

reports and observations to the group. Their basic policy line was to exclude monetary issues from UNCTAD, because this was within the exclusive competence of the IMF. DAC docs. DAC/IN(65)4 and DAC/UN(64)4.

63. This was one of the two instances in the period between Geneva and New Delhi Conferences where voting was resorted to. TD/B/42/Rev.1 (23 Dec. 1965), p. 11.

64. It has been argued that had it not been for the association of the IMF and of the developing countries with the discussions, the Special Drawing Rights (SDRs) might have taken longer to negotiate. In the IMF, the forces supporting new liquidity arrangements had more weight than in the Group of Ten. Gardner, "The United Nations Conference on Trade and Development," *op. cit.*, p. 125.

65. TD/7/Supp. 7 (2 Nov. 1967), p. IV, and *Proceedings, New Delhi*, Vol. I, p. 291.

established between SDRs and development finance, although they did not press very hard for the link at that time, partly because some of them felt that this might jeopardize the new liquidity negotiations.

Aid policies of developed countries are affected by the state of their reserves and their balance of payments situation. The slow growth of world liquidity is prejudicial to enlightened development policies, in the sense that deficit countries are prone to introduce restrictions on their aid and trade, while the surplus countries follow policies aimed at maintaining and augmenting their reserves. One of the underlying concepts of SDRs is that reserves can be created without cost of real resources. These reserves are supposed to eliminate the need for restrictive measures aimed at correcting balance of payments difficulties, which in turn will lead to the generation of additional resources and the fuller utilization of the existing ones.[66] In view of these beneficial effects of SDRs, many argue that it is logical to expect that development assistance flows will be augmented and trade policies vis-à-vis the developing nations liberalized.[67] However, the developed countries are generally unwilling to agree to the creation of a link between the new liquidity and the development finance, arguing *inter alia* that this might generate worldwide inflationary pressures.

In order to buttress their stand, the developing countries had recourse to specialist opinion again. A small group of experts was convened to carry out a study on the progress of international monetary reform, devoting particular attention to the needs of developing countries.[68]

The experts were unanimous in their recommendation that a link should be established between the creation of new international liquidity in the form of SDRs and the provision for additional and higher quality development finance. Once the agreement in principle was attained on the desirability of the link, they recommended that it be implemented either through a direct contribution by the developed countries to IDA of a uniform proportion of their annual allocations of SDRs, followed by an exchange of such SDRs into the national currencies of the donor countries concerned, or through the contribution of national currencies to IDA in a uniform proportion of their annual allocations of SDRs.[69]

On the intergovernmental level, however, agreement on the link is

66. TD/B/285 (13 Oct. 1969), pp. 19 ff.
67. Gardner, *op. cit.*, p. 125.
68. Conference resolution 32 (II), *Proceedings, New Delhi*, Vol. I, p. 43, and Board resolution 55 (VIII), TD/B/233 (21 Feb. 1969), Annex I.
69. For the summary of recommendations by the experts, see TD/B/285 (13 Oct. 1969), p. 34. The expert group included a former adviser on international monetary policy in the White House, a former German Executive Director of IBRD, member of the staff of the Bank of Italy, etc.

still very far from being unanimous. One of the strategy guidelines for the second Development Decade suggests that the question of the link be given serious consideration as soon as adequate experience is available on the working of the scheme of Special Drawing Rights.[70] Reaching the consensus, in principle, on the link is the first obstacle. Only then could serious attention be paid to working out the modalities which, depending on the type of link adopted, may require a considerable period of time before implementation could begin. As during the initial considerations of the international monetary reform and of the creation of a new liquidity, when it was argued that the link should not be pressed lest it endanger the creation of such liquidity, a similar argument is raised again. Namely, were the developing countries to push strongly for the adoption of the link principle, this would have a negative effect on the system of SDRs by intensifying the negativism of certain European countries regarding a further creation of SDRs (they are arguing against the creation of SDRs in the next round because of the large outflow of dollars from the United States). Whatever the merits of the caution and go-slow argument, its effect would be to deflate the political pressure which has been building up behind the demand for the international acceptance of the link (currently under study in the IMF), and of course, make it easier for the developed countries to continue ignoring arguments in favor of the link.

In his statement on financing at the end of the New Delhi Conference, the spokesman for the Group of 77 berated the developed countries for their "declarations of good will" which were not accompanied by "concrete measures or commitments of action".[71] At approximately the same time, the President of the IBRD spoke of the gap between the requirements for assistance, which were never higher, and the will to provide it, which was never lower.[72] We have discussed the slowly expanding consensus as regards the clarification and upgrading of aid and terms of aid targets. As in the field of commodities, however, it was difficult to establish a link between the agreement on principles and the action of states. Part of the problem lay with the objective difficulties, including the need for negotiating and setting into motion multilateral agreements based on the principle of burden sharing. However, an important impediment was to be found also in the fact that some developed countries did not take the various recommendations of

---

70. See also the second memorandum on international liquidity presented by the developing countries to the Board in September 1970. They suggested that the question of the "link" be considered at the next allocation of SDRs in 1972. TD/B/327 (30 Sep. 1970), Annex III.

71. *Proceedings, New Delhi*, Vol. I, p. 425.

72. *International Financial Survey*, October 4, 1968, p. 336.

UNCTAD seriously, nor for that matter those of DAC, and did not feel committed to follow through with action. This was especially the case with some major donors, who hold the key to overall performance in the field of development assistance.

Yet, many developed countries have improved their performance, while those which were not encouraged toward positive action, may have refrained from backsliding even further because of UNCTAD's presence—and DAC's, of course—with a battery of recommendations, a watchful secretariat, and vociferous and often embittered developing countries. The unfavorable objective circumstances in the field of development finance and the shortcomings of the present concept of aid, make it very important that new reasons be elaborated and articulated for giving, increasing and improving the flow of financial assistance to the South. UNCTAD, as an almost universal and politically sensitized forum, has an important role to play in this task. UNCTAD's influence, of course, is not directed solely at the bilateral development assistance policies of donor countries. The policy pressures emanating from UNCTAD are affecting short and long-term orientation and policies of multilateral financial institutions. In this sense, UNCTAD is being used by the developing countries to generate pressures and indirectly cause actions to be taken in those bodies where their voice is not powerfully heard otherwise.

Chapter VI

SHIPPING

The economic and commercial aspects of shipping were almost virgin territory at the time of the Geneva Conference, a forbidden land to which neither international organizations nor developing countries had easy access.[1] On the international scene it was one of the several untouched strongholds of anachronistic private enterprise and its credo of *laissez-faire*, with liner conferences enjoying oligopolistic privileges. Generally, data was scarce and there was a dearth of published materials on the economics of ocean transport. This was primarily due to the secrecy which shrouded the practices of liner conferences, price fixing and costs. The absence of reliable figures prevented developing countries from fully substantiating their grievances and suspicions about certain shipping practices.

In order to export their products, the majority of developing countries rely almost exclusively on ocean transport. However, there is a great disparity between their share in world seaborne trade and their share in the world fleet.[2] They are substantial net importers of shipping services, especially from the western maritime powers where the bulk of world shipping tonnage is concentrated, and they experience a considerable debit under the balance of payments item of ocean transport. Moreover, the costs and efficiency of shipping are very important for developing countries because the major part of their exports consists of primary commodities which are heavy and voluminous, have a

1. Note, for example, that Scandinavian countries were approached for the names of shipping experts that could collaborate in drafting the initial reports for the Geneva Conference, but they refused to cooperate. TD/B/38/Rev.1 (27 Jul. 1966), p. 9.
2. In 1967, for example, their share in total volume of international seaborne trade was 63.1% of total goods loaded and 18.7% of total goods unloaded. The corresponding figures for 1959 were 61.4% and 22.9%. TD/B/C.4/50 (24 Feb. 1969), p. 6. In 1968 only 7.4% of the total world merchant fleet belonged to developing countries (Africa—0.4%, Asia—4.3%, Latin America—2.7%). The share of the socialist countries of Eastern Europe and Asia was 8.7%; Southern Europe—7.4%; "flag of convenience" countries—16.8%; and developed market economies—59.7%.

relatively low unit value, and are usually shipped over long distances.

The developing countries are most upset over the unilateral fixing of the ever-increasing freight rates, and resent being virtually at the mercy of the shipowners from the West. In mounting their multi-pronged offensive in UNCTAD, they are trying to get a foot in the door of the chambers where conference practices and freight rates are determined. They are pressing for international regulation of a basically private industry,[3] and are hopeful that governments of developed countries will act forcefully so as to convince the shipowners of the need for reforms and innovations—all in keeping with the proclaimed goals of the international community in the field of development. They ask that procedures which are unilateral and/or collusive between shipowners (abetted by certain governments) should be internationalized and brought into the consultation machinery where the users of shipping would be in a better bargaining position. They are working on and arguing for the build-up of their own merchant fleets, thus expecting to diversify production, achieve favorable effects on their balance of payments, and improve their general economic and political position. They ask the developed nations and multilateral financing agencies for better and softer terms of loans for their shipbuilding and ship buying ventures. They also urge that changes be made in various shipping practices that are discriminatory so as to secure greater participation for newcomers in carrying seaborne trade.

The first step in this direction was made when shipping was placed as a permanent item on UNCTAD's agenda, and especially when the standing committee was created for this purpose against the opposition of maritime powers.[4] In what follows we shall deal briefly with some of the principal shipping issues with which UNCTAD is preoccupied, i.e., consultation machinery, freight rates and conference practices, merchant fleets of developing countries, and international shipping legislation.

3. It should be remembered that not too long ago, it was not generally accept-ed that governments sit to discuss and negotiate commodity trade regulation. Today, government representatives negotiate agreements and adjust rules, while private industries lobby either indirectly in the legislatures or directly through the executive. (Often, "advisers" from powerful commerce and industry lobbies sit in the delegations of developed countries to commodity negotiations.)

4. A number of developed countries, however, have predominant user interests and are in sympathy with the demands of developing nations. For example, the United States and Australia. On the other hand, the Scandinavian countries find it difficult to overlook their own interests in shipping and to ignore the pressure of powerful shipowner lobbies, which is in a marked contrast to their liberal and enlightened posture on a number of items on UNCTAD's agenda.

Consultation machinery is an organized system whereby shippers and shipowners can negotiate and reach joint agreements. It came into being because individual shippers were in a weak bargaining position against organized shipping lines, and because they had insufficient knowledge to enter into negotiations alone.[5] At the Geneva Conference developing countries complained about the lack of opportunity to take part in the decisions of liner conferences, and expressed the hope that a new system would emerge which would allow for equality and mutual consultations, with shippers getting an equal say in the decisions on shipping and freight rates. They underlined the fact that governments should be included in consultations, because dialogues between shippers from developing countries and conferences seldom gave the former satisfactory results.[6] Although the Geneva Conference agreed on the need for consultation machinery and on the issues to be considered within it, there was no consensus as to the role of governments.[7] The developed countries felt that complaints and grievances could best be solved in a machinery for private consultation between liner conferences and their customers. Although they acquiesced in the contention that governments might have to initiate action in some cases, they argued that as a rule they should not be involved in the operation of shippers' councils and consultation machinery. Moreover, the representatives of western countries insisted that their governments cannot intervene in the affairs of a private industry.

UNCTAD's Committee on Shipping agreed that consultation machinery should be established regionally and nationally in developing countries where it did not already exist; however, the role of governments in the operation of such machinery remained controversial.[8] The debate at the New Delhi Conference reflected the continuing disagreement on this issue. The Group of 77 argued that governmental participation is needed, because governments are the only reliable guardians of national interests. Among reasons mentioned were that in developing countries shippers are often foreign or foreign affiliates; nationals can pass increased shipping costs to other sectors of the domestic economy; governments take an active part in foreign trade either as exporters or importers, etc. It was also pointed out that

5. For a detailed account on the subject see TD/13 (11 Oct. 1967) and TD/13/Supp.1 (9 Nov. 1967).

6. *Proceedings,* Vol. I, pp. 226-228.

7. See "Common Measure of Understanding on Shipping Questions," A.IV.22, *ibid.,* p. 54.

8. TD/B/116 (10 Mar. 1967), Annex I.

governmental participation was necessary, because in developing countries shippers have yet to acquire sufficient organizational strength and
technical expertise to be able to negotiate effectively with the conferences. Some among the 77 suggested that developing countries should
protect their national interests by placing legislative curbs on the *laissez-
faire* practices of shipowners and conferences. The B Group, on the
other hand, conceived the governments' role as persuasive rather than
regulatory. Governments were to stimulate private initiative, and all
they should do is to encourage the formation of shippers' councils and
to induce liner conferences to accept the principle of consultation with
these councils.[9]

Although somewhat ambiguous, the resolution adopted in New
Delhi recognized the role of governments and thus represented a step
forward in the process of consensus evolution.[10] It invited the governments of developing countries to encourage the creation of shippers'
councils and consultation machinery, and to rely on the technical
assistance which can be obtained from the United Nations.[11] It asked
those governments with experience in this sphere to cooperate, while
the governments of developed countries were to "urge" liner conferences and equivalent bodies (non-conference lines and tramp interests)
to recognize shippers' councils. The unanimous adoption of this resolution was another step in the gradual recognition that effective attempts
to regulate shipping practices could only be made through intergovernmental action.[12]

It was also agreed that consultation machineries should have on their
agendas "questions pertaining to freight rates, conference practices,
adequacy of shipping services"—matters which (previously) were in
the exclusive domain of shipowners. This represented a significant
progress since the Geneva Conference, and was aimed at the shipowners who would discuss freight rates only with individual shippers,
while they would talk with shippers' councils about principles and
general terms.

The Committee on Shipping and UNCTAD's secretariat were to play
an important role in encouraging the establishment of shippers' organizations. The secretariat particularly was to gather materials relating to
the operation of the existing consultation machinery and prepare
models of such bodies adaptable to various conditions in the developing

9. *Proceedings, New Delhi,* Vol. I, pp. 307-308.
10. Conference resolution 2(II), *ibid.,* p. 45.
11. The substantive support for technical assistance in shipping was transferred
to UNCTAD at the New Delhi Conference. Resolution 6(II), *ibid.,* p. 47.
12. This added yet another to the several nails that UNCTAD has been driving
into the coffin of the shipping lines' long defended *laissez-faire* principle. *The
Economist,* April 6, 1968, p. 65.

world.[13] Although the number of national shippers' councils in the developing countries had been conspicuously on the increase, formal consultation machinery has been very slow to emerge.[14] This is the reason why the developed countries have been urged again and again to make liner conferences recognize shippers' councils as negotiating partners, and not to obstruct and delay the creation of effective consultation machinery. Thus, the Committee on Shipping at its session in May 1970 recommended that liner conferences should include in their constitutions provisions for discussion on questions relating to freight rates, conference practices, adequacy of shipping services, etc. It was also suggested that the scope of consultations be broadened so as to include interested public authorities, in addition to shippers and shippers' bodies.[15]

Freight Rates and Conference Practices

A number of grievances were voiced by developing countries at the Geneva Conference regarding freight rates. According to them, freight rates were too high, anomalous, and discriminatory. They objected on the ground that they themselves had no means to judge whether freight rate increases were justified, since these were unilaterally decided by shipowners and were put into effect arbitrarily, usually without any meaningful advance warnings.[16] Therefore, they asked that mutual consultations be held on freight rates, that methods of determining these be publicized, and that rates be registered with the competent national authorities. They proposed that freight rates be put at fair and reasonable levels; that they be fixed at lower levels for new export items from developing areas, or at least at levels equal to those for similar products of industrial nations; that changes in freight rates be made only after consultations between shipowners and the shipping interests concerned; and that promotional rates for manufactured goods from developing countries be established so as to enhance their export. While the developed countries argued that efficient transport at low cost could best be secured through free competition between shipowners, and that any interference with their activities would lead to higher costs and poorer services, the developing countries criticized the absence of free competition and the prevalence of monopoly practices by liner confer-

13. TD/B/240 (29 Apr. 1969), Annex II. The secretariat study was intended also to focus attention on the participation of governments and port authorities in the consultation machinery.

14. TD/B/257/Add.1 (25 Jun. 1969), pp. 67-68.

15. Committee on Shipping resolution 11(IV) in TD/B/301 (Aug. 1970), p. 22.

16. For the report of the Working Party on Shipping, see *Proceedings,* Vol. I, pp. 219-229.

ences. No consensus on freight rates was attained at the Geneva Conference.

The developing countries argued that the scrutiny of freight rates should be the core of UNCTAD's activities in shipping, but at the first session of the Committee on Shipping, the B Group did not agree that freight rate studies be placed on the committee's agenda.[17] A few months later, however, it was agreed in principle that such studies could be conducted in UNCTAD. However, the maritime powers considered the proposed studies on selected routes as unacceptable. They argued that this would involve a disclosure of confidential information to which governments had neither access nor the legal powers to force shipowners to divulge. In addition, they argued that such studies would be too theoretical and would yield no practical or useful results.[18]

Although the objections were methodological, in reality the maritime powers were suspicious that the findings from such studies could lead to greater intervention by governments into secretive freight rate making.[19] They feared that attempts would be made to demonstrate what "fair" rates are, and also that the UNCTAD secretariat would publish commercial secrets which could affect the competitive position of those shipowners organized in conferences, who cooperated and released the information. This objection was taken into account in the draft resolution sponsored by the 77: it stated that opinion would not be expressed on the "correctness" of any particular freight rate, and that route studies would be pilot studies based partly on simulation. The maritime powers would still not yield, a compromise could not be reached and the vote was taken. Members of the B Group were divided; those that voted in favor or abstained approved of route studies because they were interested in gaining insight into the practices of liner conferences.[20] The vote gave a mandate to the UNCTAD secretariat to

17. See TD/B/36 and Add.1 (25 Nov. 1967), p. 57. For the version of UNCTAD's program of work agreed to in 1967 see TD/B/116 (10 Mar. 1967), Annex I, while for the revised 1969 version see TD/B/240 (29 Apr. 1969), Annex II.
18. For the studies proposed by the UNCTAD secretariat and the questions of methodology, see TD/B/C.4/9 (5 May 1966).
19. See TD/B/83/Rev.1 (27 Jul. 1967), pp. 1-14.
20. This was the second instance of voting in the period between the two Conferences. It referred to paragraph 7, which dealt with route studies. The vote breakdown was as follows: in favor, 27; against, 5; abstaining, 7. Voting in favor were developing, socialist, and some developed countries (New Zealand, Canada, and Spain). Voting against were the traditional maritime powers—Norway, the Netherlands, the United Kingdom, Sweden and Denmark. Abstaining were France, Greece, Italy, Japan, F.R. Germany, Australia, and the United States. See TD/B/C.4/SR.19 (6 Jan. 1967), p. 5.

proceed with research on this key topic of freight rates.

The Algiers Conference reiterated that freight rates were rising and that they continued to be restrictive and discriminatory vis-à-vis developing countries. It asked the governments of developed countries to put pressure upon shipowners to cease imposing higher freight rates for the transport of non-traditional goods from developing countries, and to lower them on their traditional exports. They hoped that the New Delhi Conference would recognize their right to take part in any freight conference affecting their maritime traffic, on an equal footing with the shipowners from developed countries.[21]

The debate in New Delhi was a continuation along this same line; the maritime powers spoke of market forces, while the 77 claimed the existence of cartelized decisions with no reference to users from developing areas.[22] In short, developing nations called for multilateral negotiations of freight rates, and asked governments of developed countries to use their influence to press shipowners (just as they do when their own interests are at stake and when they show little reluctance to intervene).[23] The resolution adopted unanimously by the New Delhi Conference recommended that governments "invite" liner conferences "to take into account" certain areas of possible action— for example, to review and adjust freight rates which shippers consider too high; to provide special rates for non-traditional exports of developing countries; to avoid unjustifiably high freight rates, and to eliminate those practices which frustrate the exports of a developing country while encouraging exports from another country served by the same conference; to recognize port improvements which bring about a reduction of costs and adjust freight rates accordingly, etc.[24]

This same resolution directed the UNCTAD secretariat to pursue its program of work relating to level and structure of freight rates, conference practices and adequacy of shipping services. Governments were invited to cooperate with the secretariat in this endeavor, and to stimulate—within their "legal limitations"—shipowners, conferences and shippers to provide the relevant information. To obtain the needed information for its studies, the secretariat distributed questionnaires

21. TD/38 (3 Nov. 1967), pp. 18-19.

22. An example was given where freight rates were not lowered on a given route in spite of the fact that the developing country in question had improved its ports. Shipowners argue that freight rates often reflect the inefficiency of ports in developing countries, the unnecessarily long time a ship has to spend waiting, slow loading or unloading, etc.

23. For the demands of developing countries, basically a repetition of what had been said in Geneva in 1964, see *Proceedings, New Delhi*, Vol. I, pp. 309, 329.

24. Resolution 3(II), *ibid.*, p. 46.

which governments were to pass to interests concerned.[25] However, the conferences and the maritime powers were unwilling to cooperate. Only one-half of the questionnaires were returned, and the answers that were received suggested an "organized boycott of the UNCTAD probe by conference lines."[26] The most sensitive questions relating to the decision-making process, to the admission of new lines, to the revision of freight rates, and to traffic and freight sharing arrangements— received vague replies of a general nature. At the Committee on Shipping session in April 1969, the representative of UNCTAD's Secretary-General voiced the opinion that were was a "prior concertation in answering the questionnaire."[27] Also, Brazil lodged a complaint that some governments had enacted legislation to prohibit shipping lines from imparting information on freight tariffs and related matters.[28] After an acrimonious debate the Committee on Shipping adopted a resolution reaffirming the New Delhi guidelines. *Inter alia,* it asked countries that have legal measures restraining the supply of information not to allow these to hamper the efforts of the UNCTAD secretariat.[29]

At the spring 1970 session of the committee, the secretariat submitted its studies on the structure of freight rates, as well as on the liner conference system.[30] The information and facts that it gleaned from the study on liner conferences, inspired the committee to engage in a detailed debate of conference practices, and among other things to recommend that: the shipping lines of developing countries be admitted as full members of liner conferences operating in their maritime trade, and that they should have a greater and substantive participation in the transport of cargo which is generated by their foreign trade. It also recommended that whenever developing countries' lines apply for membership in way-port conferences, such applications should be

25. See TD/B/C.4/38 (16 Dec. 1968), TD/B/C.4/43 (18 Dec. 1968), TD/B/C.4/45 (24 Feb. 1969), and TD/B/C.4/47 (19 Dec. 1968).

26. *The Economic Times,* Bombay, February 2, 1969. Shipping and commercial enterprises cooperated in supplying the information.

27. See TD/B/C.4/SR.45 (17 Apr. 1969), p. 7. The Indian press was much more categorical on this issue. It stated that the Committee of the European National Shipowners' Association (CENSA) had instructed conference members on how to defeat UNCTAD's probe, and to treat the questionnaires as mere scraps of paper. They were told which questions were to get only general replies.

28. See TD/B/C.4/SR.42 (15 Apr. 1969), p. 6, and SR.43 (16 Apr. 1969), p. 6. Brazil's delegate was referring specifically to France, where shipping lines were prohibited to disclose any documents or information on trade policies of conferences, pooling arrangements, procedure for establishing and justifying freight rates, etc.

29. Resolution 4(III) in TD/B/240 (29 Apr. 1969), Annex I.

30. See "Freight Markets and the Level and Structure of Freight Rates" UN publication Sales No. E.69.II.D.13, as well as TD/B/C.4/62 (19 Jan. 1970).

considered fairly and on equal terms.[31] Regarding the freight rates, the committee recommended that the secretariat should continue to study freight markets, discrimination in freight rates, promotional freight rates, as well as the relationship between changes in freight rates and the effect on the export trade of developing countries.[32]

Merchant Marines of Developing Countries

At the Geneva Conference, the developing countries asked that their emerging fleets be treated like any other infant industry and extended all possible assistance. The build-up of domestic fleets would help them improve their balance of payments, lead to increases of national income, allow higher export earnings, and contribute to the diversification and enlargement of their economic base.[33] The developed countries offered qualified support to the establishment and expansion of developing countries' merchant fleets. They insisted that investments in shipping be based on sound economic criteria, and also argued that the effect of such fleets on the balance of payments situation would prove limited. This argument continued during the New Delhi Conference, with developing countries stating that "sound economic criteria" as understood by developed countries are not fully applicable in their case.[34] Rather, they felt that the primary guidelines should be national economic criteria (social costs and benefits), effects on the balance of payments, trade promotion, and influence of the new fleets on conference decisions.[35] Leaving aside the arguments for and against the build-up of merchant fleets in developing countries,[36] we see that the two

31. Resolution 12 (IV) in TD/B/301 (Aug. 1970), pp. 22-24.
32. *Idem.*
33. *Proceedings,* Vol. I, pp. 220-222.
34. It appears that western countries understand "sound economic criteria" to mean that new shipping companies should be established only if they can provide identical services or lower costs and prices than existing, well-established companies of traditional maritime powers. This approach, of course, ignores the infant industry argument and UNCTAD's objective of changing the international division of labor in shipping.
35. For the New Delhi debate see *Proceedings, New Delhi,* Vol. I, pp. 311-315.
36. For a thorough discussion of the subject, see TD/26 (3 Nov. 1967) and TD/26/Supp.1 (20 Nov. 1967). The secretariat concludes that there can be no general answer to the question of whether the establishment or expansion of a national merchant fleet is economically viable, or whether it represents the best use of available resources for each and every developing country. The reply is to be obtained by a feasibility study in each case. However, the conclusion of the study appears to be that when a whole set of aims is considered together (improvement of balance of payments, diversifying employment, influencing conferences, promoting national and regional economic integration, fostering trade),

most important related issues are ship finance and cargo reservation.

The developing countries demanded that it become possible for them to buy new ships on commercial deferred credit terms, through loans that are to be reimbursed over a ten-year period or longer, at low rates of interest. They hoped that regular aid funds could be used to finance ship purchases, and they expected that international financial agencies would be empowered to participate in financing the acquisition of second-hand vessels. In their draft resolution the developing countries proposed that terms on which ships are sold to them be similar to those of "soft aid".[37] The resolution adopted by the Conference invited the maritime nations in particular to consider proposals from developing countries regarding financing of their ship purchases; new vessels to be sold to them "on deferred payment terms involving repayment after delivery in not less than 10 years"; second-hand vessels to be sold on deferred payment terms of up to eight years; guarantees by national financial institutions in developing countries to be accepted as adequate for the deferred portion of payments, and arrangements to be made for the financing of second-hand ships on deferred terms.[38]

At the third session of the Committee on Shipping in April 1969, the Group of 77 pointed out that not one government of a developed country had done anything to facilitate the financing and acquisition of vessels by developing nations.[39] On the subject of payments for used bottoms, the developed countries argued that governments have no influence on the terms of contracts of these purely commercial transactions, nor are they involved in the market forces that govern the sale of second-hand vessels.[40] The 77, on the other hand, pointed out that all export credit guarantee schemes were "ultimately financed by governments and government-controlled institutions either directly or indirectly", and that governments were in a strong position to influence the terms and conditions of such transactions. The committee did not take a decision on this matter, since the developed countries stated that they would "continue to give sympathetic consideration" to the resolution adopted in New Delhi. In spite of this statement, however, the thirteen ship-exporting members of OECD signed an "understanding

---

there may be no better way of approaching them as a whole than by establishing national merchant marines. See TD/26, p. 15, and TD/26/Supp.1, p. 112.

37. TD/II/C.4/L.11, *Proceedings, New Delhi,* Vol. I, p. 314.

38. Resolution 12(II), *ibid.,* p. 49.

39. TD/B/240 (29 Apr. 1969), Chapter IV.

40. The *note verbale* by the UNCTAD secretariat regarding the proposals of the 77 contained in the resolution 12(II) received generally vague or negative answers. The major shipbuilding country, Japan, failed to submit a reply. See TD/B/C.4/44 (24 Febr. 1969) and addenda.

on export credits for ships" in May 1969, tightening the credit conditions for ship purchase.[41]

The developing nations strongly objected against being placed on a par with the developed countries under the credit conditions spelled out in the "Understanding",[42] arguing that these have adversely affected their ability to acquire new shipping tonnage and were in defiance of the New Delhi Conference resolution 12 (II). The B Group, on the other hand, felt that the "Understanding" was not contrary to the resolution 12 (II), among other things because it provides for exceptions for genuine aid reasons. The Committee on Shipping, at its fourth session in the spring of 1970, asked the developed countries to give a more precise definition of the conditions for the sale of ships to developing countries. The controversy centered primarily on the length of export credits, the down-payment, and the interest rate.[43] A limited step forward was made when it was unanimously agreed that guarantees by their national financial institutions should be accepted as adequate cover for the deferred portion of payment for new or used vessels purchased by the developing countries.[44]

Regarding assistance to shipping, the Algiers Charter provided that "all countries should recognize the right of developing countries to assist their merchant marines, including the right to reserve a fair share of the cargo transported to and from those countries." [45] The 77 pointed out that many developed countries reserved a certain percentage of incoming and outgoing cargo for their own fleets during their formative years, and some continue this practice even today. They argued that *de facto* flag discrimination in favor of shipowners from developed nations is perpetrated through the terms of shipping where the choice

41. TD/B/257/Add.1 (25 Jun. 1969), p. 72. The export credits by governments were not to exceed eight years, with a minimum down-payment of 20% and a minimum net interest rate of 6%. The aim of the "Understanding" was to gradually reduce those elements which distort normal competitive conditions in the ship-building industry, *inter alia*, by providing for equal credit terms. (See TD/B/C.4/58 (3 Feb. 1970), regarding the effect of the "Understanding" on the sale of new ships to developing countries.)

42. Due to the mobility of ships and capital, it was argued in OECD that some developed countries could exploit the situation were a differentiation between purchasers to be made.

43. The 77 reiterated their demands for the repayment periods of up to 10 years on new vessels, up to 8 years for second-hand vessels; the down-payment not to exceed 15% of the price in the case of new vessels, and 15-20% for second-hand vessels; and that rates of interest not to be higher than 5% per annum. TD/B/301 (Aug. 1970), p. 25.

44. Resolution 9(IV), *ibid.*, p. 21.

45. TD/38 (3 Nov. 1967), p. 19.

of a vessel is in the hands of importers and exporters in the West.[46] They also pointed to restrictive business practices, such as associations between traders and shipowners, conference practices, such as arrangements where shippers are penalized if they use the services of certain lines and are given special incentives to use other lines, the membership policy of some liner conferences, and so on. The maritime powers suspected that the Group of 77 in New Delhi would insist that cargo reservation (the most important type of flag discrimination) be treated in principle as equivalent to preferences for manufactures and semi-manufactures. However, there was no such concerted attempt. The resolution on the development of merchant marines in the Third World could be adopted unanimously only after the passage on cargo preferences was deleted; however, the attention of the continuing machinery was drawn to this matter.

At its third session, the Committee on Shipping directed the secretariat to prepare a study on the nature and extent of cargo reservation. The debate held in the committee in spring 1970 on the basis of this report, accentuated the divergence of views between developed and developing countries.[47] The developing countries argued in favor of government intervention to assist their national flag vessels. Cargo reservation was proposed as the most convenient measure, in view of the developing countries' inability to pay subsidies to their fleets, and also because of the fact that their shipping lines were not admitted freely into liner conferences. The developed countries were of a different opinion: cargo reservation would lead to over-tonnaging, loss of efficiency, loss of freedom for shippers, reprisals and bilateralism, inflexibility in the shipping structure, higher freight rates, and so on. The views could not be reconciled and the resolution on the assistance to shipping had to be voted through, over the general opposition of the

46. India's experience with the export of its iron ore to Japan is a case in point. Anticipating participation in the shipping, India built some vessels, but the terms of contract excluded it from shipping, and the ore went in Japanese carriers. *The Economist*, April 6, 1968, p. 65. Note that resolution 4(II) of the New Delhi Conference asked the UNCTAD secretariat to conduct a study on the terms of shipment. *Proceedings, New Delhi,* Vol. I, p. 47. For this study see TD/B/C.4/36 (13 Dec. 1968); and TD/B/240 (29 Apr. 1969), Chapter I for the discussion at the third session of the Committee on Shipping. Note that the United States practices cargo reservation with respect to aid cargoes, for example. Among other developed countries which have resorted to this instrument, Japan has abandoned it of late as part of the price to be admitted to OECD.

47. For the report of the secretariat see TD/B/C.4/63 (21 Jan. 1970). For the debate in the committee, TD/B/31 (Aug. 1970), pp. 12-13. See also "UNCTAD Success in Shipping," *Journal of World Trade Law,* Vol. 4, No. 4, July/August 1970, pp. 586-604.

developed countries.[48] It noted that the developed countries do assist and protect their shipping interests, and recognized that the developing countries have the same right. It declared that the shipping industries in developing countries require special government attention, assistance and protection, especially at the infant stage of their development. Consequently, the legislative and regulatory actions by developing countries along these lines are likely to increase. In addition to improving their bargaining power vis-à-vis the shipowners from the West, such moves could have an important indirect effect. Namely, irritated by cargo preferences and similar measures in developing countries, the governments of maritime nations might be more inclined to step in to protect the interests of their shipowners. This would mean in effect an end to their hands-off attitude and the acceptance of responsibility for what is happening in this "purely private sector".

International Shipping Legislation

The comprehensive approach to shipping requires that legal rules applying to this activity also be examined. Attempts to include the international shipping legislation on UNCTAD's agenda were initiated by the UAR in 1966.[49] The developing countries argued that the rules of international private maritime law were written by traditional sea powers (particularly the United Kingdom), and were unduly favorable to shipowners. Therefore, they asked for a review of these rules, and of the economic and commercial aspects of shipping legislation and practices, a review which would take account of the interests of the shippers and shipowners alike. They referred primarily to those aspects of shipping legislation which had a negative effect on their trade and development, in particular, bills of lading, charter parties, limitation of shipowner's liability, and international marine insurance.[50] As we shall see later, the debate on whether UNCTAD should deal with this subject and in what form, took almost three years to settle.[51] Only then could the substantive work aimed at updating the legal structure of shipping be initiated.

48. Resolution 15(IV), *ibid.,* p. 25. It was adopted by a roll-call vote of 22 in favor, 9 against and 6 abstentions. Voting against: Australia, Canada, Denmark, Greece, Japan, Norway, Sweden, the United Kingdom and the United States. Abstaining: F.R. Germany, France, Italy, Netherlands, New Zealand, and Poland. The developed countries found it impossible to arrive at a unified position in this instance.

49. For the discussion in the Committee on Shipping, see TD/B/C.4/SR. 31-34.

50. *Proceedings, New Delhi,* Vol. I, p. 315.

51. See our Chapter XI for the discussion of the institutional controversy. The maritime powers claimed that UNCTAD is a body which might produce results that are politically biased in favor of developing nations.

The first step was taken when the Working Group on International Shipping Legislation managed to agree on a work program. Priority was given to bills of lading, followed by charter parties, general average, and marine insurance. Based on the group's work, the UN Commission on International Trade Law (UNCITRAL) should prepare the necessary legal draft texts for intergovernmental consideration. It is interesting to note that at its second session in March 1971, the working group introduced a new top priority item, to wit, the subject of liner conference practices with a view to preparing a possible code of good conduct for shipowners. This was done against the strong opposition of developed countries, who were averse to any linkage of "international shipping legislation" and "conference practices", and the implied international regulation of liner conferences.[52]

The unhappiness of the developed countries, and especially the maritime powers led by the United Kingdom, over UNCTAD's intrusion into shipping was reflected through their institutional obstructionism and the refusal to discuss certain shipping subjects in this organization. Although this has been gradually overcome and shipping is now legitimized as a subject of inquiry in UNCTAD, we continue to witness heated confrontations between "haves" and "have-nots", reminiscent of the debate on preferences in its initial stages.[53] The clashes are so pronounced because shipping is a prime example of the inequities of the international division of labor, and the efforts of the *status quo* forces to preserve the system of ocean transport.

52. For the report of the Working Group on its first session see TD/B/289 (19 Dec. 1969); for the report on its second session see TD/B/C.4/86 (8 Mar. 1971). As regards the conference practices, and following the UNCTAD secretariat study on the subject, the European maritime nations and Japan (the so-called Consultative Shipping Group) took the initiative and adopted a decision in Tokyo in February 1971, asking their shipowners to formulate by the end of 1971 a self-regulatory code of conduct for liner conferences. Although these governments were to sanction such a code of conference practices, its administration was to be left to shipowners themselves. The 77 were rather perturbed by this strategy of maritime nations, and resented the possibility of being excluded from the formulation of rules vital to their interests. The decision to involve UNCTAD's Working Group on Shipping Legislation in designing a possible code of good conduct for liner conferences had to be taken by a vote; the developed countries voted against. However, a somewhat more conciliatory mood set in at the fifth session of the Committee on Shipping, held in April 1971. The 77 admitted that the Tokyo decision was nonetheless a step in the right direction, while the maritime nations apparently withdrew their opposition to the consideration of liner conference practices under the heading of international shipping legislation.

53. Note that this clash which feeds on the polarization of forces and group system in UNCTAD extends also to those shipping matters where developed and developing users have a common interest—for example, attaining rational and lowest possible freight rates.

Most shipping matters on UNCTAD's agenda find themselves in the policy-making phase of "problem recognition". Data gathering and analyses by the secretariat are among the indicators of UNCTAD's performance in the field of shipping. The secretariat thus gives the necessary direction to intergovernmental deliberations, and also provides the developing users of shipping with the sorely needed information. The opening up of additional areas to international scrutiny is yet another indication of headway being made. But the main sign of progress is to be found in the gradual emergence of consensus on a variety of recommendations and policies. Admittedly, such recommendations most of the time are incomplete, generally remain on paper, and are far from being implemented. This is primarily because of the *laissez-faire* attitude of developed countries regarding the shipping industry, and their unwillingness to make concessions and help the developing nations. On the other hand, the way to action lies through consensus on principles and policies. And if one agrees with the premise that UNCTAD aims more at long-term structural changes in maritime transport than immediate solutions of short-term problems,[54] then it can be argued that it is laying the foundation for the regulation of shipping by governments and international organizations on the basis of new principles. Thus, for example, most of UNCTAD's policy recommendations have found their way into the development strategy for the second Development Decade. In fact, some envisage a situation where shipping will be regulated through a super-conference resembling the International Air Transport Association (IATA), which would determine freight rates, shipping practices and rules, on the basis of general, open and world-wide criteria. With the emergence of developing countries' fleets and their greater determination and ability to protect their own interests, and with the continued dynamic growth of the merchant marines of the socialist countries, the changes in the present shipping system are likely to be speeded up considerably.

54. TD/B/257/Add.1 (25 Jun. 1969), p. 66.

Chapter VII

SOME OTHER ISSUE AREAS

Trade Expansion, Economic Cooperation and Regional Integration among Developing Countries

The Geneva Conference recognized that expansion of trade among developing countries could make a significant contribution to their foreign exchange earnings and to their economic development.[1] This trade flow was comparatively small—less than one fifth of the developing countries' total trade[2]—and seemed to offer plenty of scope for dynamic growth. Many advantages could result for developing countries from their mutual trade expansion and economic integration. For example, the geographic scope of their trade could be diversified, the range of exportable products enlarged, dependence on traditional export outlets lessened. Also, multinational markets could make it possible for developing countries to avail themselves of economies of scale, not attainable within their usually small national markets. There would thus be less waste of resources caused by investment in industrial enterprises working far below optimal capacity. The developing countries would be exposed to more competition, which in turn might enhance the efficiency of their production and gradually prepare their industrial products for entry into the more competitive and sophisticated markets of the developed world.

However, only in rare cases have governments of developing countries undertaken effective action for the expansion of mutual trade, and many of their schemes did not materialize. At the end of the 1960's, the small progress made contributed to a more pessimistic attitude and to doubts as to whether it was worthwhile to sustain an effort in this direction where rewards were so small.

The special difficulties that the developing countries encountered in their efforts to increase mutual trade and to integrate were among the major causes of the slow progress made. Most of them had balance of

1. Recommendations A.II.5, A.III.8, A.IV.10, and A.IV.16 in *Proceedings*, Vol. I, pp. 31, 41, 48 and 64.
2. See TD/B/309 (7 Aug. 1970), pp. 27-28.

payments difficulties, feared the harmful effects of lowering trade barriers, and only ventured into various arrangements when they felt certain that they would be compensated by additional exports of their own. Some, afraid of dislocations in their balance of payments, insisted on strict and immediate reciprocity. Customs revenue was often an important part of the total revenues of the developing countries and this acted as an additional inhibition to the reduction or removal of tariffs. Many were reluctant to expose their newly-born industrial enterprises to competition; furthermore, the products of the developing countries were not usually complementary and were banned by high protective barriers. They also suffered from the heritage of the colonial past, viz., a poor infrastructure and the high cost of transport (because the traditional trade flows were directed to the North and not to those regions in which developing countries were located), reverse preferences, links with the developed countries in marketing, banking and currency, etc. The least advanced among developing countries were reserved in their attitude to integration, demanding the equitable distribution of benefits and costs, and special measures in their favor, while countries planning their economic development usually felt that the operation of free market forces was not favorable to them. And, finally, the industrial countries were often better and cheaper sources of supply and could sell on more generous terms (offering suppliers' credits, concessional credit terms, etc.).[3]

In the early years, UNCTAD did not have a special body to deal with trade expansion, economic cooperation, and regional integration, and this item fell under the jurisdiction of various committees and of the Trade and Development Board. The lack of institutional focus kept this subject outside the mainstream of UNCTAD's activities. On the intergovernmental level work was confined to general statements about the advantages and desirability of action in this sphere. Specific action and solutions were not considered, nor were generalizations backed up by a consensus on specific matters.[4] However, the Secretary-General of UNCTAD had as early as 1965 initiated a systematic analysis of attempts at trade expansion and integration undertaken by developing countries, in an effort to draw the necessary lessons from these experiences. The documents which resulted were used in preparing the base of the labors of UNCTAD.[5]

3. See *Proceedings, New Delhi,* Vol. I, pp. 361-362, and TD/B/AC.10/2/Add.1 (7 Oct. 1970).
4. TD/15 (2 Nov. 1967), p. 31.
5. See the secretariat study "Trade Expansion and Economic Integration among Developing Countries," (UN publication Sales No. 67.II.D.20); also reports by expert groups "Trade Expansion and Economic Cooperation among Developing Countries," (UN publication Sales No. 67.II.D.2), and "Payments Arrangements

The secretariat put particular emphasis on the idea that trade co-operation and integration among developing countries could make faster progress if it became the object of convergent action by the developing countries on the one hand, and by the entire international community on the other hand. This approach was reflected in the Algiers Charter. The developing countries stated their determination to contribute toward the fulfilment of UNCTAD's objectives by stepping up their efforts with regard to trade expansion and economic co-operation among themselves. After pointing to the special problems and difficulties which they face in this field—as compared to integration processes in developed countries—they stated that the availability of appropriate external financing and technical assistance would contribute to more rapid progress. Special emphasis was given to the insistence that international support should be granted in a manner that would fully respect the right of developing countries to follow their own methods of approach. The developing countries stated that they will inform the New Delhi Conference of the efforts they are making or planning to make in this field; at the same time, they asked the developed countries to make a formal declaration of support for their efforts at cooperation and integration, specifying the nature and volume of financial assistance they were ready to grant.[6]

The UNCTAD secretariat had initially proposed that groups of developing countries should each specify negotiating targets and their objectives in the field of trade expansion and regional integration.[7] In this manner they were to demonstrate to world public opinion how they themselves, through self-help, were willing to contribute to the realization of UNCTAD goals. But, the developing countries did not show much interest in this suggestion. At the New Delhi Conference, when the Group of 77 submitted its original negotiating paper on this subject matter, it contained simply a list of things that developed countries ought to do in the fields of commercial policy, finance and credit, and technical assistance.[8] On the other hand, the negotiating paper submitted by the B Group, which was supposed to constitute the formal declaration of support requested by the Algiers Charter, was so general as to be almost meaningless in the eyes of the developing countries.[9]

---

among the Developing Countries for Trade Expansion," (UN publication Sales No. 67.II.D.6).

6. TD/38 (3 Nov. 1967), p. 24.

7. As conditions, needs and potentialities vary from region to region, it was not possible, of course, to specify targets that were the same for all regional groups. Thus, ideally, each regional body would have fixed a negotiating target for itself, to be implemented in a given period following the Conference.

8. TD/II/WG.II/Conf. room paper 15 (6 Mar. 1968).

9. TD/II/WG.II/Conf. room paper 14 (5 Mar. 1968).

The compromise resolution finally adopted by the Conference was in the form of a concerted declaration. The developing countries stated their intentions, while the developed and the socialist states indicated the manner in which they proposed to support such efforts.[10] The declaration recognized that developing countries must overcome special difficulties if they want to make progress in their mutual trade expansion and economic integration. This was in itself a sort of conceptual progress, since up to that time the developed countries did not formally recognize the existence of such special difficulties. Moreover, the developed countries expressed a willingness to consider financial and technical assistance for any concrete schemes presented to them by the developing countries. They listed certain purposes which they regarded as worthy of this support, for example, assistance to financial institutions embracing groups of developing countries, and financial assistance for the planning and implementation of regional projects; assisting infrastructure projects related to regional integration; helping the least advanced members of a particular group in sharing the benefits, etc.[11] It was conspicuous that possible support measures did not apply to schemes of inter-regional cooperation among developing countries, because of the reservations of big trading nations like F.R. Germany, Japan and the United States. It was also significant that the socialist countries of Eastern Europe stated their willingness to support economic and trade cooperation among developing countries. Earlier, they appeared not quite certain whether regionalism in the Third World was, on balance, good or bad from their perspective. As for the developing countries, they declared their determination to negotiate "further meaningful commitments" among themselves before the next Conference.

In the period following the New Delhi Conference, the frequent efforts of the developing countries to expand or initiate economic cooperation, trade expansion and regional integration continued, although in most cases progress was very slow as the participants encountered the difficulties inherent in these endeavors.[12] In UNCTAD, the secretariat moved toward granting technical assistance in this field, the

10. Conference resolution 23(II), *Proceedings, New Delhi*, Vol. I, pp. 52-53.
11. As we have seen, balance of payments problems are prominent on the list of special difficulties. The Group of 77 asked, therefore, that developed countries agree in principle to contribute financially to reserve funds for multilateral payments arrangements among developing nations. It was argued that the United States had done precisely this for the European Payments Union in the early 1950's, and that this was the condition for the success of intra-European trade liberalization. However, most B Group members were reluctant to come out unequivocally in favor of payments arrangements.
12. For a review of various developments see TB/B/309/Add.1 (16 Jul. 1970), pp. 61-72; and TD/B/AC.10/2 (9 Sep. 1970).

comparative analysis of the various experiences and problems which it had pursued previously having better equipped it for this task. On the intergovernmental level, an Intergovernmental Group on Trade Expansion, Economic Cooperation and Regional Integration among Developing Countries met in November 1970 in order to recommend ways and means to implement the 1968 concerted declaration. The agreed conclusions of the group represented, in fact, an expanded and more precise restatement of the New Delhi consensus. It is worth noting that on this occasion consensus in principle, although vague, was reached on the desirability of multilateral payments arrangements by the developing countries concerned as a means to help reduce the balance-of-payments difficulties which they often face as a result of trade liberalization and expansion commitments. Moreover, it was agreed that such payments arrangements merit international support in appropriate cases. On the other hand, agreement was not reached on a specific proposal that the IMF should support trade liberalization among developing countries by entitling them to make special drawings exclusively designed to overcome deficits resulting from trade liberalization measures. Moreover, the IMF came out very strongly against adding another financing facility (the so-called "integration tranche") to its general financing arrangements, and argued that such balance-of-payments difficulties could be taken care of through its normal financing machinery, on a flexible and pragmatic basis.[13]

In concluding, it should be noted that although the developed countries repeatedly stress the importance of trade expansion, cooperation and regional integration, one gets the impression that they are not pushing the developing countries in this direction very firmly. Their lukewarm attitude is partly caused by the fact that they may expect to be besieged by a number of demands for support.[14] Furthermore, their trade interests could be affected, since many developing countries would find new suppliers among themselves for many goods which they traditionally imported from the North.[15] The concern of some developed

13. For the report of the intergovernmental group see TD/B/333 (2 Dec. 1970), especially pp. 42-48. Also consult our Chapter XI for a discussion of the institutional controversy surrounding the creation of this group. Regarding the IMF reaction see TD/B/AC.10(I)CRP.4 (13 Nov. 1970), and the statement of its representative at the Tenth Board, March 3, 1971.

14. In this period, the various groupings of developing countries have not used the mechanism available in UNCTAD where they can bring forward concrete schemes needing international support.

15. They may also suspect that developing countries will gain more political and economic leverage as a result of their integration and trade expansion efforts. On the other hand, such anxieties may not arise, as most decision-makers in the developed countries do not believe that the developing countries will succeed in setting up powerful groupings.

countries is reflected in their reiteration of the theme that trade expansion and integration efforts should not be carried out at the expense of third countries, and that they should foster a "rational and outward-looking expansion of production and trade". They view with special scepticism any proposals for, or attempts at, inter-regional trade expansion and cooperation schemes among developing countries, out of which a special preferential trading system among developing nations might emerge, as an attempt to offset the ever-increasing massive power of the integrated North.

The Least Developed Developing Countries (LDDCs)

One of the principles adopted by the Geneva Conference provided that measures and policies emerging from UNCTAD should "take into account the individual characteristics and different stages of development of developing countries, special attention being paid to the less developed among them." [16] At the same time, the principle of "non-discrimination" among developing countries was emphasized, while many felt that any explicit differentiation between them would be harmful to the emerging Group of 77 and to its political unity.

After 1964, the question was raised sporadically in the continuing machinery how the interests of LDDCs would relate to specific measures under consideration, how they would be assured of equivalent advantages, and whether they should be entitled to special treatment in order to obtain added benefits warranted by their low level of development. The matter did not begin to crystallize, however, until the provisional agenda for the New Delhi Conference was adopted; one of the items was special measures for the least advanced developing countries. This raised two issues, first, which countries belonged to the LDDC category, and second, what would be the special measures in their favor.

The identification of the least advanced developing countries was fraught with methodological and also with political and negotiability obstacles. The methodological difficulties stemmed primarily from the fact that there was no general agreement as to what indicators were basic components of economic development, what weight was to be assigned to various indicators, where the cut-off point was to be established, etc. Even assuming that these problems could be overcome and an academically respectable list of LDDCs drawn, the crucial question of negotiability remained. Would such a list command general acceptance? How was one to draw a line to separate LDDCs from the

---

16. General principle XV, *Proceedings*, Vol. I, p. 22.

more advanced countries? Would the borderline cases which did not qualify for LDDC status reconcile themselves to the classification? An agreement could be hardly reached, especially if classification as a least developed country was to justify a claim for special outside assistance. Nevertheless, arguments were advanced in favor of a classification. It was argued that the developed countries could not consider any special measures for the least advanced without knowing exactly to which and to how many countries such measures would apply. Also, it was pointed out that once a classification was worked out, it would not be necessary to expend time and energy arguing over who they were as different items on the agenda come up for consideration. Those opposed to the all-purpose classification feared that it would draw a demarcation line in the Group of 77, and possibly set the two categories of developing countries working against each other. The UNCTAD secretariat, after some considerable internal debate, concluded that it should be up to the Group of 77 to determine pragmatically, as different measures come up for consideration, which were the least advanced countries that would qualify for special treatment.

List or no list, those countries that felt that they belonged to the LDDC category continued to press for special measures in their favor. In fact, during the Algiers Conference, the biggest controversy within the Group of 77 centered on the special measures for LDDCs. A cross-regional alliance of states from Africa, Asia, Central and Latin America fought to get their status recognized and to push through special measures which would take account of their position.[17] Special measures offered a better chance to those developing countries that felt that they would not be adequately benefited by the policies emerging from UNCTAD. This also represented a test for the Group of 77, which was meeting in full strength for the first time since the Geneva Conference. It was no longer a question of reaching agreement on a broad resolution addressed to developed countries, nor was a general diagnosis of a problem involved; rather, the distribution of "expected" gains was at stake. The UNCTAD secretariat paper—which was intended as a test balloon for certain ideas which were being considered for inclusion into the final version of a study for the New Delhi Conference—intensified

17. During the preparations for Algiers, Bolivia, Ecuador and Central American states urged within the Latin American group that the provision for special measures be included in the regional Charter of Tequendama. The more advanced countries—Argentina, Brazil and Colombia, in particular—spoke of the need for "non-discrimination" and turned a deaf ear to these demands. So, the Latin American LDDCs waited for the more responsive forum in Algiers, where the African countries arrived with the intention of asking for special measures. Of course, Africans felt that almost every country on their continent under any criteria would probably qualify for LDDC status.

the controversy.[18] It explicitly suggested that special consideration be given to LDDCs' production and export potential when export quotas in commodity agreements were being established or revised. It was not surprising, therefore, that Brazil and Colombia appeared as the most uncompromising opponents of special measures; coffee negotiations were in progress at that time and they resisted the revision of quotas in favor of smaller producers. They were also against financial and technical assistance measures which would explicitly favor the less advanced members of the Group of 77. In fact, they objected to these measures being considered globally and preferred solutions within regional integration schemes. Their policy stand was reflected in their insistence on broad formulations and vague phrases, and in their attempts to narrow down the areas to which special measures would apply. Their stand may have been inspired in part because the African countries stood to be the principal beneficiaries of such measures.

Nevertheless, the Algiers Conference made some progress. Regarding the classification of LDDCs, it was agreed that it would be undesirable "to attempt to abstract a general definition of such countries nor, at that stage, an *a priori* strict listing of such countries." [19] As for commodities, the Algiers Charter provided for special consideration of LDDCs' needs while improving access to developed countries' markets for tropical and temperate zone primary products; it also proposed a temporary refund, at least in part, of revenue charges and duties on commodities of particular interest to them.[20] Agreement was also reached on measures to enable LDDCs to share in the benefits of general preferences, viz., their less competitive products would be exempted from escape clause action, flexible time limits would apply to them regarding the duration of GSP, specific commitments would be undertaken by developed countries to supply them with technical and financial assistance for the establishment of export-oriented industries. Matters left in the air by the Algiers Conference were picked up by a working group, which met later in Geneva and conducted discussions within the "framework of unity of the Group of 77 to ensure equitable sharing of the benefits to be derived from international economic cooperation". Among the measures that the group recommended were

18. See Algiers Conference document MM.77/I/Misc.5 (5 Oct. 1967).
19. TD/38 (3 Nov. 1967), p. 27.
20. These measures, of course, were farther removed from implementation than the possible measures related to negotiation of commodity agreements. Note that the Latin American countries did not want any mention of "commodity agreements" in the text referring to special measures. "Commodity policies," suggested by Prebisch, resolved the deadlock and made adoption of the text possible.

160

the following: that the terms and conditions of basic and supplementary financing be adapted to LDDCs' needs, that the volume of development loans to them be enlarged, that when negotiating and renegotiating commodity agreements "appropriate liberal treatment" be accorded to them while account be also taken of the "trade needs of traditional producers among developing countries".[21]

The basic assumption of the UNCTAD secretariat study on the subject, prepared for the New Delhi Conference, was that special measures for LDDCs should not be isolated as an independent problem, because this would fragment the interests of the Group of 77; rather, they should be viewed as an integral part of the general measures on UNCTAD agenda.[22] The Conference itself was preoccupied with the major issues; special measures for LDDCs were on the periphery of its interests, allocated to one of the working groups.[23] However, the problem was ever present, and the question of equitable benefits for LDDCs was raised in connection with every general measure.[24] The principle of equitable benefits from UNCTAD policies for LDDCs was generally accepted; however, it was reiterated that special measures should not create discrimination against some members of the 77, nor adversely affect the development of any of them.[25] The resolution adopted by the New Delhi Conference was general in tone and did not specify any concrete measures in favor of LDDCs. Yet, it was a landmark in the sense that it represented the first international recognition of the problem and the acceptance of the necessity to pay special attention to LDDCs' needs in concrete decisions emerging from UNCTAD and other UN organs. It recommended that special measures

21. See the group's report to the New Delhi Conference, TD/38/Add.2 (7 Mar. 1968).

22. TD/17 (24 Nov. 1967) and TD/17/Supp.1 (4 Jan. 1968).

23. For the report of the Working Group II see *Proceedings, New Delhi,* Vol. I, pp. 367-370.

24. Note the case of preferences, where the draft resolution by African countries included the wording to the effect that the Conference "affirms ... the objectives of the generalized system of preferences in favour of the developing countries, and *more particularly of the least advanced of the developing countries.*" Document 77/II/9 (24 Mar. 1968). This was modified in the adopted text to read: "including special measures in favour of the least advanced among the developing countries ..." Resolution 21(II), *Proceedings, New Delhi,* p. 38.

25. It is interesting to note that among the recommendations of the Coordinating Committee of the Group of 77 for the Algiers Conference was one suggesting that the more advanced developing countries grant preferences to LDDCs within the measure by which they themselves profit from the GSP. Also, those that increase their exports as a result of the GSP should contribute to the UN Capital Development Fund; the resources thus obtained to be used for investments in those countries not benefiting equitably from the general preferences. These proposals obviously did not encounter a responsive audience in Algiers.

be devised in given areas, on the basis of proposals made by the 77 and by the UNCTAD secretariat. The least developed were to be identified in the context of each measure, on the basis of criteria relevant to the policy measure in question.[26] It was also decided that landlocking should be considered as one of the criteria in identifying LDDCs.[27]

Following the New Delhi Conference, and on the basis of its interpretation of the relevant resolution, the UNCTAD secretariat decided to publish its study, which among other things identified countries in the LDDC category.[28] It ranked countries according to the composite level-of-development index; 24 African countries, 1 from the Caribbean, 4 from Asia, and 1 from the Middle East qualified for the LDDC status.[29] Naturally, the secretariat was severely criticized, especially by those countries which felt that they also belonged to the LDDCs but were assigned a higher ranking. They questioned the authority of the secretariat to engage in the identification exercise, and argued against the choice of variables which, according to them, caused all kinds of distortions in the overall picture. The South and Central American countries in particular—recognized within their own region as belonging to LDDC category—objected vociferously.[30] Some countries pointed out that the ranking was unwise due to political and strategic reasons; they argued for a specific list for each measure only after such a measure had been decided upon. Unhappy with the UNCTAD secretariat's political judgment in this instance, the Group of 77 asked that the studies on special problems of LDDCs (although not their identification) be continued with the assistance of experts, acting in their personal capacity, selected in consultations with the heads of regional economic commissions.

26. Conference resolution 24(II), *ibid.*, p. 54. The 77 had asked that the identification be made from issue to issue, on the basis of a general classification to be worked out by them according to regional criteria and through regional machinery. The B Group, on the other hand, argued that a specific list was necessary because the nature and scope of particular measures depended on the number of countries for whom it was intended.

27. Conference resolution 11(II), *ibid.*, p. 31.

28. The wording of the Conference resolution 24(II) taken as authorization for this study was as follows: "continue studies relative to identification of least developed countries and to examine various approaches to this problem."

29. For the ranking of developing countries and the list of LDDCs see our Chapter XII. The secretariat study is in TD/B/269 (11 Jul. 1969). The composite level-of-development index was arrived at by applying factor analysis to data for six economic and social indicators: *per capita* GDP at factor cost; percentage of GDP originating in manufacturing; *per capita* consumption of energy; combined primary and secondary school enrolment ratio for population between the ages of 5 and 19; number of doctors per 100,000 inhabitants; and percentage of manufactures in total exports.

30. For the debate in the Board see TD/B/SR.216 (15 Sep. 1969), pp. 7 ff.

At its September 1969 meeting, the Ninth Board called on the UNCTAD Secretary General to submit a study on devising effective measures that would enable LDDCs to benefit from the second UN Development Decade (resolution 63 (IX)). To this end, the Secretary General appointed a group of experts acting in their personal capacity. Proceeding from the premise that the international community should have as much interest in reducing the gap among developing countries, as between the developing and the developed ones, the experts advanced a long list of special measures in each of the basic areas of interest to UNCTAD.[31] They also suggested that an *ad hoc* body be established within UNCTAD to formulate, develop and review policies and projects in favor of LDDCs. The experts were unanimous in concluding that it would be futile to define in precise terms the LDDC concept, as well as to name those countries which would qualify for this status; they also felt that drawing a demarcation line would at best be an arbitrary exercise. It was observed that no internationally acceptable solution for combining the various indicators of development into one composite index was likely to be found. They opted for a relative definition of LDDCs, in the context of each particular measure, while admitting the possibility that some countries might qualify as LDDCs in the context of all measures.[32]

Realizing that the backwardness of LDDCs extends to all sectors and phases of economic and social life, many of which were outside UNCTAD's competence, the Board also called on the General Assembly to consider what contributions other organs of the UN system could make in the solution of these problems and how. As an outgrowth of this, and on the basis of the General Assembly resolution 2564 (XXIV) of 13 December 1969, the Committee for Development Planning established a working group, which in addition to making a number of substantive recommendations, also engaged in the identification exercise.[33] It divided LDDCs into three subgroups: 1. "hard core", i.e., those that would qualify for the LDDC status by meeting all criteria and who deserve comprehensive and integrated action programs; [34] 2. "relatively least developed", i.e., those that qualify for

31. For their report see TD/B/288 (18 Dec. 1969).
32. It is worth noting that the experts concluded that special problems that LDDCs encounter are to a large extent connected with the fact that they are at early stages of development, and are frequently characterized by dependence on foreign commercial and financial institutions. Lack of national banking and financing organizations which would control domestic and capital money markets results in a steady outflow of profits and domestic savings.
33. See E/AC.54/L.36 (17 Apr. 1970), and TD/B/316 (25 Jun. 1970).
34. Basically, to be included into the "hard core" LDDC category, a country should have a *per capita* GDP of less than $100 in 1966, a literacy rate not

LDDC status within a specific field of action because they are below a cut-off point in some selected development indicator; and 3. those that might qualify as least developed within a given region, and therefore merit special treatment, for example, in the context of regional co-operation arrangements. Nonetheless, the working group also concluded that each UN body should evolve its own criteria for identifying LDDCs. As was to be expected, most developing countries in UNCTAD strongly disagreed with the identification carried out in the Committee for Developing Planning, and reiterated their policy stand that LDDCs should be identified with regard to each particular measure.[35]

If all the measures recommended by the experts could be put into effect, the LDDCs would be in a much better position to cope with their problems. Unfortunately, there is a big gap between such recommendations and the consensus on the intergovernmental level. Thus, although much greater attention is being paid to the problems of LDDCs, progress in devising and implementing specific measures in their favor is quite modest.[36] In UNCTAD, for the time being this, to a great extent, is due to the absence of concrete results in favor of the developing countries as a whole, a fact that is only incidentally reflected in the non-implementation of measures related to LDDCs.

Socialist Countries in UNCTAD

The socialist countries came to the Geneva Conference to air their grievances against import-export restrictions and discriminatory cold war trade policies perpetuated against them by the developed countries.[37] They contended that the proposals and demands of developing countries related only to the financial and trade practices of developed market economies, and therefore did not apply to them. Gradually,

---

exceeding 20%, and a share of manufacturing in GDP of 10% or less. The Committee for Development Planning suggested that the following countries "could be classified" as LDDCs: from Africa—Botswana, Burundi, Chad, Dahomey, Ethiopia, Guinea, Lesotho, Malawi, Mali, Niger, Rwanda, Somalia, Sudan, Tanzania, Uganda and Upper Volta; from Asia and Oceania—Afghanistan, Bhutan, Laos, Maldive Islands, Nepal, Sikkim, Western Samoa and Yemen; from the Caribbean—Haiti.

35. TD/B/327 (30 Sep. 1970), p. 87.

36. TD/B/309/Add.1 (16 Jul. 1970), p. 9. As we have seen in the case of preferences, no concrete and definite measures could be adopted *ab initio* and the problem of LDDCs was to be taken care of in the dynamic context of a functioning GSP. In this instance, such measures would represent an additional cost to the donors.

37. For the background information on the problem see *Proceedings,* Vol. VI, pp. 113-273.

however, they came to realize that developing nations expected positive action and commitments from them also. Near the end of the Conference they assumed certain commitments, which were incorporated into the *Final Act*. In short, the Conference recommended that the socialist countries should take the trade needs of developing countries into consideration when fixing quantitative targets in their economic plans, and that they should expand their imports of primary products from these nations. It was also proposed that they should diversify and increase their imports of manufactures from the Third World and reduce and abolish customs on such goods. As a demonstration of their good will, the USSR, Czechoslovakia, Hungary and Poland assumed certain quantitative targets to be included in their economic plans.[38]

As UNCTAD's continuing machinery was set into motion, East-South trade was not at the top of the list of priorities. Whenever the matter was scrutinized, the developing countries would ask for an augmentation of their share in the total trade of socialist countries. Some of them would object to the uneven geographic distribution of this trade flow. The socialist countries would reply that their exchange of goods with developing nations was by far the most dynamic trade flow in world commerce, that they were concluding a number of new trade agreements with these countries, and that they could not import from certain developing countries which discriminated against them unless given the right to export under the same conditions as the developed market economies.[39] As regards the various financing targets advanced in UNCTAD, the socialist countries maintained that it was the imperialist powers who bore the responsibility for the economic underdevelopment of Africa, Asia and Latin America, and refused to accept any commitment to meet the recommendations in this sphere.[40]

Since the primary preoccupation of UNCTAD was the confrontation between the 77 and the B Group, the socialist countries appeared most of the time as marginal actors, extending support to the demands of the developing countries vis-à-vis the developed nations. They expected that the 77 should treat them differently from the developed market economies, and back their demands for the removal of discriminatory practices and the normalization of East-West trade. Yet, UNCTAD is

38. *Ibid.,* Vol. I, pp. 30, 35, 40, 94-95, 183.
39. For an extensive review of trade relations among countries having different economic and social systems consult TD/B/128 and Add.1-3 (21 Jul. 1967). Also, TD/B/307 (16 Jul. 1970).
40. At the Geneva Conference, the socialist countries abstained in the vote on recommendations pertaining to aid and terms of financing. *Proceedings,* Vol. I, pp. 43-44.

an organization in which the developing countries make concrete demands on the basis of the realities of the present international economic situation. The all-consuming preoccupation of the socialist countries with East-West trade, and their often vague pronouncements regarding their own obligations and actions in the field of development dissatisfied many developing countries. Furthermore, unlike in 1964 when the 77 were trying to exploit the rivalries between the two blocs, they faced an increasing cooperation between East and West in the economic and political fields.

As a result, a change in the attitude of the Group of 77 became evident at the ministerial meeting in Algiers. Those who drafted the Algiers Charter attempted to establish a balance of obligations by all countries in the solution of economic development problems. It was therefore felt that the demands addressed to the socialist countries had to be stated explicitly. Although some developing countries argued that the socialist countries should not be mentioned at all, the majority agreed that this could be interpreted as relieving them of any responsibility to participate in international endeavors in development.[41] Moreover, many developing countries were thinking only in terms of where and how they could sell their coffee, cocoa and similar products, and not necessarily in terms of historical responsibility, political systems and alignments.

The Algiers Charter stipulated that the expansion of East-West trade should not unfavorably affect the trading possibilities of developing countries.[42] It also asked that in their plans the socialist countries should provide for the "accelerated increase of their imports of primary commodities and manufactures and semi-manufactures originating from developing countries"; that they refrain from re-exporting the goods they import from the developing countries, without the permission of the latter; that they reduce the gap between the import and sales prices of products originating from developing countries; that they grant concessions "whose advantages are at least equivalent to the effects of preferences which would be granted by the developed coun-

41. One unsubstantiated rumor of how this action started is that China and the USA were pulling strings in order to embarrass the socialist countries of East Europe. Namely, those developing countries which were the staunchest advocates of explicit demands being incorporated into the Charter could be linked by deduction to the absent superpowers.

42. Note that this has been a controversial point in UNCTAD's deliberations. The socialist states argued that international trade flows were interdependent, and that consequently any increases in East-West trade would also stimulate the trade of developing nations. However, many countries, developed and developing, contended that if special measures were not undertaken, the increase of East-West trade might be detrimental to the expansion of the South's trade.

166

tries with market economies"; that payments arrangements with developing countries be multilateralized among the socialist countries of Eastern Europe, etc.[43]

The reaction of the socialist countries to this part of the Algiers Charter was, on the whole, unfavorable.[44] They felt that there were no historical, economic or political grounds for grouping them together with the developed capitalist nations. They had achieved their progress solely through the efforts of their own peoples, without exploiting others and they did not export capital in order to gain profits. They did not create the problems of the developing countries, and they therefore had no moral or material responsibility to them.[45]

In New Delhi, it was evident that many developing countries viewed the socialist nations also as their direct competitors in the western markets with regard to a number of commodities, particularly oil, timber, and certain food products. Moreover, they feared that the export-import capacities of the socialist countries would, to a growing degree, be absorbed by their economic ties with the West and vice versa, leaving less room to sustain and expand the economic relations of the developed East and West with the developing South. They continued to express doubts that automatic benefits would accrue to them from the increase in East-West trade.[46] Nevertheless, the New Delhi Conference took an important conceptual step forward when it agreed on the interdependence of trade flows, and decided that an increase of East-West trade "would affect positively the expansion of international trade as a whole, including the trade of developing countries, provided that necessary constructive measures to promote trade and economic relations with developing countries are undertaken by those two groups of countries." Therefore, it recommended that countries participating in East-West trade ensure through positive measures that trade between them does not unfavorably affect the trade of developing countries.[47]

As far as the socialist countries were concerned in New Delhi, a prerequisite for any consideration of East-South trade—and for a

43. See the Algiers Charter, TD/38 (3 Nov. 1967), pp. 4, 11-12.
44. Especially irritating to them was the reference to the continuing wide disparity between the import prices of goods from developing countries and their domestic selling prices in the socialist countries. The developing countries argued that the consumption of their products in Eastern Europe was discouraged by high domestic prices, while the socialist countries pointed out that this argument was irrelevant because in their economic plans the element of consumer demand played no part in determining import targets.
45. Representative of the USSR in the General Assembly (fall 1967), A/C.2/SR.1159, pp. 11-12.
46. *Proceedings, New Delhi*, Vol I, pp. 337-340.
47. Conference resolution 15(II), *ibid.*, p. 32.

better and more cooperative atmosphere with the Group of 77—was that they should not be lumped together with the B Group.[48] At least overtly, developing countries complied with this wish. On the substantive side, they agreed that there is an interdependence of trade flows, and they consented, in principle, to grant to the socialist states conditions for trade no less favorable than those that they give to the developed market economies. In return, the socialist countries accepted, in a qualified form, almost all the demands addressed to them by the Algiers Charter. It must be noted, however, that unlike at the Geneva Conference, the socialist countries did not undertake any quantitative commitments to increase their imports from the developing countries,[49] although they agreed to "take duly into consideration the trade needs of the developing countries when quantitative targets are fixed in their long-term economic plans," and to promote the diversification of the structure and geographic scope of this trade. They firmly refused to accept the demand "to eliminate the margin between the import price and the domestic selling price"; they felt that this and some other "provocative" demands were tactical maneuvers by the 77 aimed at pleasing the developed countries, or instigated by the latter. Also, the socialist countries continued their rather inflexible attitude toward the aid flow target and other financing issues, arguing that this was a matter between the developing countries and the developed countries only.

The socialist countries of Eastern Europe produce synthetics, they export primary products, manufactures and semi-manufactures, and they are becoming important traders as their economic isolation ends. Their capacity as donors is growing. The reforms in their economies, i.e., various incentives, cost-considerations assuming a central place in decision-making, abandonment of detailed central planning and al-

48. The Soviet Union, in its reservation on Conference decisions in financing expressed its disagreement with the idea of dividing all countries into "rich" and "poor", or into the "rich North" and the "poor South". *Ibid.*, p. 61.

49. Until almost the last day of the New Delhi Conference, it was not certain whether the socialist countries would announce their commitment to certain quantitative targets. Their ministers of foreign trade came to New Delhi near the end of the Conference, and rumor had it that they would announce such targets. "Preferences Hold the Key," *The Economic Times* (Bombay), March 23, 1968. Many hoped that this would happen during the crucial stages of negotiations and force the developed market economies to present more generous concessions of their own. The hopes failed to materialize. Two plausible explanations were offered for this. First, the situation in Czechoslovakia prevented the D Group from assuming a united stand even though the Soviet Union was willing to consider the targets; secondly, the fact that the B Group did not offer anything to the Group of 77 meant that the socialist countries did not have to make a significant concession of their own. It was preferable to have a vague commitment rather than quantified targets.

lowing various enterprises to operate freely within broad import-export targets, are softening the special features of planned economies and making it easier for them to be integrated into the prevailing practices of international trade. The argument that it would be difficult to expand East-South trade before the liberalization of East-West trade is losing strength precisely because of the expansion of East-West trade. As a consequence, the sideline position occupied by the socialist countries in UNCTAD since 1964, is slowly being eroded.

Although rather disappointed with the way East-West trade was pushed aside in 1964, the socialist countries viewed the birth of UNCTAD as a very positive development. They considered as very progressive the fact that the Geneva Conference adopted a set of principles on international trade, including the principle of East-West trade normalization. They thought of UNCTAD's continuing machinery as a vehicle which would refine these principles and gradually lead to their implementation. In fact, for some time after 1964 they expected that UNCTAD might fulfil the role of a world trade organization, and initiate policy recommendations and actions for the normalization of East-West trade. Yet, the going was heavy for the new principles because of determined opposition from the developed countries. Moreover, the question of East-West trade could not be even included on the agenda, for several years, because the B Group refused to discuss the substance of this matter in UNCTAD. And, when after a protracted institutional battle East-West trade finally found its place in UNCTAD,[50] it remained essentially a marginal issue and not a priority topic as the socialist countries had hoped for. Consequently, their expectations were diminished and they gradually lost some of their original interest in this organization. Moreover, they were disaffected with what they considered as the "bakshish" tactics of the developing countries, feeling that the entire relationship should be based on the principle of mutual advantages.

In a sense the socialist countries continue to face the dilemma of finding their proper place and role in UNCTAD. One obstacle in their way is the fixation with the problem of East-West trade, which from their own perspective appears central to international economic relations, while they apparently relegate to a secondary plane the fundamental issue of liberating the productive and social forces that exist in the developing areas. The socialist countries are making active and sincere efforts to increase and diversify their imports from the Third World, to initiate new and varied forms of economic cooperation with many developing countries, and to implement the various policy guide-

50. See Chapter XI for a discussion of this controversy.

lines to which they have committed themselves in UNCTAD. Yet, one cannot escape the impression that they act too cautiously in this international organization. They prefer to move in the safe realm of principles and declarations, while modalities and specific decisions are left completely at their discretion. They shun controversy and get upset whenever exposed to some pressure. They even appear moderate, if not conservative at times, in the UNCTAD context, often patterning their response on the basis of B Group actions.

It should be recalled that the socialist countries played a crucial role in the making of UNCTAD. They are in a position to assume once more the positive role of initiator and innovator, by underpinning their declarations with specific commitments, concrete substantive goals, quantified targets, and subjecting their actions to an effective implementation review. In this manner, among other things, they would create a politically competitive situation in UNCTAD, forcing the hand of the developed countries, and thus improving the chances for substantive progress on a much broader front.

Part II

CONCLUSION

The magnitude of the development problem and disagreement among
governments as to what should be done about it have imposed limits on
the achievements of the international organization. Working in an
environment highly unfavorable to its goals, UNCTAD could not in
the short run bring about the restructuring of the international economic
system, change the international division of labor, nor even create
significant obligations on the part of states toward the economic development of the Third World. Yet, the interaction of ideas and the
conflict of interests in UNCTAD have speeded up the evolution of
thinking in the field of trade and development. UNCTAD has played
a most crucial role in this process, as it has helped structure the political
communications among the developed and developing countries, allowed the developing countries to aggregate and articulate their demands forcefully, while compelling the developed countries to listen and
to respond to specific demands addressed to them.[1]

As we have amply demonstrated in the previous pages, UNCTAD
has been rather successful in opening up new grounds for collaboration
and in bringing about consensus evolution on a great variety of subjects.
Studies, long debates and discussions, and a long list of recommendations adopted, have not produced many concrete results so far. But,
conceptual and intellectual progress is essential if actions are to follow,
and UNCTAD has been laying the basis on which decisions to act can
be made, or even are already being made. Some significant progress in
understanding has been achieved on a number of issues, and ideas and
proposals formerly held heretical are being legitimized and gradually
accepted by many people in the developed countries.[2] As a result, the

1. See an excellent study by R. S. Walters, "International Organizations and
Political Communications: The Use of UNCTAD by the Less Developed Countries," forthcoming in *International Organization*.
2. The most notable instance of this is the Pearson Commission Report,
which, it has been argued, has lent respectability to UNCTAD's recommendations
in the West. In fact, there are a few recommendations in this report "which had
not previously been put forward in an identical or analogous form by UNCTAD."
D. H. Pollock, "Pearson and UNCTAD: A comparison," *International Develop-*

developed countries have been generally on the defensive, no longer able to dismiss the majority of the demands of the developing countries as unrealistic and irresponsible, and many of their decisions have been influenced to varying degrees by UNCTAD's outputs. Moreover, the existence of UNCTAD has helped usher in modifications in the orientation and policies of certain international organizations. These organizations are engaging in new activities, their orientation has been changing in the direction of the needs of the developing countries, even their terms of reference are being gradually adjusted to take account of the whole new dimension brought about through the articulation of Third World demands. This is obviously an important, though indirect qualitative change that can be attributed to UNCTAD and the forces behind it.

On the other hand, the process of consensus building in UNCTAD has usually been excruciatingly slow,[3] the decisions embodying consensus were in many instances burdened with qualifications, were too general, or depended for implementation on the voluntary action of states, while those decisions directly linking the consensus in principle with action and implementation were most difficult to obtain. These two problems, speeding up the consensus building, and establishing a firmer link between UNCTAD's decisions and their implementation, loom large in this organization. These are however the issues that shall be discussed in the chapters that follow.

---

ment Review, Autumn 1970. In an annex, the author gives a comparative list of excerpts from the Pearson Commission Report and selected UNCTAD documents.

3. At least part of the difficulties could be attributed to those directly involved, foreign trade and financing ministries' officials, economists, bankers, experts, etc., who may suffer from the constraints of their professions and of the system which they help run and according to which they have learned their trade. These professional drawbacks often prevent them from perceiving things in a politically imaginative and innovative way. When they do, however, vested interests of the countries that they represent restrain their initiative.

PART THREE

The Institutionalization of UNCTAD

> With the requisite good will, the creakiest of international machinery will
> operate fairly satisfactorily. Without that good will, the best machinery will
> fail to produce the desired results.[1]

During the Geneva Conference representatives from the developed
countries often argued that a new international organization should not
be established if the major trading nations did not exhibit a commitment
to its purposes and goals and if they opposed its creation. The developing countries, on the other hand, asserted that a competent institutional framework was a prerequisite for action in the field of trade
and development. They reasoned that the international system and
policies of governments are dynamic; therefore, a new organization in
an area ridden with controversy could contribute to propitious policy
changes.[2] Both viewpoints contained some degree of truth: the lack of
political will on the part of the developed countries caused UNCTAD
to be less than prolific in the substantive sphere; but, as we have seen,
a number of new policies and principles are receiving recognition or
are on the way toward implementation—precisely because the developing countries now have UNCTAD as the institutional focus for
the promotion of their demands.

When states agree on the goals to be attained, they usually attempt to
create an efficient machinery best suited to their needs. Such was not
the case at the Geneva Conference where the views of North and South
were polarized on matters of substance. The result was that UNCTAD
was born in an unfavorable political atmosphere as an institutional
compromise. The developed countries generally considered it an un-
wanted intruder, to be kept in a state of institutional weakness and
underdevelopment. The developing countries, on the other hand, saw it

1. Report of the Group of Experts, *op. cit., Proceedings,* Vol. V, p. 401.
2. The reader should recall our discussion in Chapter II. The developing
countries dramatically emphasized the institutional question at the Geneva Conference only after it became clear that there would be no breakthrough on substantive issues. The argument held was that permanent machinery was the only
way to continue efforts at agreement on measures and policies which would make
it possible to implement the objectives of the Final Act.

as just a point of departure from which to proceed step by step to an international organization which would fully correspond to their needs and goals. A paragraph in General Assembly resolution 1995 (XIX) left the institutional question open-ended:

> The Conference will review, in the light of experience, the effectiveness and further evolution of institutional arrangements with a view to recommending such changes and improvements as might be necessary. To this end it will study all relevant subjects, including matters relating to the establishment of a comprehensive organization based on the entire membership of the United Nations system of organizations to deal with trade and with trade in relation to development.

It does allow for institutional review as and when needed and also for the potential creation of a comprehensive trade and development organization.

The developing countries assume that a bigger and stronger institution will contribute more to the achievement of their own goals, and they continuously urge that UNCTAD be vested with additional powers and its scope widened. The developed countries find it difficult to control UNCTAD, both on the secretariat level and on the intergovernmental level and generally feel that their participation in this organ is more of a burden than anything else. As a result, they prefer to see it limited institutionally to the lowest common denominator of agreement—as elaborated in General Assembly resolution 1995 (XIX).

In Part III we shall focus on the evolution of UNCTAD as an organization—that is, its institutionalization. Institutionalization is here taken to mean the consolidation of the machinery, changes in its prerogatives, and the acquisition of new responsibilities. The principal questions that will be asked are the following: (1) What is UNCTAD's place and status in the family of international organizations? (2) Have UNCTAD's functions been amplified, and have its methods of work been improved in order to make it more effective and powerful? (3) Has the scope of UNCTAD's activities expanded—i.e., what instances of task expansion have been recorded? The overall question, in short, is whether UNCTAD bears a greater resemblance today to the image of the institution that the developing countries desire than it did when it started.

176

Chapter VIII

UNCTAD WITHIN THE UNITED NATIONS

The relationship between UNCTAD and its parent body, the General Assembly, has essentially been a troublefree and complementary one. The General Assembly has not engaged in any detailed supervision of UNCTAD's activities, nor has it attempted to resolve specific issues from UNCTAD's agenda. Its role has centered mainly around giving guidelines of a general nature to the Board and its subsidiary bodies, and in this manner it has partly filled the vacuum created by a three to four year gap separating the UN Conferences on Trade and Development. It has also been used as a political forum, to dramatize certain unresolved problems of UNCTAD and to generate additional political pressure when necessary.[1]

UNCTAD's relations with the ECOSOC, on the other hand, have not been wholly free of controversy. And to this problem we turn our attention now.

It is only because of the pressure from the smaller powers at the San Francisco Conference that ECOSOC was elevated to the status of a principal organ of the United Nations.[2] However, neither the United Nations nor ECOSOC was allowed by its principal members from the West to play a significant role in world economic relations. As we have already pointed out, the policy of the western powers was to keep sensitive matters of international trade and finance within the purview of those international organizations which they fully dominated. Efforts in the early 1950's to discuss in ECOSOC a global approach to such questions as employment stability, industrial production, commodity prices and economic growth were effectively blocked by the United States,[3] and arguments that the United Nations is the proper forum for decisions on economic matters affecting all countries went unheeded. Seeing that little could be achieved in the central UN organs, where

1. For a very thorough study of the legislative history and institutional developments in UNCTAD since the Geneva Conference consult D. Cordovez, "UNCTAD: From Confrontation to Strategy," mimeo.
2. See Townley, op. cit., p. 217.
3. Haas, Tangle of Hopes, op. cit., p. 127.

consensus did not even exist on the proposition that economic development was a major problem, the developing countries pressed for the creation of regional economic commissions in addition to the one set up for Europe. It was in spite of western opposition that ECAFE and ECLA, and eventually ECA, were established. Although set up by ECOSOC, these commissions began to act in a quasi-autonomous manner, submitting annual reports on their activities and plans to their parent body.[4] The moving of developing countries to their own regional forums weakened the already shaky role of ECOSOC. It also became clear that the developing countries would not always respect the recommendations of ECOSOC since it did not represent their interests, being small in size and overshadowed by the big western powers.[5] When dissatisfied, they would simply take matters to the Second Committee of the General Assembly to obtain a different ruling. It was in the late 1950's when the pressure for institutional changes began to mount that the developed countries tried to revive and activate ECOSOC as the central UN organ to deal essentially with problems of economic development. They did not succeed.

In Geneva in 1964 the developing countries attempted to sidetrack ECOSOC and to limit its role but did not have the strength to do so. Yet, they succeeded in preventing it from becoming UNCTAD's parent body, which further undermined its status as one of the principal organs of the UN and reduced its prestige. This uneasy compromise reflected the desire of developed countries to preserve the central position for ECOSOC in face of the developing countries' determined drive to have UNCTAD endowed with all the necessary powers to deal with the problems of economic development. As explained in Chapter II, UNCTAD was established by the General Assembly, through its

4. See R. Gregg, "Program Decentralization through Regional Economic Commissions," in G. Mangone, *UN Administration of Economic and Social Problems* (New York: Columbia University Press, 1966), pp. 234-239. Although the staffs of regional commissions are units of the Department of Economic and Social Affairs at Headquarters, the developing countries tried to enhance their independence. The drive for decentralization on the secretariat level gained momentum in the early 1960's when regional commissions assumed an enlarged operational role in the field of technical assistance. See W. R. Malinowski, "Centralization and Decentralization in the United Nations Economic and Social Activities," in *International Organization* (1962), Vol. XVI, No. 3.

5. At that time, ECOSOC still had 18 members. According to an unwritten convention, the Big Four were always elected and were *de facto* permanent members. The western powers were usually able by various means to manipulate some of the ECOSOC members so as to prevent decisions contrary to their policies. This caused the center of gravity on development to move first to regional economic commissions and then to the Second Committee of the General Assembly.

power to create subsidiary organs (Article 22); this meant that it was *sui generis,* neither a specialized agency based on a classical model, nor an economic body formed by and responsible to ECOSOC. The developed countries felt that it was against the UN Charter for UNCTAD not to be under ECOSOC, but their interpretation of the Charter provisions did not meet with widespread support. In fact, the Group of 77 contended that ECOSOC should assume only "residual functions" in the field of trade and development. This is one of the reasons for the continuing controversy on the UNCTAD-ECOSOC relationship.

According to General Assembly Resolution 1995 (XIX), the Board reports to the General Assembly through ECOSOC. For the B Group this meant that ECOSOC was to supervise the Board and UNCTAD, while for the 77 it meant that ECOSOC should act only as a "post office" to transmit the Board's reports to the General Assembly without making any recommendations as to their contents. The latter viewpoint generally appears to have prevailed so far and ECOSOC in fact has performed a perfunctory function in this respect. When a Board report is considered in ECOSOC, delegates avoid going into substance and details because soon thereafter it is to be on the agenda of the Second Committee of the General Assembly. A brief debate and a short resolution to transmit the report to the General Assembly is the customary procedure in ECOSOC, although it may occasionally express its opinion, as it did in 1967 on the preparations for the New Delhi Conference. Whereas it may have appeared on the surface that a detente between ECOSOC and UNCTAD had set in, this was hardly so. The underlying problem as to which of the two UN organs should occupy the central position for the coordination of international policies on trade and related problems of economic development was not solved.

It may be recalled that at the Geneva Conference the developing countries argued that UNCTAD should be endowed with extensive coordinating powers and with overall responsibility in the field of trade and development. The developed countries wanted to keep this role exclusively for ECOSOC; for according to their interpretation of the UN Charter, ECOSOC was the principal UN organ for maintaining order and coordination in the sphere of economic and social activities.[6] The provision adopted by the Geneva Conference accommodates both viewpoints. UNCTAD is:

> generally to review and facilitate the coordination of other institutions within the UN system in the field of international trade and related problems of

---

6. For an extensive discussion of ECOSOC's role see W. Sharp, *The United Nations Economic and Social Council* (New York: Columbia University Press, 1969), pp. 94 ff.

economic development, and in this regard to cooperate with the General Assembly and the ECOSOC, with respect to performance of their responsibilities for coordination under the Charter of the United Nations.[7]

The developing countries were accused of disregarding the Charter provisions by denying the coordinating powers and functions of ECOSOC, reinterpreting the Charter as vesting the General Assembly with all responsibility for economic and social matters, and encouraging UNCTAD to take over the work and functions of other bodies rather than trying to coordinate with them.[8] The issue was primarily that of influence. ECOSOC's membership was limited and the developing countries did not have an absolute majority there until its recent expansion, and in their opinion the key offices of the Department of Economic and Social Affairs were staffed by officials adhering to the western point of view.

Before we turn to the outstanding controversy on the respective roles of ECOSOC and UNCTAD in the preparation of the second Development Decade, it is relevant to briefly draw attention to UNCTAD's budget and the location of its secretariat, which are of importance for the understanding of UNCTAD's situation in the UN. We shall also speak of relations between international organizations in the field of economic and social development.

The Location of UNCTAD Headquarters

At the Geneva Conference, the developed countries argued that the secretariat for the continuing machinery ought to be part of the Department for Economic and Social Affairs (ESA), while the developing nations asked for an independent secretariat. The compromise provides for a separate unit which is nonetheless an integral part of the Secretariat of the United Nations, but in no way subordinate to the Department of Economic and Social Affairs.[9] Since the developing countries did not secure a fully independent status for the UNCTAD secretariat, it could be expected that a campaign would be waged to remove it from the New York Headquarters and to place it in a milieu more conducive for independent action and growth.[10] The question of the secretariat's

7. General Assembly resolution 1995 (XIX).
8. See Kotschnig, *op. cit.,* pp. 30 ff.
9. General Assembly resolution 1995(XIX) does provide for close cooperation and coordination between the UNCTAD secretariat at the Department for Economic and Social Affairs, a provision requested by the developed countries. (See Chapter XIII for our discussion of the UNCTAD secretariat.)
10. The influence of the United States and the daily competition and strife with other units of the UN Secretariat were considered undesirable. Subjective motivations also played a role. Many international civil servants and delegates

location occupied two sessions of the Board and *de facto* prevented the consideration of substantive issues. Most developed countries, with the exception of France which was allied with the 77 and the socialist states (because of its traditional preference for Geneva), put up stiff opposition to any move from New York.

Once the decision was taken to transfer UNCTAD's headquarters to Geneva,[11] a liaison office was still maintained in New York to coordinate and cooperate with the other units of the UN Secretariat, and informally to test the pulse of the central UN organs. The division for financing related to trade of the UNCTAD secretariat was also left in New York because of the proximity of international monetary and financial institutions located in Washington; it was later merged with the liaison office. A small part of the UNCTAD Secretary General's office was also kept in New York as a separate unit.

The transfer of UNCTAD to Geneva was important to its development. On the intergovernmental level, the political winds of the General Assembly that sway UNCTAD are significantly reduced by the simple fact that the same men are not engaged in both forums.[12] The new

---

consider New York highly unfavorable not only for "biological survival", but also for independent status because of the "role" (official or unofficial) of the host country.

11. The initial decision of the Board (passed by vote) was to have UNCTAD headquarters located in Geneva. However, there was often xenophobic opposition from the Genevese population to having yet another international organization in their midst and the matter had to be reconsidered. Rome was the most serious candidate, and Italy fought very hard to have UNCTAD there. But after the strategic moment for the vote was lost, the number of city candidates mushroomed. London, Accra, Lagos, Addis Ababa and Mexico City were proposed. Many developing countries requested a site in the Third World, which should provide a more "salubrious" atmosphere for UNCTAD's functioning. In the end Geneva won the vote anyway, being technically and practically the most convenient location; besides, the Swiss government finally gave its assurance that UNCTAD would be welcome. See Cordovez, "The Making of UNCTAD," *op. cit.*, pp. 321-323, summary records of the Board, TD/B/70 (Aug. 1966) and TD/B/L.65 (15 Oct. 1965).

12. One of the arguments for keeping UNCTAD in New York was that if it were to succeed, most of its decisions would have to be political rather than mainly economic. Therefore, its headquarters should be established at the center of political activity. However, the greater politicization of UNCTAD's work which would probably have resulted in New York might not have been beneficial for the majority of highly technical matters on its agenda. Note, however, that politics follow the subject matter and that UNCTAD politics are considered as exaggerated by many who are used to the relaxed functional style of the Geneva scene prior to 1965. For the impact of UNCTAD on the number, life style and composition of permanent missions in Geneva see J. Siotis, "Les Missions Permanentes à Genève et la CNUCED." A preliminary report (Geneva: Carnegie Endowment, 1968).

location for the UNCTAD secretariat was meant to boost its operational autonomy, among other things by removing it from ESA as well as from the UN Headquarters administration, and thus reducing the opportunities for organizational and jurisdictional disputes and administrative interference.

The UNCTAD secretariat, however, remains a part of the UN Secretariat and it cannot extricate itself completely from the various links and obligations that this entails. The Secretary-General of UNCTAD is subordinate to the Secretary-General of the United Nations, who also appoints him. When some important decision is taken or some kind of a special authorization given, this is done by the Secretary-General of the United Nations himself.[13] The UNCTAD secretariat does not have the power to hire and promote its personnel (although in this respect it is much better off than the regional economic commissions, which have to go through the ESA first, before arriving to the final authority at the Headquarters). In fact, for internal administrative purposes it is considered as a department of the UN Secretariat. Nonetheless, the UNCTAD secretariat has, so far, enjoyed a large degree of *de facto* operational autonomy. This was partly due to the nature of UNCTAD's budget, a matter which will be discussed in the next section. It was also a result of the ability of the UNCTAD secretariat and in particular of Prebisch to exploit the objective circumstances and resist the determined efforts of the larger UN bureaucratic framework to suppress or hamper any attempts at decentralization. Tight centralized administrative control from the Headquarters may have merits from the point of view of bureaucratic efficiency, and the order and allocation of scarce resources, yet in the final analysis it leads to a substantive control of a given department and decreases its flexibility. The UNCTAD secretariat has therefore been hard pressed to preserve what operational autonomy it had acquired from being eroded. In this sense, it finds itself at a disadvantage when compared to UNIDO which is in Vienna, because it has to face the outpost of the UN Headquarters Secretariat, namely the European Office of the United Nations.

13. For example, when the question arose whether UNCTAD's secretariat could service the Algiers Conference, this had to be cleared by U Thant. Note that Prebisch consulted U Thant on legal and political matters, but was given full autonomy in the economic sphere. This was sometimes dubbed as "intellectual autonomy". Prebisch and De Seynes cooperated on many occasions, but took no orders from each other.

At the Geneva Conference, some developing countries argued that while the United Nations would carry all the expenses of the proposed machinery, the new organization and its secretariat should have an appropriate budget of their own and complete autonomy in its use.[14] These initial, somewhat unrealistic, proposals were based on the expectation that UNCTAD would have an independent secretariat. In the negotiations that followed, the main issue actually was whether a separate UNCTAD section should be opened in the UN budget, or the financial estimates for UNCTAD be simply incorporated in the UN budget (which is not arranged by departments, but by objects of expenditure, e.g. salaries, travel, etc., covering all organizational units) and identified in a separate annex, as advocated by the developed countries.[15] Eventually, it was decided that separate budgetary provision should be opened for UNCTAD expenditures within the regular UN budget.[16] Members of UNCTAD are not assessed with particular reference to UNCTAD, although those that are not members of the United Nations make contributions according to the UNCTAD appropriations section (the same method was already being applied to the International Court of Justice).

Some observers have argued that UNCTAD resembles a specialized agency because there is comparatively little control over its budget by the General Assembly and over its budget's administration by the UN Headquarters Secretariat. These remarks were inspired by the early years of UNCTAD, when as a "baby" organization it had a relatively smooth sailing through the budgetary maze of the United Nations. Gradually, however, the attitude of both the General Assembly and of the Headquarters Secretariat became more inquisitive and controlling, basically reflecting a considerably tougher stance of the principal budget contributors.[17] Nonetheless, the "budget within a budget" has proved of considerable practical value to UNCTAD, in

14. *Proceedings,* Vol. I, p. 252.

15. For the UN budgetary process see J. D. Singer, *Financing International Organization* (The Hague: Martinus Nijhoff, 1961).

16. Other UN organs having separate budgetary provisions are the Office of the UN High Commissioner for Refugees, the International Court of Justice and (following the UNCTAD precedent) UNIDO.

17. In 1966, i.e., the first year in which UNCTAD operated at full strength, the expenses amounted to $5.4 million. In 1969 the expenses were $7.9 million ($156.7 mil. for the UN as a whole). Appropriations for 1970 were $8.9 million ($168.4 mil. for the UN). Estimates for 1971 were $10.7 million, later scaled down tot $10.0 million ($184.0 mil. for the UN). See UN doc. A/8006, p. XVII.

addition to the symbolic element of singling it out as a distinct entity within the UN institutional hierarchy.

The UNCTAD draft budget is prepared by the UNCTAD secretariat. During the preparations of the draft budget, the UNCTAD secretariat is not formally entitled to discuss it with governments; informal consultations do take place, however, at least with the most important delegations. On the intergovernmental level, the work program (number of posts, man-months needed for various projects, etc.) which serves as the basis for the compilation of the budget, is submitted to the Board for information and comments.[18] And although the Board does not engage in a real budgetary scrutiny of figures, this offers the first opportunity to governments to express themselves publicly on UNCTAD's program of work and the projected needs.[19] Many delegations usually reserve their position until the Fifth Committee of the General Assembly considers the UN budget as a whole. However, it is important that the initial considerations be undertaken by the delegates who are familiar with UNCTAD's work, and that a degree of political support for various items be built up already at the level of the Board. Thus, for example, the Advisory Committee on Administrative and Budgetary Questions (ACABQ) takes into consideration what happens in the Board when it engages in the trimming exercise. Once the debate on the UN budget is opened in the Fifth Committee of the General Assembly, the fact that the UNCTAD section is clearly visible makes it possible for the delegations to identify the requests of the UNCTAD secretariat, and for the developing countries to defend resources sought for trade and development.

When the UN budget is approved by the General Assembly, the UN Controller allots the UNCTAD share directly to UNCTAD's Secretary-General, to be administered in accordance with the normal UN practices. Although the UNCTAD Secretary-General does not have the

18. Before the work program goes to the Board, it has to be approved by the UN Controller. (One should differentiate between the budgetary process and the scrutiny of the work program, on the one hand, and the rules of procedure on financial implications, on the other. Before any proposal involving expenditures is approved, the UNCTAD Secretary-General is to circulate a report on the estimated costs involved and the administrative and budgetary implications, with reference to existing authorizations and appropriations. The developed countries usually object to the financial implications of various resolutions that are passed or studies that are proposed. In return for their consent, they often obtain substantive concessions.)

19. At one time, the UNCTAD secretariat submitted figures of the draft budget to the Board. This is done no longer, primarily because it was not possible by the time the work program had to be finalized to have all the necessary elements to prepare the draft budget. The new practice reflects also the hardening of the UN budgetary procedure.

freedom to use the appropriations at his discretion (he is formally supervised by the UN Controller and is supposed to use the monies within the approved allocations under each item), he enjoys autonomy within these broad limits. The fact that the UNCTAD Secretary-General has the available funds at his disposal means a great deal in terms of more efficient daily administration, greater flexibility and enhanced autonomy. The situation can best be understood by envisaging how UNCTAD would have fared had its expenditures been simply included into the UN budget. First, some of its funds (primarily those for conference services and printing) would have been allotted directly to the European Office of the United Nations. Not only would have this affected negatively its efforts at self-identity, but would have decreased its bargaining power vis-à-vis the European Office in terms of services that it wants (the power which it now has because it reallots the money itself), and in fact curtailed its autonomy because for any related expenditure the approval of the European Office would have been needed. Secondly, all other expenditures would have been authorized by the UN Secretariat at the Headquarters. Thirdly, since UNCTAD's costs would not have been identifiable within the overall UN budget, some of its resources could be easily shifted to other sorts of expenditures.[20] Moreover, in that sort of a situation, one is never quite sure how big a slice of the available resources he will obtain for a given purpose. The strategic location of a given department (or individual) in relation to those who allot funds may often be of greater importance for obtaining monies than the substantive value of a request by another department.

Duplication/Coordination Problem

The UN network in the field of economic and social development has been described as a pluralistic system. Less politely, it has been labelled a decentralized, feuding and "imperialistically" inclined group of bodies, not prepared to accept guidance and directives from any policy center. Constitutional provisions and agreements on their mutual relations did little to remedy an essentially anarchic situation between the specialized agencies and the UN; the various organizations tended to engage in disputes over their respective competence.

The problem was essentially twofold: to determine the respective

20. Note that the new budgetary procedures under consideration include, for example, a proposal that UN regional economic commissions be treated in a similar manner as UNCTAD and UNIDO. The program budgeting would make it possible for governments to have an insight into the cost of these commissions.

fields of jurisdiction and to coordinate the efforts of the various organizations in the same general field.[21]

The coordinating efforts were overshadowed by the existing functional decentralization. Actually, the meaning of "coordination" was not quite clear, and in practice it appeared to mean no more than consultations or liaison.[22] ECOSOC's efforts at coordination remained basically ineffective, with little impact on the activities of either the specialized agencies or the United Nations. During its first year ECOSOC established the Administrative Committee on Coordination (ACC). A body at the senior secretariat level, the ACC was to provide ECOSOC with reviews of inter-agency programs; it was to be chaired by the Secretary-General of the UN and composed of executive heads of various agencies and commissions. Also a Sessional ECOSOC Committee on Coordination was established at the intergovernmental level.[23] The ACC is the highest inter-secretariat forum for the examination of jurisdictional disputes between agencies—a "body of elders" operating on the basis of persuasion.[24] Attempts are made to iron out disputes through informal inter-agency agreements, secretariat initiatives, and often through joint working groups or committees. It is interesting to mention that coordination activities in recent years have achieved significant proportions.[25] However, the time and resources

21. J. G. Hadwen and J. Kaufmann, *How United Nations Decisions Are Made* (Leyden: A. W. Sijthoff, 1960), p. 22.

22. It is argued that lack of coordination involves a waste of resources, overburdening of governments, proliferation of conflicting and repetitive voices, multiplication of conferences, and so on. Gardner, "The United Nations Conference on Trade and Development," *op. cit.*, p. 128. But in a situation where "coordination" is of a "consultative-persuasive nature" rather than a "vertical diktat" these phenomena are to be expected. See T. Meron, "Administrative and Budgetary Coordination by the General Assembly," in Mangone, *op. cit.*, p. 38. See General Assembly resolution 2188(XXI) (13 Dec. 1966) which outlines the improvements needed to avoid program duplication and to ensure coordination in economic, social and technical cooperation.

23. The ACC reports are reviewed on the intergovernmental level by ECOSOC and its Coordination Committee. More recently the Committee on Program and Coordination (CPC) was established, which has a broader membership than ECOSOC.

24. Many observers have said that the main function of the ACC is to use sweet words to conceal the total lack of coordination. Others have noted that the heads of various agencies treat each other in a suspicious manner, as if they were representing sovereign states vitally concerned with their spheres of influence. See A. Schonfeld, *The Attack on World Poverty* (New York: Random House, 1960), p. 187.

25. These activities occur on three levels: the secretariat level (the ACC system and De Seynes' meetings with the executive secretaries of regional commissions); the intergovernmental level (Coordination Committee of ECOSOC, CPC, and enlarged CPC); and the mixed level (meetings of the president and

expended on coordination appear to be in inverse proportion to results; the substantive activities appear to be less and less coordinated, while the effect of coordination is often that no project can be carried out by one agency alone. Thus, the question arises in the minds of those directly involved, and especially international civil servants, whether a certain amount of duplication is not preferable to the paralysis which appears to be emerging from "excessive" coordination.

Governments and international civil servants, each in their own way contribute to the duplication/coordination difficulties. It is said that neighboring states usually harbor ill feelings toward each other. In like manner, the secretariats of international organizations with similar and/or overlapping terms of reference are occasionally on less than cordial terms; they compete with each other for financing (especially technical assistance funds), for political support for their work programs, projects, personnel, etc.[26] They often believe that their own activity is the most important one, purposely ignore other organizations' activities and studies, and jealously guard their jurisdictional domain while trying to expand it as much as possible by acquiring additional responsibilities. When secretariats are on good terms, they may do a research project together, help each other service meetings, engage in informal consultations and even join forces to counter some government pressures.[27] Secretariats headed by men of complementary outlooks are more likely to cooperate.[28] Secretariats and departments within the United Nations usually make common cause against an

---

vice-presidents of ECOSOC with the ACC). Note also that the situation was somewhat improved by EPTA and the Special Fund, which managed to coordinate the activities of various bodies to a certain degree by establishing UN standards as a prerequisite for the disbursements of their resources. Money may be the best coordinator yet, but there is the inherent danger of major contributors attempting to impose their policy preferences under the guise of coordination.

26. For instance, an UNCTAD official complained that various departments in the UN secretariat deal with similar matters, regardless of whether they are sufficiently competent in a particular field. Therefore, it was concluded that there is a need to advertise UNCTAD's capabilities to governments, not only against GATT but also against other parts of the UN Secretariat, an undertaking that would not be necessary were all of them to adhere strictly to those matters which are within their competence.

27. They all share in the frustration caused when sovereign nation states place obstacles in the path of the more efficient functioning of international organizations; in that sense they belong to the conspiracy against the parochial representatives of governments.

28. Personal links also play an important role. For example, the fact that both Prebisch and some of his close collaborators in the UNCTAD secretariat had a background in ECLA assured a close cooperative relationship between the two organizations.

"outsider", e.g. a specialized agency; this, however, does not prevent them from engaging in "civil confrontations" the rest of the time.[29]

In the background of problems caused by international civil servants one usually finds ambiguous directives that international organizations receive from governments. In addition to the objective causes—such as the different views of the developed and developing countries on the role of various international organizations in the field of economic development, or the different memberships of various institutions—we can note that some governments consider duplication and overlapping as functional to their goals (either to stall and confuse, or to spur the activity of the organization that feels challenged). One also sometimes notes that delegations from the same country in different international forums advocate different approaches and make inconsistent demands, maybe because of lack of coordination on the home front (where various ministries cannot agree among themselves or lack means of coordination between each other),[30] or because delegates to a given organization become loyal to it, acquire a vested interest in its performance and want to see it in the center of the stage. Hence, it has been argued that many difficulties could be alleviated if governments would only coordinate the activities of their representatives in different international organizations.[31] Actually, as early as 1947, the General

29. Thus, for example, numerous jurisdictional disputes have occurred between the UNCTAD secretariat and the Department of Economic and Social Affairs at the Headquarters. This in spite of an informal agreement reached during the closing days of the Geneva Conference among Prebisch, De Seynes (the Under-Secretary for Economic and Social Affairs), and Narasimhan (the Under-Secretary for General Assembly Affairs) on the division of responsibilities between the two secretariats. (The agreement was subsequently approved by U Thant.) Part of the problem is caused by the fact that the developing countries continue to ask that UNCTAD infringe upon what have been traditional though neglected spheres of ECOSOC and Department's activities. The more notable instances of jurisdictional conflict occurred in the field of invisibles (shipping, insurance, tourism) where the Department of Economic and Social Affairs felt that the UNCTAD secretariat was intruding into its domain. The dispute was solved through an agreement negotiated with De Seynes at the New Delhi Conference which placed insurance, maritime shipping, and ports responsibilities in UNCTAD, while ESA kept coastwise and shortsea services and inland transport. The competence of both was recognized in tourism, although in 1970, the Secretary-General of UNCTAD agreed that his secretariat's activities for tourism be transferred to ESA. Another serious bone of contention was the substantive support for technical assistance in shipping and port improvement; this category was finally transferred to the UNCTAD secretariat and integrated with its program of research on shipping and ports.

30. See Hadwen and Kaufmann, op. cit., p. 23. There are differences in the way that specialists in various areas and foreign ministry officials perceive problems. This often results in contradictory instructions to representatives in different agencies.

31. Meron, op. cit., p. 44.

Assembly called on member governments to achieve a coordinated policy among their delegations in the United Nations and in the specialized agencies.[32]

The political implications of the duplication/coordination phenomenon have become very pronounced since UNCTAD was born. Two international organizations may overlap institutionally, legally and technically, but their outputs can vary significantly, depending on which coalition of countries is dominant, and on the quality and especially the organizational and political ideology of their staff. One of the implicit goals of UNCTAD and of the forces behind it was to intrude into the previously sacrosanct empires of various international bodies, whose principles and practices were not fully congenial to the goals of economic development, and whose outputs of interest to developing countries were either non-existent or insufficient. Furthermore, UNCTAD was intended as an antidote for the dispersion and overlapping of activities in this field, a synthesizer leading to a coordinated global approach. UNCTAD thus had to come into conflict with the vested interests of other organizations, which awoke to the fact that economic development had become one of their principal spheres of competence only in 1962, when the decision was taken to hold the Geneva Conference. Moreover, the developed countries who were attempting to preserve the jurisdiction of the traditional organizations, saw the duplication of UNCTAD's tasks by other bodies as one way to place obstacles in the path of the "rampant" majority of developing nations and their newly created forum. These jurisdictional problems can drain the energy and patience of the participants, and together with conflicting outputs and advice, the staggered consideration of the same subject by different bodies and the blurring of issues, can contribute to frustration, stalling and the postponement of substantive action. As a result, the duplication/coordination controversies in which UNCTAD was involved assumed strongly political overtones. We shall focus on two such prominent cases: first, UNCTAD's role in the second UN Development Decade; and, secondly, UNCTAD's relationship with GATT (though we shall discuss the latter issue in the next chapter since GATT is not within the UN system).

UNCTAD and the Second UN Development Decade

Experience of the first Development Decade has created a consensus that there is a need for a coordinated, centralized and planned approach to the

32. General Assembly resolution 125(II). If UNCTAD's group system were extended to other agencies and organizations, coordination on the governmental level could improve.

problem of economic development on the international level, a rationing and careful distribution of the limited resources available for this purpose, a general direction of the entire effort, and an overall scheme of interrelated measures.

Some members of the group of experts which analyzed the institutional issue prior to the Geneva Conference felt that the effectiveness of international efforts would be enhanced if an organization with "the necessary executive power and machinery" were established to consider the activities of multifarious organizations and give them positive guidance to enable them, in their limited fields, to function in harmony with the over-all policies designed to promote trade and development.[33] The developing countries wanted to ascribe this role to UNCTAD, while the West argued that this is an overarching concern which belongs to the UN as a whole, and especially to ECOSOC and most of the specialized agencies, and opposed any attempts to place UNCTAD in a "commanding position".[34] Most of the developed countries, who preferred a less assertive body more amenable to their control considered that the program and organizational ideology of UNCTAD, the alignment of states within it, and the nature of its secretariat, made it an undesirable candidate to lead in the preparation and execution of the second Development Decade.

Thus the problem of strategy formulation for the second Development Decade rekindled the unsettled institutional issue of the responsibilities of the General Assembly, ECOSOC and UNCTAD, and of their relationship within the UN hierarchy.[35] This problem overshadowed the substantive issues for a while, or—to put it more correctly—it masked the deeper problem of the specific responsibilities that nation-states should assume in promoting international economic development. A statement by the spokesman of the developing countries indicated their conviction that all attempts to preclude UNCTAD from playing an important role in the preparations of the second Development Decade stem from a clear-cut policy:

> to reduce the influence of UNCTAD, to deprive the organization of a leading role in the struggle against under-development and to concentrate inter-

---

33. *Proceedings*, Vol. V, p. 414. In this connection, it has been argued that coordination should no longer be considered purely as a procedure for settling jurisdictional and institutional disputes, but as a mechanism for harmonizing the various components of a program, i.e., various programs that constitute the development strategy. Cordovez, "UNCTAD: From Confrontation to Strategy," *op. cit.*, Chapter II, p. 28.

34. See, for example, Cordovez, "The Making of UNCTAD," *op. cit.*, p. 298. and Kotschnig, *op. cit.*, p. 33.

35. See Cordovez, "UNCTAD: From Confrontation to Strategy," *op. cit.*, pp. 32-38.

national action in institutions which possess neither its dynamism nor in-
dependance, and which do not have the same ability to view historical events
in a modern light.[36]

The Prebisch Report to the New Delhi Conference, titled "Towards a
Global Strategy for Development", was intended to stimulate the
Conference to contribute to the preliminary framework on an international development strategy for the 1970's and to elaborate the
elements within the sphere of competence of UNCTAD.[37] Although the
atmosphere in New Delhi was not favorable to discussion of a global
strategy, and the report was not considered, Prebisch's lines of thinking
were of central importance in the subsequent debates on the second
Development Decade.

Another of Prebisch's concerns was the role of UNCTAD in the
formulation and execution of development strategy, and his report was
an opening shot in the institutional battle. A certain amount of the
preparatory work on the second Development Decade was done by
ECOSOC's Committee for Development Planning, composed of non-
governmental experts [38] with the close collaboration of the Department
for Economic and Social Affairs. The expert approach and the lack of
visible progress, however, displeased most governments who thought
that the committee was approaching this matter as if it were a mere
econometric exercise. They resolved, therefore, that work should be
initiated on the policy level. In the summer of 1968, after the New
Delhi Conference, ECOSOC decided that its Economic Committee
should meet inter-sessionally to consider the problem.[39] The question
immediately arose as to what should be the role of UNCTAD's Board,
because in terms of the UN hierarchy it had only an ambiguous and, at
most, but a distant relationship with the Economic Committee of
ECOSOC. The developing countries argued that the Board could not
report to the Economic Committee, and since the Board was meeting

36. Remarks by the representative of Chile, TD/B/SR.182 (5 Feb. 1969).

37. General Assembly resolution 2218(XXI) (19 Dec. 1966) stressed that one
of the reasons for the slow progress during the first Development Decade was
the absence of a framework of international development strategy; the UN
Secretary-General was therefore asked to elaborate a preliminary framework
of such strategy for the 1970's. Resolution 2305(XXII) (13 Dec. 1967) called for
the preparation of the second Decade, *inter alia*, on the basis of the results of the
New Delhi Conference.

38. This committee was originally supposed to advise governments on planning,
but later its emphasis shifted to strategy for economic development and the designing of models for the world economy.

39. ECOSOC resolution 1356(XLV) (2 Aug. 1968). ECOSOC instructed its
Economic Committee to formulate an outline of international development policy,
incorporating concerted action by member states, and to make suggestions on
methods and means for its evaluation and implementation.

in September 1968, *inter alia*, to consider UNCTAD's contribution to the Second Development Decade, this had to be one of the issues on its agenda.

The background for the deliberations of the Seventh Board was set by a special report of Prebisch on the role of UNCTAD in the preparation and execution of the second Development Decade.[40] Prebisch based his report on the premise that although UNCTAD's sphere of competence was mainly in the field of trade and development, it was not possible to isolate these from the whole group of problems to be covered by a global strategy. He distinguished between a strategy spelling out the broad guidelines of intergovernmental action, and the plans to be drawn-up by various specialized agencies in their respective spheres of activity; he claimed that the latter should be subordinate to the former and not vice-versa, as had often been the case in the past. Prebisch furthermore claimed that the global character of the strategy for the Decade, even when limited to its purely economic aspects, required that all elements be taken into account at the same time, both in their formulation and execution.[41] He stressed the need for comprehensiveness and for a central body that would coordinate and guide the actions of various sub-centers and place them in proper perspective. Prebisch, however, left the question open as to which intergovernmental body was to undertake this task, especially in respect to reviewing the execution of goals and targets for the Decade.[42] Nonetheless, many interpreted the report as favoring UNCTAD as the intergovernmental body to examine the execution of the strategy. Alarm bells sounded in the specialized agencies and the UN departments, as well as in the capitals of various developed countries: UNCTAD was trying to assume the central institutional position and to dominate the planning of the second Development Decade, by ignoring the UN Charter and by exceeding its own jurisdictional competence!

In his speech to the Seventh Board, Prebisch begged them not to misinterpret his reports. Although he maintained that it was impossible to separate development strategy as a whole from the trade and financial measures which were within UNCTAD's jurisdiction, he did not advocate that his organization go beyond its terms of reference.[43]

40. See TD/B/186 (21 Aug. 1968).
41. *Ibid.*, p. 33.
42. Note that the report was much more specific on reviewing internal action in developing countries. It singled out regional economic commissions and other regional bodies, and possibly the use of independent experts. For some interesting proposals on this matter see M. F. Millikan, "Comments on a Procedure for Reporting and Evaluation of Development Progress during the Nineteen Seventies," E/AC.54/L.28 (22 Apr. 1968).
43. See TD/B/189, p. 7.

On the question of periodic reviews of policy execution, Prebisch mentioned basic analyses and reports, produced on the regional level, assessed by a group of experts, and communicated to "UNCTAD or ECOSOC, or to the combined attention of both".[44] As a matter of fact, it appears that Prebisch had in mind some sort of joint UNCTAD/ ECOSOC committee, which would act as a principal organ in the formulation and execution of the Development Decade.[45]

The developing countries were much more assertive. They stated that since UNCTAD has a coordinating function in the field of trade and development, it should play a central role not only in the planning of the strategy for the next Development Decade, but also in the major part of its execution, by putting into practice those items within its competence. Moreover, the developing countries argued that UNCTAD should be the organ to initiate and take action on the strategy, and that it should make recommendations to ECOSOC. The Group of 77 proposed that the Secretary-General of UNCTAD convene an inter-governmental group to assist him in his preparation for the Decade and formulation of proposals and objectives in the field of trade and development.[46] Most of the developed countries—particularly the United States, France and Great Britain—opposed the establishment of such a group, and reiterated their view that the UNCTAD discussion of the Decade strategy was inappropriate and premature in view of the fact that ECOSOC had assigned the main coordinating role to its Economic Committee.[47] They argued that such a group should not be convened until the UN family as a whole had defined its approach to the Decade. It was impossible to achieve a compromise, and the draft proposal of the developing countries was passed by a vote. A vain attempt to placate the developed countries was made by including a qualifying clause to the effect that the Secretary-General of UNCTAD should continue his preparatory work within this organization's compe-tence and with due regard to the activities of other UN organizations, the Board's deliberations and the role of ECOSOC's Economic Com-mittee.[48]

44. *Ibid.,* p. 13.
45. He also expressed sympathy for the proposal for a "World Development Council," consisting of distinguished international public figures, and serviced by an independent professional staff which would draw on the statistical, analytic and reporting services of the entire UN family. For the details of this interesting proposal made by M. F. Millikan, see E/ AC.54/L.28, *op. cit.,* pp. 5 ff.
46. See their draft resolution TD/B/L.129 (13 Sept. 1968) and Rev. 1 (21 Sept. 1968).
47. See the report of the Seventh Board (Sept. 1968) on this item, A/7214, pp. 53-57. See also *International Conciliation,* No. 574, (Sept. 1969), pp. 128-131.
48. The draft resolution was adopted by 33:0:15. Belgium, Greece, and Spain

Some of the sponsors of this resolution intended to use the intergovernmental group as a bargaining weapon in the General Assembly in order to extract a joint UNCTAD/ECOSOC body (which however was hardly acceptable to the developed countries because it implied equal coordinating powers for the two organs toward, for example, the specialized agencies), or some other compromise solution such as a committee in the General Assembly. Complex negotiations followed in the Second Committee. The representatives of the specialized agencies lobbied against UNCTAD's coordinating role; [49] the major developed countries continued their opposition and argued that UNCTAD's role should not be defined until the general directives of the Decade were established, while the socialist countries endorsed a central coordinating role for ECOSOC under the UN Charter.

A compromise emerged, whereby the General Assembly would ask ECOSOC to double the membership of its Economic Committee from 27 to 54, the extraordinary members to be designated by the President of the General Assembly annually until the completion of the preparatory work.[50] This enlarged body was to be called the Preparatory Committee for the Second Development Decade, and be responsible to the General Assembly, although reporting to it through ECOSOC.[51] In its work, the Committee was to be assisted by the Department of Economic and Social Affairs *and* by the UNCTAD secretariat, and was to meet as appropriate, both in New York and in Geneva. One of the

together with the 77 and the socialist countries voted for. The Nordic countries, the Netherlands, and F.R. Germany, although inclined to accept the demands of the 77 abstained for reasons of group solidarity. The paragraph on convening the intergovernmental group was adopted by 33:7:7. Belgium, Greece, the Netherlands, and Spain from the B Group voted for, while Australia, Canada, France, Italy, Japan, the United Kingdom and the United States voted against. (See A/7214, pp. 86-88).

49. As an observer put it, the specialized agencies feel annoyed even by the innocuous coordination that ECOSOC is exercising, and they were not too eager to see UNCTAD, its secretariat and the Group of 77 allied, preying on everybody in the role of coordinator.

50. General Assembly resolution 2411(XXIII) (17 Dec. 1968).

51. In 1966, also, a similar question arose as to whether the General Assembly or ECOSOC should be primarily responsible for the coordinating function, when the former decided to undertake a review of the economic and social activities of the UN. The West wanted this to be entrusted to ECOSOC's Committee for Coordination, while the developing countries proposed an *ad hoc* committee to be appointed by the Assembly. A compromise provided for the ECOSOC Committee to be enlarged by an additional 5 members, designated by the President of the Assembly. The Committee so constituted would be responsible to the Assembly and under its authority to ECOSOC. General Assembly resolution 2188(XXI) (13 Dec. 1966). See Cordovez, "The Making of UNCTAD," *op. cit.,* p. 311.

elements in the compromise was a paragraph on the role of the Board, which asked that it continue its efforts to reach agreement on the issues remitted to it by the New Delhi Conference and which are of "basic importance for the elaboration of the international development strategy for the 1970's." In this deal the developing countries apparently accepted that a basically ECOSOC body should be endowed with the central coordinating role in the preparation of the Decade, as re-compense for their increased participation.[52] They also agreed that in addition to states who are members of the UN, member states of the specialized agencies and IAEA should be eligible for membership of the Preparatory Committee. This meant that F.R. Germany could become a member of the committee, which would have been unacceptable to the socialist countries, who consequently voted against the resolution.[53]

When the B Group proposed F.R. Germany as one of its candidates for a seat on the Preparatory Committee, the socialist countries failed to submit their nominations and threatened to abstain from participating in the work of the committee. The Preparatory Committee could not be constituted, and UNCTAD's intergovernmental group remained as the only mechanism for the preparation of the Decade. According to the compromise reached in the General Assembly, UNCTAD's inter-governmental group was to be abolished in due time. The failure to constitute the Preparatory Committee led the developing countries (and especially those who were opposed to the compromise reached on the Preparatory Committee) to press for the convening of the intergovern-mental group.[54] All the B Group members (including those who usually do not participate even as observers in UNCTAD's labors) showed up

52. It is interesting that the developing countries did not appear very coor-dinated on this occasion. Some felt that ECOSOC should be the primary organ for coordination. This might have been related to their membership in ECOSOC, and it might also have been a desire for a compromise with the western group.

53. General Assembly resolution 2411(XXIII), 17 Dec. 1968. The D Group voted against the resolution because of the "illegal procedure of appointment" which made it possible for non-members of the UN to participate in one of its principal organs on an equal footing with its members. The socialist countries felt that this move was discriminatory against them, and especially against the German Democratic Republic. Our account is based on Cordovez, "UNCTAD: From Confrontation to Strategy," *op. cit.*, pp. 35-38.

54. Prebisch was delaying the convening of the intergovernmental group, fearing the injection of the East-West dispute in its work. It is interesting that throughout this period, both the western and socialist camps strongly pressed the developing countries to support their respective positions. At some points it even appeared that the developing countries would be drawn into the dispute and that their unity of action would be undermined. Yet, they maintained their concern for the speedy initiation of effective preparations for the Decade, and refused to have this tied to the controversy over West German seat in the Preparatory Committee.

195

in the intergovernmental group, not to discuss the substance of the development strategy but to demonstrate as a bloc against the group's existence. The "Big Four" of the B Group took an inflexible position against any substantive discussion until the Preparatory Committee was constituted. After a very short session, the intergovernmental group passed the entire matter to the Board, which discontinued the group's existence and took over responsibility for preparing UNCTAD's contribution to the second Development Decade. However, agreement could not be reached on the convening of the Board to proceed with the Decade work. The United States, France, F.R. Germany and the United Kingdom argued that the resumed session of the Board should not be held without explicit reference to the functioning and timetable of the Preparatory Committee. They thus attempted to assert the supremacy of the committee, and to prevent the Board from initiating its work until F.R. Germany obtained its seat.[55] Although the draft resolution did not explicitly link the Preparatory Committee's work and the convening of the Board in connection with the Decade, the text implied that the Board would not proceed independently or in an enhanced capacity. This was acceptable to all B Group members but the "Big Four" who pressed for a vote in order to underline their position, in spite of the requests by many delegations that there be no voting and that reservations be reflected in the summary records.[56] The amendment by the United States that the Board resume its eighth session only after the program of work and calendar of meetings of the Preparatory Committee had been established was defeated by a vote of 10:29:8, while the draft resolution of the 77 was adopted by 38:4:6.[57]

55. See TD/B/233 (21 Feb. 1969), pp. 8-9. The United States would not support any UNCTAD meetings (except those regularly scheduled) until the Preparatory Committee convened in New York and laid down guidelines, presumably for UNCTAD also to follow. Apparently, the "Big Four" in the B Group hoped that by delaying the resumed session of the Board they could enlist the support of the developing countries to have F.R. Germany placed on the Preparatory Committee. The 77 rejected delay, arguing that East-West quarrels did not belong in UNCTAD. "West Loses Vote in U.N. Aid Board," *The New York Times,* February 9, 1969.
56. It is interesting that these countries which always argued against voting in UNCTAD, made use of the voting procedure in this instance.
57. The conciliatory approach of the 77 won them the support of the moderates in the B Group, who generally sympathized and cooperated with the developing countries in their efforts to obtain a larger role for UNCTAD in the preparation of the second Development Decade. Voting in favor of the draft amendment were Australia, Germany, France, Greece, Italy, Japan, New Zealand, Spain, the United Kingdom, and the United States. Austria, Belgium, Canada, Denmark, Finland, the Netherlands, Sweden and Switzerland abstained. Germany, France, the United Kingdom and the United States voted against the draft resolution. Australia, Austria, Greece, Italy, New Zealand and Switzerland abstained.

Eventually, acting upon the advice of the UN Secretary-General's Legal Counsel, the President of the General Assembly appointed F.R. Germany to the Preparatory Committee. The proposal to appoint the German Democratic Republic was turned down, and the socialist countries refused to participate in the committee's work. The committee, nonetheless, proceeded with its work and submitted to the General Assembly a draft of the second Development Decade strategy, which contained *inter alia* recommendations by the Trade and Development Board.

At the resumed session of the Eighth Board, a memorandum submitted by the 77 contained a proposal that UNCTAD should make suggestions on the general framework of the Decade. The major developed countries insisted that this would be contrary to the coordinating role of the Preparatory Committee, and that UNCTAD's effort should be limited to reaching the maximum agreement on the issues remitted to it by the New Delhi Conference. Having failed to obtain for UNCTAD the desired role of central leader and coordinator in the preparation of the second Development Decade, the 77 directed their efforts at defining the list of measures within its competence needed to help attain the targets of the Decade. The debates held in the Board and the proposals made, had a decisive influence on the Preparatory Committee, ECOSOC and the General Assembly. In fact, the essence of the most important provisions of the international strategy of development adopted by the General Assembly at its 25th session and contained in its resolution 2626 (XXV) was negotiated in the UNCTAD Board. As for the institutional dispute, although the developing countries failed to propel UNCTAD to the central position, ECOSOC's constitutional role in the organizational set-up dealing with development was seriously challenged. Moreover, the question as to which organ, and through which kind of procedures, the implementation of the second Development Decade strategy will be reviewed could not be settled by the General Assembly at its 25th session. Indubitably, the problem of relations between UNCTAD and ECOSOC, their respective roles in the Decade and ECOSOC's place in the UN system will be the subjects of discussions for years to come.[58]

Voting in favor, together with the 77 and the D Group were Belgium, Canada, Denmark, Finland, Japan, the Netherlands, Spain and Sweden. TD/B/233 (21 Feb. 1969), p. 12. For the explanation of voting see TD/B/SR.192 (13 Feb. 1969). See also Board resolution 57(VIII) in TD/B/233, Annex I.

58. Indicative of this was the US proposal to enlarge the Council's membership (from 27 to 54), in order to reassert its "leadership and authority" and to make it into an "effective force for leadership in the second Development Decade." Press Release USUN-63(71), May 17, 1971.

Chapter IX

RELATIONS BETWEEN GATT AND UNCTAD

In the first two chapters we examined critically some of the aspects of
GATT. We also found that the developing countries' attack on GATT
prior to and during the Geneva Conference was highly symbolic and
ideological: GATT was the fortress which generated, preserved and
enforced the rules and concepts of the existing international economic
relations which developing countries found disadvantageous and discriminatory. As an organization (in spite of its ICITO umbilical cord),
GATT was outside the UN and fully controlled by the developed
countries, with the developing countries having only a very minor
influence on its decisions. Its secretariat staff, and especially its top
echelon, was almost entirely from the West and largely committed to
the traditional trade philosophy.

At the Geneva Conference the developing countries, supported by
the socialist countries, tried but did not succeed in reducing GATT
to some subordinate role vis-à-vis UNCTAD, nor in establishing a
formal link and defining a relationship between the two organizations.[1]
GATT remained on the scene; and, reformed through the adoption of
Part IV, under the title "Trade and Development", it was prepared
to challenge or to meet the challenge of UNCTAD. Observers from the
developed countries felt that UNCTAD and its supporters were trying
to take over GATT's work and functions,[2] while others argued that
GATT's rapid task expansion into the field of trade and development
and its operational activities were deliberate political moves intended
to confront UNCTAD with systematic competition. UNCTAD's sym-
pathizers asked: why should the developed countries, which at the
Geneva Conference were cool or opposed to most developing countries' proposals, quickly, thereafter, allow the essence of the *Final Act*
to be transferred into a contractual instrument such as the General

1. GATT is not explicitly mentioned in General Assembly resolution
1995(XIX). (For a thorough discussion of UNCTAD-GATT relationship and the
chronology of events see Cordovez, "UNCTAD: From Confrontation to Strategy,"
op. cit., Chapter III.)
2. Kotschnig, *op. cit.,* p. 35.

198

Agreement? The developed countries may have begun to take the new concepts more seriously, but they also wanted to buttress GATT, to rebuild its image, to help it maintain its position as the central body for trade, and to equip it for the forthcoming fight with the "aggressive forum of the poor". Furthermore, they needed an authoritative source to help them argue with the developing countries, as well as to contradict (if necessary) and criticize UNCTAD's research, studies and proposals. Through jurisdictional disputes and competition, they may have wished to play GATT and UNCTAD against each other and to maneuver between the two organizations.[3] Indubitably, the developed countries preferred GATT to UNCTAD—that is, GATT was an old institution, whose serviceability to them was well-tested, while this new organization was unpredictable, ideologically repugnant, its key positions mainly staffed by "subversive" international civil servants, and not easily controllable.

Part IV marked the enlargement of GATT's competence and its greater orientation toward the problems of developing countries. The expansion of its tasks often meant a duplication of the mandate, functions, and work of UNCTAD. Since this study is primarily concered with the institutionalization of UNCTAD, we look at the task redefinition and task expansion of GATT as a challenge to UNCTAD. Hence the question: how did the controversy over duplication between GATT and UNCTAD unfold, and how did UNCTAD meet the challenge?

The basic point at issue was the respective roles UNCTAD and GATT would play in the field of trade and development. Prebisch voiced the view of many developing countries when he said that the parallel course undertaken by some governments in GATT was a deliberate move to secure for it an image similar to that of UNCTAD— i.e., the image of an organization concerned with Third World problems —although in reality the two organizations remained far apart in outlook and in their basic orientation toward international economic relations.[4] The developed countries and the GATT secretariat claimed,

3. "... for nothing rejoices the heart of a government more when confronted with an awkward problem than to have it discussed simultaneously in several institutions. This enables you to move from one to the other and, with a sufficient amount of agility, you may avoid dealing with the problem in any of them." Statement by Wyndham White at the Geneva Conference, *Proceedings,* Vol. II, p. 437.

4. Speech by Prebisch to GATT's Committee on Trade and Development, TD/B/114 (30 Jan. 1967), p. 14. GATT was based on the assumption that on the basis of the MFN clause, the obligation to negotiate, listen to complaints of others and use dispute-solving methods, world commerce would develop favorably for all countries. UNCTAD's philosophy, in contrast, calls for direct intervention

however, that there was in fact no duplication between GATT and UNCTAD, and that their functions were demonstrably complementary. According to them, UNCTAD should be the policy forum for intensive, comprehensive and wide-ranging discussions on trade and development, while GATT should pursue the technical and practical tasks of sponsoring trade negotiations, assisting in the application and administration of agreements resulting from these negotiations, and engaging in various operational activities. UNCTAD would launch ideas, but would try not to replace the specialized bodies by performing their tasks and would not become involved in practical details.[5] The developing countries rejected this limitation of UNCTAD.[6] If UNCTAD were to be confined to discussions and debates and prevented from producing tangible results, its meaningfulness, authority and reputation would suffer. Above all, there was no guarantee that the ideas generated by UNCTAD would be fully implemented in GATT, which was a specialized body, controlled by different mandatory rules, a different set of actors, composed of a partly different membership, and guided by different philosophical concepts and policy priorities. In addition to these basic issues, GATT's search for a role, the policies of developing countries, and the relations between the GATT and UNCTAD secretariats, played a part in shaping the UNCTAD/GATT duplication controversy.

GATT's Search for a Role

UNCTAD was a dynamic newcomer on the international scene, facing a myriad of fresh and challenging problems. GATT's position was quite different. At the time of UNCTAD's birth, it had been on the pedestal for almost twenty years. The Kennedy Round brought industrial tariffs down to levels where, in many instances, they represented smaller obstacles to trade than some non-tariff and paratariff devices. However, international action regarding these other barriers was rather ineffective as shown, for example, by GATT's un-

---

in world trade so as to bring about certain effects favorable to developing countries. J. Kaufmann, "Trade Policies for Less Developed Countries," in H. B. Chenery, F. Baade, J. Kaufmann, I. M. D. Little, L. H. Klaassen, and J. Tinbergen, *Towards a Strategy for Development Cooperation* (Rotterdam: Rotterdam University Press, 1967).

5. For example, see the speech by GATT's Director General, Sir Eric Wyndham White, "Whither GATT?", press release GATT/1006 (19 Oct. 1967), and J. Royer, "Reforming the Institutional Machinery of World Trade," GATT doc. Spec(63) 264 (14 Oct. 1963), p. 15.

6. See our discussion of UNCTAD's functions in Chapter X.

happy experience with quantitative restrictions during the Kennedy Round, and presupposed a long preparatory work of identification. In addition to non-tariff barriers another area of possible action centered on agricultural protectionism. This was apparently yet another insuperable barrier for GATT, for it was an area where its rules had been flouted for a number of years, and which required long-range, comprehensive measures. The Contracting Parties recognized this fact and agreed that it would be unrealistic to expect any significant initiatives for the multilateral and comprehensive reduction of tariff and non-tariff barriers to trade in the near future.[7] In other words, in pursuit of its primary objective of liberalizing world trade by means of negotiations, for the time being, GATT was running out of things which it could do successfully. This was reflected in the limited scope of the work program it adopted in this area in the autumn of 1967.[8] The situation was different when it came to the trade of developing countries. Here, the Contracting Parties could specify a number of institutional and substantive provisions which represented a significant workload that could keep the GATT staff busy (the staff had expanded significantly due to the Kennedy Round negotiations).[9] This could assure GATT of a relatively active life, in contrast to the stagnant atmosphere which might have set in had it been confined principally to the administration of the Kennedy Round results.

Developing Countries in GATT

We have noted the enmity and suspicion of many developing countries toward GATT, both before and at the time of the Geneva Conference, and their extended efforts to create their own organization. How, then, is one to explain the fact that they also support and often initiate task expansion in GATT? We shall later discuss the efforts of the GATT secretariat to gain the confidence and trust of the other side, efforts

7. See "Review of the work of the Contracting Parties through the last two decades and conclusions on their future work programme" (November 1967). GATT press release GATT/1012 (30 Nov. 1967).
8. An Agriculture Committee and a Committee on Trade in Industrial Products were to be established to examine and explore the opportunities for progress in these areas. An objective analysis of the tariff situation after the Kennedy Round results were implemented was to be conducted, and an inventory of non-tariff and para-tariff barriers was to be taken. *Ibid.*
9. In addition to the advance implementation of the Kennedy Round results for developing countries, there were provisions referring to the reactivation of the Special Group on Tropical Products; the establishment of panels of government experts to examine problems related to products of interest to developing countries; the initiation of trade negotiations on expansion of trade among developing countries; the Trade Center; preferences; cotton textiles, etc., *ibid.*

which helped improve the image of the organization in the eyes of many developing countries. At this point it may be useful to mention some other elements.

Although the Group of 77 has a strong political preference for UNCTAD, this is not reflected in organized opposition by the developing countries in GATT to its task expansion. The group discipline common in UNCTAD is not present in GATT and it is possible for individual developing countries to assume differing positions. A developing country may be somewhat uncertain of its policy on a given issue, or its delegations in GATT and UNCTAD may be uncoordinated.[10] It may feel that UNCTAD is better equipped politically to accomplish a given task, while in fact, GATT is technically more competent. It may judge that the commitment of the West is much stronger in GATT, that this is the forum more likely to produce concrete results, and that, however limited they may be, it is results which count in the final analysis. It may espouse the strategy of "playing on two pianos"—i.e., exerting pressure in two organizations as a spur to activity and the speedier maturing of ideas.[11] As a result, some developing countries exhibit a degree of "inconsistency" both in UNCTAD and in GATT; they apply pressures toward task expansion in the two organizations, and displease international civil servants who as a result get enmeshed even more in jurisdictional disputes. Thus, paradoxically, the initiation of a given activity in GATT which is simultaneously on UNCTAD's agenda may be considered functional by a developed and a developing country, but for different reasons. The former may see it in the diffusion of pressure and a counteraction of UNCTAD, while the latter hopes that it will intensify pressure on the

10. Note, for example, the statement by the representative of Chile that GATT is the best suited international organization to examine the problem of the technological gap from the point of view of international trade. He therefore proposed that this subject be included on the GATT agenda as an item well fitting the new stage into which GATT had moved following the Kennedy Round. (GATT doc. TD/W/67). At approximately the same time, Chile was cosponsoring a resolution to create a committee on science and technology in UNCTAD.

11. "Ideas and concepts have to be put out in several forums. What does not succeed in one forum may succeed in another ... Certainly limited available resources should be put to the best possible use. There should be no waste and there should be no real duplication. But ... particularly *new* thoughts and ideas have to be put out, discussed and crystallized in many forums to achieve success ... What is important is not who will do something, but that something should be done and done quickly." Statement read on behalf of India's Minister of Commerce at the XXIV session of the Contracting Parties, 22 November 1967 (mimeo). Based on the "two-pianos" strategy, the developing countries initiated the consideration of non-tariff barriers and restrictive business practices in UNCTAD's Committee on Manufactures, even though these subjects were already on GATT's agenda.

West and increase the chances of progress. In general it appears that developing countries would like to avoid a situation where they would be forced to choose between GATT and UNCTAD; they would like to be parties to all possible advantages that may stem from membership of both organizations, even though they generally disapprove of GATT and of what it stands for.

Relations Between the GATT and UNCTAD Secretariats

Until very recently, the GATT secretariat was led and generally manned by an expert core of Anglo-Saxons, and its philosophy of trade closely reflected the views of two major trading nations, the United States and the United Kingdom. For a long time GATT's secretariat had been a source of unhappiness for those men in the United Nations concerned with the promotion of the Third World cause. Most members of the acting secretariat of the Geneva Conference had actively cooperated with the developing countries for many years. Their activities on the institutional issue during the preparation of the Geneva Conference and during the Conference itself were especially regarded as hostile by the GATT staff, who were fighting for the future of their own organization. The accumulated ill feeling and mistrust were carried over into the post-Conference period, since the acting secretariat formed the core of the secretariat in the newly-created UNCTAD machinery. GATT's top leadership continued to collaborate very closely with the principal western governments, while the UNCTAD secretariat had firm links with the Group of 77. An additional element in the strained relationship between the two secretariats [12] was the personal animosity of their leaders: Prebisch, a Latin American economist, a flamboyant leader and the ideologue of the rising forces and demands of the Third World, vs. Wyndham White, a British lawyer with a Foreign Service background, a pragmatist, a bureaucrat, entrusted with the administration and preservation of a given system which he had helped to restore, stabilize and mold after the war, and who basically continued to view Third World problems as being of peripheral importance and concern. Furthermore, their past contacts, when Prebisch had been the head of ECLA, and especially at the time of LAFTA's creation, had apparently not been to their mutual satisfaction.

GATT had been waging a campaign to win over the developing countries: even before the Geneva Conference there had been a tendency to be less strict on standards of admission so as to attract new

12. UNCTAD's hostility was much more open and frank, and was generally reflected in its studies and documents. GATT's staff was under instructions not to retort openly, but to maintain a posture of frigid indifference.

members and GATT began to open participation in certain of its activities to non-members.[13] Staff was also recruited from developing areas (but good care was taken to see that such men entertained no "subversive" ideas), and some attempts were ostensibly made to give more attention to demands for a representative geographical distribution. During the Kennedy Round, the GATT secretariat extended substantive support to many developing countries, and with the full connivance of developed countries [14] it showed many of them where their own negotiating possibilities lay.[15] In addition to the genuine concern that some of the top men in the GATT secretariat exhibited for the problems of developing countries, one of the important reasons for such behavior was the wish to "guard the rear" and to avoid any accusations of indifference toward the problems and difficulties of developing countries. Such actions were bound to have an impact: although their institutional loyalty continued with UNCTAD, many developing countries ceased to view the changing GATT secretariat with the same hostility as in the past.

While fighting for a clientele, each secretariat deliberately ignored the activities of the other organization. The GATT leadership in particular acted as if UNCTAD did not exist,[16] an approach consistent with their expectations that UNCTAD as an organization would not last too long. The secretariats also engaged in something that we could call "beating each other to the punch". Their calendars were not coordinated, and on occasions meetings would be scheduled so as to precede or coincide with a similar session of the other body. This appears to have been the favorite tactic of the GATT secretariat.[17] At

13. For example, the services of the GATT Trade Information Center were made available to all developing countries, irrespective of their membership in GATT. Also, non-members were invited to participate in the trade negotiations among developing countries. See TD/50 (3 Jan. 1968), on the activities of GATT in the field of trade and development in the period 1964-1967.

14. See Curzon, "The GATT: pressures and strategies of task expansion," *op. cit.,* p. 10.

15. Some developing countries lacked the necessary technical skill for effective participation in these negotiations, had limited manpower, and often had no clear instructions from home. The GATT secretariat helped them draft their request lists and advised them during the negotiations. It chaired meetings, helped delegates to find solutions, etc.

16. Note the curious fact that GATT's *Review of International Trade* did not include UNCTAD in the list of acronyms which precedes the text.

17. GATT's Committee on Trade and Development held one session in Punta del Este, an unorthodox practice for this organization. Some interpreted this as a means to build up GATT's popularity in Latin America, which had the highest percentage of non-members of GATT of all developing continents. On another occasion (in the summer of 1967), Wyndham White proposed that GATT hold

other times they would engage in competition over some substantive matter—for example, the case of the Kennedy Round evaluation, where the UNCTAD secretariat succeeded in turning out its study before the one by the GATT secretariat.[18] One of the main results of UNCTAD's evaluation, was to provide the developing countries with solid data and ammunition with which to substantiate the disappointment they expressed at the end of the negotiations.[19] The premises and methods on which the UNCTAD study was based guaranteed that its results would differ somewhat from those produced by the GATT secretariat, which appears to have been guided by the position of developed countries that the negotiations as a whole afforded substantial benefits for the Third World.[20] What effect this duplication had on governmental policies is hard to assess, but it is quite evident that on precisely the same question different conclusions were sometimes arrived at due simply to the different policy orientations of the two secretariats.

---

a ministerial meeting (sessions on the ministerial level have higher prestige and greater importance) to survey the principal problems regarding action in GATT after the Kennedy Round. Many saw this, rightly or wrongly, as an attempt to steal the limelight from the approaching New Delhi Conference, and the proposal did not receive general support.

18. The developed countries did not approve of such a study being done by UNCTAD, and the proposal had to be voted through against their opposition. (TD/B/120, (5 Jun. 1967) p. 10). For the UNCTAD evaluation see TD/6 (4 Sep. 1967), and the supporting documents; for the GATT evaluation see COM.TD/48 (19 Oct. 1967), and Rev.1.

19. This was considered as important in view of the forthcoming debate on the subject in GATT. The UNCTAD secretariat also wanted to show that additional measures were necessary to promote the industrial exports of developing countries, and that the results of the Kennedy Round did not weaken the case for preferences.

20. The initial statement released by the GATT secretariat was to the effect that the outcome of the Kennedy Round for the developing countries did not differ greatly from the overall results of the negotiations. GATT press release GATT/992 (30 Jun. 1967). Among other things, GATT's overall and major products summaries were given in terms of frequency distribution which was useful in building up a general picture of the results of the Kennedy Round, yet it did not permit any simple overall assessment of the results for the developing countries, and did not provide for any comparison with the results for the developed countries. UNCTAD's study, on the other hand, disaggregated to the fullest extent possible and in this manner showed the effect of the Kennedy Round on the various tariff rates on selected products and drew conclusions as to the increase in market access achieved and the degree of protection retained (i.e. the extent of tariff and non-tariff barriers that remained and called for further action). Also, UNCTAD's study provided simple overall assessments by means of trade-weighted average rates before and after the Kennedy Round, the averages being given for all products as well as for products of interest to developing countries, thus permitting a comparative analysis.

Chapter II disclosed some of the similarities between the *Final Act* of UNCTAD and Part IV of GATT. In institutional terms, there are several areas where the activities of the two organizations touch upon or overlap each other, or where some confusion exists about their respective competence. More specifically, these are commodities problems, preferences for the manufactures and semi-manufactures of developing countries, trade expansion and integration among developing countries, and export promotion and technical assistance in the field of trade.[21]

Commodities—Wheat. In contrast to UNCTAD's overall coordinating role, which is very controversial and not accepted by developed countries, there seems to be general agreement that this organization has the mandate for sectoral coordination in the field of commodities.[22]

The memorandum on wheat, which embodied all the essential ingredients for a commodity agreement, was negotiated during the Kennedy Round without consulting UNCTAD.[23] Some countries, as well as the UNCTAD secretariat, felt unhappy about this approach which undermined UNCTAD's prestige and authority. They claimed that the United Nations was the recognized machinery for the negotiation of commodity agreements, and that it had been deliberately kept out of the picture in this case. But, the role of the United Nations is controversial: developed countries argue that neither the UN nor UNCTAD have the exclusive competence to convene commodity conferences.[24] In fact, there is no provision or rule which explicitly states that commodity agreements must be negotiated under the auspices of the United Nations, although this has been a common practice and this responsibility has been

21. For the terms of reference of GATT's Committee on Trade and Development and its subsidiary bodies, see *Basic Instruments and Selected Documents* (BISD) (1965), 13th Supplement. Also see TD/50 (3 Jan. 1968).

22. The Committee on Commodities is to coordinate the activities of all bodies involved in the commodity field, including the appropriate organs of the FAO, autonomous commodity councils, study groups and other commodity groups, and any commodity activities within GATT. See Board Resolution 9(I) in TD/B/70 (Aug. 1966). Also see the terms of reference of ICCICA and CICT whose functions were assumed by UNCTAD's Committee on Commodities.

23. When GATT's Group on Cereals began to operate in 1965, the FAO and the International Wheat Council representatives participated as advisers to the Director General of GATT. The UNCTAD secretariat was not invited, and only near the end when the basic features of the memorandum had already been decided upon, were its representatives allowed in.

24. The USSR went to the other extreme and argued that to convene the wheat conference was an unquestionable prerogative of UNCTAD. See TD/B/120 (5 Jun 1967), Annex II, and TD/B/L.103 (1 Sep. 1967).

exercised by the UN since 1946. In the end, however, and in deference to the customary procedure, the wheat agreement was not formalized in GATT; instead a "negotiating" conference was held under the aegis of the International Wheat Council and with the cooperation of UNCTAD.[25]

Wheat was an important item in international trade and had to be dealt with as a part of the overall deal in the Kennedy Round package, the United States had insisted that the agreement be finalized in GATT, and this agreement could be negotiated by major producing and importing developed countries while disregarding others. The USSR was the only country that strongly espoused the role of UNCTAD, while the developing countries did not appear too concerned. Although the 1967 wheat agreement was an exception because of the special occasion and the nature of this commodity, institutionally it represented a setback for UNCTAD, and it could serve as a precedent for any future attempts to endow GATT with a larger role in the field of negotiating commodity agreements.[26]

Trade Expansion among Developing Countries. A few months before the Geneva Conference, GATT began to consider the exchange of tariff preferences among developing countries.[27] In 1966, during the Kennedy Round, the chairman of an informal group of developing countries started to prepare the ground for negotiations on mutual exchange of tariff and other concessions on a preferential basis among developing countries. In November 1967, at the 24th session of the Contracting Parties it was decided to establish a Trade Negotiations Committee (TNC) and to initiate such negotiations, whereupon the Director General of GATT sent out invitations to the developing coun-

25. We shall return to this problem in the next chapter, when discussing UNCTAD's negotiating function.

26. It is interesting to note that in his speech to the Geneva Conference, Wyndham White said that GATT had shown a "self-denying" attitude by not arrogating to itself the right to deal with commodity questions which have been entrusted to the UN organs. (*Proceedings,* Vol. II, p. 436). He gave the impression of leaving the door open for GATT to be invited to fulfil additional responsibilities in the sphere of commodities, in marked contrast to the exclusion of commodities from GATT's agenda in the past. As we know, this was not acted upon and CICT and ICCICA functions were transferred to UNCTAD. (During the Kennedy Round, the EEC had also proposed that a sugar arrangement be negotiated in GATT. However, this proposal was not accepted.)

27. In March 1965, a Working Group on Expansion of Trade among Developing Countries was set up. It embarked on a discussion of a number of points other than tariffs but related to the expansion of trade among developing countries, which *inter alia,* included payments unions, export credits, untying of aid, etc. See our Chapters VII and XI for a discussion of UNCTAD's activities in the field of trade expansion among developing countries.

tries.[28] As for UNCTAD, its secretariat and a group of experts had produced two studies in the field of trade expansion and integration among developing countries which were intended to encourage and serve as guides for such efforts. Therefore, UNCTAD secretariat members were displeased with the fact that GATT meetings on this matter were called without prior consideration of UNCTAD's progress in the same field. They felt that governments, because of inertia, take into account only the documentation of the organization in which they are working at a given moment, and that a formal mention of UNCTAD's documents did not ensure that they would be considered. The UNCTAD secretariat also argued that the proposed negotiations might prejudge matters for those developing countries which were not members of GATT, and was furthermore upset at neither receiving relevant information, nor an invitation to participate in these meetings.

Before GATT's Trade Negotiations Committee was established, the UNCTAD secretariat had hoped that such trade negotiations among developing countries as a whole would be a task that would typically fall within the framework of UNCTAD, all the more so because many developing countries interested were not members of GATT, and that the UNCTAD secretariat had made some specific suggestions on the type of concessions that could be negotiated. But the Secretary-General of UNCTAD, overburdened with many other problems, did not act with the determination necessary to ensure that UNCTAD's central role be advocated by the developing countries. When GATT acted to establish the TNC, it merely invited the UNCTAD secretariat to participate as an observer. The UNCTAD secretariat did not find this satisfactory, and it asked at that late stage for a negotiating committee jointly serviced by GATT and UNCTAD. Such a solution was unacceptable to Wyndham White; he expressed concern that UNCTAD's participation might compromise the GATT tradition of secret negotiations, and argued that the GATT secretariat alone should service negotiations, while UNCTAD could possibly be associated to make it easier for non-GATT members to participate, without being involved in the consultations. After some prodding from the UNCTAD secretariat, the developing countries asked that their mutual trade negoti-

28. GATT document TN(LDC)/5 (8 Dec. 1967). Each country was asked to establish for every other developing country a list of products which it exported or believed it could export. The "pragmatic" approach—i.e., without studies, reports, drafting of the Committee's terms of reference, etc.— was intended to initially expedite things and differed significantly from the UNCTAD style. However, by the nature of things these negotiations did not appear to be expeditable. This lack of preparation and of awareness of the special difficulties involved appears likely to have been one of the reasons why these negotiations took many years to get off the ground.

ations on an inter-regional basis be carried out in a joint GATT-UNCTAD framework in order to allow all the interested parties to participate on an equal basis.[29] As a result, Wyndham White improved the status intended for the UNCTAD secretariat by indicating that it would be associated with the preparation and servicing of these negotiations.[30] But in actual fact, GATT continued to act on its own, with UNCTAD's secretariat being denied access to these negotiations. The UNCTAD secretariat has, however, helped some developing countries non-members of GATT, who are taking part in TNC, to prepare their lists of requests and offers. On the other hand, it has not had enough resources and determination to press for a larger role of its own in these negotiations.

Technical Assistance and Export Promotion. Prior to 1964 GATT had no technical assistance operations other than training programs which were partly financed by the UN.[31] The establishment of the Trade Promotion Center was among other things intended to improve GATT's reputation by making it useful to developing countries. The Center's original activities of providing market research and information services were soon expanded to include a trade promotion advisory service and technical assistance.

Suggestions were made that even though GATT was not a part of the UN family, the UN Development Program (UNDP) should rely on its rechristened International Trade Center and perhaps use it as an executing agency for its technical assistance activities in the field of trade.[32] The GATT secretariat staff advertised the practical actions performed by the Center to show that its organization was accomplishing something tangible for developing countries, while UNCTAD still remained in the clouds.

Prior to 1966 UNCTAD was not entitled to extend technical assistance because there were no corresponding provisions in its terms of reference. When this changed, due to the pressure from the Group of 77 and the realization of the UNCTAD secretariat that UNCTAD had to do something practical for developing countries, UNCTAD was in a better position to compete with GATT.[33] Though the GATT Center

29. GATT document W. 24/9 (15 Nov. 1967).
30. A/7214, p. 39. The USSR objected to the servicing of the meetings by the UNCTAD secretariat within the GATT framework.
31. The UN paid for travel and the *per diem* expenses of trainees, while GATT bore the rest of the cost.
32. See GATT document Spec(67)3 (20 Jan. 1967). Note that the GATT Center depended on irregular grants from individual governments for its financing.
33. GATT and UNCTAD were competing with each other on who would send a technical assistance mission to some developing countries. Apparently, GATT was more successful because of its independent financing and the ability to

was sometimes resented as a thorn in the side of the UNCTAD secretariat, which was trying hard to take to operational activities in a meaningful way, it obviously could not be banned from the scene. Some means therefore had to be found to neutralize it. At a special meeting of the executive heads of UNCTAD, UNIDO, the UN regional economic commissions and UNDP in January 1967, in view of the fact that various organizations were providing technical assistance in export promotion, a decision was taken to combine and coordinate these activities and resources in a UN program for the promotion of exports from developing countries.[34] One of the reasons for starting this program was also to improve UNCTAD's bargaining position vis-à-vis GATT, which in a sense was claiming to be the only international organization which could do a proper job in the field of export promotion. The aim was to pull GATT into this overall effort. Wyndham White "welcomed" the coordination of his organization's trade promotion activities with the UN program—note that within the ACC, GATT is treated as a specialized agency for the purpose of coordination. Much more effective was the next step, that is, Prebisch's proposal to set up a joint center, because, according to him, the problem of duplication between GATT and UNCTAD could not be resolved by simple coordination within the UN Export Promotion Program. After informal negotiations in ACC, GATT's Director-General and UNCTAD's Secretary-General reached an agreement in principle and jointly announced in ECOSOC in July 1967 that they would present their governing bodies with a plan for merging GATT and UNCTAD export promotion activities, and transforming the GATT Center into a joint GATT/UNCTAD Center.[35] However, this was done only after a delay during which Wyndham White took a dim view of the proposal.

UNCTAD and GATT each had its own reasons for entering into this partnership. We have already noted the desire of the UNCTAD secretariat members to associate their organization closely with the operational stage of activities, and to offset GATT's drive to build up its own popularity at the expense of UNCTAD. In addition, GATT's expertise, its 20 years of experience and its developed network of contacts with

---

respond quickly to demands, while UNCTAD was shackled by the UN red tape. UNCTAD was not able to respond to a sudden requirement in West Africa, and the countries involved had recourse to GATT which was able immediately to put a 2-man team from its staff in the field. (See our Chapter XI for a discussion of technical assistance in UNCTAD.)

34. See E/4337. This was done primarily to help smooth out the jurisdictional difficulties between UNCTAD and UNIDO over technical assistance projects on export promotion.

35. See TD/B/156/Add.1 (5 Sep. 1967).

governments could be put to very valuable use in an area where experts are difficult to find.[36] The GATT secretariat has always claimed to possess the necessary expertise to perform the backstopping activities for the UN technical assistance work in the field of trade, but not being part of this organization, it had no institutional channel to UNDP financing. When the Board asserted in 1966 that the UNCTAD secretariat should be able to provide the backstopping required, and when the question was raised in UNDP in the spring of 1967 as to why UNCTAD was being denied the function of providing professional support in this field, an institutional tussle was thought to be imminent. In order to avoid this, and to secure access for the GATT Center to UNDP funds—which it could not have in direct competition with UNCTAD, a UN organ—the developed countries yielded to demands for a joint center. Most of all, they feared that if a joint center was not formed, the developing countries and Prebisch would attempt to form a separate one within UNCTAD.[37] They must also have figured out that in any kind of joint arrangement, the GATT secretariat would have the upper hand. Actually, they wanted to ensure this by drafting the terms for the joint relationship in a manner that would favor GATT. This maneuvering occurred at the intergovernmental level in UNCTAD, GATT and the General Assembly.

When the joint center proposal (within the framework of the UN Export Promotion Program) was presented to the Fifth Board in August 1967,[38] there was general approval for this cooperative GATT-UNCTAD effort. The Group of 77 hoped that it would get an immediate "go", so that the joint center would begin operating as of January 1, 1968. The major developed nations were opposed to this; they claimed that additional information was necessary on the center's financing, its relationship to the UN Export Promotion Program and to UNDP, and governmental supervision. At the 24th session of GATT's Contracting Parties in November 1967, the developed countries favored delay, but the pressure from the developing countries was too strong, so a working group was constituted to consider the proposal.[39] On two crucial

36. Since such experts have to come mainly from the West, there was the problem of the developed countries' mistrust of UNCTAD, and their possible reluctance to supply the men that the UNCTAD secretariat might ask for. Such an attitude was not likely over a demand originating from the GATT secretariat.

37. For example, a provision of the Algiers Charter asked to "take into consideration the establishment of a single export promotion centre within the United Nations family under the auspices of UNCTAD." TD/38 (3 Nov. 1967), p. 13.

38. TD/B/133/Add.1 (29 Aug. 1967).

39. Proposals of GATT's Director-General are contained in GATT documents L/2839 (31 Aug. 1967), and L/2890 (6 Nov. 1967), while the report of the Working Group is to be found in L/2932 (22 Nov. 1967).

questions, namely, the direction of the center, and the appropriation and control of its budget, the group did not express itself very precisely, while the provisional nature of its report in effect meant delay in the initiation of a true joint operation.

Upset over this outcome, Prebisch indicated during the informal negotiations in the General Assembly that, according to GATT's Working Group report, UNCTAD's role was conceived more as a participatory one than that of an equal on a contractual basis. He argued that this meant the rejection of the original agreement, and he even hinted that UNCTAD would pull out from the arrangement. It was felt that the developed countries were attempting to gain access to the UNDP for GATT and to relegate UNCTAD's secretariat to a secondary role in the entire operation.[40]

Finally, after prolonged maneuvering in the corridors of the General Assembly, the UNCTAD forces prevailed: the resolution that was adopted provided that the Center be operated jointly by UNCTAD and GATT "on a continuing basis and in equal partnership".[41]

The unusual setup of a Center with two parent bodies has proved capable of functioning and the Center's activities underwent rapid expansion after joint operations were initiated. Although certain operational features have proved a bit cumbersome (for example, the consideration of the budget, primarily because UN/UNCTAD budgetary procedure takes too long),[42] various difficulties are being gradually sorted out. Most important of all, the original institutional controversy was defused and lost in intensity.

Preferences. In the early days of the debate on preferences, the unsettled issue was whether GATT would have a role to play in determining the contents of the general scheme on preferences, or whether it would simply have to grant a waiver once the matter had been decided in UNCTAD. Many developed countries argued that GATT should not put aside its examination of generalized preferences for manufactures of developing countries, even though this matter was being discussed in UNCTAD.[43] However, GATT's Working Group on

40. This interpretation is supported by Wyndham White's statement at the 24th session of the Contracting Parties: he said that one could hardly conceive of a more foolish proposal" than the one made by Prebisch for a joint center, because in business one chooses the organization that will do the most efficient job. He also crticized Prebisch and his concern for parity in financing and expressed doubts about a center supervised by the two organizations.

41. General Assembly resolution 2297(XXII) (12 Dec. 1967).

42. A joint budgetary machinery for the Center is under consideration. See UNCTAD documents TD/B/239/Rev.1. (13 May 1969), TD/B/256 (3 Jul. 1969), and TD/B/267 for the information on the activities of the Center.

43. GATT document L/2410, paras. 35, 37.

Preferences remained inactive.[44] The developed countries used the venue of their own circle in the OECD, while the consultations with the developing countries took place in UNCTAD. In view of this, GATT was no longer involved in the preference game. GATT's limited membership, its continuing and open reservations vis-à-vis the principle and usefulness of general preferences (for example, the refusal to include the concept of preferential treatment for the products of developing countries into Part IV), and the fact that the developing countries had no political weight within this organization, were among the reasons which precluded GATT from playing any role in the determination of the system of general preferences. Thus, the problem of duplication with UNCTAD never arose, whereas the recent decision to entrust UNCTAD with the review and supervision of GSP could possibly mean that GATT's role would not extend beyond granting the legal coverage.[45]

Evolution of GATT-UNCTAD Relations

The leaders of UNCTAD and of GATT gave conflicting interpretations of the problems in the relations between the two institutions. Prebisch felt that governments caused problems since they gave parallel instructions to UNCTAD and to GATT, and he felt, therefore, that it was up to the governments to improve the situation by eliminating the causes of duplication. Prebisch thought that there was no great difficulty in ensuring collaboration on the secretariat level, but that collaboration would be fruitless as long as there was no underlying concept of the respective functions of the two organizations.[46] He argued that duplication was not desirable and that those governments causing it often

44. The only GATT action related to general preferences was on the application by Australia in 1965 for a waiver to introduce preferential rates of duty on imports of certain manufactures and semi-manufactures from developing countries. The Contracting Parties granted the waiver, and are reviewing the matter annually.

45. The question that remains open is whether and to what extent the Contracting Parties want GATT to be involved in this matter. For the time being, all indications are that GATT would play a marginal role. The simplified waiver granted to GSP in GATT does provide for a general review procedure, which should be undertaken without duplicating the work of other international organizations. Also, bilateral consultations may take place between a preference-giving country and any Contracting Party which considers that benefits from the General Agreement are being impaired "unduly" as a result of GSP. (Note that there were apparently some attempts to have a rather systematic review of GSP in GATT. However, during the discussions in OECD this approach was rejected.)

46. See TD/B/82/Add.3 (20 Jul. 1966), paras. 38, 39; TD/B/114 (30 Jan. 1967), pp. 14-15; and TD/B/133 (3 Aug. 1967), p. 13.

did so on purpose. Wyndham White, however, repeatedly stressed that jurisdictional disputes could be solved at the secretariat level, and that some parallelism between the basic juridical texts of the two organizations was not totally undesirable and did not necessarily mean that there would be any duplication or overlapping.[47] In his view, duplication did not really exist because UNCTAD was a forum, while GATT was the place where things were implemented.

The UNCTAD secretariat was basically oriented to preventing matters of principal concern to developing countries from coming within GATT's purview. After all, GATT had failed to fulfil expectations in this field, and that was one of the reasons why UNCTAD had been created—i.e., to assume all the responsibilities regarding trade and development. It is no wonder then, that Prebisch viewed the "aggressive expansionism" of the GATT secretariat with alarm, especially since it was aided and abetted by developed countries, and by developing nations, "playing on two pianos". GATT, on the other hand tried to assume additional responsibilities in this field, especially the operational ones which, through concrete pay-offs, would make it more acceptable to the Third World. In addition, GATT leadership originally tended to believe that UNCTAD's collapse was inevitable—a view later replaced by a more realistic appraisal of UNCTAD's viability. In line with this, a policy was adopted to preserve a certain exclusiveness for GATT, and through rivalry and duplication to dominate the "inferior" UNCTAD.

The "not-on-speaking-terms" relationship between the two secretariats which followed the confrontation at the Geneva Conference was gradually becoming normalized.[48] In 1966, discussions were initiated between Prebisch and Wyndham White aimed at making constructive cooperation possible between the two organizations. As a matter of fact, Wyndham White proposed at the 23rd session of the Contracting Parties, held in April 1966, that a programming committee (nicknamed "committee on coexistence") be established. Composed of senior UNCTAD and GATT officials, this committee was to be responsible for guiding the study and discussion on trade and development, comparing and examining related projects and proposals on the agendas of the two organizations, with the aim of achieving constructive collaboration and avoiding wasteful duplication.[49] The UNCTAD secretariat,

47. See GATT document SR.23/10 and UN document E/4337, pp. 15-17.
48. Note that at least some government representatives were annoyed at what they felt were the attempts by international civil servants to pull them into various jurisdictional disputes. The international civil servants, on the other hand, felt that they were simply exposing contradictions inherent in the positions taken by governments in UNCTAD and GATT respectively.
49. GATT doc. SR.23/10. This proposal was in harmony with the Part IV,

however, did not show great enthusiasm for this suggestion. The secretariat saw it as a tactical move which would present GATT and UNCTAD as having equal responsibility in the field of trade and development. It feared that formalization of the proposed relationship could infringe upon UNCTAD's status as the central body on trade and development. By the time the matter was brought to the attention of the Board, some developed countries had also withdrawn their support from the Wyndham White proposal. The primary reason for this was apparently the question of the committee's membership, supposed to include the Chairman of the Contracting Parties and the President of the Board, in addition to the officials of the two secretariats. Certain developed countries considered as unacceptable the possibility of a representative from a socialist country—in the capacity of the President of the Board—taking part in the proposed programming committee.

Informal discussion between the GATT and UNCTAD secretariats continued, however. At the ACC session in the spring of 1967, and after some pressure from the executive heads of other agencies, it was agreed that arrangements should be made for appropriate officials from the two secretariats to meet periodically, on an informal basis, to review outstanding problems in the areas of export promotion, trade expansion, preferences, and to explore possible common action. Their conclusions would be submitted to governments for approval and action.[50]

This acquiescing of the UNCTAD secretariat in a pragmatic approach to duplication activities represented an important change in its tactics. One of the reasons why it initially (1965-67) did not like a possible division of tasks with GATT, was that it felt that this could possibly limit UNCTAD's growth as a new organization. Only when UNCTAD had consolidated its institutional structure and had entered all fields of its interest, did the secretariat feel prepared to cooperate and negotiate from a position of strength with GATT. Also, many developing countries felt that duplication between GATT and UNCTAD was often detrimental to their interests since it allowed the developed countries to play on two stages and escape responsibility, and that it constituted a waste of energy for both organizations. Therefore, they proposed action to achieve harmonious cooperation between the two organizations, so that their work and studies would complement rather than parallel, or compete with each other.[51]

---

which called for collaboration of the Contracting Parties and other international organizations whose activities related to trade and development.

50. TD/B/133 (3 Aug. 1967), paras. 43-46.

51. See the report of the Coordinating Committee of the Group of 77 for the Algiers Conference (Algiers document 77/22/SC.1/3) (July 1967).

GATT could not be neutralized or eliminated, its task related to the problems of developing countries appeared to expand constantly,[52] and the duplication feud presented a costly proposition. Therefore, the UNCTAD secretariat decided it would be wise—and the Group of 77 actively supported it—to enter into a "symbiotic" relationship with GATT in those areas where overlap existed. The accent was placed on the positive elements of the GATT-UNCTAD duality, on their joint actions, and not on their separate ones, in those areas where their interests, concerns, and mandates were identical or parallel.[53] Therefore, UNCTAD adopted a less dogmatic approach and envisaged joint actions including coordinated calendars of meetings, negotiation machinery, and the means of providing technical assistance to developing countries. The GATT secretariat and the developed countries did not appear too enthusiastic with the demands for joint activities, as we have seen in the specific cases of the Trade Center and in the trade negotiations among developing countries. Joint action would indeed have been more than simple cooperation on the secretariat level; GATT's operational exclusiveness was being challenged, and its supporters suspected that this was also a move toward a long-range goal that many developing countries continue to entertain, that of subordinating GATT to UNCTAD.

While fighting, the two organizations were also engaged in emulating each other. GATT was trying to improve its image in the light of UNCTAD's goals, and to appear a "me-too" advocate of developing countries' needs. Thus, it underwent some changes and multiplied its activities regarding trade and development. UNCTAD, on the other hand, already had developing countries' loyalty and the "correct" philosophy of trade was on its side, but it lacked the proper institutional prerogatives. What it lacked it could easily observe next door, in the contractual and operational forum of GATT. Both GATT and UNCTAD faced serious difficulties in their attempts at imitation. Any institutional improvements or task expansion in UNCTAD were opposed by the developed countries, while GATT's attempts to accommodate the developing countries' demands through technical assistance and various other ways, could not conceal the fact that the great majority of these efforts were of only marginal importance for North-South trade relations, and that the content and concepts of the General

52. Generally, task expansion in this field was much easier to attain in GATT than in UNCTAD. In GATT, developed countries were most often favorably disposed toward such demands since UNCTAD appeared on the scene; in UNCTAD, as a rule, they exhibited a negative attitude.

53. Report of the UNCTAD secretariat on improvement of the institutional machinery and the methods of work. TD/B/173 (31 Jul. 1968), p. 24.

216

Agreement continued to represent the international economic system which the developing countries were trying to reform. This was all too evident in the failure of the Kennedy Round negotiations to fulfil the expectations of the majority of developing countries, as well as in the lip service being paid to GATT's Part IV.

Attempts by UNCTAD to contain GATT through a frontal attack failed, and the style of "diplomatic non-recognition" did not prove effective. The change to more subtle tactics of cooperation represented what many thought to be a much better approach. In practice, however, symbiosis and cooperation meant no more than a truce. The GATT secretariat was hardly in a mood to cooperate with UNCTAD, having, to begin with, unwillingly entered into the joint Trade Center venture. As for UNCTAD, with the departure of Prebisch, there was no more drive in the secretariat for pursuing a policy of active (aggressive) coexistence vis-à-vis GATT. This made it easier for GATT, also under a new leadership, to ignore UNCTAD and to assume a posture of cold indifference. The joint Center had to be kept going, but this cooperative effort was considered a mistake which would not be repeated again. The fear of UNCTAD as a challenger has all but disappeared. On the other hand, the developing countries' presence and activities in GATT are often felt to be bothersome, and are viewed as a threat by the GATT secretariat. This for the simple reason that they tend to politicize the atmosphere in this contractual body, prompting the developed countries to discuss and decide various problems in the more congenial club asmosphere of OECD, thus reducing and undermining the central role of GATT.

In the final analysis, the UNCTAD-GATT relations depend on what is decided on the intergovernmental level. However, the governments so far have preferred to leave the *modus vivendi* between the two organizations undisturbed. Provided that the issue is raised again one day, UNCTAD's position is not an uneasy one. Its long-range trump cards are its (soon to be) universal membership, its strong roots within the UN system, its ability to mobilize political support and generate political pressure, its progressive trade philosophy, and certainly also the continuing slow erosion of GATT's rules.

Chapter X

UNCTAD—A NORMATIVE FORUM OR . . .

During the deliberation stage of the policy process in an international organization, problems are defined, factual data obtained, points of consensus among states sought, and recommendations made. In general, this is how the United Nations' organs work. However, what lies beyond persuasion, initiative and pressure in an eminently practical field such as trade and development? What happens when studies, analyses and debates are successfully completed on a given issue and when consensus on a certain principle is to be translated into action? Logically, this should be followed by the stage where states undertake the obligation to act in a prescribed manner, and then by the execution of the negotiated agreement.

The developing countries feel that UNCTAD's activities should not be confined to unenforceable and inoperative recommendations, and that it should be endowed with negotiating and implementing functions. They see this as a way to create a stronger and more consistent link between UNCTAD's principles and the actions of states. The developed countries, on the other hand, have traditionally been reluctant to have UNCTAD vested with any of the prerogatives of a specialized agency or contractual organization. Moreover, they are suspicious of any moves which could heighten their obligation to act along policy lines emerging from UNCTAD. In fact, many of them would prefer to see UNCTAD in a state of controlled "immobilisme", a "talk-shop" which would serve also as a safety valve for the frustrations of the developing world.[1]

In the pages that follow, we shall inquire whether UNCTAD's negotiating and implementing functions have got beyond the limitations imposed by the developed countries' interpretation of its constitutional text.

1. It has been often argued that the establishment of an organization creates the illusion of attacking the problem, and thus tends to satisfy demands for action.

Implementation

General Assembly resolution 1995 (XIX) provides that the Board:

> shall keep under review and take appropriate action within its competence for the *implementation* of the recommendations, declarations, resolutions and other decisions of the Conference . . .

When the continuing machinery began to operate, the developing countries raised the issue of implementation of the *Final Act*. Their demands, however, faced several obstacles. Many provisions of the *Final Act* were not adopted unanimously,[2] and even when they were, their wording was often ambiguous and concealed substantive differences of opinion among developed and developing countries. They also included qualifying clauses such as "to the extent possible", a phrase which in UN parlance tended to mean no commitment to act. Furthermore, the developed countries contested the binding nature of recommendations emanating from UN organs.[3] The developing nations nonetheless argued that the adoption of a recommendation implied *ipso facto* the acceptance of a corresponding commitment by governments to implement relevant measures—particularly when a recommendation was adopted unanimously. The developed nations, on the other hand, pointed out that the provisions of the *Final Act*, as distinct from multilateral contractual instruments, were not obligatory and could claim only a moral and political force.[4]

Realizing that the only "sanction" at their disposal was the censure of world public opinion and the loss of political prestige which the developed nations did not relish, as well as intensified political pressure, the developing countries attempted to establish an effective review of how the recommendations of the Geneva Conference would be implemented. Some of them wanted the Board endowed with powers which would enable it to hold individual countries responsible. They also wanted to establish procedures for clearly determining government responsibility with regard to implementation. They asked that infor-

2. Of the 15 general principles which were supposed to reflect political agreement on the new approach to international trade, only one was adopted without dissent. Of 13 special principles, only two were adopted unanimously. There were 57 substantive recommendations, and 29 were adopted unanimously. On 28 occasions voting was resorted to, 15 of which were by roll-call.

3. According to an extreme interpretation, the *Final Act* did not represent joint solutions but ideas, suggestions and requests, which anybody could interpret in his own way. Representative of Belgium, TD/B/SR.101, p. 58.

4. Even so, at the Geneva Conference many developed countries voted against certain recommendations or general principles, because if implemented these would impose what they felt were unacceptable financial burdens upon them, or they would limit their maneuverability. See J. Kaufmann, *Conference Diplomacy*, (Leyden: A. W. Sijthoff, 1968), p. 69.

mation supplied by governments be closely related to each particular recommendation, and that detailed progress reports be requested from every government.[5] The developed countries saw things differently. According to them, a formalized reporting procedure on the implementation of the *Final Act* recommendations would give these a character quite different from recommendations by the UN bodies. They argued that the Board should not be converted into "an inquisitorial body to carry out a detailed country-by-country examination of the extent to which recommendations adopted by the Conference have been implemented or were being complied with." [6]

The "implementation crisis" persisted during the first two sessions of the Board, held in 1965.[7] No rapprochement could be attained. The developed countries maintained that implementation reporting is a misconception of UNCTAD's role, and that GATT, as a contractual organization, is the only proper place to review the implementation of trade measures.[8] The resolution adopted by the Second Board reflected an implicit recognition by the developing countries that for the time being they could not compel the developed nations to submit their policies and actions to detailed scrutiny in UNCTAD. According to this resolution, the Secretary-General of UNCTAD is to prepare an annual report on international trade and economic development, on the progress made in the economic development of developing countries, and on their trade and development needs. On the basis of this report, which would be based among other things on information provided by member states (in a form which they find appropriate), the Board should fulfil its task of periodically reviewing and assessing the progress of the implementation of Final Act recommendations. However, as is customary in a situation where real consensus cannot be achieved, the equivocal wording of the resolution left the meaning of implementation in doubt.[9]

5. See comments by Brazil and Pakistan (TD/B/SR.94, pp. 9-10) and Ghana (TD/B/L.31 (17 May 1965)).

6. Comments by the United Kingdom, TD/B/L.63, Add.4, (11 Oct. 1965), p. 14.

7. For the debate at the Second Board, see TD/B/SR.27-35.

8. Note that GATT's Part IV (Art. XXXVII, paras. 1 and 2) provides for reporting procedure on implementation in the Committee on Trade and Development. The GATT secretariat is to circulate the notifications that it may receive from governments when effect is not being given to relevant provisions of Part IV. Contracting Parties are requested to give notice of any actions which they may undertake in pursuit of their commitments under Part IV. On the basis of various information, the GATT secretariat should submit reports summarizing the latest situation on tariff or quota barriers which affect developing countries' exports. (GATT doc. L/2410).

9. See Board resolution 19(II), in TD/B/71 (Aug. 1966).

The review of implementation in GATT apears to be truly effective only in those areas where a state is exposed to retaliatory measures from the other parties to the agreement. Therefore, it is not surprising that GATT's Part IV, in spite of its contractual nature, suffers from the same lack of implementation as various UNCTAD recommendations. In some international organizations of a non-contractual nature—most notably the International Labour Organisation (ILO) and the OECD—member states agree to submit reports and information on the measures they have undertaken to implement given recommendations or constitutional provisions.[10] DAC procedure in the OECD closely resembles what developing countries had in mind for UNCTAD.[11] DAC members undergo the scrutiny of their peers, and common standards are applied to assess their aid programs. Each country is examined by the entire committee, while three delegations have special inquisitorial responsibilities. However, DAC is like a family: discussions and criticisms are private and informal, and the language used is mild and feelings are rarely hurt. Even so, some governments in DAC continued for a long time to harbor suspicion about the entire procedure and felt that their sovereignty was being infringed. Thus it was hard to imagine that developed countries would willingly subject a broad range of their policies in sensitive areas to the scrutiny of a hostile forum like UNCTAD. They naturally interpreted Board resolution 19 (II) to mean that there should be no formalized procedure of evaluation, and that there could only be a general debate rather than a case-by-case examination of policy measures applied by individual countries.[12]

The report by the UNCTAD secretariat has to be the basis for any implementation procedure. It would be a significant step in the direction of a stronger international community if international civil servants could actively seek, obtain and use information on the policies of individual countries free of constraints. However, a vague and weak mandate given by resolution 19 (II), plus the uncooperative attitude of the developed nations, preempted such a possibility. While preparing the first implementation review, the UNCTAD secretariat felt that what was required of it was a fairly comprehensive survey, rather than a direct comparison of the way in which individual countries had imple-

10. Members of the ILO agree to make annual reports on the measures they have taken to give effect to the provisions of the conventions to which they are party. As the ILO matured, this procedure became more thorough. One of the means established to exert moral pressure on states is a blacklist of delinquents. For details see E. B. Haas, *Beyond the Nation-State* (Stanford, Cal.: Stanford University Press, 1964), pp. 248-269.

11. For a description of DAC procedure, see Rubin, *op. cit.,* pp. 73 ff.

12. TD/B/L.63 (11 Oct. 1965), paras. 6-7. For the discussion at the Third Board, see TD/B/SR.62,63,65,67.

mented each recommendation.[13] In its preparation of the report, the UNCTAD secretariat depends mainly on the information that governments supply it with, although it collects its own information from various sources against which it checks the government replies. However, according to the developed countries, reporting is not an obligation but an enlightened practice, and governments individually have the latitude to decide on the nature, form and definition of information that they will offer.[14] Therefore, the developed nations procceded to supply data which was of a general and positive nature, and made it clear that such data was given voluntarily and should be used mainly to find the fields in which it might be possible to organize concerted action. As a result, the end product was an overall view of trends and patterns of international trade and development and the causes underlying them, rather than a tool to spur individual governments into action and to expose their respective policies to the detailed scrutiny of an international forum. Even in its very general form, the first implementation report encountered the criticism of the developed countries.[15] They frowned upon the use of information not supplied by governments,[16] and they felt that the report was too negative in its tone and

13. TD/B/SR.104, p. 84.

14. Only 40 governments furnished answers to the questionnaire on implementation for the 1966 review. Many developing countries failed to do so, as they may have felt that the questionnaire did not apply to them. Besides the information on their own policies, they could also have supplied valuable data on some actions of developed countries—for example, on reverse preferences. UN Doc. A/6135, p. 89.

15. TD/B/82 (20 Jul. 1966) and addenda. Note that the annual report consists of two parts, one on trends in trade and development, and the other on trade policy developments.

16. Note a very interesting case where the UNCTAD secretariat attempted to use unofficial information in the first implementation report. Paragraph 115 (TD/B/82/Add.2 (20 Jul. 1966)) claimed the existence of a *sub rosa* vertical preferential agreement between the United States and Venezuela. Quoting a German source—*Nachrichten fur Aussenhandel*, 2 May 1966— the secretariat claimed that about 1,500 American products enjoyed reverse preferences in Venezuela, in return for special access privileges granted to certain Venezuelan products in the US. The UNCTAD secretariat wanted to show one Latin American country "guilty" of a special arrangement with a developed country, and in this manner to relieve some of the pressure exerted on the African states associated with the EEC. Soon after the report was made public, a corrigendum was issued deleting paragraph 115 without any explanation. Strong pressure by the United States forced the secretariat to yield. American representatives argued that the use of a newspaper source was unwarranted, and that such an arrangement did not exist. (A later check confirmed that the information was to a large extent correct *de facto*. Venezuela applied a conditional MFN regime, and the tariff concessions that it granted to the United States—647 positions, according to the commercial treaty between the two countries renegotiated in 1953—were extended automa-

did not adequately reflect the progress actually made.[17] The Group of 77, on the other hand, objected to the passivity of the developed countries and to their "platonic" statements.

As a result of the initial criticism, the annual implementation reports prepared by the secretariat were significantly toned down, and they are for the time being no more than very general reviews of international trade and development and related policies. At the intergovernmental level, debate is general and vague, as is customary in a situation where implementation review is not focused on the performance of an individual country. The exchange resembles any other general debate in UNCTAD, where developing countries attack overall performance and trends, while developed nations protest their good will, sincere efforts and positive actions.

At present, UNCTAD is removed from the task of supervising, criticizing, or investigating in detail the implementation of its recommendations by individual states. The developed countries claim that agreement on a system of reporting and consultation can come about only through concerted actions and negotiations on the level of plenipotentiaries, where the rights and obligations of states on a given matter would be defined. In other words, until negotiations promoted by UNCTAD or organized under its auspices have borne fruit, members are not expected to say what practical steps they have taken in order to carry out the policies defined by UNCTAD, since this remains within the domain of their autonomous action.[18]

We have reversed the logical order and discussed implementation before negotiation. This, however, reflects the situation in UNCTAD, where the developing countries had hoped to impose greater commitment to action by the developed countries, by creating a direct link between policy recommendations and implementation, without necessarily going through the rule-making stage. As we have seen, their efforts have fared poorly so far.

The question is: what are the present obstacles to the institutionalization of an effective implementation procedure in UNCTAD? The answer is simply that the developed countries feel that their political

---

tically and without compensation to other countries with which it had commercial relations on the basis of the MFN clause, i.e. Belgium, Bolivia, Spain, El Salvador, the United Kingdom and Italy. Since Venezuela did not pursue an active policy of concluding trade agreements, these countries in fact enjoyed a preferential access to its market.)

17. Doubt was cast on the technical quality of the report, especially by the United Kingdom (TD/B/SR.96) and by Belgium (TD/B/SR.101). For the debate at the Fourth Board, see TD/B/SR.93-104, and the Board report in A/6135/Rev.1, Part Two, Chapter I.

18. Statement by the representative of Switzerland, TD/B/SR.33, p. 49.

and economic interests would be adversely affected by such a procedure; besides, they are unwilling to subject themselves to any "ignominious" treatment in this forum of "the poor". There would be fewer difficulties if, first, the implementation procedure were to lose its present connotation for developed countries as constituting persecution against them and, secondly, if these countries were offered some incentive to make them agree to subject a range of their policies to such a review. In this connection, it is important to note that the UNCTAD secretariat envisages the increasing review of policy implementation by *all* countries as one of their organization's basic roles.[19] The secretariat based its thinking on "convergent measures", a concept advanced by Prebisch in his contribution to the preparation of the second Development Decade. He spoke of development as involving mutual responsibilities, and the adoption of a series of concerted measures by peripheral countries and by industrial centers, all as a part of a global strategy.[20] The developing countries would pledge to mobilize their internal resources and commit themselves individually and as a group to a set of policies; in return, the industrial countries would pledge to mobilize international resources to help the others in this endeavor. As part of the strategy and in the name of global interest, all groups of countries would consent to submit their policies, actions and compliance with the guidelines, to detailed international scrutiny and routine assessment in UNCTAD.

This proposal, if put into practice, would represent not only a significant accretion to UNCTAD's prerogatives, but also a higher form of international cooperation. The idea, in fact, acquired a wider meaning during the preparatory work for the second Development Decade. It became generally accepted that one of the ways to give some teeth to the broad guidelines of the development strategy would be through a regular appraisal of the actions taken by *all countries*. The General Assembly resolution 2626 (XXV) speaks of the appropriate arrangements "to keep under systematic scrutiny the progress toward achieving the goals and objectives of the Decade", as well as "to identify shortfalls in their achievement". UNCTAD evidently will pursue the implementation review within its own field of competence, the results to be eventually submitted to the General Assembly, through ECOSOC, for overall appraisals of the development strategy which should take place every two years. Whether the implementation review in UNCTAD will be reinvigorated, made effective and given a true meaning under the umbrella of the second Development Decade still

19. TD/B/173 (31 Jul. 1968), p. 13.
20. Prebisch, *Towards a Global Strategy of Development, op. cit.,* Part V.

remains to be seen.[21] What is more important for the time being is that as a result of UNCTAD's debates and experiences, the concept of implementation as related to "non-binding" recommendations of the UN bodies, is gradually beginning to gain a more widespread acceptance in principle.

Negotiations

General Assembly resolution 1995 (XIX) provides that UNCTAD will:

> initiate action, where appropriate, in cooperation with the competent organs of the UN for the negotiation and adoption of the multilateral legal instruments in the field of trade, with due regard to the adequacy of existing organs of negotiation and without duplicating their activities.

This paragraph reflects the disagreements at the Geneva Conference. The developing countries demanded that the framework for the negotiation of legal instruments or multilateral agreements be set up as required within the permanent machinery of UNCTAD; developed countries argued that UNCTAD could only study the bases of multilateral agreements, and recommend the establishment of *ad hoc* negotiating machinery to ECOSOC, in cases where such machinery did not already exist. After the New Delhi Conference, the developed nations continued to insist that UNCTAD is a body for collective thinking, which should leave others to negotiate policy and concrete measures and to supervise their execution.[22]

A "semantic" dispute has been raging in UNCTAD over the meaning of "negotiations". The B Group insists that negotiations in UNCTAD cannot go beyond the concept as traditionally accepted in the United Nations, which is a deliberative organization with non-committal resolutions as its immediate result. The developed countries criticize the developing countries for their attempts to legislate actions on the part of member states in UNCTAD, and to establish new, binding

---

21. During the debates on the second Development Decade, the developed countries appeared less reluctant to accept the possibility of an implementation review, provided that the self-help efforts of developing countries would be also scrutinized. The developing countries, on the other hand, although very sensitive over the question of their economic and political sovereignty, were apparently ready to consider "paying the price" and having their development policies evaluated in return for an effective implementation procedure. See Cordovez, "UNCTAD: From Confrontation to Strategy," *op. cit.,* Chapter II, p. 12.

22. See TD/B/173 (31 Jul. 1968), p. 6. The functions of the OECD, as seen by the West, may as well refer to UNCTAD. Accordingly, the OECD is not charged with a specific task which it accomplishes with greater or less efficiency; rather, it is a forum to structure communication among members, enhance comprehension of issues, at best leading the members into greater agreement. Ohlin, *The Global Partnership, op. cit.,* p. 242.

principles.[23] One of the main issues before the New Delhi Conference was whether it would be a "negotiating" one. Prebisch expressed the feelings of developing nations—and what he considered to be a widespread understanding—that negotiations in New Delhi would not be solely a reconciliation of views on resolutions and recommendations, as had been the case in Geneva in 1964. According to him, ideas had matured on some issues, and this made it possible to envisage negotiations directed toward an agreement—not necessarily a full draft agreement, but an agreement on basic principles to guide negotiations after the New Delhi meeting.[24] Also, the President of the Fifth Board, in his September 1967 statement which was supposed to reflect the consensus of the participants, said that one of the aims of the Conference was to achieve "specific results" through "appropriate forms of negotiations".[25]

The New Delhi story is well known. The developed countries evidently interpreted the term "negotiations" in its widest sense—i.e., "the sum total of talks and contacts intended to solve conflicts or to work towards the common objectives of a conference,"[26] or, more specifically, a process of achieving agreement on the formulation of recommendations. They thought of the Conference as a deliberative meeting where countries could exchange points of view and engage in general discussion. On the other hand, the Group of 77 hoped that the Conference would have some quasi-legislative traits and make at least certain decisions and/or recommendations which would commit the developed countries to a given course of action.[27] The difficulty was that for the West, negotiations in the economic sphere essentially meant a *quid pro quo* bargaining process leading to a balanced set of mutual concessions,[28] a definition hardly applicable in the UNCTAD context. However, this issue will be further discussed later on.[29] Our main

23. Kotschnig, in *The Global Partnership, op. cit.*, p. 29.

24. TD/B/SC.5/1 (12 Sep. 1966), pp. 9-10.

25. TD/B/SR.151. Also, General Assembly resolution 2206(XXI) (17 Dec. 1966) provided that the Conference should achieve "practical and concrete results by means of negotiation aimed at securing the greatest measure of agreement." However, note that "securing the greatest measure of agreement" was a "chapeau" which diluted the meaning of "negotiation".

26. Kaufmann, *Conference Diplomacy, op. cit.*, p. 23. Also, see his comments as the representative of the Netherlands, TD/B/SR.161, p. 5. [It is interesting that before this semantic dispute flared up, an OECD document assessing the Geneva Conference spoke of "three months of work, discussion and *negotiation* at Geneva." OECD doc. TC(64)14 (1 Jul. 1964), p. 1.]

27. For the distinction between deliberative and legislative conferences see Kaufmann, *op. cit.*, pp. 25-28.

28. The Netherlands' *note verbale* in TD/B/175/Add.3 (3 Sep. 1968), p. 5.

29. See Chapter XIV for a discussion of the nature of negotiations and of the bargaining power of the developing countries.

concern here is the role UNCTAD has played in the negotiation of multilateral instruments.[30]

Let us focus first on commodities. This is relatively the least controversial area because negotiations to conclude commodity agreements are classical in nature, in the sense that they are based on reciprocity. Here, UNCTAD's terms of reference are least circumscribed (such agreements were previously negotiated under the auspices of the UN) and it is a field in which it impinges the least upon the jurisdictional domain of other organizations.

Thus far, several commodity conferences have been held under the auspices of UNCTAD—for tin, olive oil, sugar, cocoa and wheat.[31] For our purpose of defining UNCTAD's role, it is useful to identify those commodities where no agreement is as yet in existence—for example, cocoa, oilseeds, oils and fats, natural rubber, iron ore, etc. Sugar should be included in this group, because the sugar agreement was inoperative and the International Sugar Council was hibernating when UNCTAD tackled the problem. There is a second group of commodities, for which agreements are in existence and are actively administered by appropriate commodity councils. Coffee, wheat, and tin are the three most relevant items here, while olive oil is of marginal importance.

Regarding the first group (i.e., commodities where no agreement exists), it can be asserted that *de facto* negotiations are being, or can be held in UNCTAD. The negotiating conference of plenipotentiaries is convened only after very long periods of preparatory work in UNCTAD during which the necessary documentation is prepared, consultative and commodity study groups meet to assess the possibility of an agreement, secretariat members carry out missions to key capitals to sound out governments, and also act as mediators among participants.[32] Only then does a preparatory committee meet, to be followed

30. Thus far the only multilateral legal (contractual) instrument outside of the commodity agreements negotiated under UNCTAD's auspices has been the Convention on Transit Trade of Land-Locked Countries. On the basis of the recommendation of the Final Act, an *ad hoc* negotiating conference was convened in the summer of 1965 (it was preceded by the meetings of a committee which prepared a draft convention). It adopted the Convention, which, having received a required number of ratifications, entered into force in June 1967.

31. However, representatives from developed countries usually point out that governments attending such commodity negotiations are participants of a conference, not of an UNCTAD body. Statement by the delegate of Japan, TD/B/SR.165, p. 6.

32. Prebisch was very active as a mediator, especially for cocoa and sugar. Many admit that his efforts were of great importance for the conclusion of the sugar agreement. For example, in the case of sugar, he made a recommendation to governments on the basic export tonnages to be allotted to exporters. Obviously,

227

by a negotiating conference if sufficient consensus is achieved on the draft agreement.[33] As we saw in the case of cocoa and sugar as well, the stage of paving the way for the conclusion of the agreement was entirely within UNCTAD. The negotiating conferences were convened under its auspices (i.e., the auspices of the United Nations), serviced by its secretariat, and held in its headquarters. If the conference fails to produce an agreement—as was the case for cocoa and sugar on several occasions—the matter "returns" to UNCTAD, and consultations continue there until the conference is reconvened by its Secretary-General. It is UNCTAD that gets either the credit or the blame, depending on whether negotiations succeed or fail.[34]

If an agreement is concluded, an autonomous commodity council is established to administer and supervise its operation. The Havana Charter provided that such councils would report to the ITO, but there is no such explicit provision in UNCTAD's terms of reference. Although UNCTAD is supposed to facilitate coordination in the commodity field,[35] this does not imply a hierarchical relationship with the councils and UNCTAD *de jure* has nothing to do with the operation of a commodity agreement. However, when an agreement approaches its expiration date (the usual duration is five years), it should be renegotiated under UN, i.e. UNCTAD auspices, where a negotiating conference is convened. As we noted when discussing the wheat agreement, in practice there are several options on this point. Thus, consultations and renegotiations can be held in the UN, or they can be held in the commodity council, to be followed by a negotiating conference under UN auspices. There is also a third possibility: the renegotiating confer-

---

in a sphere where concrete bargaining over prices, tonnages, and the like is involved, the UNCTAD secretariat can play a role very similar to that of the GATT secretariat in trade negotiations.

33. For the description of preparations for a commodity conference, the negotiation of an agreement, and its operation and renewal, see "Intergovernmental Commodity Agreements," *Proceedings,* Vol. III, pp. 113-139.

34. For example, UNCTAD was held responsible for the many frustrations connected with the sugar negotiations. "Sir Harold: UNCTAD Is a Failure, Agency Blamed for Lack of Sugar Agreement." *The Trinidad Guardian,* May 19, 1967. Once the agreement was concluded, UNCTAD was highly praised by many developing countries, including Trinidad's neighbor, Jamaica, whose Minister of Industry and Trade called it "a victory for UNCTAD." UNCTAD, *Monthly Bulletin* (November 1968).

35. As we have already seen, the terms of reference of the Committee on Commodities provide that it coordinate the activities of all bodies in the commodity field, including therein both the autonomous commodity councils and GATT. However, it should do this within the competence of the Conference which, in turn, is "generally, to review and facilitate the co-ordination." See TD/B/61/Rev.1 (17 Feb. 1966), and General Assembly resolution 1995 (XIX).

ence can be held outside the UN, and under the auspices of the commodity council.

We have already noted that tin and olive oil agreements were re-negotiated or extended (where the content of the previous agreement had not substantially changed) at UNCTAD sponsored conferences. However, in regard to both coffee and wheat (in 1967), UNCTAD was prevented from exercising its negotiating function. It faced the obstacles of the strong and institutionalized commodity councils,[36] jealous of their prerogatives, and the desire of principal producers and consumers to conduct renegotiations elsewhere. In the case of the 1967 wheat agreement we saw that UNCTAD played only a marginal role. Similarly, when the coffee agreement was being renegotiated, UNCTAD was limited to the status of observer. Discussions on the renewal of the coffee agreement, which was due to expire in September 1968, took place in the International Coffee Council (ICC). According to the UNCTAD secretariat, even though the Coffee Council was concerned with the renewal of the coffee agreement, the accepted procedure was to convene a United Nations conference, both to review the old agreement and to negotiate a new one. Could the council, which was responsible for the administration of the agreement, undertake the review of its operation alone, or should this function be performed by a broader forum with the council's cooperation? [37] Developed countries and some developing ones argued that renewal negotiations should be held in London, and that a UN conference could perhaps be called at a later stage if desirable. Legal authority, historical precedent and the prestige of UNCTAD and of the Coffee Council were at stake, and all related to the equality of participation and equal opportunity in negotiations. The major producers (particularly Brazil and Colombia) and consumers preferred the International Coffee Council because of the weighted votes and their voting strength there. The smaller producers (African countries and some Latin American ones) favored UNCTAD, because a conference under its auspices would be based on the principle "one country, one vote", and because through UNCTAD they had a better chance of exercising political pressure in favor of their demands.[38]

36. Many developing countries have complained that developed countries, particularly the United Kingdom, exercise considerable control over the commodity councils and groups which are located mainly in London. It has also been argued that the technical nature of these bodies hampers them from assuming an overall view of the needs of developing countries.

37. See TD/B/157 (4 Sep. 1967), p. 6.

38. For example, Ecuador, Uruguay and Peru suggested that the agreement be renegotiated under the auspices of UNCTAD because this would give it greater political weight. *The London Times,* May 31, 1967.

In brief, the venue of renegotiating commodity agreements is controversial and UNCTAD's record so far is mixed. However, its future claims to sponsor renegotiating conferences for those agreements born under its auspices will be much stronger. Another very important point in favor of UNCTAD is the need to have the socialist countries participate in commodity conferences. As we have seen, the USSR has followed a consistent policy line of being prepared to take part only in commodity negotiations sponsored by UNCTAD. This was one of the very important reasons why UNCTAD was chosen as the venue for the 1971 Wheat Conference.[39] What this means in fact is that UNCTAD is likely to gradually seize for itself the negotiation and renegotiation of all international commodity agreements.

Turning our attention to subjects other than commodities, we notice that preferences and supplementary financing represented the two most notable instances where consensus evolution in UNCTAD had proceeded far enough so as to make concrete multilateral action possible. These issues, like most other issues on UNCTAD's agenda, involved a qualitatively new type of negotiations: ideally, the motor force and incentive for states to act would be provided by their overarching goal, the necessity to cope with the problems of economic development multilaterally and in a concerted manner.

In New Delhi, during what was mistakenly felt to be the final stages of negotiations on supplementary financing, developing countries claimed that the scheme which had originated at the Geneva Conference should be completed in UNCTAD, and that any other course would constitute the gravest injustice to UNCTAD's institutional machinery.[40] They asked that the Intergovernmental Group on Supplementary Financing be "authorized to negotiate and decide" on the features of the machinery for supplementary financing, including draft statutes and proposals for the financing of that machinery. This agreement was to be approved by the Trade and Development Board and by the Governors of IBRD, which then would be followed by governmental ratifications.[41] The B Group opposed this proposal, so the New Delhi resolution on supplementary financing contained no provisions regarding

39. In a turnabout, as compared to 1967, the International Wheat Council requsted that UNCTAD convene a conference, and submitted a provisional negotiating text. The UNCTAD secretariat agreed to convene the conference under its auspices only after it was given firm assurances by IWC that there was a good chance of concluding an agreement. This was apparently a self-protective measure against a possible failure of negotiations.

40. Statement on behalf of the Group of 77 by the delegate of Ceylon, TD/SR.78 (27 Mar. 1968).

41. Draft resolution of developing countries (TD/II/C.3/L.18), *Proceedings, New Delhi*, Vol. I, pp. 295-296.

the negotiation of the scheme, or the adoption of an agreement.[42]

As we have already seen, in September 1969 the Ninth Board agreed to ask IBRD to work out arrangements for supplementary financing "on the basis of the conclusions of UNCTAD's Intergovernmental Group." [43] In one sense, UNCTAD had lost the institutional battle because it cannot decide directly on the specific features of the arrangements, as the developing countries might have wished it could. On the other hand, if the recommendations of its intergovernmental group are incorporated basically unchanged into the multilateral agreement on supplementary financing, one can argue that by and large the crucial part of negotiations was completed in UNCTAD, the outcome containing sufficient commitment on the part of the developed countries to assure implementation of the agreement.

For the time being, however, the way the question of supplementary financing has been treated by the IBRD illustrates quite well what is involved behind the interminable institutional disputes between the developed and developing countries, and the efforts of the latter to keep things in UNCTAD. The Bank, contrary to expectations, deferred the detailed consideration of the scheme because there was no support among the majority of potential donors for contributing resources to supplementary financing.[44] The decision of the Bank management, although possibly sound from a banker's point of view, contributes to delay and the reduction of pressure in favor of supplementary financing. In other words, by not drawing up a scheme on the basis of UNCTAD's conclusions and making an estimate of its cost, the Bank has deprived the developing countries of a definite model for which to seek political and financial support, and temporarily postponed a clear-cut debate on the matter.

Regarding preferences, the Algiers Charter asked that negotiations leading to the conclusion of an agreement should be held in UNCTAD, while the developed countries stated categorically in their 1967 OECD report that there should be no binding commitment to grant special preferential treatment to developing nations. Consequently, the resolution on preferences adopted in New Delhi mentions neither "negotiations" nor "agreement"; instead, it points to necessary "consultations" to be held in the Special Committee on Preferences.[45] It differed significantly from the 77's draft resolution, which had asked that a special "negotiating" committee on preferences be established in

42. Resolution 39(II), *ibid.,* p. 42.
43. Board resolution 60(IX), TD/B/(IX)/Misc.9 (24 Sep. 1969), Annex I.
44. See TD/B/327 (30 Sep. 1970), pp. 45-48 and Annex IV. Some observers have interpreted the action as an attempt at pigeonholing.
45. Resolution 21(II), *Proceedings, New Delhi,* Vol. I, p. 38.

UNCTAD, in order to "negotiate" a draft agreement on GSP. After it had completed its work, a conference of government plenipotentiaries was to be convened.[46]

As we have seen, the "consultations" took place in the OECD where the B Group elaborated a joint strategy, and in UNCTAD's Special Committee on Preferences where a mutually acceptable system of generalized preferences was finally agreed to. In UNCTAD, the developing countries criticized the deficiencies of each submission and specified their additional demands, while the scrutiny of unresolved problems continued. Throughout the process, the developed countries scrupulously avoided the term "negotiations". They made a subtle distinction: when parties "negotiate" they agree in the end to something which is binding on both, while in UNCTAD a common understanding was being reached through consultations and consensus, with the donors granting preferences on a purely voluntary basis, with no binding obligations involved.

Yet although no negotiations were involved which would result in a binding legal instrument,[47] *de facto* negotiations on preferences were held in UNCTAD. The process which in 1964 began merely in the form of phrases that representatives hurled at each other in plenary debates, moved to the stages where highly technical and specialized issues were considered and states engaged in complex and hard bargaining. The difference was to be found in the end product; i.e. the political/economic agreement, based on a lesser degree of obligation than a legally binding international treaty, underlined the novel conditions which characterize UNCTAD's work.

The fact that preferences were conceived and brought to fruition in UNCTAD was borne out by the unanimous agreement which stipulated that there should be an appropriate machinery within UNCTAD to review and evaluate the effect of GSP.[48] However, though the countries agreed on what UNCTAD should do, they differed on the nature

46. Draft resolution TD/II/C.2/L.5, *ibid.,* p. 278.

47. The result is simply an "understanding" contained in the report of the Special Committee on Preferences, rather than a protocol or a final document. Note that the spokesman of the B Group argued that the procedure of consultation used in the instance of preferences could not be considered as a precedent for other UNCTAD meetings. TD/B/300/Add.1 (27 Apr. 1970), p. 25.

48. As recently as 1967 many felt that it would be almost impossible to obtain the role of a supervisor of the GSP for UNCTAD, and the Algiers Charter proposal that in due time a suitable machinery be established in this organization to "supervise and ensure the effective implementation" of the GSP was deemed excessive. As a compromise, some thought of UNCTAD/GATT cooperation in this endeavor.

of the machinery to fulfil the task.[49] Another institutional controversy? Yes, but organically related to the problems that we have been discussing, namely, the negotiating and implementing functions of UNCTAD.

In brief, the developed countries argued that the generalized preferences could be reviewed satisfactorily in the Committee on Manufactures, while the 77 wanted a special machinery for this purpose, and proposed that the Special Committee on Preferences become a permanent organ which would be entrusted with this task.[50] In essence, the developed countries were against a committee on preferences because it would have offered a convenient institutional focus for a full-fledged critical and probably acrimonious examination of the general preferences, and a host of related issues. They shun any sort of "implementation" procedure precisely because preferences are granted voluntarily, as a unilateral concession, and since, in their opinion, there are no mutual rights and obligations, the donors should be free to do as they please. Another drawback of the special committee, as far as the B Group is concerned, is that it would make it institutionally easy for the 77 to "negotiate" continuously and to press for additional concessions. In contrast, the Committee on Manufactures has a number of items on its agenda, and there preferences would be treated only as part of the routine business, receiving comparatively less attention and time. Moreover, placing preferences on its agenda would help overload the Committee on Manufactures and cause its other pursuits to be deranged and slowed down. This refers especially to non-tariff barriers, a very sensitive area into which the developed countries would like to prevent UNCTAD from probing too deeply. In view of the above, it is self-explanatory why the Group of 77 is waging a battle for a special machinery. The developing countries also feel that proceedings in the Special Committee on Preference have helped them gain considerable negotiating experience and knowledge, and would like to have this learning process continue so as to be better equipped for future rounds of consultations on similar subjects. Whatever the outcome of this controversy, the fact that UNCTAD has been entrusted with the reviewing and supervising role is an important institutional gain for this organization.

49. See TD/B/329 (12 Oct. 1970), pp. 13-15; also Add.1, p. 20, and Add.4, pp. 8-11. The decision on the matter has been postponed until the Eleventh Board. TAD/INF/463 (13 Oct. 1970).

50. The D Group originally favored the Committee on Manufactures, but it came to support the view of the 77 in the end. (See TD/B/300 (27 Apr. 1970), p. 122.) Of late, the socialist countries have exhibited a pronounced coolness to institutional growth in the UN because of financial implications, and also due to the problem of effective participation by member governments.

During one of the more frustrating moments in New Delhi, one African delegate interpreted the acronym UNCTAD to mean "Under No Circumstances Take Any Decisions". His sarcasm was directed at the major developed countries which adhered to the theory that UNCTAD was a normative forum for the discussion and formulation of policies, and not a negotiating and operational mechanism for co-operation in trade and financing. Our examination of the instances where the issue of negotiations was involved showed that UNCTAD has been moving away from being a purely deliberative forum.

The resolution unanimously adopted at the Seventh Board in September 1968, included a provision that "the task of negotiation, including exploration, consultation, and agreement on solutions, is a single process," and that the "achievement of solutions was and re-mained the primary objective of UNCTAD." [51] Juridically, this text added nothing new, yet its adoption reflected general recognition of the fact that the policy process is continuous and that subjects which have matured in UNCTAD over a period of years cannot be easily severed from it at the point when they require action. It may be technically difficult in some instances to split the process artifically and transfer "hard" negotiations into some other forum, especially when consideration of a given subject has reached an advanced stage in UNCTAD. It may be impractical because of the varying memberships of organizations in this field. And it may be politically difficult to do so because of the opposition of the developing countries, for example, in those instances where a specialized negotiating forum had shown reservations against solutions advanced in UNCTAD, or when they shun a given organization simply because of their own inability to mobilize sufficient bargaining power in favor of their demands within it.

In a number of areas the evolution of substantive consensus is approaching a point where concrete action will have to be undertaken; the contention that UNCTAD can only discuss, review and initiate but not complete the action will thus be challenged more persistently. The problem is likely to be resolved gradually, by creating precedents which would enable UNCTAD to relate more intimately and firmly with negotiating responsibilities.

The "Streamlining" of UNCTAD's Machinery

The techniques and apparatus used to deal with trade, aid and de-velopment have a considerable and sometimes a decisive impact on the efforts to reach conceptual consensus, especially when it comes to

---

51. Board resolution 45(VII), A/7214, p. 93.

translating consensus into practical action.[52] A complicated, unwieldy, inefficient and overburdened machinery can add to the difficulties already inherent in the subject matter. The failure of the New Delhi Conference was ascribed primarily to the lack of political will on the part of the developed countries to meet the demands of the Third World, but some of the exasperation and frustration of the delegates was also due to the lapses in organizational set-up of the Conference.[53] One of the items on its agenda was institutional review, but this matter was in the background while the delegates focussed their attention on the numerous substantive problems. Moreover, the developing countries did not prepare a joint position on the institutional matter, and the secretariat did not present a study of its own.[54] Yet as the end of the Conference approached and disappointments accumulated, the institutional issue became very germane. However, due to the lack of time and delays within the Group of 77, the Conference could only refer the belated draft resolution by India and Chile containing various proposed measures for the improvement of UNCTAD's work to the Board for further action.[55]

Would institutional improvements be directed solely at the "mysterious sterilizing hand of UN procedures", which was manifested in New Delhi (among other things) through a waste of time and energy on procedural matters, repetitive debates and speeches, and an immense agenda? Or would it also involve adding new functions to UNCTAD's arsenal? The B Group members generally felt that the functions and organizational set-up of UNCTAD should remain unchanged,[56] while the developing countries advocated a sweeping review. The thrust of

52. A communication by the government of the Netherlands, TD/B/175/Add.3 (3 Sep. 1968), p. 4.
53. We shall discuss the informal group system in Chapters XII and XIV. It also contributed to the difficulties experienced in New Delhi.
54. Apparently, the UNCTAD secretariat wanted the matter toned down, so as not to detract attention from the urgent and pressing matters of substance. Prebisch gave the green light to his staff on this only during the session in New Delhi.
55. TD/L.30 in *Proceedings, New Delhi,* Vol. I, p. 407. It is interesting to note that the initiative in this matter was undertaken by the secretariat, which passed the original draft to the Indian and Chilean delegations some four weeks before the end of the Conference. When the two countries managed to produce a joint draft, the end of the Conference was already near, and there was no time or desire to consider their proposal in depth in the Group of 77. One of the reasons for the delay was also the wish to see what the substantive outcome of the Conference would be, and to base the proposals for institutional review on the outcome.
56. A communication by the government of F.R. Germany, TD/B/175 (22 Aug. 1968), p. 9. Note that some developed countries commended UNCTAD and stated that it had fulfilled the hopes and expectations. This effort to present UNCTAD in a generally positive light was intended to counter the 77, which painted a bleak picture and asked for concomitant improvements.

their demands was aimed at introducing into UNCTAD "certain well-known techniques for specific action, such as reporting, initiating concrete action plans, consultations, negotiations, and reviewing and overseeing," thus enabling it to reach decisions and come to positive conclusions.[57] In essence, the developing countries questioned whether the UNCTAD machinery, broadly patterned after the General Assembly, was quite appropriate and sufficient for dealing with the problems of trade and development.

Their proposals for improvements went along four basic lines. Primarily—and this was the area where the debate centered—they wanted UNCTAD to be recognized as an action-oriented negotiating body, capable of reaching decisions and positive conclusions.[58] As regards the operational function, mainly because of pressures from its more progressive members upon the reluctant delegations of the United States and the United Kingdom, the B Group conceded that UNCTAD should become a participating agency in the UNDP.[59] However, on questions of negotiating and implementing functions, the B Group insisted on its traditional interpretation of UNCTAD's role as an organ to assist in the continuing process of dialogue.[60]

The second aim of the Group of 77 was to reduce the frequency and duration of meetings, and to improve the process of deliberation, so as to release energy, time and resources which could be devoted to the tasks of exploration, consultation and negotiation. It was agreed that the triennial conference should be shortened to 3-4 weeks, that its agenda should be limited to fundamental matters mature for settlement, and that it should be preceded by a short preparatory meeting which would deal with organizational and administrative matters (in New Delhi these subjects had taken a great deal of precious time). The Board is to hold one meeting a year instead of two, to concentrate on substance [61] and on working out agreed solutions, and to ensure the

57. See TD/L.30, *op. cit.,* and the draft resolution of the 77 at the Seventh Board, TD/B/L.126 (3 Sep. 1968).

58. The work of the Seventh Board in the fall of 1968 was based on governments' comments on the India/Chile proposal contained in TD/B/175 (22 Jul. 1968), and addenda, and the study by the secretariat, TD/B/173 (31 Jul. 1968). The resolution adopted by the Board (45(VII)) is in its report (A/7214, pp. 93-96). For a thorough analysis of the review of institutional arrangements that took place at the Seventh Board see Cordovez, "UNCTAD: From Confrontation to Strategy," *op. cit.,* Chapter VII, pp. 158-192.

59. We shall discuss this development in the next chapter, which deals with task expansion.

60. Comments by the United Kingdom government, TD/B/175/Add.1 (1 Aug. 1968), p. 9.

61. For example, the elections of officers, representation of intergovernmental and non-governmental organizations, review of coordination, calendars, work

holding of meetings on a high political level whenever an issue of great importance is on its agenda. The main committees are also to meet once a year, ahead of their parent body.

This underaccentuation and rationalization of the traditional UN deliberative procedure was to be accompanied by a wider practice of consultation through *ad hoc* bodies, such as intergovernmental groups, expert groups and working parties; this, in fact, was the third aim of the Group of 77. They proposed that these groups be small in size (not more than 12 delegations, according to the secretariat paper on the subject), that they meet in private, and that they have precise terms of reference and a deadline for the completion of their task. These proposals must have struck the developed countries as an attempt to introduce certain working methods into UNCTAD which have proved highly useful in GATT. In general, the B Group felt that organizations other than UNCTAD offered opportunities for consultation on financial and trading issues, and that such efforts could be undertaken in UNCTAD only in those circumstances where the inadequacy of other forums was established. Furthermore, such meetings could be convened only if the governments most concerned agreed to it.[62] The developed countries pointed to the agreement reached in New Delhi which authorized the Secretary-General to arrange for intergovernmental consultations in the field of commodities,[63] while on other matters the standing organs of UNCTAD could fulfil the role. The compromise reached provided that the terms of reference for the Committees on Manufactures, and Financing and Invisibles be so altered so as to enable them to set up intergovernmental groups to perform specialized work without further approval by the Board.[64] These groups, however, were not to be vested with any consultative prerogatives and had to be patterned according to the typical UN bodies of that kind.

The fourth aim of the developing countries was to define with more precision the role of the secretariat, since the relevant provisions of the General Assembly resolution 1995 (XIX) were rather vague. The secretariat members were on many occasions not quite certain how to

programs and financial requirements could be all disposed of at a short special session of the Board, or simultaneously with the work of the Second Committee of the General Assembly.

62. Comments by the government of the Netherlands, TD/B/175/Add.3 (3 Sep. 1968), p. 6. The Brazilian viewpoint was that such groups should meet at the request of one or more of the developing countries, and not just of any member of UNCTAD, since this organization's task is primarily to help the developing countries. TD/B/175 (22 Jul. 1968), p. 6.

63. Resolution 16(II), *Proceedings, New Delhi,* Vol. I, p. 36.

64. The Committee on Commodities and the Committee on Shipping already had such provisions in their terms of reference.

behave, and were often attacked for overstepping their prerogatives. The developed countries especially, lost no opportunity in critizing a secretariat which they considered as activist and the right arm of the 77. The draft resolution of the Group of 77 provided that UNCTAD's Secretary-General be authorized to appoint and convene meetings of intergovernmental groups and similar bodies whenever in his judgement the need arose to do so; he should also take the necessary initiative and participate fully in discussions and negotiations. These proposals were hardly reflected in the resolution adopted by the Board: the Secretary-General could arrange for intergovernmental consultations only in the field of commodities, and only after having taken into account the views of any commodity group or council concerned, consulted with interested governments, and done the necessary preparatory work.[65] Regarding discussions and negotiations, he would take initiative and be appropriately represented, rather than participate fully at all stages as the developing countries had suggested. It is interesting to note that, in conformity with GATT practice, the Secretary-General was given the authority to fix and modify the dates of UNCTAD meetings, after consulting with the chairmen of the organs concerned.

Many observers felt that the failure of the New Delhi Conference on substantive issues and the consequent disenchantment of developing countries, would make it necessary for the B Group to be more conciliatory on the institutional issue at the Seventh Board. However, the developed countries apparently felt that making a single concession —that on UNCTAD's status as a participating agency in the UNDP— would be sufficient. The reduction of the frequency and duration of sessions of the Conference and its organs was basically non-controversial.[66] This was also true of the clarification of the Conference's role—it would primarily review and ratify policies and give general guidelines, while the continuing machinery would do the main work and produce results.[67] Some flexibility was introduced through the

65. The developed countries were rather unwilling to consider giving more flexibility and greater latitude to UNCTAD's Secretary-General for convening such meetings. They apparently feared a possibility of such meetings being convened without the support of all governments. Moreover, they associated the proposed prerogatives not with the office of the Secretary-General in abstract, but with Prebisch himself.

66. Note that long meetings brought out in bolder relief UNCTAD's image as a debating club, and too many meetings reduced the level of representation. The Board meetings in 1969 were especially long, and resort was made to the so-called "resumed session" due to the controversy over UNCTAD's contribution to the preparations for the second Development Decade.

67. Before the New Delhi Conference, the work of the continuing machinery almost ceased, with everybody waiting for the big meeting which was expected to achieve concrete results.

238

Secretary-General's new prerogative of changing dates of meetings, as well as convening commodity consultations. (Previously, a special session of the Board was necessary to authorize such consultations.) Yet, no truly qualitative changes occurred in UNCTAD's machinery which were commensurate with its task. In addition to lack of progress on negotiating and implementing functions, the developing countries failed in their attempt to gain acceptance for a widespread use of inter-governmental groups as a means to introduce priorities and functional specificity into the decision-making process and to overcome obstacles to meaningful negotiations inherent in the unwieldy size of deliberative bodies. The proposals advanced by the developing countries had to be shelved until a more favorable opportunity came for institutional innovation, while UNCTAD continued along the lines characteristic of its work during the previous period. The Group of 77, however, has adopted the tactics of keeping the institutional question constantly alive. This, in fact, is an incremental method of improving UNCTAD's machinery, because limited concessions can always be extracted from the developed countries. Consequently, it is to be expected that one of the important proposals at the next Conference will be to amend and go beyond UNCTAD's terms of reference as prescribed in General Assembly resolution 1995 (XIX).

Chapter XI

TASK EXPANSION

The scope of UNCTAD's activities has been controversial ever since the idea of new machinery was advanced in the early 1960's. The developed countries argued, among other things, that a wider scope could be achieved only at the expense of efficiency. They originally insisted that UNCTAD's continuing machinery be confined to the field of commodities, because a mandate in other areas related to development would cause it to duplicate the work of other international organizations. In contrast, the developing countries asked for a global, centralized and coordinated approach through a single institution devoted to development, an institution which would take an overall view of the legal, economic, financial and commercial aspects of their situation. In other words, almost any subject which would be subsumed under the heading of improving their lot in world economy could be considered for inclusion among UNCTAD's activities.[1]

We have defined "task expansion" as those instances where a new assignment was not explicitly provided in UNCTAD's terms of reference, and therefore represented their amplification; or where it was not to be found among UNCTAD's activities in the earlier period. Although task expansion is not necessarily accompanied by the creation of a new organ, the developing countries almost invariably ask for a working group or a committee, because they feel that unless a special institutional focus is created, the matter will not receive the attention that it deserves.

The situation in UNCTAD could briefly be characterized as one where the developing countries press for task expansion, while the

1. This, of course, does not exclude functionally specific pressures through a decision on priorities—i.e., concentrating in a given period on the realization of a limited number of objectives. In GATT, for example, which to begin with does not have a very diversified task, two important problems are seldom dealt with at the same time, and strategy, timing and priorities are crucial. Prior to the New Delhi Conference, the major developed countries tacitly supported a mushrooming of the agenda, expecting that this would lessen the pressure upon them, increase their maneuverability, and not permit concentration in depth on any subject.

240

developed countries resist such proposals. There are many reasons why the developing countries behave as they do; among other things, through inertia they want to bring into UNCTAD almost everything that concerns them, as this is the only international organization where they possess a degree of control both over the machinery and over the secretariat. They follow the premise that chances are higher for a "learning process" to take place if a matter is dealt with regularly in its own institutional niche. Finally, dissatisfied with the performance and progress of other international organizations, the developing countries are attempting to intensify political pressure and achieve more by bringing certain matters into UNCTAD. Additional causes of task expansion, of course, are both the new and pressing needs that keep appearing and generating further pressures to this end, and the vulnerability of the UNCTAD secretariat to the expansionist bent of international civil servants.

In view of the usual attitude of the developed countries, which is to prevent UNCTAD from getting additional mandates and to bypass it if at all possible, the 77 have adopted the tactic of constantly exerting pressure for task expansion. The developed countries make small concessions which are incorporated into decisions, but the 77 return with a new demand, and so on. Compared to the original proposals of the developing countries, the instances of task expansion in UNCTAD are usually diluted compromises, with both the substantive scope and the institutional features circumscribed. Compared with the previous situation, however, they represent significant progress.

Technical Assistance

After 1960 the developing countries pressed for "devolution" of the UN's operational responsibilities in the economic and social field to regional economic commissions.[2] They wanted to secure a larger measure of control over the UN programs of technical and preinvestment assistance by taking them out of the jurisdiction of the Department of Economic and Social Affairs, where the influence of the conservative donors was very strong, and where at that time all senior posts were filled by western staff members. The opponents of decentralization did not wish to yield control of these programs to those UN organs which, according to them, lacked the proper skill and expertise, sound economic judgement and political responsibility.[3] Al-

2. "Devolution" means a transfer of power to make final decisions, while "deconcentration" refers to administrative delegation without a final transfer of power.
3. Gregg, *op. cit.*, pp. 232 and 272. Note the statement by the UN Under-

though the various recommendations of the Final Act mention technical assistance and its role in the development of the Third World, the institutional provisions are silent on UNCTAD's operational role in this field.[4] The reason for this was that at that time the developing countries concentrated on substantive matters and therefore considered this task as being of marginal importance. They also feared that by making premature reference to technical assistance they might endanger the extremely frail compromise on the establishment of the continuing machinery. After the machinery came into being, and as the secretariat was gradually constituted, developing countries made it amply clear that they expected technical assistance from UNCTAD, and they actually came up with specific requests. The B Group, however, maintained its position that UNCTAD was a policy-formulating and deliberating organization, not to be endowed with operational functions.

At the Fourth Board in September 1966, the secretariat submitted a document which stressed that UNCTAD was in a strong position to render technical assistance in the field of trade and invisibles, because of its broad membership, its close working arrangements with regional economic commissions, and its close relations with the newly formed UNIDO.[5] After protracted informal negotiations, the developed countries yielded and the resolution adopted by the Board empowered UNCTAD to give technical assistance related to export promotion, trade expansion and integration among developing countries, shipping, insurance and tourism. This represented a qualitative change in UNCTAD's terms of reference and started the chain of events which led to the status of a participating agency in the UNDP in 1968.[6]

However, the first step had to be modest. The draft resolution circulated privately by Chile asked that UNCTAD become a participating agency in the UNDP, and UNCTAD's Secretary-General a member of the Inter-Agency Consultative Board (IACB) of the UNDP. At that time only the second part of the proposal could be agreed upon.[7] As a concession to the B Group, Prebisch made a statement

Secretary for Economic and Social Affairs to the Second Committee in 1960, to the effect that regional commissions should devote themselves to research and study, and be barred from operational responsibilities. (A/C.2/L.518). Quoted in *ibid.*, p. 273.

4. Recommendations A.II.4, A.II.5, A.III.3, A.III.4, A.III.8, A.IV.23, A.IV.24, and A.IV.25, in *Proceedings*, Vol. I, pp. 31-57.

5. TD/B/97 (15 Aug. 1966).

6. Board resolution 31(IV), in A/6135/Rev.1, Part II, Annex A. Only a brief mention of these negotiations is to be found in the summary records (TD/B/SR.107 and 110.) A compromise with the B Group was made possible by withdrawing the request for a "participating agency" status.

7. See Board resolution 31(IV) and General Assembly resolution 2207(XXI)

to the effect that although he considered the full membership of UNCTAD's Secretary-General in the Consultative Board of the UNDP to be essential for his organization to play its substantive role effectively, he did not see a link between this membership and UNCTAD's status as a participating agency. The United Nations is a participating agency, and UNCTAD is part of the UN; therefore, it would use the UN's various operational and administrative services. The UNCTAD secretariat would give full substantive support to technical assistance activities, but would not add any further machinery to what already existed.[8] Under this arrangement, technical assistance projects in the field of trade and invisibles were allocated to the United Nations, while UNCTAD acted as one of the substantive departments of the UN Secretariat, to which the Office of Technical Cooperation (OTC) of the Department for Economic and Social Affairs turned for advice. In other words, UNCTAD had no operational and administrative machinery to render technical assistance.[9] Unlike UNIDO, UNCTAD had no funds of its own to provide technical assistance projects, and it had to refer either to the UNDP or to the regular technical assistance program of the UN—in either instance through the Department for Economic and Social Affairs.

In the initial stages, the UNCTAD secretariat had no serious difficulties in performing its substantive support role—with the exception of some projects where speedy action was required and where delays occurred due to the lengthy procedures that its requests had to follow. Informally, however, the developing countries and the secretariat kept mentioning a participating agency status for UNCTAD in the UNDP. They pointed to UNIDO, which gained this prerogative *ab initio*,[10]

(17 Dec. 1966). See TD/23 (3 Nov. 1967) for a concise review of this matter. Under the instructions of the General Assembly, the UNDP amended rule 6 of its rules of procedure, so as to include UNCTAD among the UN organs which could send representatives to the meetings of its governing council.

8. Substantive support means, *inter alia,* advising governments on how to formulate requests, advise the UN Office of Technical Cooperation (OTC) and the UNDP on requests received from governments, evaluate candidates for a given mission and for export promotion projects, brief experts, maintain contact with them while they are in the field, support their activities with information, review their reports, etc. In addition, on a more general level, the secretariat could collect the available data and experience, and make it available to developing countries (TD/B/139 (28 Jul. 1967) and TD/23 (3 Nov. 1967)). The Prebisch statement is reproduced in TD/23, Annex 1, p. 1.

9. Decisions were still taken by OTC and the Department of Economic and Social Affairs (in more important cases by De Seynes himself, but never by Prebisch).

10. General Assembly resolution 2152(XXI), 17 Nov. 1966.

but the B Group argued that UNCTAD had no problems in obtaining UNDP funds.

By 1968 the situation had changed significantly. When the joint GATT/UNCTAD center was considered, some developed countries (the United States in particular) suggested the possibility of the proposed center becoming the executing and participating agency of the UNDP, so that it could directly carry out the technical assistance programs funded by the UNDP.[11] This was a controversial proposal, aimed at allowing the center direct access to UNDP funds, while UNCTAD would remain at its former status. In fact, this was a tactical move to divert the UNDP funds primarily to export promotion projects, while sidetracking and neutralizing UNCTAD and its projects which were likely to dwell on trade policies, and fundamental and structural problems of international trade and invisibles.[12] The proposal could not go unchallenged, since it was more logical for UNCTAD, one of the parent bodies, to become a participating agency. Also the New Delhi Conference marked the end of the jurisdictional dispute between the Department of Economic and Social Affairs and the UNCTAD secretariat, and the transfer to the latter of the research responsibility and substantive support in technical assistance for shipping and the improvement of ports. Therefore, it was expected that the demands for technical assistance from UNCTAD would increase substantially as the GATT/UNCTAD Trade Center began its work, and as various programs of integration, foreign sector planning, shipping, ports, insurance, etc., were initiated in the developing countries.

The UNCTAD secretariat felt that it would be impossible to obtain technical assistance financing when faced with the entrenched positions of other agencies if UNCTAD did not become a participating agency of the UNDP.[13] The developing countries adopted the same view and at the Seventh Board in September 1968 included it as one of their major demands for institutional improvements in UNCTAD.[14] Their demand was supported by the socialist states, France, and the Scandinavian countries. The principal opponents of the proposed solution— the United States and the United Kingdom—yielded eventually. Thus the Board adopted a resolution asking the General Assembly to promote UNCTAD into a participating and executing agency of the

11. See GATT document L/2932, and UN document A/C.2/239, para. 20.
12. Export promotion has been labelled the "opium of the people".
13. At that time, the participating agencies in addition to the United Nations and UNIDO were ILO, FAO, UNESCO, ICAO, WHO, IBRD, ITU, WMO, IAEA, UPU and IMCO.
14. See the draft resolution of the Group of 77 (TD/B/L.128 (10 Sep. 1968), which heavily relied on the original secretariat memorandum.

UNDP.[15] Again, however, the Secretary-General had to undertake certain commitments as a concession to the opposition. He promised that UNCTAD's new status would not lead to the establishment of additional administrative services, that export promotion projects would be executed primarily through the UNCTAD/GATT Trade Center,[16] and that no changes would be made in the handling of projects under Chapter V of the UN budget. Regarding this last point, Prebisch said that he would not suggest any modification of the practice of handling projects in the fields of trade and development in the UN Regular Programme of Technical Co-operation, that he would not seek to earmark a specific portion of Chapter V in advance for such projects, and that he would not try to have a part of the funds in Chapter V taken and assigned to UNCTAD under another heading.[17] This actually meant that regarding the regular technical assistance program the UNCTAD secretariat would not disturb the *status quo* in relation to the Department for Economic and Social Affairs.

However, as is usually the case, a commitment undertaken by an international civil servant—even though its wording was very closely negotiated by all concerned—does not have to be honored by governments. In the Second Committee of the General Assembly which approved UNCTAD's status as a participating agency in the UNDP in December 1968,[18] the developing countries, supported by France, asked that the annexed statement by Prebisch and any reference to it be deleted from the resolution. As a compromise, the statement was deleted, although the preambular paragraph referring to it remained. One delegation even expressed the view that the annex would stand only while Prebisch was in office, and that his successor would not have to abide by it. Obviously, the 77 anticipated further institutional developments in this area, with UNCTAD slowly gaining ground.

Appearing in its full right as a participating agency of the UNDP, was a significant point for UNCTAD in its attempts to climb up and establish itself in the institutional hierarchy of international organi-

15. Board resolution 44(VII), in A/7214, p. 84. France played a crucial role in this process.

16. See appendix to resolution 44(VII). The Secretary-General emphasized that the GATT/UNCTAD Center is responsible for export promotion with neither GATT nor UNCTAD having activities of their own.

17. Trade is in Section 13, which includes economic development, social development, and public administration. A separate section for industrial development was opened by the General Assembly resolution 2298 (XXII) (12 Dec. 1967). Industrial development is reviewed by UNIDO's Industrial Development Board, and is handled directly by the UNIDO secretariat without having to go through the Department for Economic and Social Affairs.

18. General Assembly resolution 2401(XXII), 13 Dec. 1968.

zations. By acquiring its own identity within the UNDP—previously it was the UN representative who spoke in its name—UNCTAD has gained the chance of imparting to governments its ability to provide technical assistance, and engaging in "agency salesmanship".[19] Of course, this is essential, because in order to obtain the bigger share of technical assistance funds for those areas of activity for which UNCTAD is responsible, the requests have to come from the governments in order to be honored by the UNDP.

Since 1969 technical assistance projects carried out by UNCTAD have mushroomed and diversified, an important change in view of the previously limited number of UN projects in the field of trade and invisibles. Thus in 1970, the UNCTAD program of technical assistance amounted to almost $ 2 million, and was primarily financed by the UNDP resources.[20] So far the UNCTAD secretariat has respected the original agreement and relied on administrative, financial and recruitment machinery of the UN Headquarters (OTC and the Technical Assistance Recruitment Services (TARS)). But due to the New York-Geneva gap some difficulties were experienced in the administrative and financial servicing of UNCTAD's operational activities, and for the sake of administrative sanity some functions were transferred to Geneva.[21] The UNCTAD secretariat has already suggested that this matter should be eventually reconsidered, and moves toward decentralization can be expected. Regarding the regular technical assistance activities of the United Nations, a downward trend in the planned resources for trade and invisibles projects to be executed in the year

19. Some psychological imponderables are involved here, including the question of prestige.

20. By UNDP criteria, UNCTAD is a small operational agency. The big ones are FAO, UNESCO, ILO, WHO and the UN. For 1970, there were 91 projects for 58 countries, and 20 inter-country projects, as well as 134 individual assignments to technical assistance missions and 399 fellowships for training activities. The projects fell into the following main categories: export promotion and marketing; trade policy, planning and projections; trade expansion and integration; shipping and ports; and, insurance and reinsurance. As of 30 June, 1970, the total for the year 1970 stood at $1,760,900. Of this the UNDP funds accounted for $1,454,900, while $306,000 came from the regular UN program. Of this total sum, $868,000 was for the export promotion projects carried through the UNCTAD/GATT Center (supplemented by another $1 million in voluntary contributions by the developed countries). For an extensive discussion of technical assistance activities of UNCTAD see TD/B/315 (22 Jul. 1970). For the framework and procedures of the UNDP see P. Berthoud, "The United Nations Development Programme," *Journal of World Trade Law*, Vol. 4, No. 2, March/April 1970, pp. 155-191.

21. A Technical Assistance Co-ordination Unit has been established in the Office of the Secretary-General of UNCTAD. It is responsible for UNCTAD's technical assistance activities.

246

1971, has led the UNCTAD secretariat and some countries to suggest that a way should be found to endow trade and invisibles with a greater share in this program. Presumably, this could involve changing the procedure under Chapter V of the UN Budget and earmarking in advance a part of the funds for this purpose. Yet, the fact remains that the regular UN program has been stationary for the past 6 years—at $ 6.9 million, of which $ 1.5 million was earmarked for UNIDO. Obviously, this is not where the future of UNCTAD's technical assistance lies, and its eye will be turned primarily to the expanding extra-budgetary resources of the UNDP which amounted to approximately $ 230 million per year as the 1970's set in.

International Shipping Legislation

The field of shipping offers a good example of the task expansion process in UNCTAD. Following the usual scenario, at the First Board in 1965, the developing countries proposed the establishment of a separate committee on shipping,[22] while the developed countries argued that shipping matters should be included on the agenda of the Committee on Invisibles and Financing, because any proliferation of committees and subsidiary bodies of the Board would decrease its effectiveness and dilute the resources of the secretariat.[23] Yet the Group of 77 succeeded in obtaining a committee on shipping, equal in status and terms of reference to the other standing committees in UNCTAD. The beginning of the committee was difficult, and it took a first session and a special session to adopt a program of work. There was a lot of opposition to the committee and the secretariat undertaking substantive work. However, the 77 were quite successful in initiating dialogue in UNCTAD on a variety of shipping subjects which the maritime powers had had no intention of discussing a few years earlier. Using the committee as the institutional focus, the developing countries and the secretariat gradually brought a number of substantive issues into UNCTAD.

In 1966 the Group of 77 raised the question of international shipping legislation, which was not covered by the adopted program of work. It was argued that the comprehensive approach to shipping in

22. TD/B/SR.10, p. 62. Recommendation A.IV.21 of the Final Act called for intergovernmental machinery on the economic aspects of shipping to be established.

23. TD/B/L.23 (27 Apr. 1965), p. 9. The other way to look at this matter, of course, is to say that the Committee on Invisibles and Financing, by being overburdened with a variety of subjects, would actually be paralyzed and made more inefficient.

UNCTAD required that legal rules also be examined. As we have seen, the B Group countries firmly objected to UNCTAD's undertaking any activities in this sphere, because they felt that the existing bodies could be used for the resolution of the controversy. They referred to the International Maritime Committee, but since this was a non-governmental organization, the 77 insisted that it could not fulfil this function.[24] Another possibility was the legal committee of the International Maritime Consultative Organization (IMCO). The developing countries refused to consider this solution saying that IMCO deals with purely technical questions of shipping and their legal implications, and that the IMCO Council which runs this organization is not representative, since the majority of its members are elected from countries owning the largest merchant marines. As a last line of defense, the developed countries singled out the UN Commission on International Trade Law (UNCITRAL), a newly formed organ of the UN General Assembly responsible for the activities in the field of international trade law.[25] They continued to stress that UNCTAD's Committee on Shipping was not specialized enough for this matter, and that the UNCTAD secretariat had no competent staff for the task.

In New Delhi the developing countries pointed out that UNCITRAL did not include shipping legislation as a priority item on its work program, and they felt that UNCITRAL's work on the economic and commercial aspects of international shipping legislation would be dormant for a long time unless UNCTAD took the initiative.[26] The draft resolution submitted by the 77 asked that a standing committee on international shipping legislation be formed within UNCTAD, for the purpose of reviewing the commercial and economic aspects of

24. The International Maritime Committee was established in Brussels at the end of the ninetheenth century, and is composed of lawyers and shipowning, cargo-owning, banking, insurance and shipbuilding interests. Its drafts are submitted to governments through the Brussels diplomatic conference which meets every four or five years. Legal rules and conventions prepared by it traditionally were biased in favor of the carrier (shipowner) and against the shipper (cargo-owner).

25. As a sidelight, it is interesting to note that at the Fourth Board, responding to General Assembly resolution 2102(XX) (20 Dec. 1965) on the progressive development of private international law with a particular view to promoting international trade, developing countries sponsored a draft resolution (TD/B/L.98 (22 Sept. 1966)) which states that according to its objectives and composition, UNCTAD is the most appropriate body for the examination, on a permanent basis, of the unification, harmonization and modernization of international trade law. However, the General Assembly established UNCITRAL to undertake this task. (General Assembly resolution 2205(XXI) (17 Dec. 1966)).

26. For the summary of the debate in the Fourth Committee of the New Delhi Conference, see Proceedings, New Delhi, Vol. I, pp. 315-317.

shipping in relation to legislation; to indicate what modifications and what new legislation might be necessary; and to issue directives for UNCITRAL to follow.[27] If UNCITRAL's work proves unsatisfactory, or if it is not capable of fulfilling the task, the standing committee should itself undertake the drafting of legislation. The revised draft of the 77 asked for a working group in lieu of a committee. However, no meeting ground could be established, primarily because of the United Kingdom's inflexibility, and as a result the resolution asking the Board to establish the working group was voted through at the plenary of the Conference.[28]

At the end of the New Delhi Conference it was not quite clear whether the developed countries would attempt to obstruct the formation of the working group, boycott its work and fail to participate in its financing (as they threatened), or whether they would engage in further bargaining over the nature of its program of work and its terms of reference. The first possibility was highly unlikely, because whenever an international machinery is created, even though its opponents threaten not to participate in its work, they usually fail to carry out their threats. In this instance, such a move would have been politically costly. Besides, many developed nations were quite sympathetic to the goals of the proposed body. Actually, the 77 intended the vote in New Delhi to be a method of speeding up the process of consensus attainment,[29] and of improving their bargaining position. The issue was discussed again at the Seventh Board, where unanimous agreement was finally reached on the establishment of a working group. However, its composition, terms of reference and work program were left to the decision of the Committee on Shipping as its parent body.[30] Once more, the developed countries reiterated that there was no need for UNCTAD to be involved in this specialized subject, and that although it could act as a catalyst to stimulate improvement and innovation in international maritime law, substantive work should be carried out by other "competent" international bodies.

Before the Committee on Shipping met in the spring of 1969,

27. TD/II/C.4/L.15, *ibid.*, pp. 317-318. This was a maximal institutional demand, because it was very unlikely that a standing committee would be created for such a limited task.

28. Resolution 14(II), *ibid.*, pp. 50-51. Most members of the B Group voted against it (Austria, the Holy See, and New Zealand abstained), although many of them sympathized with the demands of the 77.

29. Remember that the process of conciliation does not apply to procedural and institutional matters, except in amending General Assembly resolution 1995(XIX). A vote can be pressed at any time.

30. See A/7214, pp. 41-42. The 1969 session of the Committee on Shipping was to interpret resolution 14(II) passed by the New Delhi Conference.

UNCITRAL under the beneficial influence of the duplication threat (or in spite of it), created an *ad hoc* working group on international shipping legislation and included shipping legislation as one of the priority items on its agenda.[31] In the Committee on Shipping the 77 asked that the UNCTAD Working Group on International Shipping Legislation review the economic and commercial aspects of this legislation from the standpoint of shipping and development of developing nations, and then make recommendations to UNCITRAL; if necessary, it should draft new legislation and prepare documentation which would serve as a basis for further work to be carried out by both UNCTAD and UNCITRAL.[32] In addition UNCTAD was to examine the feasibility of drafting a general instrument on maritime transportation development, an instrument which would deal with international relations in shipping. In contrast, the draft resolution submitted by the B Group was mainly concerned with the institutional problems of avoiding a duplication of activities, and with the size and composition of the working group.[33]

The compromise resolution adopted by the committee contained no mention about "drafting", nor did it speak of further work "to be carried out by both UNCTAD and UNCITRAL" once recommendations were made by the working group.[34] The membership of the group was set at 33, a figure much larger than the 20 advocated by the developing countries. No reference was made on the feasibility of a general convention or agreement on maritime transportation and development. This compromise reflected the three persistent elements in the attitude of the B Group: confine UNCTAD to its deliberating function; generally oppose improvements in its working methods which might bring it closer to a negotiating forum;[35] and resist any incorpo-

31. The decision in UNCITRAL was taken in March 1969. See the statement of UNCITRAL's chairman to the Committee on Shipping (TD/B/240 (27 April 1969), Annex IV). General Assembly resolution 2421(XXIII) (18 Dec. 1968) recommended that UNCITRAL include international shipping legislation as one of its priority items.

32. TD/B/C.4/L.40, in TD/B/240 (27 Apr. 1969), Annex V.

33. TD/B/C.4/L.43, in *idem*.

34. Committee on Shipping resolution 7(III), *ibid.*, Annex I. The UNCTAD secretariat and the UN Office of Legal Affairs will jointly provide services for the working group. *Ibid.*, p. 34. For this purpose a secretariat joint unit was established and located in the UNCTAD headquarters in Geneva. (See our Chapter VI for a discussion of international shipping legislation from the substantive point of view).

35. It has been argued that the expanded membership of the working group was promoted by the developed countries not only to secure a seat for all those vitally concerned with the issue of international shipping legislation, but also to transform it into a large committee *de facto*. The political tension that inevitably

ration of an overall set of principles on development into an international convention or agreement.

It took three years for the subject of international shipping legislation to earn its place on UNCTAD's agenda, and more than four years before the substance of the issue was really tackled in depth. The group's terms of reference were significantly diluted from what the developing countries considered to be a satisfactory institutional framework. On the positive side, however—and this is important—by raising the issue of international shipping legislation, the 77 brought it onto the international scene and prepared the ground for its re-examination from the point of view of the economic development of the Third World. The duplication threat generated by UNCTAD helped force action in UNCITRAL; that is, it resulted in indirect task expansion (or "cross-fertilization"). Obviously, its long-term effects on international private maritime law will be significant.

Trade Expansion and Integration among Developing Countries

As we indicated in Chapter VII, with the exception of secretariat studies,[36] some limited technical assistance activities, and two expert group meetings, the matter of trade expansion and integration among developing countries received very cursory attention in various UNCTAD bodies until the New Delhi Conference. As a matter of fact, it was not quite clear what role UNCTAD could play in view of the efforts already in progress on the regional and subregional levels. At the Algiers Conference, the developing countries proposed that a permanent committee be established in UNCTAD to study all questions related to their mutual trade expansion and integration. The committee's activities would include, *inter alia*, centralization and dissemination of information, studies on the possible establishment of export and import groupings by one commodity or by a group of commodities (among developing countries), studies on the improvement of the infrastructure of transport and communications among developing countries, and so on.[37]

accompanies the deliberations of such large bodies could possibly hamper it from adopting the technical and specialized approach necessary for its successful functioning. This did not happen, however, and the group is apparently performing its task on a high technical level.

36. It is interesting to note that in the beginning years the secretariat had only one consultant working on this matter.

37. TD/38 (3 Nov. 1967), p. 25. Note a detail in the wording of a provision to establish a special center to train experts in the field of economic cooperation and integration: the center should be under the auspices "of UNCTAD, and of *other* specialized agencies."

In New Delhi, the representative of the Secretary-General gave an elaborate report on the institutional possibilities within UNCTAD,[38] mainly dealing with the measures that could be adopted to facilitate the implementation of the declarations of support for the trade expansion and integration efforts of developing countries.[39] According to the secretariat, UNCTAD's main role would be to mobilize attention and to offer a focus where developing countries could present schemes that needed international support, instead of (or in addition to) going through bilateral channels. The question raised was whether the existing bodies were sufficient or whether a new one should be set up. The secretariat clearly favored the latter solution, arguing that in trade among developing countries, trade in manufactures and commodities, as well as finance and payments matters were interrelated, and should be considered together, in a body to be attended by specialists familiar with the situation in various groupings.

The New Delhi Conference was apparently not prepared to tackle the institutional matter. It was agreed that UNCTAD would have a role to play, but even though some of them indicated that they were open to conviction, the developed countries reiterated that a proliferation of new bodies should be avoided. The developing countries, on the other hand, supported a permanent committee within UNCTAD.[40] The Conference adopted a resolution which recognized that trade expansion and economic integration were essential to the development strategy of developing countries, and that this subject should therefore be handled on a continuing basis. UNCTAD's competence was recognized for providing support, encouragement and periodic reviews. It was also decided that appropriate institutional arrangements should be set on a permanent basis before the end of 1968.[41]

In the paper prepared for the Seventh Board, the secretariat expressed the view that an intergovernmental meeting should be convened, first to examine questions which could usefully be considered in UNCTAD and which were amenable to international action, and then

38. TD/II/WG.II/Conf. Room Paper 13 (4 Mar. 1968). The opening sentence was apologetic: "In a situation characterized by a scramble for ever-more proliferating activities, to which international organizations are inevitably subject, secretariat utterings will be considered as reflecting some degree of institutional self-interest."

39. Other institutional matters requiring attention were UNCTAD's participation in the multilateral negotiations among developing countries—negotiations which were initiated in GATT—and expansion of the secretariat's activities for improved technical assistance backing.

40. For the Working Group II report, see *Proceedings, New Delhi*, Vol. I, pp. 365-366.

41. Resolution 23(II), *ibid.*, p. 53.

to decide on the establishment and scope of the permanent machinery.[42] Some developing countries were prepared to accept this solution, while others wanted a permanent body immediately; some developed countries were prepared to consider a permanent committee, while others doubted its usefulness.[43]

The eighth session of the Board held in February 1969, ratified the consensus which had already crystallized at the Seventh Board. It was agreed to convene an intergovernmental group in 1970, to examine the outstanding questions and to recommend ways and means to implement the concerted declaration of the New Delhi Conference. It was not however decided how trade expansion and regional integration among developing countries would be dealt with in UNCTAD in the future, although the possibility was left open to the Secretary-General of UNCTAD to convene *ad hoc* working parties when requested to do so by developing countries members of a specific grouping, on the basis of their concrete proposals needing international support.[44]

The Intergovernmental Group on Trade Expansion, Economic Cooperation and Regional Integration among Developing Countries met in November 1970.[45] During the debate on the institutional problem, some delegates expressed doubts whether the group should be convened again. The secretariat, in a marked shift of attitude, also questioned the usefulness of a permanent organ; in fact, it considered

42. See secretariat report TD/B/183 (1 Aug. 1968) and Add.1. According to the secretariat, once such machinery was created, it would not enter into negotiations on specific commitments. Rather it would support negotiations undertaken elsewhere, encourage new approaches, and help eliminate the various obstacles that developing countries face. The role of the UNCTAD secretariat as envisaged in the report, provided for research, dissemination of research results and information, and technical assistance and advisory services. The possibility was advanced that the Secretary-General would act as a point through which developing countries could channel their requests for support from developed countries. He would also give service to groups that need assistance for presenting their demands, offer training and seminars, etc.

43. For the report of the Seventh Board see A/7214, pp. 34-36. One country suggested that the Board appoint an *ad hoc* sessional committee to deal with this subject as necessary.

44. When requested to convene a working group, the Secretary-General should also consult the developed countries concerned, and would be able to convene such a group only if substantial number of developed countries concur. See Board resolution 53(VIII) in TD/B/233 (21 Febr. 1969), Annex I. Also see pp. 30-32.

45. See the report of the group TD/B/333 (2 Dec. 1970). The group *inter alia* reviewed the progress made and the problems encountered since the New Delhi Conference, untying of development finance and trade expansion among developing countries, payments questions, and UNCTAD's program of work in this field. (Note that the possibility of convening *ad hoc* working parties has not been made use of in the period under survey.)

the preparation of such meetings as interfering with its research and technical assistance activities in this field.[46] Many developing countries, on the other hand, felt that the working group should meet annually. A compromise emerged, whereby the authority to call together another group, when and if necessary, was given to UNCTAD's Secretary-General.

The spokesmen for the Group of 77 had claimed all along that more could be done to promote trade expansion among developing countries with an adequate machinery in UNCTAD, and also that it was important to have a forum for debating implementation of the concerted declaration on the subject adopted by the New Delhi Conference. One of the motivating factors was to create a point from which to pressure the developed countries into helping alleviate the special difficulties that various trade expansion and regional integration schemes encounter. Yet, the Group of 77 as a whole did not exhibit a strong interest in this matter, and it is interesting to note that a great deal of impetus behind this push for task expansion was due to the efforts of the UNCTAD secretariat, which in the beginning vigorously promoted the role of its organization in this sphere. Moreover, the idea of a concerted declaration originated with the secretariat, fitting into Prebisch's concept of a "global strategy", whereby all groups of countries would commit themselves to achieve a given goal. As for the B Group, at least some of its members were reserved toward the efforts of developing countries at mutual trade expansion and economic cooperation; also, in addition to their standing objection to new bodies and functions because of fiscal implications, they were less than cheerful at being "annoyed" in yet another place where the various developing countries' groupings might seek support. Thus their renitency to this instance of task expansion in UNCTAD.

Although its role has not fully crystallized so far, UNCTAD has gained a more or less defined institutional mechanism to deal with the problem of trade expansion, economic cooperation and regional integration among developing countries, an important item in the global strategy of development.[47]

46. Note that following the New Delhi Conference the capacity of the UNCTAD secretariat was enlarged by setting up a special program to deal with the trade expansion and economic integration of developing countries. The special program has since become a full-fledged division.

47. Due to the possibilities that this cooperation offers to developing countries in the long run, one might conceivably envisage the creation of a machinery where they would be the sole members. Under those conditions, there would be the possibility of discussing a large number of topics of common interest and common actions, which are difficult to include on the agenda of an UNCTAD organ in which the developed and socialist countries also participate.

254

During the New Delhi Conference, Brazil and Chile, supported by India and Pakistan, proposed that UNCTAD should deal on a regular basis with the transfer of technology to developing countries.[48] Since UNCTAD was the central UN organ for all matters related to economic development, these countries emphasized that it also had a role to play in the transfer of technology. Therefore the sponsors felt that the Board should consider establishing a committee on science and technology.[49] They argued that although ECOSOC's Advisory Committee on the Application of Science and Technology to Development (ACAST) performed a useful function, it was composed of non-governmental experts acting in a personal capacity, and, like other international bodies concerned with the issue, it concentrated on the scientific and technical aspects, while neglecting the all important political and economic ones. Furthermore, they felt that there was a need for central coordination since these activities were distributed among a number of UN bodies, and that this function should be performed at the intergovernmental level where policy decisions are taken. The general response of developed countries to this was that the subject should be tackled through the existing organizations, on a step-by-step basis. The Conference did not have enough time to consider the proposal and referred it to the Trade and Development Board.[50]

48. The Group of 77 could not achieve unanimity on this proposal. Within the Latin American subgroup, Argentina blocked the proposal. Nevertheless, against the practice of group solidarity and the unanimous backing of various demands, the four sponsors presented the resolution to the New Delhi Conference on their own. (Note that the Geneva Conference had adopted a recommendation on the transfer of technology. See A.IV.26, *Proceedings*, Vol. I, p. 57.)

49. For the report of the Working Group I see *Proceedings, New Delhi*, Vol. I, pp. 353-355. For the draft resolution see TD/II/WG.I/L.4/Rev.1, in *ibid.*, pp. 357-358. The committee's main functions would be to review basic activities in this field; to see how technology and know-how could be transferred on reasonable terms to the Third World; to study the costs and burdens of the transfer of technology on the balance of payments, and to examine the effects of existing international legislation on the protection of industrial property upon the economic development of developing countries. It would also review the implementation of recommendations. (It is interesting to note that during the first session of the Committee on Invisibles and Financing related to Trade, no agreement could be reached on the proposal that transfer of technology, know-how and patents be one of the items included in the program of work in the field of invisibles. A sentence was included, however, stating that this committee should establish such a program in "due time". TD/B/42/Rev.1, p. 23. Thereafter, it never returned to this question.)

50. *Proceedings, New Delhi*, Vol. I, pp. 388-389. It is interesting that the UNCTAD secretariat advised that the Conference should not take any action

The argument voiced at the Seventh Board (September 1968) and the approaches by the developed and developing countries were reminiscent of the preparatory stages for the Geneva Conference.[51] The B Group was opposed to any role being played by UNCTAD in this sphere; interestingly enough it found a measure of support among the socialist countries.[52] It was pointed out that UNCTAD action would duplicate and overlap the work of UNIDO, UNESCO, ECOSOC's Advisory Committee, and the International Union for the Protection of Industrial Property; it would also have significant financial consequences. The developed countries favored delay, and suggested waiting for the outcome of ECOSOC deliberations. The 77 reiterated their familiar argument: the existing institutional arangements were not adapted to their requirements, no duplication would occur, and there was a need for machinery to keep the whole question under continuous review, since the subject was at present considered piecemeal by different bodies—bodies which moreover did not deal with the terms and conditions of the transfer of technology. According to the 77, other international organizations did not take an overall view of the legal, economic, commercial and financial aspects of the matter. The balance of payments and trade aspects especially, they argued, which were not considered elsewhere, fell squarely within the competence of UNCTAD. In order to understand the motivations of developing countries, one should remember that only limited practical effect was given to the decisions of the 1963 UN Conference on the Application of Science and Technology for the Benefit of Less Developed Areas, and that the subsequent recommendations of the General Assembly and of ECOSOC had encountered a similar fate.

The B Group sponsored a draft resolution which did not mention

that might lead to "unnecessary" duplication in the UN. This was actually a rather cryptic statement, implying that some action could be taken which would not cause real duplication. Of course, a discussion of the political and economic elements would hardly have duplicated the work of any other organ. See TD/84 (19 Mar. 1968). (Note that the representatives of the UN Department of Economic and Social Affairs lobbied among delegations against the proposed draft resolution. They felt that the transfer of technology fell under the strict jurisdiction of ECOSOC. Also, the paper by the UNCTAD secretariat on the subject was inspired by a desire to be on good terms with the Department and to respect the above mentioned 1964 agreement on the division of responsibilities.)

51. For the report of the Seventh Board on this issue, see A/7214, pp. 44-47.

52. See the statement by Bulgaria that the proliferation of UNCTAD's permanent organs is undesirable, and that things can be discussed in *ad hoc* machinery when required. *Ibid.*, p. 46. The socialist countries suggested that perhaps the Committee on Invisibles and Financing could be used, and that a new body should not be established before it was clear that this would be a wise use of financial and other resources.

UNCTAD, welcomed the initiative of ECOSOC to strengthen the UN activities in this field, and asked for further study.[53] This draft was rejected by a vote: the B Group voted for, the 77 against, and the D Group abstained. The draft resolution of the Group of 77 stressed the need to establish an appropriate intergovernmental machinery within UNCTAD to study the general question of the transfer of technology which would be likely to promote the economic development of the Third World. It was proposed that final action be taken on this matter no later than September 1969, at the ninth session of the Board. This draft was adopted by a vote: the 77 voted for, the B Group against, and the D Group abstained.[54]

At the Ninth Board (September 1969) the spokesman for the 77 stated that technology should be given as much importance in the field of development as trade and financing. The developing countries felt that their growth rested on three "pillars"—financing, trade and technology.[55] Since no consensus could be reached, the matter was postponed again, this time for the Tenth Board, and the secretariat was asked to prepare a study on this subject.[56]

At the Tenth Board (September 1970) the developing countries proposed that a main committee of all UNCTAD members be established to deal with the transfer of technology. They argued that this most important subject could be discussed meaningfully only in a permanent committee, and recalled that in spite of the objections raised against the creation of the Committee on Shipping, this committee engaged in very fruitful work once it was set in motion. The developed countries were generally of a different view.[57] It was pointed out that discussion was going on in other intergovernmental organizations, with a view to changing their machinery in favor of the demands of the Third World, and that UNCTAD, therefore, should not prejudge the issue by establishing a permanent committee. Instead, a temporary machinery was proposed by some—either a sessional committee of the

53. *Ibid.*, p. 123.
54. Resolution 48(VII), *ibid.*, p. 89.
55. See A/7616, Chapters I and III. (Note also that Prebisch in his speeches continuously emphasized the technological gap and the transfer of technology themes. Again, he played the role of a leader and spokesman, gradually mobilizing the developing countries.)
56. Resolution 62(IX), *ibid.*, p. 74. For the position of the 77, see their draft resolution TD/B/L.189/Rev.1, in *ibid.*, Annex V. For the detailed chronology of developments concerning institutional machinery see TD/B/310 (1 Jul. 1970), pp. 3-9.
57. For the summary of the debate at the Tenth Board see TD/B/327 (30 Sep. 1970), pp. 56-69. For the secretariat study see TD/B/310 (1 Jul. 1970). Note that several developed countries expressed sympathy for a permanent body in UNCTAD, and Spain—the B Group member—openly sided with the 77.

Board or an *ad hoc* group of governmental experts—to help define UNCTAD's role. They generally felt that no decisions should be taken in UNCTAD until the General Assembly and the ECOSOC had decided on future work in the field of science and technology in the UN system.[58] Thus a draft resolution by Belgium, New Zealand and the United States advocated further study of the role of other international bodies and that a report be submitted to the Eleventh Board. One of the reasons for the strong B Group negativism was apparently the anxiety that UNCTAD would interfere in the area where big corporations and so-called international companies operate, often exploiting the inexperience and lack of knowledge in most developing countries.

The compromise which emerged provides for a 45-member Intergovernmental Group on the Transfer of Technology. After an organizational and two substantive sessions there would be a review of its work and purpose, including the institutional solution in the framework of UNCTAD.[59] Thus, although there was no definite consensus on the standing institutional machinery and on the precise work program of UNCTAD, this organization's pursuits have expanded into a new area.[60] The institutional solution is temporary, yet UNCTAD's role has been placed on a "continuing basis" and in view of the seriousness of the problem and the growing concern with what has been called "technological colonialism", the transfer of technology could become an important UNCTAD endeavor. With the help of political pressure, this area could be gradually opened up for systematic exploration and research, as in shipping.

The pattern of task expansion in the case of technology transfer is typical of UNCTAD in general. The developing countries perceive a substantive problem, want to do something about it, and propose a

58. The socialist countries also felt that another main committee in UNCTAD would mean heavy cost and a serious burden on its calendar of meetings. Obviously, the opposition of the socialist countries weakened the bargaining power of the Group of 77.

59. See Board resolution 74(X) in TD/B/327 (30 Sep. 1970), Annex I, pp. 10-12. It is interesting that some developed countries argued that because the group was temporary, the UNCTAD secretariat should not engage additional permanent personnel for the transfer of technology and that it should rely primarily on consultants. The 77 felt that this suggestion was irrelevant since UNCTAD would deal with the subject on a continuing basis, irrespective of the institutional machinery established, and that the staff resources would have to be expanded. The latter view prevailed, and the secretariat will have a small nucleus to service the group and to prepare the necessary documentation.

60. Among UNCTAD's functions is the identification of obstacles and problems that may limit the transfer of technology to developing countries. Also, it is to consider various forms of the foreign exchange costs of the transfer, licensing and similar arrangements, and, to suggest international and national action to overcome obstacles. *Ibid.*

machinery with an extensive mandate within UNCTAD. The B Group's reaction to such a proposal is divided into stages. Initially, it rejects the idea *in toto*, arguing, *inter alia*, that any such machinery would cause unnecessary duplication with other international organizations which are already fulfilling the task in a satisfactory manner. After a while, since the developing countries do not reduce their pressure, the developed countries usually accept the inevitable and become reconciled to the fact that some sort of machinery will be created within UNCTAD. Nevertheless, they first have recourse to a variety of tactical delaying devices. When these maneuvers are exhausted and more time has elapsed, the fight begins over the terms of reference and the work program. As a rule, the developed countries attempt to ensure that the proposed body be generally innocuous. Only after this phase of the institutional battle is over—and on the average this appears to be three years from the beginning—consensus emerges and some sort of a machinery is created to deal with the substantive problem which caused the commotion to begin with.[61] If we agree that the institutional battle is primarily the reflection of the underlying substantive disagreement, and from the B Group's point of view one of the ways of delaying the consideration of specific policies, we can then argue that once the process of task expansion is completed, the developed countries begin yet another stage of opposition—i.e., an attempt to neutralize the new machinery and to avoid significant policy changes in spite of its existence. However, this tactic already belongs to the phase of substantive consensus building, a topic that we have dealt with previously.

East-West Trade

At the Geneva Conference, Czechoslovakia submitted a draft resolution on trade among countries having different economic systems; it asked that the proposed machinery discuss obstacles and limitations which hamper this trade, and that within its framework a consultative procedure be established to deal with the problems of inter-systems trade. However, due to an unfavorable political atmosphere, this draft was never discussed, and it was referred to the continuing machinery.[62]

61. Note that additional complications were encountered during the election of members to the intergovernmental group. First, Portugal was advanced as one of the B Group candidates. This caused a very negative reaction of the 77, and of the Africans in particular. Later, Portugal's candidacy was withdrawn, but the B Group did not present candidates for all the posts it was entitled to. Consequently, three places remain unfilled. The United Kingdom, for example, has refused to take part in the intergovernmental group.

62. *Proceedings,* Vol. VIII, p. 86, and Vol. I, pp. 94-95. See also E. M. Chossudovsky, "UNCTAD and Co-existence," *Co-Existence,* Vol. 6, pp. 97-118.

During the Board debates held on the subject, the socialist countries asked for action and concrete recommendations by UNCTAD on the normalization of international trade among countries having different economic and social systems, and the removal of discrimination and artificial obstacles to this trade. The developed countries, supported by some developing nations, opposed the suggestion; they argued that UNCTAD's work should focus on East-South trade problems and not on East-West issues which were already under consideration in the UN Economic Commission for Europe (ECE).[63]

For some time UNCTAD was excluded from any substantive discussions of East-West trade. A small step forward was made at the Third Board in 1966: it was agreed that on the basis of periodic reports by the UNCTAD secretariat, East-West trade problems would also be discussed—with specific attention paid to the trade interests of developing countries and to the work of UN organs in this field.[64] This qualification reflected the feeling of many developing countries that UNCTAD should concern itself predominantly with their problems; it also meant that the developed countries had softened their approach as they now recognized that the ECE was not the sole UN body for the multilateral consideration of East-West trade, and that UNCTAD as a universal institution could also discuss the matter. This reflected a certain thaw in East-West relations, and a gradual rapprochement on the economic and political levels. As we have already noted, it is at this point that some developing countries began to voice suspicions that a rapid expansion of East-West trade might be detrimental to their interests.

At the Fifth Board in 1967, a brief substantive discussion of inter-systems trade was initiated on the basis of the secretariat report. The majority of the developed countries reiterated their opinion that the scrutiny of East-West trade belongs to the ECE. But, as some observers noted, in UNCTAD the developed countries argued that questions of improving East-West trade belong to the ECE, while in the ECE, they sat passively and were scarcely responsive to initiatives on this matter. As a group they were not eager to meet the demands of the socialist countries for the normalization of commercial relations, and tactically they were not willing to be exposed to pressures in UNCTAD, where the socialist countries might have enlisted the political support of some developing countries, especially those that are their important trading partners.

63. See reports of the First and Second Board (A/6023/Rev.1), Chossudovsky, *op. cit.*, p. 114, and J. Siotis, "ECE and the Emerging European System," *International Conciliation*, No. 561 (January 1967).

64. A/6315/Rev.1, Part One, para. 15.

In New Delhi, the concerted declaration on East-West-South trade provided that the Board periodically convene a sessional committee on the expansion of East-West and East-South trade.[65] This, together with the recognition of the interdependence of trade flows, was considered a significant gain by the socialist countries. The Eighth Board (February 1969) moved another step in the direction of a fuller recognition of UNCTAD's role in this sphere. It was decided to convene a sessional committee of the Ninth Board (September 1969) which would engage in consultations and the elaboration of proposals on the expansion of East-West and East-South trade. It would also provide a place for bilateral consultations on more specific matters. Such consultations would be confidential, voluntary and non-commital in character, and would be held parallel to the work of the sessional committee.[66]

Although a temporary solution, the sessional committee which was convened for the first time during the Ninth Board provided the institutional focus for the first intensive considerations of inter-systems trade within UNCTAD's continuing machinery.[67] Some six years had passed since UNCTAD was established, and it was almost 15 years ago that the socialist countries began to press for the consideration of East-West trade in a universal forum, preferably in the ITO. A circumscribed institutional foundation had finally been laid in UNCTAD for the fulfillment of their wishes. Multilateral discussions accompanied by mutually agreeable consultations on trade matters that are of specific interest to the parties involved may form a basis for new East-West and East-South trade links. On-the-spot consultations in UNCTAD do offer a chance for easy contact, something that is usually not the case because of political obstacles. Institutionally this may yet prove to be one of the more significant instances of task expansion for UNCTAD. For the time being, however, this has not been the case. Some developed countries continue to be reluctant to discuss East-West trade in the sessional

65. Resolution 15(II), *Proceedings, New Delhi,* Vol. I, pp. 33-34. During the Conference France and Austria were the only developed countries supporting the demand that UNCTAD be empowered to deal with the substance of East-West trade. Only during last minute negotiations was consensus reached on the role of UNCTAD.

66. Note that the ECE had previously arranged for similar consultations under its auspices. See Chapter VIII of the report of the Eighth Board (TD/B/233 (21 Feb. 1969)).

67. For the report of this committee, see Chapter II of the Ninth Board's report (A/7616). Note that during the first part of the Ninth Board, parallel to the multilateral work of the sessional committee, more than seventy bilateral consultations, involving 43 countries, took place on specific trade matters. The socialist countries had sent their deputy ministers to this session. (UNCTAD press release TAD/415 (15 Sep. 1969).) It is interesting that 26 developing countries and 10 developed market economies took part in these consultations.

committee, arguing that this matter should be discussed in the first place in the ECE, while UNCTAD would concentrate on questions of East-South trade. Other developed countries, however, share the opinion of the D Group and of the 77, that UNCTAD has a useful role to play in this field.[68]

In concluding this chapter, the question should be asked whether task expansion in UNCTAD is a sign of success, or whether it is maleficient because it heaps additional burdens on an already overloaded organization. Obviously, had UNCTAD concentrated on only one or two subjects, consensus building probably would have been faster than in a situation where it has to worry about a score of other issues. The argument of narrow functional specialization is, however, an academic one. UNCTAD is there precisely because it was intended to be global in scope, and because the problems that it tackles are interrelated and of a global nature. Furthermore, individual developing countries face different problems, and it would not be politically feasible to omit any of these. We assert that instances of task expansion in UNCTAD are generally a sign of success, in the sense that they imply the recognition of a problem and the need for international action. Setting up the machinery has negative financial implications, it strains the manpower resources of governments and international secretariats, and does not mean that the problem will be solved; but will better results be achieved with the machinery than without it? UNCTAD's task expansion into a new area opens the path toward consensus building and action—that is, through task expansion the 77 attempt to pull developed countries into a dialogue on a given issue which had previously been approached from a perspective other than that of Third World needs. The difficulty, of course, is that instances of task expansion in UNCTAD are usually distorted and are often a pale reflection of what the sponsors originally had in mind. In any case, the UNCTAD "technique" of task expansion is more efficient than the usual approach of ECOSOC or of other UN bodies, where issues are usually settled by the adoption of a resolution without establishing some sort of permanent institutional focus. Moreover, once a new body is established in UNCTAD, chances are higher that it will eventually perform many of the functions which the 77 originally envisaged.

68. Typical of the political issues involved is the comment by some developed countries that the documentation submitted by the secretariat was biased, while the socialist countries and some other developed countries commended the same documentation as containing valuable information and being of practical importance. See the report of the Tenth Board TD/B/327 (30 Sept. 1970), pp. 70-82. At the consultations which took place during the Tenth Board, 29 developing countries and only 3 developed market economies participated.

Part III

CONCLUSION

In an interview in 1967, Prebisch said that UNCTAD should (1) provide a political and ideological frame for practical action in the field of trade and development; (2) define and orchestrate the new approach; and (3) act as a coordinator of the existing organizations, agencies and bodies. In addition to shaping policies, UNCTAD should also be instrumental in negotiating and implementing the corresponding practical measures.[1] In the preceding pages we have attempted to depict the extent to which the supporters of UNCTAD have succeeded in securing such roles for their favorite organization. The institutional growth and consolidation were slow insofar as the aspirations of the 77 were concerned, primarily because the developed countries were not inclined to permit the expansion of UNCTAD's prerogatives, considering it an organization of the Third World whose underlying premises and goals they viewed with scepticism. Some members of the B Group have generally espoused a more conciliatory line on institutional matters and have often been responsive to the wishes of the 77 in this sphere,[2] yet since the Geneva Conference the overall mood of the developed countries has not changed significantly.[3]

1. Interview given to *The Manchester Guardian* on 12 January, 1967.
2. It should be recalled that the pressure from these "dissenters" helped convince others in the B Group that UNCTAD should be granted the status of a participating agency in the UNDP. Occasionally, France is to be found in this group. According to a French delegate, yielding on institutional matters to the 77 is like putting a sugar coating over the substantive cracks. Also at issue is the French disaffection with "Anglo-Saxon" organizations—i.e. those organizations which France thinks are controlled by the United Kingdom and the United States, including GATT.
3. Typically, the 77 and the B Group could not see eye to eye as to what role the UNCTAD secretariat should play in informing the world—about UNCTAD's objectives and the problems of development—and especially the peoples in the developed countries whose negative pre-disposition, it is claimed, prevents the western governments from entering into commitments along policy lines advocated in this organization. See the report of the Ninth Board (A/7616, Chapter V and Annex V) and the report of the Tenth Board (TD/B/327 (30 Sept. 1970), pp. 98-99). The B Group generally argued that the UNCTAD secretariat, instead of playing a direct role, should publicize its aims and activities through the newly

By way of summary, we would first like to point out several prominent milestones in UNCTAD's brief history which had an impact (or will have one in the long run) on the evolution of its role, functions and authority.

1. Resolution 19 (II), adopted by the Second Board in September 1965, ended the implementation crisis. It was, in effect, a tacit, though reluctant recognition by the developing countries that UNCTAD would not be allowed to make a detailed scrutiny of the policies of the developed countries in order to pressure them to implement the *Final Act* recommendations. Its adoption also meant the end of an atmosphere of bitter confrontation which had been carried over from the Geneva Conference into the continuing machinery.[4]

2. The decision to move UNCTAD away from New York was an effort aimed at achieving and asserting organizational, intellectual, political and administrative independence.

3. Resolution 31 (IV) on technical assistance, adopted by the Fourth Board in September 1966, ensured the operational and service functions for UNCTAD, led to its joining forces with GATT to operate the International Trade Center (thus decreasing friction between the two organizations), and qualified it to attain the rank of a participating agency of the UNDP and thus be able to expand and finance adequately its technical assistance activities.

4. The New Delhi Conference in 1968 made everybody acutely aware of the shortcomings of UNCTAD's machinery and made the question of institutional improvement an important item on the agenda. Although the Conference is and remains the principal organ,[5] it has been recognized, as a result of the New Delhi experience, that the backbone of UNCTAD is the continuing machinery which performs all the necessary tasks and prepares the foundation for any concrete achievements.[6] The accent was shifted from "sporadic" to "permanent".

---

formed Centre for Economic and Social Information (CESI) at UN Headquarters, and the regular Office of Public Information (OPI) programs.

4. The initial period—i.e., between the Geneva Conference in the spring of 1964 and the adoption of resolution 1995(XIX) in December of that same year—was a critical period, as were the first two sessions of the Board in 1965. At that time, a threat to UNCTAD's survival still lingered in the air, and the impalpable feeling of uncertainty prevailed among those involved.

5. In 1964 some western representatives felt that a triennial conference supported by a small and weak continuing machinery would not represent a serious institutional challenge to GATT and other organizations. Actually, the provisional nature of the Conference was one of the reasons why the West was willing to accept it as an institutional compromise.

6. Often, the Geneva Conference is referred to as UNCTAD-1, and the New Delhi Conference as UNCTAD-2. We have avoided this because the acronym

5. General recognition that UNCTAD has a role to play in the international action on East-West trade might eventually bring it somewhat closer in scope to the ITO.

6. The retirement of UNCTAD's Secretary General Dr. Raúl Prebisch in 1969, marked the end of an era of dynamic leadership and norm articulation at the secretariat level.[7]

7. The sugar agreement of 1968 was the first sign that UNCTAD was not just a talk-shop devoid of concrete achievements. The 1970 agreement on preferences is in fact a landmark in the evolution of this organization, which has greatly heightened its prestige. It is a proof that practical achievements can be attained in UNCTAD, for that matter very important and even unexpected ones. The way "negotiations" were completed and the fact that UNCTAD will be entrusted with the review of the system of preferences, are indicative of a somewhat more positive attitude of the developed countries toward this organization.

In general, we can conclude that UNCTAD has evolved into a hybrid, semi-autonomous agency with a large administrative apparatus, a steadily growing budget, rapidly expanding servicing activities, and an ever-proliferating network on the intergovernmental level. It has definitely gone beyond a simple parliamentary diplomacy forum, a role to which the developed countries tried to confine it. It differs from the political organs of the United Nations in the sense that it is less political, more functionally specific, and technically oriented; in addition, *de facto* negotiations are conducted in it to an increasing degree. On the other hand, it differs from the general type of specialized agencies because it is less independent, more intensely political, more functionally diffuse, and less technical at this stage of its growth.[8]

This mixture of "styles" is partly the consequence of UNCTAD's organizational set-up, but it primarily reflects the nature of its goals, the subject matter with which it deals, and the response of states to its aims. Even if a specialized agency had been created in 1964, its style and work would have differed little from what we have witnessed in UNCTAD—with the possible exception of institutional squabbles—because in this instance "technical" cannot be isolated from "political". Quoting Keynes, Prebisch said that people who pretend to be engaged in a highly specialized and practical approach actually follow ideas and concepts that had been prescribed some time ago.[9] Things may be

---

UNCTAD is associated primarily with the continuing machinery and the secretariat.

7. See chapters XIII and XIV for a discussion of the UNCTAD secretariat.

8. As we have seen, this varies depending on the phase of the policy process where a given subject matter finds itself.

9. *Far Eastern Economic Review* (April 6, 1967), p. 20.

amenable to a purely technical approach only in a situation where the basic values and the existing relationships are not questioned. It is precisely because of this crucial link between the political and the technical that the developing countries would like to have UNCTAD control policy development, the translation of the policy into rules and their implementation, for this organization is politically sensitized and responsive to their needs. Can a debating and political pressure forum coexist in the same organization with a negotiating, implementing and servicing framework? There is nothing inherently impossible in this proposition. In the case of UNCTAD the obstacles are essentially politico-economic. Therefore, UNCTAD can look forward to a better institutional future provided that the political mistrust some major developed countries harbor toward it fades, and they ease their "as-a-matter-of-principle" opposition to this organization and its endeavors.

PART FOUR

Actors and Conflict Resolution in UNCTAD

In this final section we focus our attention on the principal actors in UNCTAD and their pattern of interaction, in order to provide an additional insight into the conflict/conciliation process in this organization.

The peculiarity of decision-making in UNCTAD, compared to other international organizations, derives from the polarization between developed and developing countries, and the disparity in economic and bargaining power between the two sides. This disparity has resulted in the group system of negotiations, where the developing countries use the Group of 77 as an instrument to enhance their leverage vis-à-vis the complacent and unhurried developed nations. In fact, the basic factor which shaped the emergence of the group system as we know it today was the developing countries' premise that their only effective bargaining weapon against the West was their unity; consequently, a common front had to be established and maintained at all costs. The behavior of the 77 at the Geneva Conference brought about counter-measures by the western countries, which also began to take up joint negotiating positions in an attempt to shield themselves from the assault by the developing countries. What emerged in Geneva—and what was new compared to the groupings operating previously in the General Assembly and elsewhere—was the cohesiveness of all groups, a common front concealing in-group differences, the discipline among group members, and the rigidity of group positions.

The group system in UNCTAD is informal and has no official standing. But the existence of groups was implicitly recognized in UNCTAD's constitutional document (General Assembly resolution 1995 (XIX)). The four lists of states established for election purposes correspond very closely to the group divisions in UNCTAD. The exceptions are Cuba, Taiwan, Israel, Mongolia and South Africa, which are on either the A or C lists, but which are not included in the membership of the 77. The B list is almost identical with the B Group; Cyprus is the exception, having signed the Declaration of the Seventy-Seven in 1964. The D list too is almost identical with the D Group, the exception here being Albania, which does not participate in its activities and meetings.[1]

Our aim is to depict and analyze the groups, the UNCTAD secretariat, and to point out the characteristic traits of the group-system method of bargaining and negotiations. It need not be emphasized that these topics represent the intimate side of the life of an international organization, and are not fully accessible to outsiders. One must depend mainly on information benevolently supplied by others—and the greater the degree of sensitivity of a question, the greater the interviewee's reluctance to reply. Matters are particularly complicated in UNCTAD due to the variegated decision-making situations, the multiple levels of decision-making, and, of course, the ideological polarization which may complicate an individual's quest for objective information. Yet a student of international organization has to rely on the means available, and in the absence of better evidence he must use the soft data which he obtains through interviews.[2] This chapter is based primarily on such interviews, as well as on limited personal observation. Because of varying accessibility to information on different aspects of the subject, the treatment of issues involved is somewhat uneven. Our primary task is to deal separately with the three groups and the UNCTAD secretariat. This should provide us with the background for a brief discussion of their interaction on the decision-making level.

1. A gentlemen's agreement is in force, whereby countries proposed by one group for membership in various UNCTAD bodies are accepted by other groups. (Portugal is an exception, because when it was nominated by the B Group for a seat in two committees, the African countries asked for a vote and Portugal failed to obtain the required majority. The B Group has ever since refrained from nominating Portugal, except, as we have seen, in the case of the Intergovernmental Group on the Transfer of Technology.) However, this informal understanding is challenged by Israel and Cuba because their candidacy is never advanced by the Group of 77, which nominates from lists A and C. (Before the current practice took hold, Israel was elected member of two committees at the First Board.) Of course, Cuba is being ostracized by the Latin American group, and Israel by the Arab states. Many developing countries are sympathetic to either Cuba or Israel, or both, but for reasons of group unity they cannot support them. As a result, Cuba and Israel for the time being attend the meetings of various subsidiary bodies of the Conference as observers only, unless of course such bodies happen to be open-ended in terms of membership (for example, the Special Committee on Preferences).

2. The problem of research on international organizations has been dealt with elsewhere. See, for example, C. Alger, "Systematic Research on International Organizations" (paper presented to the Seventh World Congress of IPSA Brussels, September 1967).

Chapter XII

THE GROUPS IN UNCTAD

The Group of 77

The Joint Declaration of the Seventy-Seven Developing Countries issued at the end of the Geneva Conference stated that:

> The unity (of the developing countries in UNCTAD) has sprung out of the fact that facing the basic problems of development they have a common interest in a new policy for international trade and development ... The developing countries have a strong conviction that there is a vital need to maintain, and further strengthen, this unity in the years ahead. It is an indispensable instrument for securing the adoption of new attitudes and new approaches in the international economic field.[1]

In the post-war international system, groups coalesced according to common political, ideological, and/or geographical traits, and each group was usually led by a big power. The Group of 77, in contrast, is characterized by a heterogeneous composition, by vast political, ideological and cultural differences, by varying levels of economic development, by large numbers, and by the absence of leadership by a big power.[2] The basis for the 77 was their shared interest in rising above the peripheral and unfavorable position which they occupied in the world economy, and their common approach to world economic

1. *Proceedings,* Vol. I, pp. 67-68. The possibility of allowing Israel, Cuba, Mongolia, South Korea and South Vietnam to join the group was mooted when the Conference was about to end. The problem was resolved by asking the regional groups to pass judgment on those countries geographically belonging to them. The Asian group did not object to the candidacies of South Korea and South Vietnam. The Vietnam war had not as yet flared up in 1964, and the developing countries were eager to show that political differences did not affect the group's functioning. This made possible the political oddity of South Vietnam's (and South Korea's) presence in the Group of 77. However, their "illegitimacy" in the eyes of many developing countries bars them from playing an effective role in the group. (See Chapter II for a discussion of developing countries at the Geneva Conference.)

2. The Group of 77 consists of the countries that signed the 1964 Declaration and any additional countries whose attendance at the group meetings is not objected to by the regional group to which they belong geographically. Although the group has come to number more than 90 countries, the original name was maintained for symbolic reasons.

271

problems. The awareness of a common interest, as we have seen, was greatly furthered by various UN publications and by the writings of Prebisch. The Group of 77 was born as an *ad hoc* group of co-sponsors of the 1963 declaration, but soon evolved into a permanent instrument to systematically articulate the demands of the developing countries, and to improve their negotiating capacity; its unity was cemented by the intransigence of developed countries at the Geneva Conference.

The Physiognomy of the Group of 77. One of the characteristics of the Group of 77 is its non-institutionalized nature. The lack of organizational focus was accentuated in the initial stages by the jurisdictional conflict between the Geneva and New York "branches" of the 77. The New York-Geneva dichotomy was generated by several factors. The temporary headquarters of UNCTAD immediately after the Geneva Conference were in New York, and this is where the initial activities of the 77 took place; moreover, when UNCTAD was moved to Geneva many developing countries did not have permanent missions in this city. The prestige of some ambassadors was also involved, since many of those assigned to their countries' permanent missions in New York were aspiring to a leadership role in the Group of 77.[3] The fact that UNCTAD's parent body is the General Assembly, to which the Board reports regularly, added to the confusion. But most important of all, no formal decision was taken by the 77 on the division of responsibilities between the two cities. The result was that no one was quite certain where the authoritative voice of the 77 was located. The jurisdictional controversy became very intense during the preparations for the Algiers Conference. The permanent missions in New York expressed the view that the Geneva group should be subordinated to them, on the grounds that many developing countries were not represented in Geneva.[4] The matter was formally put to rest by the decision taken in Algiers that the Group of 77 should meet on the ministerial level whenever this be deemed necessary, and always prior to the UN Trade and Development Conference; otherwise, for the formulation of joint positions on issues within UNCTAD's purview,

3. Many of these personalities played a prominent role during the Geneva Conference in 1964, for example, Hakim of Lebanon and Pinera of Chile. Envoys to the UN Headquarters are more likely to be of the "diplomat-politico" type, with political ambitions at home, in contrast to the career-type men and specialists found in Geneva.

4. See Siotis, "Les missions permanentes à Genève et la CNUCED," *op. cit.*, p. 18. During this period the New York group refused to recognize the decisions taken in Geneva, while the delegates in Geneva were accused by some of trying to set the date for the Algiers meeting so that it would coincide with the General Assembly session, in order to prevent the New York ambassadors from being present.

the competent authority is the "Group of 31" in Geneva, consisting of the developing countries members of the Board.[5]

The gradual shift of responsibilities to Geneva reflected several facts: (1) the number of missions of developing countries in this city started increasing steadily; (2) there was a growing specialization in UNCTAD's work, while the New York "generalists" were usually not familiar with the technical intricacies of the issues involved; and (3) men physically away from the UNCTAD seat could not be expected to cope with its daily problems in a satisfactory manner. The choice of Geneva also meant a greater degree of isolation from the highly politicized atmosphere prevalent among developing countries' delegations in New York,[6] as well as a somewhat greater independence for UNCTAD (the New York group feels that UNCTAD's links with the General Assembly should be strengthened, while the Geneva delegates prefer to see their organization more independent from New York).

Another general trait of the Group of 77 is its regional orientation, and the fact that the regional groups tend to be more institutionalized. The Latin American group, for example, possessed a rudimentary organization as far back as 1946. Even its membership has changed little since then, except that Cuba has been excluded, and the English-speaking states of the Caribbean have been admitted.

(1) *The Latin American Group*: ECLA continues to play a very important role in the Latin American group. It deals with technical and economic matters on UNCTAD's agenda, and establishes the technical base for the intergovernmental coordination which takes place in the Special Commission on Latin American Coordination (CECLA).[7] The work of CECLA, which is done on a ministerial level,

5. TD/38 (3 Nov. 1967), p. 28. Note, however, that this decision has been contested by non-members of the Board. The composition of the "Group of 31" in the period 1968-1971 was: Afghanistan, Algeria, Chad, Ghana, India, Indonesia, Iran, Iraq, the Ivory Coast, Madagascar, Malaysia, Mali, Nigeria, Pakistan, the Philippines, Rwanda, Senegal, Somalia, Syria, Tunisia, Uganda, and Yugoslavia from list "A"; Brazil, Chile, Colombia, Costa Rica, Guatemala, Jamaica, Mexico, Peru, and Venezuela from list "C". The developing countries who are not members of the Board attend the meetings of the "Group of 31" as observers.

6. Many a delegate working in the atmosphere of the General Assembly is appalled by the fact that the delegation of South Vietnam attends the meetings of the 77 in Geneva. In other words, the more functional surroundings in Geneva made it easier to overlook certain political problems. This is very important, as the *sine qua non* of the group's organizational unity was precisely that it be shielded as much as possible from divisive political issues.

7. Created just before the Geneva Conference, CECLA was first composed of governmental experts. In 1964, the Latin American countries realized that they needed a body where they could coordinate their economic policies in international forums, but without the presence of the United States (and Cuba). The

is supplemented with on-the-spot coordination by Latin American delegations in Geneva, guided by CECLA's substantive decisions. The relative institutionalization of the Latin American group is aided by a common language, historical, cultural and economic ties, the long experience of working together in various international forums, and perhaps also by the focus that their regional integration efforts have offered.[8]

(2) *The African Group*: Formally, it is the Economic Commission for Africa (ECA) and the joint meetings of the ECA Working Party on Intra-African Trade and the *Ad hoc* Committee of 14 of the Organization of African Unity (OAU) that undertake to elaborate concrete proposals and recommendations on all issues of interest to the African group. The meetings of this mixed group were not regular in the beginning, partly because of financial problems and partly because some African countries did not show great interest in UNCTAD, seeing it as an organization with too many costly meetings and very few concrete payoffs for their continent. The coordination and attempts to form a coherent position were further hampered by the sometimes varying interests, and the traditional mistrust and lack of effective communication between the English- and the French-speaking countries. In New Delhi, however, the African group was very well prepared and coordinated, and it was effectively backstopped by the ECA secretariat. Since then, it has met regularly prior to each session of the Board.

(3) *The Asian Group*: This group is the least homogeneous ideologically, politically and culturally.[9] It has no true organizational focus. ECAFE has not established itself as a coordinating instrument, partly because not all the group members belong to it,[10] and partly, of course,

---

Lima Declaration of 1964 describes CECLA as the Latin American forum for trade and development, where ministers and their deputies meet whenever necessary. CECLA has no secretariat, and it is the ECLA secretariat that acts in an advisory capacity to the Latin American delegations in CECLA as well as in UNCTAD. See TD/B/185 (23 Jul. 1968), Annex V.

8. The English-speaking states of the Caribbean do not quite fit into this "club".

9. Informally, three broad groupings in the Asian group are usually taken into account for the purpose of elections for UNCTAD posts. West Asia: Afghanistan, Iraq, Jordan, Kuwait, Lebanon, Saudi Arabia, Syria and Yemen; Far East and South East Asia: Burma, Cambodia, Indonesia, South Korea, Laos, Malaysia, Maldive Islands, Philippines, Singapore, Thailand and South Vietnam; and the third group made up of Ceylon, India, Iran, Nepal, Pakistan and Yugoslavia.

10. The Arab states of West Asia, for example, fall under the jurisdiction of the UN Economic and Social Office in Beirut (UNESOB).

because of the presence of certain developed countries. ECAFE has, however, organized ministerial meetings to consider UNCTAD matters. The Asian group operates mainly during the various sessions of UNCTAD, without any regular attempts to coordinate its position in advance.[11] This, however, has not prevented it from achieving effective coordination during UNCTAD meetings, and it has apparently done so with greater ease than either the Latin American or the African groups.

The growing strength and rigidity of regional groups among the 77 was quite evident in New Delhi. Their ascendance implied that yet another very important level of decision-making had emerged in UNCTAD. To arrive at decisions in regional groups and then to attempt to iron out the differences in the Group of 77 is a complicated process, especially due to differences in interest, the rigidity of the regional group positions and a lack of procedures for a more effective decision-making process. In view of this, the coordination of the overall group position, which mainly takes place during UNCTAD meetings, and the irregular and sporadic efforts in the interim periods are likely to prove an unsatisfactory arrangement in the long run. This is precisely the reason why suggestions have been made to establish a secretariat and a permanent consultative machinery for the Group of 77.[12] A secretariat would place the action of the 77 on a steadily continuous and stable basis, bolster the group's negotiating ability and technical preparedness, and somewhat offset the centrifugal forces at work. The consultative machinery would ensure continuity and stability of the group's decision-making and would represent an additional filter through which internal differences among developing countries could be cleared prior to meetings of the UNCTAD bodies. Obviously, this would allow more time and energy for contacts and negotiations with developed and socialist countries at these meetings.

The developing countries are fully aware of the benefits which could stem from such a machinery; after all, they have to look no farther than the OECD and the role it plays for the B Group. Yet, they have neglected this option, so far. The 77's need for their own secretariat was made less pressing by the fact that the UNCTAD secretariat could be relied upon for certain services. Moreover, the situation is not propitious for a decision to constitute formally the organization of the 77. Practical difficulties in drawing up the terms of reference, financing

11. For example, many group members were not present in Bangkok when the declaration for the Algiers Conference was adopted.

12. Some African countries in Algiers proposed the establishment of a common secretariat and a common center for information of the 77, but they did not find a receptive audience.

the cost (including travel), and deciding on a location for such a machinery are not to be underestimated. Some developing countries—especially among those that are politically and ideologically close to the West—are averse to any formal institutionalization of the group, mainly because such a move would carry political overtones with which they are not willing to be associated.[13] Other developing countries may feel that such an organization would restrict their freedom of action[14] and limit the group's flexibility, or they may identify organizational continuity as being typical of the present day blocs. An additional obstacle, and a crucial one for that matter, is the opposition of the major developed countries to any steps towards institutionalizing the Group of 77 along the lines of the OECD or the CMEA.[15]

The Leadership of the 77. Its large numbers and its basically unstructured operation, the absence of great powers, the cleavages among its members, and the over-accentuation of the concept of sovereign equality are not conductive to the development of a pattern of authority in the Group of 77. Leadership in the group is subtle, and as a result, is difficult to pinpoint. In this context, to lead means to be able to exert a degree of political and intellectual influence on the group's policies over a period of time.

There are several leadership resources that play a significant role in the Group of 77. Economic strength and size is one of them. Provided that a country possessing these attributes decides to do so, it can become a contributing member of the loose grouping which appears in the forefront of the 77. Such a country may be prevented from positive leadership because of a lack of coordination on the national level and because of jurisdictional disputes among its various ministries (e.g., Mexico), or because of its ambivalent attitude toward the action of the group (e.g., Argentina[16]). A country with clear political objectives and

13. This partly reflects the cleavage in the Group of 77 between the non-aligned and other developing countries. For an interesting discussion of the organizational framework for the continuing collaboration of non-aligned nations see L. Mates, "Non-Alignment After Lusaka," *Review of International Affairs* (Belgrade), December 5, 1970, p. 8.

14. A permanent machinery would among other things accentuate the problem of the group leadership, as it would tend to bring forth those who would "run the show". Of course, any emergence of a well-defined leadership elite would be resented by those on the outside.

15. Certain developed countries would be quite upset were such an organization ever to come into being; in fact, even the amorphous Group of 77 appears very bothersome to many. Their opposition could not be ignored and it could be very effective, since such pressures are usually expressed through bilateral channels.

16. Although Argentina encounters many economic problems common to those of other developing countries, emotionally it classifies itself as belonging

which plays an important role in the non-aligned movement is in a good position to exercise influence on the orientation of the 77 (e.g., India, Yugoslavia, the UAR [17]). A defined program, technical preparedness and clear instructions to its delegates are still other important and crucial assets; Brazil, Chile, India, Pakistan and Yugoslavia belong to those excelling in this respect. Actually, one could consider their various ministries as performing the role of secretariat for the 77. Specialization is respected within the group, and some countries play a much more important role in particular areas; for example, Ceylon has always been in the forefront on matters of financing. Specialization is that much more important if related to a country's specific economic interests—Chile, Brazil, India and the UAR are prominent on shipping, Afghanistan and Bolivia on landlocked countries, Argentina and Uruguay on temperate zone products, Ghana and the Ivory Coast on cocoa, etc.[18] Another objective factor of importance for the leadership role is a country's membership in a formal body of UNCTAD (especially in the Board), plus the fact that it has a competent permanent mission in Geneva.[19]

Personality attributes and individual skills are of great importance.[20] Only the most able diplomats can effectively contribute to the conciliation of views during the usually precarious decision-making situations

---

to the developed western world. In fact, it would probably feel much more comfortable in the halls of the OECD than it does in the sessions of the 77. The frequent fierce competition between Brazil and Argentina for leadership in Latin America is therefore not evident in UNCTAD. During the Geneva Conference, when the Goulart regime was overthrown in Brazil, Argentina did not use the opportunity to take over the leadership of the Latin American group. In fact, today it is not even a member of the Trade and Development Board— at the New Delhi Conference the Latin American group failed to advance it as one of its candidates.

17. The UAR role has faded somewhat since the 1967 war. Changes of regimes in Ghana and Indonesia have weakened the roles of these two countries.

18. It is interesting that the "general" leaders tend to stay in the background on the specific issues, where they have no direct interests. Brazil, of course, is an exception, being involved in almost every item on UNCTAD's agenda at the present time.

19. Those permanently stationed in Geneva were at the source of events and had a definite advantage over the periodic guests. Many African countries, for example, did not have missions in Geneva; as a result, in the early years of UNCTAD Nigeria appeared on many occasions as the sole spokesman for sub-Saharan Africa.

20. Among the personality attributes considered helpful in conference diplomacy are charisma, administrative competence and expert knowledge, long association with the organization in question, negotiating ability, personal stature in international circles, etc. See R. W. Cox and H. K. Jacobson, "Decision-Making in International Organizations: An Interim Report" (paper presented to the Sixty-Fifth Annual Meeting of APSA, September 1969), p. 21.

within the Group of 77.[21] The role of some countries is to an important degree due to the personality of their delegate.[22] In some instances, in fact, a change of representative diminished or terminated a country's influence.[23] One additional point should be made: those delegates who do not have very strict instructions from their governments at home are more free to exercise their subjective judgment, and have an advantage in some decision-making situations because of their greater freedom of maneuver.[24]

The somewhat cohesive and authoritative leadership which emerged among the developing countries and operated during the Geneva Conference in 1964 has not managed to endure: the prevalent atmosphere in the Group of 77 today is one of egalitarianism and pluralism. In general, most group members exhibit open resentment toward a country which throws its weight around and attempts to exercise the leadership function too conspicuously. Would-be leaders were often exposed to attacks, and this taught them to be very cautious when launching initiatives.[25] India did not take this into consideration and, as a host country, attempted to direct the course of the group on almost every issue during the New Delhi Conference; this generated an adverse reaction among the developing countries and resulted in a notable decrease in India's influence on the course of group policies.[26] Furthermore, several major developing countries occasionally seem jealous of one another. Thus, for example, the Latin American countries in

21. Some of the notable and influential names that were or still are associated with the Group of 77 include: Silveira of Brazil, Lall of India, Stanovnik of Yugoslavia, Santa Cruz of Chile, Brillantes of the Philippines, Adebanjo of Nigeria, Mahmood of Pakistan, etc.

22. The Philippines is a good example in this instance.

23. Lebanon was very prominent both during the Geneva Conference and in the New York branch of the Group of 77, due to the ability of Ambassador Hakim. At present its role is practically nonexistent, although it has a mission in Geneva.

24. It has been suggested in the case of Adebanjo of Nigeria that his personal expertise and experience and position as spokesman for the African group were all complemented by the absence of effective communications with the Lagos government, which was preoccupied with the civil war. All this, plus the fact that his superior officer (the Nigerian ambassador to Switzerland) showed no interest in UNCTAD matters, made Adebanjo one of the more influential delegates in the Group of 77. This is all the more interesting in view of the fact that he only held the rank of a counsellor in the Nigerian permanent mission.

25. For example, a number of delegates did not like the great drive and personal initiatives of Silveira of Brazil, or in some cases of Lall of India.

26. Aware of this situation, the Yugoslav delegation, which submitted the draft on preferences within the Group of 77 in New Delhi, "carried the ball" only until the group's negotiating stand crystallized. Thereafter, it prudently withdrew from such an exposed and vulnerable position.

Algiers were upset over what they interpreted to be the efforts of the "three" (India, the UAR, and Yugoslavia) to control the course of the conference.

In general the leadership centers of the 77 are in the regional groups. Brazil and Chile can be singled out in the Latin American group; Nigeria, Ghana, Algeria, and the UAR stand out in the African group; and India, Pakistan, the Philippines and Yugoslavia [27] head the Asian group. In addition, mention should be made of the spokesmen for the sub-group of the least advanced countries, mainly Ethiopia, Tanzania, Bolivia, Ecuador, El Salvador and Guatemala.

Cleavages and Differences in the Group of 77. Three main types of cleavages can be distinguished in the Group of 77: (1) those that are political and ideological in nature, (2) those between the more and the less advanced countries in the group, and (3) those resulting from the links of certain developing countries with certain developed ones.

The underlying cleavages in the group are political and ideological. It was possible to consolidate the Group of 77 in 1964 because of the tacit understanding that these differences must be glossed over, a *sine qua non* for its existence and operation.[28] Purely political matters seldom appear on its agenda; when they do, an attempt is made to dispose of them quickly and efficiently, and they are usually not allowed to excessively obstruct the regular business of UNCTAD.[29] (UNCTAD is probably not the best place to observe the political differences among the members of the Group of 77. However, a study

27. During the initial stages of the Geneva Conference, Yugoslavia "belonged" to the African group. In the closing stages it was moved to the Asian group, and it is from this group's quota that it continues to be elected to various posts in UNCTAD. (It has been alleged that some western countries at times foster a notion that Yugoslavia is not a developing nation. This has been interpreted as an effort to undercut the role of this country, which is an important source of initiatives, ideas, information and skill within the group.)

28. Illustrative of the situation is the fact that the Saigon government's delegation represented South Vietnam in UNCTAD and in the Group of 77, while at the Third Conference of Non-Aligned Countries held in Lusaka in September 1970, South Vietnam was represented by the NLF delegation.

29. The inability of the Algerian government to "guarantee the security" of the South Vietnamese delegation which arrived at the ministerial meeting of the 77, the delegation's absence from the conference hall, etc. caused a big uproar. Some Latin American and Asian delegations were rather upset, warnings of boycott were heard, and it appeared that the conference was on the verge of a breakdown. The matter was settled rapidly, however, by putting the South Vietnamese delegation on a plane on its "own volition", and allowing the South Korean representatives to remain in Algiers. The conference was thus free to turn to its business—something that concerned everybody—and it did so as if nothing had happened. The entire meeting could probably have been torpedoed over the South Vietnam incident, if anybody had so wished.

of their behavior in the non-aligned countries' movement, and in the General Assembly on purely political matters, could yield a precise analysis of this issue.) Most important for the functioning of the 77, however, is the fact that political cleavages are generally not so evident in economic matters. In fact, in a number of instances the demands and proposals, the bargaining tactics and style, and the rhetoric of various countries are almost identical, even though they may be at different ends of the political spectrum. In many cases, Brazil's style could in fact be labelled "radical" or "extreme" in the UNCTAD context.[30]

The question in the long run is not so much whether these cleavages will undermine the Group of 77 for the developing countries can continue to practice the present approach, that is, to ignore political and ideological differences in order to seek common economic interests. The question is rather whether, in spite of these differences, it will be possible to involve all developing countries in joint activities in the "purely" political sphere, as a means of increasing the group's bargaining power in UNCTAD and sharpening its thrust.

Although loyalty to the regional groups is strong among the 77, during the Algiers Conference we saw that a cross-regional alliance was forged among the least advanced countries (LDDCs). We have already discussed the political and methodological difficulties that arose in attempts to arrive at an objective list of LDDCs. Depending on the particular measure under consideration, a country may qualify for this status. Furthermore, the political support that a country can muster is at least as important as the objective criteria. Thus, Guatemala in 1965 had a *per capita* GDP at factor cost of $ 277, and it ranked as number 38 on the list worked out by the UNCTAD secretariat; therefore, it was far above the cut-off point dividing the LDDCs from the others. Still, the most important element was that in the Latin American context Guatemala is considered as an LDDC.

Since the Group of 77 has opted for the approach to designate LDDCs for each item as it becomes ripe for action, it is logical to expect some sort of selective coalition politics to emerge, rather than an across-the-board confrontation of the more developed versus the less developed group members. On the other hand, the possibility remains that an exchange of support and a more or less permanent alliance will occur within this broad coalition of states, which in one respect or another fall into the lower reaches of the classification.

30. While at the Geneva Conference one could argue the case that the majority of "radicals" were to be found on the political left, in the continuing machinery of UNCTAD "radical" has come to mean the one who presents extreme demands vis-à-vis the B Group, and it is not necessarily related to the political system and orientation of the developing country in question.

The problem of LDDCs is further accentuated by the fact that it is superimposed on regional cleavage. Most African countries find themselves *de facto* in the indefinite category of LDDCs. Thus, for illustrative purposes, it is worthwhile reproducing the tentative ranking worked out by the UNCTAD secretariat in 1969 on the basis of a composite level-of-development index.[31] (See Table I, page 282.) It is useful to compare Table I with Table II (page 283) which ranks developing countries according to their per capita GDP at factor cost.

It is true that a stratification exists within the Group of 77 which is diffuse and difficult to pinpoint. However, it does not necessarily have to harm the group's unity of action, and it will not do so if most of its members feel that they are obtaining adequate advantages from the policies that emerge from UNCTAD and are brought about by their group's pressure. A resolution for this, however, will have to be worked out through a series of coordinated and balanced measures, perhaps even a definite strategy.

Cleavages most consequential to the unity of action of the group are those which result from the non-complementary character of their short-range economic interests—especially those which derive from special ties with developed countries. Of particular importance is the cleavage between the African and the Latin American groups, fueled, it should be recalled, by the dispute over the special preferences some African states enjoy in the EEC market. The EEC associates and the Commonwealth members in the African group act according to a tacit understanding not to attack each other regarding special preferences, and their group acts in a united manner on this issue. The conflict between the Latin Americans and Africans often becomes emotional, and tends to spill over into other areas, such as special measures for the LDDCs. The Latin Americans have often not shown a special awareness of or understanding for the problems of the African states, and have generally failed to make any conciliatory gestures; the Africans, on the other hand, continue to view most Latin American states as the "middle-class" of the 77, disguised as developing countries only in order to obtain various advantages. This cleavage seriously hampers the functioning of the group, consumes precious time, and often due to the exaggerated rhetoric and negotiating tactics of the two regional groups, it seems to assume crisis proportions. The Asian countries try to

31. The comparative classification is to be found in UNCTAD document TD/B/269 (11 Jul. 1969), p. 21. For the definition of the composite level-of-development index that was used in the classification, see Chapter VII. Evidently, there is nothing sacrosanct in the index chosen by the UNCTAD secretariat, and any modification of the criteria that were used could produce a different ranking of many countries.

TABLE I

Rank of developing countries, members of the group of 77, according to the composite level-of-development index (1965 or nearest year) *

1. Argentina	30. Guatemala	55. Haiti
2. Yugoslavia	31. Syria	56. Lesotho
3. Uruguay	32. Gabon	57. Madagascar
4. Chile	33. Western Samoa	58. Togo
5. Mexico	34. Congo (B.)	59. Nepal
6. Cyprus	35. Honduras	60. Central African
7. Panama	36. Bolivia	Republic
8. Singapore	37. Ghana	61. Uganda
9. Jamaica	38. Liberia	62. Mali
10. Lebanon	39. Pakistan	63. Afghanistan
11. South Korea	40. Ceylon	64. Malawi
12. Peru	41. Zambia	65. Sierra Leone
13. Costa Rica	42. Morocco	66. Ethiopia
14. Guyana	43. Congo Democratic	67. Rwanda
15. Philippines	Republic	68. Guinea
16. Colombia	44. Cameroon	69. Nigeria
17. Barbados	45. Kenya	70. Laos
18. Brazil	46. Swaziland	71. Tanzania
19. UAR	47. South Vietnam	72. Burma
20. Paraguay	48. Thailand	73. Gambia
21. Ecuador	49. Ivory Coast	74. Dahomey
22. El Salvador	50. Indonesia	75. Sudan
23. Dominican Republic	51. Equatorial Guinea	76. Burundi
24. India	52. Cambodia	77. Chad
25. Mauritius		78. Mauritiana
26. Tunisia	*LDDC category*	79. Niger
27. Nicaragua		80. Upper Volta
28. Jordan	53. Senegal	81. Somalia
29. Malaysia	54. Botswana	82. Yemen

* Algeria, Iran, Iraq, Kuwait, Libya, Saudi Arabia, Southern Yemen, Trinidad and Tobago, and Venezuela were not included in the comparative classification because of their atypical economic and social structures which are due to their dependence on petroleum and petroleum products. We have also excluded from the list those countries that are not members of the Group of 77.

TABLE II [32]

Rank of developing countries, members of the Group of 77, according to their per capita GDP at factor cost in 1965 (in US $)

Per Capita GDP		Per Capita GDP		Per Capita GDP	
1. Kuwait	4,434	33. Ivory Coast	217	63. *Sudan*	99
2. Venezuela	1,255	34. Ghana	215	64. *Madagascar*	98
3. Argentina	778	35. Jordan	214	65. *Togo*	98
4. Libya	755	36. Algeria	214	66. India	97
5. Trinidad &	682	37. Honduras	209	67. *Gambia*	92
Tobago		38. Zambia	207	68. *Botswana*	90
6. Cyprus	614	39. Paraguay	207	69. *Guinea*	88
7. Uruguay	559	40. Ecuador	200	70. *Haiti*	86
8. Singapore	528	41. South Yemen	200	71. *Indonesia*	85
9. Chile	493	42. West Samoa	200	72. *Niger*	84
10. Panama	479	43. *Senegal* *	198	73. *Uganda*	83
11. Jamaica	465	44. Tunisia	187	74. Congo	
12. Yugoslavia	460	45. Swaziland	184	Democratic	
13. Mexico	441	46. Morocco	180	Republic	75
14. Costa Rica	373	47. Congo (B)	177	75. *Nigeria*	74
15. Barbados	369	48. Syria	170	76. *Mali*	74
16. Gabon	367	49. UAR	167	77. *Dahomey*	72
17. Lebanon	363	50. Equatorial		78. *Nepal*	68
18. Nicaragua	323	Guinea	160	79. *Chad*	66
19. Colombia	315	51. Bolivia	154	80. *Laos*	63
20. Guyana	297	52. *Sierra Leone*	142	81. *Lesotho*	63
21. Iraq	283	53. Ceylon	138	82. *Burma*	62
22. Malaysia	280	54. *Mauritania*	137	83. *United*	
23. Guatemala	277	55. Cameroon	125	*Republic of*	
24. Liberia	259	56. Cambodia	120	*Tanzania*	61
25. Peru	253	57. South		84. *Ethiopia*	58
26. El Salvador	249	Vietnam	119	85. *Afghanistan*	55
27. Philippines	246	58. Thailand	117	86. *Somalia*	54
28. Iran	242	59. *Central*		87. *Yemen*	50
29. Saudi Arabia	240	*African*		88. *Malawi*	45
30. Dominican		*Republic*	113	89. *Burundi*	45
Republic	231	60. South Korea	107	90. *Upper Volta*	42
31. Brazil	230	61. Pakistan	101	91. *Rwanda*	42
32. Mauritius	230	62. Kenya	99		

* Countries in italics have been identified as LDDCs in the UNCTAD secretariat study.

32. TD/B/269, Annex, pp. 1-3.

contribute their share and to mediate in the dispute; however, they sometimes have no choice but to stay on the sidelines and observe the goings-on.[33] Another dangerous cleavage exists between the land-locked developing countries and their transit partners, also developing countries.

Besides the overall cleavages in the Group of 77, one can also mention the varying interests among the developing countries: each one has different priorities, depending on the nature of its economy, the level of its development, and the structure of its exports. These, too, may affect group action. Before 1967, for example, preferences did not occupy an important place on the list of African priorities; as a result, they showed no zeal in this matter.[34] But, as we have seen, once a demand for full product coverage was included, they exhibited a much greater eagerness. Another source of disputes, which may grow in importance as various measures in UNCTAD ripen for implementation, is the distribution of benefits among the developing countries. All these problems are obviously subject to conciliation, with smaller groups of countries coalescing around a common denominator and attempting to work out the best possible deal for themselves.

Before we proceed to an examination of the decision-making process in the Group of 77, it is important to mention two factors which contribute to the difficulty of reaching in-group consensus, or undermine it once it is achieved: (1) the parallel use of bilateral and multilateral approaches to the problems of development by decision-makers of individual developing countries, and (2) the attempt of some developed countries to neutralize and undermine the common front of the Group of 77. Regarding bilateral/multilateral strategy, there is a dichotomy in the policies of most developing countries. They look for solutions to their problems via bilateral channels, and at the subregional level; in many instances they seek privileges through close association with a given developed country or grouping. Simultaneously, they take part in UNCTAD's work, where the indivisibility of the solution to development problems is paramount, and where strengthening multilateralism

33. Lall of India and Brillantes of the Philippines, who in Algiers acted as appointed mediators in the very heated dispute between the Africans and the Latin Americans over special measures for LDDCs, preferred to remain passive observers in this instance. In fact, it was Prebisch who helped to find a verbal compromise solution.

34. The list of African priorities was as follows: financing; getting developed countries to commit themselves to enter into commodity agreements; technical assistance; industrialization and transfer of technology; shipping and invisibles; and (only at the end of the list) special measures for the least advanced in the preferential scheme. See E/CN.14/WP.1/13.

and generating joint Third World actions comes first. This behavior is quite logical and there is nothing inconsistent about it. A developing country may believe in the value of UNCTAD's approach, and it may expect a number of benefits to result from global action in this forum,[35] but it will simultaneously pursue its own limited and short-range goals.[36] As a matter of fact, some developing countries often try to exploit the pressures generated in UNCTAD to obtain various advantages on the bilateral level, even if this is to the detriment of other developing countries. Success in this is usually followed by a period of passivity in their role in UNCTAD. Also, it has been suggested that some developing countries, in order to gain or preserve favorable consideration from international financial organizations, sometimes show a tendency to tone down their position in UNCTAD.

It is precisely on this note of bilateral advantages that some developed countries play when promoting their divisive tactics vis-à-vis the 77. It is an easy task, since weak nations are more vulnerable either to threats or warnings of punishment or to promises of advantages.[37] The persuasive power of a major developed country is not negligible; the object of persuasion may modify its stand accordingly. By influencing some developing countries, western powers can affect the position of the 77 and increase the divisive trends in the group.[38]

As a consequence, the developing nations will consume more time and energy trying to achieve in-group consensus, while at the same time finding it more difficult to exert sufficient pressure on the B Group. Furthermore, one of the rules of the group system as it has evolved in

35. The payoffs of collective action are often more difficult to pinpoint than are those a country obtains bilaterally; however, the issue is different. Here one is not talking so much about the dollars-and-cents payoffs; what is at stake are structural changes for which bilateral action is totally ineffective.

36. Note, for example, that a quest for short-range advantages caused the Cocoa Producers Alliance to fail when some of its undisciplined members fell to the temptation of temporarily high cocoa prices.

37. One of the leaders of the Mexican revolution described his country's position as being far from God, but close to the United States. Many developing countries find themselves in a similar situation in their relations with certain developed countries. In such instances, the "persuasiveness" of messages received increases manyfold.

38. This is usually done by individual developed countries, although the move can in some instances be previously cleared by several of them. For example, the 18 associates of the EEC travelled to New Delhi via Paris. It has been argued that the French gave them a "talk" on the issue of general and vertical preferences. (An interesting remark appeared in the journal *Marchés Tropicaux et Meditérrannéens* (14 Oct. 1967) just before the New Delhi Conference. The editor deplored the fact that in Geneva in 1964 many of the African associates were influenced by other developing countries, and he felt that more efficient coordination among the "24" (6 + 18) was essential in New Delhi.)

UNCTAD is that the developed countries usually are not expected to act until the Group of 77 presents a common stand on a given issue. Thus by delaying, or preventing, consensus among the developing countries, any action on substance is postponed still further into the future. Let us now turn to the decision-making process within the Group of 77.

Decision-Making in the Group of 77. At the early stages of the Geneva Conference the Group of 77 operated as a loose caucus, where initiative by individual countries was common.[39] Near the end, however, the group appeared monolithic and two rules of behavior came into force. First, all proposals had to be cleared by the Group of 77 before they were thrown into the wider arena of negotiations with the developed countries. Secondly, all proposals had to be unanimously endorsed by all members of the group; consequently, if a country, or a group of countries, opposed a proposal, it would remain under consideration until consensus was achieved. When the permanent machinery of UNCTAD came into being, the Group of 77 continued to adhere to the in-group decision-making rules which had emerged in Geneva.

During the meetings of UNCTAD's main bodies (here we primarily mean the Conference and the Board), the work of the Group of 77 goes on at two levels, i.e., the regional groups and the plenary of the 77.[40] Attempts were made to decentralize the decision-making process in the group, so as to adapt it to the specialized requirements of the agenda; there was little success in most instances because the plenary of the 77 prefers to make the decisions itself rather than delegate them to smaller representative bodies.[41] As we have seen, the regional groups are growing in importance: even the smallest proposals are referred to them

39. It should be recalled (Chapter II) that Burma's draft resolution on institutional matters was submitted to the Fourth Committee of the Geneva Conference without ever being shown to the 77 as a whole. Had the sponsors done so, the draft would probably never have seen daylight and could not have been effectively used as a bargaining weapon to help crystallize the position of the 77, and to influence the developed countries.

40. At the Board, for example, the regional groups would meet at 8 a.m., to merge into the Group of 77 an hour or so later, and only when this meeting was over would they proceed to the formal body. (The group is at its full strength only during the Conference, and of course, at the ministerial meetings, like the one held in Algiers. At the Board sessions, the Group of 77 consists of the 31 developing countries members of the Board, plus those which are at the Board as observers and take part in the group proceedings on the basis of an internal agreement.)

41. At the Fifth Board (August 1967) several working parties were appointed; however, they either never met or failed to contribute to the work of the 77. In fact, time was mostly wasted in trying to select which countries were to be their members.

for clearance, and only later do they find their way to the meeting of the group as a whole.[42]

One of the problems plaguing the Group of 77 is the relative inefficiency and slowness of in-group decision-making. There are several reasons for this situation, above and beyond the substantive disagreements which must be reconciled. Often a discussion of non-substantive matters is allowed to divide the group and divert attention from the central issues;[43] an inordinate amount of time is wasted on procedural issues and chairmanships. Some African and Latin American delegates appear to have a special flair for these subjects. The high rate of turnover of delegates also causes problems: those more familiar with the scene have to spend time explaining things to newcomers and trying to restrain them from actions which might disturb a consensus already crystallized. Many delegations often lack specialist skill and adequate preparation.[44] The group is also characterized by a certain lack of inhibition on the part of some delegates. As a result, their behavior does not on every occasion conform to "accepted" parliamentary norms.[45]

42. Consensus achievement within regional groups is a story in itself, and it often stalls the work of the Group of 77. For example, Latin Americans have an unconscionable compulsion for oratory. Speeches are associated with the prestige and ego of the delegates; thus, even though the group acts as a family, the members find it necessary to give lengthy exposés which are often no more than repetitions of what the previous speaker has already said. Their meetings last longer as a result; they use more time than is warranted, and often make other members of the 77 wait. The African group is plagued by suspicion and differences between Anglophone and Francophone Africans, the latter being suspected of often acting under French influence. Furthermore, in any regional group even one opinionated member may frustrate taking a decision, because decisions are taken by consensus.

43. For example, during the closing stages of the New Delhi Conference, when a number of crucial issues were awaiting urgent action, an entire meeting of the 77 was used up in a debate over an organizational suggestion. It was proposed that, in order to save time in the plenary, the group have a delegated spokesman on each issue. This caused a heated and wasteful debate on how to choose such spokesmen, whether this was a good idea or not, etc. The turmoil was partly due to the fact that the proposal was interpreted as a challenge to the leadership of the chairman of the 77 at that time, Silveira of Brazil.

44. In some instances certain delegates did not receive the documentation in their capitals and/or read given documents for the first time when they arrived at a meeting. This, of course, pre-empted them from participating constructively in the work of the group. Others took position without ever reading the pertinent documents.

45. The mistrust and problems existing between the African and Latin American groups contribute to the frequently tumultuous atmosphere of these meetings, and generate unnecessary conflict over minor issues. The somewhat strained relations between delegates of India and of some African countries are yet another obstacle to a more efficient conciliation of views; this is especially

The regional groups are the main sources for proposals in the Group of 77. They also channel the initiatives of the various governments, either via meetings in the regional context, or directly in UNCTAD. The UNCTAD secretariat can likewise be an important initiator of proposals; various delegations may be willing to cooperate and sponsor draft resolutions or ideas emanating from the secretariat and coinciding with their interests. "Pet projects" from a given country, or from a group of countries—those which are not controversial within the group and in which most other countries are not greatly interested—used to get unanimous group support. This was gradually modified so as to increase the resort to a type of barter: those not directly interested in a proposal agree to support it for a *quid pro quo* from the interested countries on some other issue. This practice has been extended to encompass occasional "package deals" within the group. We have already mentioned, for example, how the African group in Algiers accepted that studies be conducted on the effects of special preferences, and how it exhibited a much more conciliatory attitude on the issue of phasing out the vertical preferential arrangements. They conceded this on condition that a satisfactory solution be worked out to the problem of special measures for LDDCs.[46] Part of the deal also included an agreement to insist on full product coverage in the preferential scheme. Although explicit "package deals" are usually frowned upon, this general method is likely to be used continuously, because one of the underlying, though theoretical, goals of the Group of 77 is for all its members to obtain more or less equivalent advantages from the policies that emerge from UNCTAD. Obviously, it becomes very hard to satisfy this requirement if an issue is treated in isolation. The difficulty with the "package deal" approach, however, is that when the 77 engage in this exercise, their main goal is to reach internal consensus, and they may fail to take sufficient account of the position of the developed countries. Moreover, the negotiations with the B Group must be subject by subject, as in no case would the developed countries accept a package simply because it is essential for the unity of the 77. Often the solution of one problem is delayed until all the elements of the package deal are

---

true because India aims at a leadership role which, for the above reason, it occasionally finds difficult to exercise. (The reasons why some African countries mistrust India are probably related to the question of the Indian minority in East Africa, India's role as a global power, its efforts to be an effective leader, and perhaps the fact that India's diplomats, trained in the British tradition, at times underestimate their less experienced colleagues.)

46. Similarly, at one of the Board meetings, the African group agreed to give its support to the draft resolution on the transfer of technology in return for the acceptance of its draft resolution on LDDCs.

agreed upon. Of course, there is always a possible way out of a predicament; in this case through deferred benefits.[47] However, the question remains: how satisfied will those countries be that get their payoffs only in the future? In fact, the situation might be somewhat easier to cope with had the developing countries adopted one of the principles of nineteenth century collective bargaining, namely, the slogan of the labor movement: "all for one, one for all". However, it is states that are involved here, and their behavior is different from that of labor unions. They are more likely to be guided by such mottos as, "if I do not get it, neither will you" or, "your thing will not go through unless mine does", and they do not always consider a given proposal purely on its own merits.

In elaborating general demands and principles, the Group of 77 encounters no serious difficulties. But to work out more specific proposals and to take the interests of various countries into account is something else again. When there are conflicting interests among the factions within the group, there is a tendency toward "splitting the differences".[48] Typically, in the case of special preferences for manufactures, both sides made concessions in New Delhi in order to attain the agreement. The Latin Americans agreed not to press for the immediate abolition of special preferences and accepted a transitional period; the Africans, in spite of their previous reluctance to record any commitment, agreed that five years after the initiation of the general preferences, special preferences should come up for international review, with the aim of eventually eliminating them. The conflict was at least temporarily resolved, not on the basis of the will of the least cooperative party, but somewhere in between the two bargaining positions. The "splitting of differences" is a more logical mode of conflict resolution than is the "minimum common denominator", since both sides are likely to benefit, and since it is in their mutual interest to arrive at an internal solution.

Conflicts within the group which relate to the question of how a given demand is to be formulated are, in most instances, resolved on the basis of the maximum common denominator. This is especially the case with complex proposals; they are made up of several components in which different countries exhibit a greater or lesser amount of interest. The sum of the specific demands results in a maximum

47. In the case of preferences, for example, we noted the proposal to extend the duration of the scheme for the LDDCs, in order to take account of their later maturation and their inability to take immediate advantage of the scheme.

48. For the concepts of "splitting the differences" and "minimum common denominator" see E. B. Haas, "International Integration, the European and the Universal Process," *International Organization*, Vol. XV, No. 4 (Autumn, 1961).

common denominator proposal. Many additional factors are responsible for this type of consensus formation within the group, and for maximizing the demands raised vis-à-vis the developed countries. For example, there is the classical bargaining element of "over-stating the claim" in order to obtain the maximum possible concession. The 77 are generally unwilling to compromise the goals and general principles elaborated in 1964. They have a strong preference for "universal" solutions (i.e., those requiring action by all the developed countries, and intended to benefit all the developing countries), and they perceive the entire negotiating process with the West as one thesis prevailing against another. Therefore, there is a definite tendency within the group to produce a maximum common denominator position. The crucial question thus appears to be: how flexible is this position once the confrontation with the B Group is launched?

The maximizing of demands and a rigidity in position tend to be more pronounced on matters of principle and on issues of global impact involving the majority of developing countries; conversely, of course, the degree of flexibility is greater when a functionally specific issue is under consideration, for example, the sugar agreement or supplementary financing. Moreover, when a global issue or a matter of principle is considered with a view to implementation, the 77 tend to assume a more flexible and conciliatory attitude. Contrast, for example, their rigid position on preferences adopted at the New Delhi Conference, with their flexibility during the finalizing of the agreement in UNCTAD's Special Committee on Preferences.

Two final points are worth making before we conclude our discussion on decision-making in the Group of 77. A degree of permanence and stability in the operation of the 77 has come through better knowledge of each other, the educational effect of working together, and the experience with group action since the Geneva Conference. This is especially evident at the Board level, where a smaller group of developing countries has been closely associated for a number of years. It is precisely this greater stability and relaxation on the working level that has contributed to a thaw of the previously rigid rules of group behavior among the 77—rules stressing that each proposal be cleared by the group first before being thrown into the wider arena, and that every proposal be unanimously endorsed. The first instances of the change began to appear in New Delhi,[49] and there is an apparent trend

49. For example, India and Chile submitted their proposal on institutional matters without obtaining unanimous group support (among others, the African group had no time to decide, while Argentina cast a negative vote within the Latin American group). Also, the proposal of the committee on the transfer

in the continuing machinery, for regional groups to speak independently on those issues where it has proven difficult or impossible to obtain unanimity in the Group of 77.[50] These changes have also come about after the experience of a paralysis caused by some of the rigid traits of of the group system.

The Unity of the 77. When the Group of 77 was born, some observers from developed countries argued that its unity was a matter of rhetoric, that the cohesiveness of the poor was a transient phenomenon not to be taken seriously, that it was diplomatic in nature rather than derived from a fundamental community of interests, and that although it could be maintained while the discussion was generally on the level of principle, it would not last once concrete offers were made, since they would bring about a real conflict of interests among developing countries.[51] This argument was partly inspired by the confrontation atmosphere prevalent at the time, and by the ill-will of many in the West toward UNCTAD and the Group of 77.[52] It differed markedly from the view of the other side, expressed succinctly by Prebisch: "whatever may divide the 77 it will always be far outweighed by what are the permanent economic common denominators uniting them." [53]

The monolithic behavior of the 77 at the Geneva Conference crystallized around slogans aimed at tearing down traditional institutions, dogmas, concepts and practices, inspired even more by the intransigence

---

of technology was submitted to the plenary without unanimous support from the members of the group. Note, however, that these first mild transgressions in group behavior occurred in non-substantive areas, where the interests of group members were not really opposed to each other.

50. Note, for example, the Declaration of Santo Domingo, issued by the Latin American group just before the Seventh Board in the summer of 1968, and just following the New Delhi Conference and the unhappy experiences with the functioning of the group system. It stated that when it is not possible to agree with other regional groups within the 77, the Latin American group would put its views forward directly to the B Group, because it is important to maintain the necessary flexibility and freedom of action.

51. "US Economic Policy Towards the Developing Countries," summary proceedings of the conference sponsored by the Brookings Institution, Washington, D.C. (9-10 December, 1965), pp. 5, 7-8.

52. In 1964 and immediately thereafter, speculations were rife in developed countries about the pending breakdown of UNCTAD. Such arguments may have contained a dose of wishful thinking, but they failed to take account of the tenacity of an international organization with significant support behind it (and although a UN machinery is difficult to set up, it is even more difficult to destroy); nor did they bargain with a considerable and persistent unity of interest and action among developing countries; finally, and primarily, they did not grasp the fact that because of the maturing of certain forces, UNCTAD itself was only a manifestation of a more fundamental historical process.

53. *Far Eastern Economic Review,* April 6, 1968.

of the West, and made more conspicuous because of the "en bloc" voting of the developing countries. Under those conditions it was not difficult to maintain the appearance of total unity within this heterogeneous coalition. Yet, even at that time differences were often manifest when a concrete policy matter, in contrast to a general principle, was considered.[54]

The insistence on strict group unity and discipline, common in the early years of UNCTAD, was a carry-over from the Geneva Conference, and was related to the premise that the unity of the 77 was their only effective bargaining weapon in the confrontation with the developed countries. Moreover, the newborn and still fragile Group of 77 protected itself in this manner against unnecessary shocks and strains. It was also relatively easy to maintain a monolithic posture, as almost all the issues on UNCTAD's agenda were passing through the "problem recognition" and "recommendation" stages of consensus evolution. Another contributing factor to this response of the 77 was the prevailing inflexibility and negativism of the B Group vis-à-vis the policies advocated in UNCTAD.

During the 1967 ministerial meeting of the Group of 77 held in Algiers, differences of interest were revealed regarding certain concrete proposals; sharp disputes occurred too. In fact, not only did the group weather the "family quarrels" and emerge unscathed, but, its operational unity was strengthened and it gained self-assurance. Following the Algiers Conference, it gradually became possible not to consider internal disagreements, deviation or lack of discipline as a threat to the existence of the group. Today, in spite of the lesser frequency of a monolithic consensus, the developing countries continue to negotiate joint drafts, act together as sponsors, delegate spokesmen and negotiators, and vote as a group. The monolithic unity has been replaced by a more realistic concept of solidarity centering around two basic factors: (1) the position of developing countries in the world economy and their quest for change; and (2) a general agreement that the Group of 77 is a valuable policy and pressure tool, that it should continue to be active, that it is contributing to the slow learning process of all those involved in development cooperation in UNCTAD and elsewhere, and that it aids the acceptance and implementation of at least some measures that the developing countries desire. Consequently, the correct question to be asked while considering the unity of the 77 is not whether the group

54. Differences among states are much more likely to appear in a situation where concrete measures are being considered, since these tend to affect their well-being in a different manner. The problem is accentuated by wide differences between members of the 77, disparity in size and income, the nature of their economies, geographic locations, etc.

will continue as a viable unit, but rather as to how successful are the developing countries in reconciling their differences and conflicts of interest.[55] In other words, how successful are they in working out a joint strategy on a given policy issue and accommodating specific interests within this framework?

The B Group

For a number of years, the western countries have been consulting each other on economic policies, first in the OEEC, later in the OECD. We have already mentioned how they met in 1964 in the OECD to discuss the forthcoming Geneva Conference, and how they attempted to establish some generally accepted guidelines. The loose, consultative nature of the western caucus was characteristic.

Owing to the polarization of forces at the Geneva Conference, and especially the emergence of the Group of 77 and its unity, the developed countries began to assume rigid collective positions in order to better resist the pressures emanating from the developing countries.[56] After the Conference was over, the B Group became formally institutionalized: a special ministerial decision was taken to have the OECD serve as its instrument. Within the OECD's Trade, Maritime Transport, and Development Assistance (DAC) committees, special working groups were formed for UNCTAD matters, i.e. commodities and manufactures, shipping, and financing.[57] The OECD secretariat was assigned, *inter*

55. The complexity of the task varies according to the issue on the agenda. Some matters interest only a small number of states (e.g. a commodity agreement). On others it is relatively simple to achieve unanimity (e.g. terms of aid). However, especially difficult are those problems like preferences, where one has to take account of the conflicting or competing interests of a number of countries, the global nature of the proposal, and the necessity to satisfy most group members. Any future exercises of "dividing up the pie" as various measures keep maturing for implementation may entail some hard bargaining and conflict among the 77. It should also be recalled that a broad distinction already exists in UNCTAD between those policies which are directed at the regulation of the overall international economic environment, and those, for example, which are of direct interest only for a group of countries.

56. One of the sentences in the report of the above-mentioned OECD group which met before the Geneva Conference was: "... it will profit nobody to have competition between member countries to obtain the approval of the less developed countries. The differences in view on certain points cannot by any means justify such an attitude." OECD doc. TC(64)4, p. 6. Although jockeying for favors among developing countries was thus apparently frowned upon, individual action by a developed country on substantive matters was common before the rigidities of the group system took hold.

57. The membership of the OECD is not exactly the same as the membership of the B Group. Australia and Finland are associate members, while New Zealand

293

alia, the task of conducting analyses, collecting information on the attitudes of developing countries regarding various matters on UNCTAD's agenda,[58] and servicing the B Group meetings, both in the OECD and in UNCTAD. In the OECD, through the exchange of information and a reconciliation of the positions on both substance and negotiating tactics, the developed countries decided to coordinate their policies regarding UNCTAD. One of the working rules provided that any important proposal or intended initiative by one country should first be communicated to the OECD for consultation.[59]

Within the OECD, a decision on the general policy line is taken; it is on the basis of this decision that the B Group in UNCTAD adjusts its position to the dynamic elements that arise. The static context in the OECD and the absence of the other negotiating party usually necessitate a departure from the original position. However, as we saw in the case of preferences, when an important issue is involved, and when the position reached in the OECD is in the form of a package deal among the developed countries, the changes can only be nominal or tactical in nature.[60] It should be noted that some members of Group B hold consultations prior to the OECD meetings. This is especially the case with the Nordic countries. They maintain constant communications between responsible ministries concerning UNCTAD matters; they

---

is an observer. Originally, there was some confusion about their participation, but today they take part in the OECD consultations on UNCTAD matters. Some OECD members—Greece, Iceland, Ireland, Luxembourg, Spain, Switzerland and Turkey—are not members of DAC, but participate in the working party on UNCTAD within this committee. See OECD doc. DAC/UN(64)1.

58. Individual developed countries also have access to detailed information on the events in the Group of 77, information which they may obtain through their favored developing countries. Developing countries, on the other hand, gather only fragmented information about what is going on in the B Group, and this places them at a disadvantage in the negotiating process.

59. Originally, it was the heads of the OECD missions in Paris that attended the B Group meetings. This proved unsatisfactory, however, because they were not thoroughly familiar with the UNCTAD scene. Today, it is the heads of the B Group delegations that meet in Paris prior to any meeting of UNCTAD. In addition, meetings of the B Group permanent delegations in Geneva are held on a more or less regular basis. This practice was initiated in Geneva on the suggestion of the United Kingdom. The meetings are held on a very informal basis in various missions. One of the reasons for this is not to give the impression to the 77 that UNCTAD policy issues can be discussed in Geneva during the periods between various meetings.

60. Several problems arise with on-the-spot changes of such decisions. First of all, it is necessary to obtain a clearance from home; however, on any complex issue of substance it is often difficult to achieve this in the very short time that any meeting lasts. Secondly, it is then necessary to produce yet another group position on the same issue, and this involves further in-group bargaining.

divide up tasks and prepare common positions. As we have seen, the Nordic countries presented a joint submission on preferences. The EEC members also hold consultations among themselves on certain UNCTAD matters, and the EEC Commission prepares background studies and even makes policy proposals on given issues. Of course, the Common Market countries have to coordinate their position on the proposals which directly affect their common policies, for example, the policies relating to tariffs, or to agricultural products.

Among the cumulative institutional advantages that the B Group possesses vis-à-vis the 77 are: the institutional focus that it has in the OECD; the secretariat that prepares studies, obtains necessary information on other groups and services meetings; the availability of information; the possibility of continuous intra-group consultations; long experience in mutual consultation; special divisions within the ministries dealing with UNCTAD affairs; a continuity of representation, and a relatively high level of expertise.

In search of the B Group leaders, of course, one looks to the major western powers. In fact, the composition of the small negotiating group which elaborated the proposal on preferences within the OECD, is a good indicator of the actual leadership. Originally, it was proposed that this group should consist of the "big three"—the United States, the United Kingdom, and France. West Germany objected and gained access to this inner circle. Japan likewise contended that it should participate, but it was refused this privilege, because its reservations against general preferences would have caused the already low common denominator to be even lower.[61] Basically, it is the interaction between the giant trading nations that determines the position of the B Group.[62] The United States—as the most important trader with and donor of aid to the developing areas—the United Kingdom and France carry a great amount of influence, and are the veto powers among the developed countries.[63] However, in spite of the veto power, the ability of each one of them to determine the group's policy along the lines it desires is not always so great. The most notable example of this is Washington's

61. Japan felt slighted, especially since the general scheme on preferences would significantly affect its interests. Many argued that had Japan been included in this narrow negotiating group, no agreement would have been reached; once the scheme was adopted by the "big four", Japan had little choice but to join.

62. On certain issues, of course, the EEC and its Commission play a crucial role. The Nordic countries acting together have also increased their weight in the deliberations of the B Group.

63. Yet, sometimes half-way solutions can be attained without their participation. For example, neither the United States nor the EEC are parties to the sugar agreement.

policy on preferences: although it could indefinitely stall the crystalli-zation of the group position, it gradually had to change its own approach to the issue. In fact, even the veto powers do not like to be isolated in their negative attitude for too long. On the other hand, and viewing things from the positive angle, if one of these countries supports a given principle or policy measure, the chances that it will be agreed upon are much brighter.

Status as a big trading nation is not the only leadership resource. The special interests of smaller countries are recognized on specific issues, and they are then permitted to play a central role, e.g., Norway in shipping. One could also speak of a certain "spiritual leadership" in the B Group composed of countries that are favorably oriented to the demands of the Third World. As we saw in the previous chapters, among the prominent members of this group are the Netherlands, Sweden and Norway. Belgium and Switzerland often assume an inter-mediary position between the Nordics and the Netherlands, on the one hand, and the veto powers on the other.

Even though the developed countries share the common desire to maintain the *status quo* in international trade, finance, and division of labor, this does not mean that the B Group is not ridden with differ-ences. In spite of the common denominator of the *status quo*, its relatively small size, the fact that its leadership is composed of the major nations, and of course, the common politics and ideology, many argue that in the UNCTAD context, the B Group is less cohesive than the heterogeneous Group of 77. One of the in-group cleavages arises out of the level of development: the views and interests of Turkey, Greece, and Spain are in many instances identical with those of the 77. Although they have generally stayed in the shadow of the B Group, they have occasionally aired views similar to those of the developing coun-tries—especially on matters of financing—even in the meetings of UNCTAD's formal bodies. Another important cleavage is between the EEC and the rest of the B Group, most visibly manifested in the perennial friction between France and the United States. It was reflected in UNCTAD primarily over the issue of special and reverse preferences. Also of consequence is a line which separates those who argue that "the developed countries should do more for the developing world than they are doing now," from those whose motto is more like "the best we can do for the developing world is to maintain our own prosperity, and to do what our economic situation allows us to do at a given moment." [64] To what extent do the former influence the behavior

64. Another way to express the same would be: "we want to do it, but we cannot." The Indian delegate at one of the Board sessions distinguished between

of the more conservative leadership of the B Group? It has been argued that their effect is mostly of an "embarrassment value", that it can change the policies of the major countries only on marginal points.[65] As a matter of fact, when they are too persistent, the leadership of the group attempts to impose some discipline and bring them back into line—by twisting arms if necessary. In New Delhi, for example, the very cooperative attitude of Sweden and the Netherlands vis-à-vis the demands of the 77 on aid targets, caused some ire on the part of the United States and the United Kingdom, which were particularly sensitive on these issues because of their balance of payments diffi-culties.[66] Although Sweden and the Netherlands (among others) ex-pressed a forceful commitment to the 1% target, at the end of the Conference they assumed a subdued role in negotiations with the 77, and they went along with their group. The major developed countries especially were irritated by the lack of discipline, and by what they felt were demagogic attempts of some group members to "ingratiate" them-selves with the developing countries in order to gain political credit which they could then use for various purposes, including the opening up of new markets. This was especially so because the major donors felt that they themselves would have to bear the principal costs of the proposed measures.[67] Besides, they considered as inconsistent the attitude of some of the dissenters on matters vitally concerning them, e.g., that of the Nordic countries on questions of shipping, where the views of the United States appeared to be much closer to those of the

---

a "political desire" to see developing countries develop rapidly (and there is plenty of desire in the West), and "political will", meaning a determination to take all the necessary steps, however unpopular, to help the Third World achieve its goals. According to him, public opinion should not lead, but should be led. (TD/B/SR.167, p. 12).

65. J. S. Nye, "UNCTAD: Populist Pressure Group," (manuscript). Note the example of UNCTAD's role in planning the second Development Decade. Even though the more conciliatory countries were joined on this occasion by Italy, Japan and Canada, they could do little to impress the United States, the United Kingdom and France. In contrast to the B Group, small and medium countries in the Group of 77 have enough weight to stall an initiative or to prevent a consensus from emerging.

66. Some delegates were upset with Sweden in particular, especially because its previous aid performance was poor in comparison with many other developed countries. The more positive members of the B Group earned a chiding nickname of "boy scouts", and were proposed for "honorary membership" in the Group of 77.

67. Of course, this touches upon the very complex question of burden sharing. For example, setting aside 1% of its GNP may be more difficult for a small country than for a large one. Also, foreign trade represents a much larger per-centage of their national income than it does for a country like the United States.

77.[68] It is customary, however, for individual developed countries to be more progressive on those issues which primarily affect the others.

The decision-making process in the B Group differs in some important respects from that in the Group of 77. The OECD secretariat contributes to the planning, organization and efficiency of the B Group meetings. The relatively small membership makes the process easier to manage and more rational. Little time is expended on procedural matters, personality clashes are less obvious, and they interfere less with the group proceedings. Delegations are well prepared, their specialist level is generally high, and they usually have clear and firm instructions from their respective governments. A country's political and economic weight is important in determining the role its delegation plays, but the personalities of individual delegates are not to be ignored, although they are of lesser importance than in the Group of 77.[69] There is a definite structure of authority within the group, which makes it possible to delegate the negotiating mandate to the big powers; the US, the UK and France, if they so desire, obtain a seat in each contact group. The smaller countries rarely express jealousy toward the leaders, in contrast to the Group of 77. Actually, the feeling could be characterized as one of resignation.[70]

The decision-making situation in the B Group was relatively simple during the initial period of acute polarization between the developed and the developing countries. The response from the developed countries on such occasions was mainly geared toward turning down the demands without incurring significant political costs; in other words, it was almost purely a matter of tactics. However, once the threshold of "problem-recognition" is crossed on a given issue and a real dialogue begins with the developing countries (first on the agreement on principle then on working out provisions for concrete actions), the decision-

68. Gradually, however, under the pressure of public opinion, the original negativism of the Nordic countries on shipping, inspired by private shipowner interests, has been somewhat softened.

69. For example, Forthomme of Belgium, Golt of the United Kingdom, Reed of Norway, Jolles of Switzerland, Viaud of France, have or had a special influence within the B Group. France's position has been somewhat modified since the death of A. Kojève, a counsellor on its delegation who played a very important intellectual role within the B Group.

70. For example, we saw how the "big four" elaborated the B Group position on preferences. It would be hard to imagine a similar situation in the Group of 77, e.g., having India, Brazil, Nigeria and Yugoslavia elaborate the group's position on the same issue. Note that the Nordic countries (among others) have complained of not being represented on the small negotiating groups which establish contacts with developing countries; these seats are virtually pre-empted by the major powers.

making situation within the B Group becomes much more complex. Since the concrete interests of nations are at stake, every proposal is carefully weighed in terms of costs, benefits, and other consequences. The complexity arises especially from two sources: first, to change established domestic policies in highly advanced nations is a very involved process, further complicated by the various international arrangements which also come into question, secondly, states must weigh the actions proposed and the costs to be incurred as a result, and balance the two according to the criterion of "equivalent burden sharing".

Similar to the maximum common denominator process that occurs within the Group of 77, resolution of conflicts in the B Group is usually achieved via the "minimum common denominator"—i.e., the sum of the most negative positions [71] on the different components of a proposal. The tendency for decisions to crystallize around the minimum common denominator is accentuated by the search for unanimous group decisions [72] and the least costly alternative, and it is strong primarily because the most powerful members of the group are usually at the negative end of the continuum of possible solutions. The B Group position tends to crystallize at the level of consensus where the positions of all the major countries intersect, i.e., *their* minimum common denominator.[73]

Another very important element in B Group decision-making is the so-called "system of internal balances", which ensures the solidarity of group members on specific issues. Implicitly, it is a give-and-take of support. For example, although the United States is relatively progres-

71. Of course, a minimum concession by a country at a given point in time may be brought to a higher level through the process of intra-group bargaining.

72. In New Delhi, for example, the B Group search for unanimity often made the group position more vague and non-committal in order to accommodate the views of just one or two members. The declaration of support for the cooperation and integration of developing countries could have been more explicit had the position of Japan not been taken into account. For understandable reasons of national interest, Japan did not favor a strong resolution on trade expansion among developing countries. Such trade expansion, of course, involves possible discrimination against its own exports which tend to compete with those of the more advanced developing countries.

73. Conversely, one could posit a situation where the major countries would opt for a more positive alternative. Then, it would matter little if some less important group members preferred to remain at the more negative position. We saw how the common denominator rose in the case of preferences when the United States changed its strategy: it mattered little what Switzerland (to mention a smaller country) thought in this instance. This does not mean, however, that ideas launched by smaller countries do not occasionally exert influence on the B Group position.

sive on matters of shipping, it nevertheless supports the position of maritime nations, with the tacit understanding that these nations, in turn, will not "stir up trouble" in the area of aid performance, which has been its sore point in the last few years.[74] The system of internal balances is yet another factor which contributes to the minimum common denominator trend. In addition, it is coupled with a dictum that no group member should raise its grievances against another developed country.[75] Whenever this balance is disturbed, some progress is recorded on the intergroup level.

Since the bitter confrontation with developing countries in the initial period of UNCTAD's operation, the B Group has been showing increasing signs of declining unity. Some of its dissenting members have in several instances sided with the opponent, not only by expressing a different opinion from the B Group as a whole, but also by voting differently in some cases where a vote was taken.

Entangled in the web of group system rules (mainly the one which makes group unanimity a prerequisite for action), some observers and participants have argued that B Group unity is of the utmost importance, because its disunity means non-action.[76] Why, then, would the developing countries and the UNCTAD secretariat greet any disunity in the ranks of the B Group as a positive sign? The entire matter is easily explained by the level of the common denominator. The B Group unity has thus far hovered around the minimum common denominator, which reflects the views of the major and most conservative developed nations. Such a common denominator obscures the position of those group members which tend to be more responsive to the demands of the developing countries. Therefore, any sign of disunity is generally of a positive nature, because it reflects the decision of some group members to detach themselves from the minimum common denominator position. This, of course, adds to the bargaining strength of the 77, since the pressure on the more reluctant developed countries increases to a corresponding degree. This differentiation in the B Group is more

74. At the New Delhi Conference, the US chose to be rather conciliatory vis-à-vis France regarding special and reverse preferences. In return, France did not agitate too much on the issue of financing, the weak point for the United States. This gentlemen's agreement worked to the satisfaction of both countries.

75. If this were not true, one could envisage a potentially overt alliance between the primary exporters from developing and developed countries against agricultural protectionism and for more favorable conditions of product access to the markets of the EEC, for example.

76. In fact, some think of group system rigidities as a blessing in disguise for the major developed nations. They buttress their own position by positioning all B Group members behind a given policy stand; they can also stall action forever, simply by disagreeing among themselves.

easily obtained in a less polarized situation, especially in those instances where the developing countries impress some moderate B Group members with the reasonableness of their demands, and even get them to "lobby" with their more unwilling colleagues.

Like the Group of 77, the developed countries maintain the fundamental solidarity which stems from their position in the international economy. However, there is a definite move away from the monolithism exhibited in the commencing years of UNCTAD. So far, deviations from the group line have centered mainly on institutional subjects and on substantive issues of marginal importance. Yet, as various measures approach the stage of implementation, and provided the system of internal balances and group loyalty could be disturbed more often, a greater and more open competition could ensue among the developed countries (in the UNCTAD context) for economic and political advantages in the Third World, and/or for meeting the needs of the developing countries. Naturally, this would create a situation more propitious for substantive policy advances. Something of this sort appears to have happened in the case of preferences, where the donor countries competed with each other for popularity in submitting their offer first, argued the relative superiority of each individual submission, and made goodwill gestures to the 77 by trying to implement the agreed measures before the others did so.

The D Group

The socialist countries of Eastern Europe have always acted as a tightly knit group in the various international forums. In the General Assembly they have been described as the most tightly organized and cohesive group: they vote identically on key issues and coordinate their tactics in presenting their position in procedural, as well as in substantive discussions.[77] This pattern fits readily into UNCTAD's style of work. The D Group uses the Council for Mutual Economic Assistance (CMEA) as its organizational focus, with the CMEA secretariat providing the technical servicing. CMEA, however, does not play as important a role as does the OECD for the B Group. The D Group is usually called together by the CMEA secretariat prior to the more important UNCTAD meetings, so as to coordinate positions on various issues. Because of its very small size, it has been able to act in a rather informal manner, particularly during the UNCTAD sessions. Its consultations can be held in lounges or at dinner tables, free from the formal

77. See T. Hovet, Jr., *Bloc Politics in the United Nations* (Cambridge, Mass.: Harvard University Press, 1960), p. 47.

conference atmosphere prevalent in the meetings of the 77 and of the B Group.[78]

The dominant role of the Soviet Union is strongly felt in the D Group; a dissenting member usually can hardly do more than to contact a delegate from one of the other two groups informally, and give a hint that his country's position does not exactly correspond with the rest of the D Group. Yet, smaller group members have on occasion prevented the Soviet Union from imposing a given policy line. In New Delhi, for example, the Soviet Union appeared willing to consider quantitative commitments for the import of commodities from developing countries, but the D Group as a whole could not take a joint stand on import targets because Czechoslovakia and Hungary were opposed.

The question of D Group unity is a relevant one. In general, the members exhibit considerable solidarity on purely political matters, but this "political discipline" is not necessarily always reflected in the economic sphere.[79] Romania plays a maverick role. It attends the D Group meetings within CMEA, but it usually sends a third string delegation, in order to accentuate its unwillingness to be committed by the decisions reached there. In UNCTAD it also participates in the D Group meetings, though it acts independently in the formal organs of this organization. It often joins the Group of 77, primarily in voting on matters of financing, although this is an issue area where the D Group abstains as a matter of principle. Of course, Romania has been claiming since 1964 that it is a developing country, and that its place is really with the Group of 77. There are a number of other substantive disagreements within the D Group which seldom come to the surface.[80] On matters of East-West trade, for example, the smaller group members are more interested in the practical aspects of the "thaw" and see it as more urgent than does the Soviet Union.

Thus far, the operation of the D Group in UNCTAD has centered primarily around three areas: supporting the demands of the 77 vis-à-vis

78. In contrast to the 77, but very much like the B Group, the meetings of the D Group are characterized by their very confidential nature.

79. In fact, it is precisely on the "General Assembly" type of issues that the D Group achieves a monolithic unity in UNCTAD. For example, regarding Cuba's candidacy for the Board in New Delhi, the D Group mounted a co-ordinated and very strong attack against the Group of 77.

80. A slight indicator of this, but an indicator nevertheless, was the fact that in New Delhi both Czechoslovakia and Hungary voted for the resolution on the mobilization of domestic capital, which was within the package of resolutions on financing. The other D Group members, as a matter of principle, abstained from voting on this resolution, while Czechoslovakia and Hungary were attempting to show a greater degree of flexibility. However, they too abstained from voting on the other resolutions which were part of the package.

the West; attempting to use the disagreements between the 77 and the B Group; and studying the implications of the various proposals made by the 77 as they affect its own interests. Following the Algiers and New Delhi Conferences and greater confrontation with the Group of 77, and because of the task expansion of UNCTAD into the field of East-West trade, the focus of D Group activities could eventually shift to a more active and involved participation in UNCTAD endeavors. For the time being, it is important to note a change in the posture of the D Group away from the relatively simple one of supporting the 77 on every issue across the board.[81] In fact, in recent years the D Group has tended on some occasions to support the B Group discreetly and this has led to disappointment among the 77.

81. Note that D Group members generally do not like to have concrete demands addressed to them by the developing countries. Technologically they lag behind the West, and are trying to catch up; besides, they are overburdened with their own development as well as with armaments expenditures. Moreover, there is a good deal of political disillusionment with the Group of 77, which has sometimes been compared to a simple squeezing device without a clear-cut economic and social policy orientation. The D Group's disillusionment also spreads to the politics of most developing countries, and as we have seen, it is particularly upset by what it considers as extravagant and irrelevant claims against it by some among the 77, claims which it feels are brought up in order to please certain B Group countries.

Chapter XIII

THE UNCTAD SECRETARIAT

It should be recalled that during the Geneva Conference Dr. Raúl Prebisch headed the temporary secretariat, which was composed mainly of officials from the UN Department of Economic and Social Affairs and from regional economic commissions. Many of these men joined UNCTAD when the decision was taken to establish the continuing machinery. Prebisch, as the Secretary-General, was faced with expectations of high-level recruitment for the secretariat, which had to be organized and fully staffed very rapidly because a complex intergovernmental machinery was already functioning.[1] However, a number of difficulties were encountered in the attempts to staff the nascent organization. The delay in deciding where UNCTAD headquarters would be located impeded many prospective candidates from making up their minds. There was a general shortage of manpower: first-rate specialists were hard to find, and if available, they were not always eager to come to UNCTAD because of the diminishing covetability of employment in the United Nations. Also, the governments of developed countries were not particularly cooperative in releasing qualified men from the jobs they were working on for a round of duty with UNCTAD. The attempt by Prebisch to apply systematically the geographic criteria in the distribution of senior secretariat posts caused additional difficulties because men needed for given offices were not always available in some areas,[2] while some of those that were recruited were not equal to their tasks.

---

1. Fashioned according to the machinery and tasks of UNCTAD, the secretariat was composed of the following substantive divisions: office of the Secretary-General (Geneva and New York), manufactures, invisibles, commodities, trade policies, trade with socialist countries, research, conference affairs and external relations, and the New York liaison office (containing the finance division). After the New Delhi Conference the trade policies division has been progressively dissolved. As a follow-up to New Delhi conference resolution 23(II), a special program on trade expansion and integration among developing countries was set up.

2. For example, the trade policies division was supposed to be headed by an

The nationalities of the directors of the various secretariat divisions reflected the balance of power (if not the equitable geographical distribution); each major country or region got at least one such post.[3] Also, an attempt was made to apply the geographical key to the staffing of the principal divisions within the secretariat. It is interesting to note that the two divisions reputed for their quality—invisibles and finance—recruited staff on the basis of competence, rather than any other criteria. This led the "developing world quota" and "socialist quota" to be filled in the middle and junior level positions. This was to be expected, as shipping and insurance experts, for example, were almost impossible to find in developing countries. Besides, the senior international civil servants that headed these divisions refused to yield to governmental pressures and recruited only the men they thought were qualified. They realized that although the strict application of the geographical distribution of posts was necessary from the political point of view, it could not yield optimal results in a highly technical organization such as UNCTAD. They maintained that eventually governments judge the work of a division on the basis of quality of research and studies, rather than on geographic distribution of its staff members.

Before the secretariat was fully staffed, it had to rely extensively on the services of consultants, and it underwent a somewhat disorganized and hectic initial period.[4] The staffing exercise was a politically sensitive one, with all governments carefully watching the distribution of posts. The developing and socialist countries were particularly eager to obtain more posts than they had in other international secretariats which were originally staffed according to different geographical keys and did not reflect the influx of new nations into the world body.[5]

African. The search took quite a while because few people could be found with the necessary trade policy experience.

3. The distribution was as follows: conference affairs—France, research—the United States, finance—the United Kingdom, trade with socialist countries—USSR, commodities—Australia, manufactures—India, trade policies—Ethiopia, shipping and invisibles—Poland. Of course, the Secretary General was from Argentina.

4. Some have contrasted the early days of the UNCTAD secretariat with the smooth operation of the GATT secretariat in the late 1940's. They apparently overlooked the fact that the GATT secretariat at that time had only six professional posts, and was not in charge of a full-blown international machinery. Moreover, GATT's membership was small, composed mainly of western states, rather homogeneous in their tradition, culture, and level of income.

5. The UNCTAD secretariat was at its planned strength for the first time in 1966. It had 361 established posts, 164 of which were on the professional level. The corresponding figures for 1968 were 454 and 256 respectively. See TD/B/181 (2 Aug. 1968), Annex. In 1968, 22 of the 48 highest UNCTAD staff were from the B Group countries, 8 from the D Group, and 18 from the 77 (7 from Africa,

ORGANIZATIONAL CHART OF THE UNCTAD SECRETARIAT

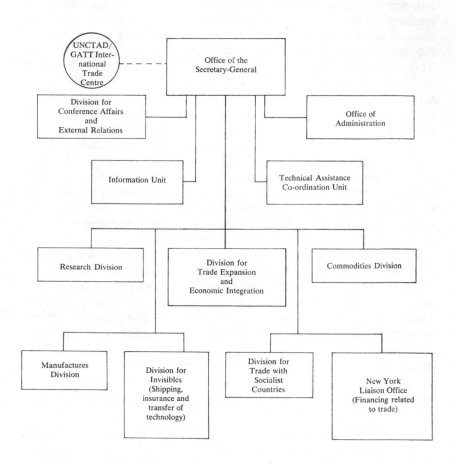

The UNCTAD secretariat was almost totally identified with the person of its first Secretary-General, Dr. Raúl Prebisch. His tireless efforts during his many years in the international field, particularly in Latin America, had contributed significantly to UNCTAD's creation and its physiognomy. His missionary zeal had inspired many; his ideas and studies—usually a few years ahead of their time—had raised important questions, stimulated a search for solutions, and helped formulate new policies at both the international and the national levels.

From the time international organizations appeared on the scene in the early part of this century, the claim has been made that there are two general types of leaders in international secretariats. First there are those who emphasize the administrative side of their function, faithfully executing the tasks assigned by governments to their organizations, and usually interpreting them in a narrow and pedestrian way; secondly, there are those who look for new initiatives and try to persuade governments to adopt them, they are men who are articulate on matters of policy and who offer a dynamic leadership.[6]

Prebisch's background, his predilection to formulate ideas and launch new policies rather than to work within the bounds of the existing ones, and his view of the international civil servant's role placed him in the latter category. Throughout his career he had assumed the role of a promoter of ideas and of an active participant. He thought of the international secretariat as being above national interests, advocating things ahead of time, and generating new ideas and concepts; in UNCTAD's case, the secretariat also served to synthesize the ideas and grievances of developing countries into a coherent set of proposals. Prebisch's independent initiatives were intended to contribute to the reshaping of governmental policies. This approach ran counter to the more traditional and conservative role of a secretariat as a passive servant only of the collective will of sovereign governments, and made UNCTAD a conspicuous example of the new trends in the concept of an international secretariat.

Although everybody recognized Prebisch's dynamic leadership quali-

---

6 from the Asian group, and 5 from Latin America). Compare this with the GATT secretariat, where 35 of the 44 highest staff in 1968 came from the West, only 9 from the developing countries, and none from the socialist states. Based on Nye, *op. cit.*

6. Kaufmann, *Conference Diplomacy, op. cit.*, p. 107, cites I. L. Claude, Jr., *Swords into Plowshares*, pp. 176-177. Claude makes a contrast between Sir Eric Drummond, the Secretary-General of the League of Nations, as an example of an efficient administrator with a British Civil Service background, and Albert Thomas, the Director-General of the ILO, a dynamic man who had once been a labor activist and politician in France.

ties, it was often stated that he was not the best possible organizer and administrator for his secretariat.[7] There were two inhibiting factors: the organizational lacunae in the secretariat, and Prebisch's own work style. Regarding the former, there was no "second in command" in UNCTAD. The original documents dealing with the organization of the UNCTAD secretariat provided for a Deputy Secretary-General (with a UN Under-Secretary rank), and later they also contained a slot for a director of coordination. Prebisch first intended to appoint one of his closest collaborators, W. R. Malinowski, as the deputy, then decided that this post should go to a small western country, while Malinowski would become the director for coordination. The D Group found this unacceptable, and offered its own candidate for a deputy in addition to a western deputy;[8] some regional groups of developing countries did the same. What emerged was the "troika" deadlock, and the appointment of a deputy did not prove politically feasible. Furthermore, the western countries strongly objected to Prebisch's choice of a director for coordination, so even this post was abolished.[9] As a result, there were no second and third men in the secretariat to whom the Secretary-General could delegate responsibility, and whose task it would be to attend to organizational matters, coordinate the work of the numerous divisions, and replace him during his frequent trips away from Geneva. Prebisch, too, began to have second thoughts about the entire idea of a deputy, especially after he was warned that the "second in command" from a B Group country could complicate the situation and even challenge his authority and leadership.

As regards Prebisch's work style, he believed in direct contacts with high government officials in the capitals of developed countries; he also spent a good deal of time in the UN Headquarters (and even in ECLA,

---

7. According to the *Australian Financial Review:* "The Secretary-General is a visionary man who has served UNCTAD well in its foundation. But he is no organiser and much will depend on his successor." (April 19, 1968).

8. The socialist countries did not accept the argument that because Malinowski was from Poland, he would represent their geographical grouping as a whole in the top echelon of the UNCTAD secretariat. They pointed out that he had been in the international civil service for almost twenty years. Malinowski had, however, the support of the Polish government.

9. Malinowski, who became the director of the Division for Invisibles of the UNCTAD secretariat, had incurred the wrath of De Seynes and of the West during his long tenure in the Department for Economic and Social Affairs. He was behind the move to decentralize the various activities of this department and transfer them to the regional economic commissions. During the Geneva Conference he collaborated very closely with the developing countries, and the developed countries (the US in particular) were angered by what they considered his "political" activities. The B Group ascribed to him the responsibility for the Burmese draft resolution on the creation of a permanent machinery.

where he continued as the Director of the Latin American Institute for Economic and Social Planning). He was thus very often absent from Geneva. During his absence, there was nobody with sufficient authority to direct matters and authorize actions.[10] Much business was conducted over the phone and via telex, but bottlenecks could still not be prevented. Furthermore, Prebisch appeared unwilling to delegate authority to the majority of his subordinates, and always asked to be informed on everything that was happening in the secretariat.[11] Too many things concentrated on him, and Prebisch often found himself overloaded, without clearly established priorities.[12] He preferred to work primarily with the small group of men with whom he had been associated before UNCTAD started and whom he could trust.[13] Only occasionally did he meet with all the directors of the divisions, and he had relatively little contact with the staff.

GATT and UNCTAD have been compared and contrasted in many ways, and their executive heads were also scrutinized. The most frequent comparison established Prebisch as a leader and Wyndham White as an administrator. This was not quite apt, in the sense that neither Prebisch nor Wyndham White were really interested in the petty details of administration. Apparently, Wyndham White delegated the administrative functioning of the GATT secretariat to his deputy, who did a competent job. Prebisch had no such recourse, and this is where the difference between efficient and non-efficient administration lay. A more relevant dichotomy between Prebisch and Wyndham White— partly generated by the different tasks of their organizations—was to be found in their relations with governments: Wyndham White was a negotiator and a mediator, Prebisch a heretic and a prophet.

The various criticisms addressed to the UNCTAD machinery, to the group system, and to the secretariat after the New Delhi Conference, brought about a reappraisal of the secretariat's internal operation. Partly as a result of this, and partly because Prebisch had already made

10. The more timid directors were reluctant to undertake independent initiatives and matters remained static until Prebisch's return; others acted on their own, subject to subsequent approval by Prebisch.
11. It is said that Prebisch would get rather upset when not informed about some developments in the secretariat and would exclaim: "Le cocu est toujours le dernier a le savoir!" He used to read many memos and some documents and make comments on them.
12. For example, his report for the New Delhi Conference was written at the last minute, and there was not sufficient time for governments to consider it before the meeting started.
13. Some of the more familiar names in the group close to Prebisch were: P. Berthoud, D. Cordovez, S. Dell, C. Eckenstein, R. Krishnamurti, W. R. Malinowski, J. Stanovnik (while he was in the UNCTAD secretariat), and J. Viteri.

up his mind to leave UNCTAD and wanted to ensure a smooth transition, two task forces of secretariat officials were established: one to coordinate the substantive work of the secretariat divisions on a regular basis; the other to be concerned with the administrative side of business. Also, many delegates—and Prebisch himself—informally voiced the suggestion that a deputy to the Secretary-General be chosen as soon as possible.[14] In fact, the suggestion was formalized in one of the resolutions passed by the Seventh Board. However, there was no chance to consider formally the matter before Prebisch suddenly announced his retirement in late 1968.

Prebisch and his secretariat were frequently criticized for not being fully impartial, and were identified with the developing countries' objectives. Some observers posed the question whether it was more apt to think of the UNCTAD secretariat or "sectariat",[15] and argued that the concept of international officials working objectively in the interest of all members was replaced in the UNCTAD secretariat by the concept of advocacy on behalf of a group of countries.[16] Replying to the charges Prebisch stressed that his "partiality" was for UNCTAD's goals—i.e., the new trade and development policy. He gladly confessed his "bias" for development, and insisted that "one could not be impartial when he saw a child beaten by an older man."

14. The question of a deputy was then a very touchy one politically, since the man who would get the job would be a likely successor to Prebisch, whose retirement was approaching. Therefore, it was expected that the person appointed would be of a very high caliber. (Among the strong candidates mentioned were Stanovnik of Yugoslavia and Lall of India.) Choosing a deputy would then have involved a complex bargaining exercise between the three groups of states, unless the appointment were to be announced without consulting them. Also, assuming that a deputy were selected, the balance would have been disturbed in the UNCTAD secretariat, which continued to be a one-man show. (It has been suggested that Prebisch usually helped choose men of lesser stature as his successors in the various posts he had occupied before coming to UNCTAD, and this produced a contrast between his reign and those that followed him.)

15. Gardner, in *The Global Partnership, op. cit.,* p. 106. Gardner suggested elsewhere that the West should protest violations of Article 100 of the UN Charter (secretariat impartiality) and make a greater effort to place qualified western officials in key positions, and alleged that the quality and impartiality of the UN secretariat were getting worse as the first generation of western officials retired or prepared to retire.

16. Of course, it may be argued that if a government cannot control or sufficiently influence an international secretariat, it is more likely to declare this secretariat as "partial". A senior French official commenting on the notion of "sectariat" pointed out that all secretariats are motivated by the interests of some special group, and that developing countries have long been complaining about the "partiality" of some secretariats that the developed countries consider as prime examples of objectivity and impartiality.

The dislike of many B Group members for the UNCTAD secretariat dated back to the Geneva Conference when some members of its staff cooperated very closely with the developing countries. It was related to the continuing close ties between the secretariat leadership and the Group of 77, to the secretariat's advocacy of a "harmful" and "mistaken" doctrine of trade and development and its pronounced hostility to the *status quo* in the international economic system, and to the fact that it openly took sides in the controversy among states.[17]

The mutual mistrust between many delegates from developed countries and many UNCTAD secretariat members, was in marked contrast to the close and friendly ties of the latter with the Group of 77. Following the ECLA practice, where the secretariat traditionally extended help to developing countries, the UNCTAD secretariat offered specialized advice to the 77 as well as to individual developing countries, helped them draft resolutions,[18] consulted them on matters of policy. Prebisch personally enjoyed the confidence of the Group of 77, which sometimes relied on his mediating efforts to settle disputes within its own ranks. The UNCTAD secretariat also provided its administrative services to the meetings of the 77. Some developed countries questioned the appropriateness of the secretariat's servicing of the meetings of the Group of 77, although they had no objections regarding similar servicing of informal meetings of the developing countries in GATT by its secretariat.[19] However, the services of the UNCTAD secretariat are available to all groups and individual countries that ask for them, provided that the cost is within the budgetary appropriations approved by the General Assembly.[20]

As it went through a period of initiation, adjustment and learning,

17. A western delegate complained that in the initial period after the Geneva Conference, the principal role of the UNCTAD secretariat was to pick up a set of figures and then try in its studies to interpret them in the bleakest possible manner, in order to artificially introduce urgency into a given situation. Others were unhappy about paying for the maintenance of a secretariat which was allegedly organizing the developing countries against the West.

18. Such drafting of resolutions, with the help of secretariat officials, is a commonplace in various UN organs. As a matter of fact, in all complex multimember organizations, the secretariat often leads delegates, since it is a permanent force on the scene. Kaufmann, *Conference Diplomacy, op. cit.,* p. 79.

19. In GATT, servicing was provided by substantive personnel, while in UNCTAD the Conference Affairs Division responsible for servicing could seldom offer more than procedural assistance.

20. The UNCTAD secretariat serviced the Algiers Conference, after being authorized to do so by U Thant. The expenses were borne by the Algerian government, and not by UNCTAD's budget.

the UNCTAD secretariat was closely scrutinized and exposed to criticism.[21]

One of the important problems in any international organization is to maintain effective two-way channels of communication between its secretariat and member governments. The GATT secretariat is perhaps the best example of an international secretariat that has given careful attention to the attitudes of important governments. The UNCTAD secretariat seldom took the opinions of governments into account in the same way, and its studies, reports and proposals usually were not informally explored or cleared with governments before being made public. The secretariat members on the whole did not practice maintaining systematic contacts with national delegations.[22] In an atmosphere of hostility and mistrust, it would have been difficult to imagine a "fruitful association" between the secretariat and the B Group delegates. Yet, even though it had good relations with the 77, the secretariat did not maintain close contacts with the delegations of developing countries either, and it failed to map carefully their thinking. The consultations with the developing countries appeared limited to Prebisch, Malinowski and a very few others, who continued their traditional relationship with the Group of 77.[23]

This general posture of the UNCTAD secretariat was to a certain extent also caused by its internal staff problems, by the fact that it had made studies and reports a basic policy weapon of its organization, and by the stage of consensus evolution through which various subjects on UNCTAD's agenda were passing at the time.

The servicing of UNCTAD meetings requires personnel skilled not solely in procedural matters but also in the specialized subject matter under consideration. Traditional conference servicing by personnel with a general background—the practice transplanted from the ECOSOC

21. Often UNCTAD personnel were contrasted with GATT personnel, who were said to be more useful in negotiations and more competent in specialized subjects. Yet no comparison of the two secretariats should have overlooked GATT's 20 years of experience, its functionally narrow task, and its non-application of geographic criteria in recruitment.

22. It has been found that the UNCTAD secretariat had almost no social relations with the representaives of various countries, developed and developing, with the exception of a small group of Latin American ambassadors. In contrast, the GATT secretariat members were rather active socially in the Geneva circles. See Siotis, "Les missions permanentes à Genève et la CNUCED," op. cit., p. 14.

23. Each division in the secretariat had its peculiar style of relations with the 77, which usually depended on its director, his personality and his background. Therefore, it is interesting to note that in the initial years the division on commodities had relatively weak links with the Group of 77, even though it dealt with a subject vitally important to the majority of developing countries.

312

and the General Assembly—did not suit UNCTAD's purposes, particularly in the course of highly technical deliberations. It often happened that "generalist" staff members could not extend efficient help to the delegates, could not establish a good working relationship with the expert government officials, and found it difficult to comprehend all events. The other side of the problem was that the secretariat ranks contained many research specialists,[24] who had little chance or no practical experience in relating to government representatives.

The foremost goal of the UNCTAD secretariat in the beginning was to focus international attention, through its studies, on a host of issues that had previously received only cursory consideration, and to initiate a systematic study of trade and finance in relation to development.[25] The secretariat's aim was to yield new data, to analyze problems, to provoke discussion and spotlight specific issues, rather than to present negotiable solutions within the existing framework. In this instance it was not really so vital to examine every proposal with governments, or to be excessively mindful of their opinions and feelings. Yet, with experience the secretariat found that in furthering the goals of the organization, tactless advocacy had only a limited success and antagonized the already sensitive western governments, and that more sophistication must be applied in a situation where the international civil servant continues to be dependent on the representatives of sovereign states. In fact, the evolution of the secretariat, its attitudes and approach, has paralleled the evolution of UNCTAD: a more subtle approach in pursuit of more effective results was gradually replacing the sharp confrontation with the developed countries. The secretariat's treatment of preferences was a good example of this process, and of adapting its research to changing needs. In 1967, when the matter descended from

24. In contrast to the few "practitioners", with the foreign trade ministries' and/or GATT background, the research specialists were not too mindful of the limits imposed upon the freedom of action of individual governments. The "practitioners" by definition tend to be more conservative as they speak in terms of what is in their opinion "possible", rather than what is "desirable".

25. A number of shortcomings have been attributed to the UNCTAD secretariat in this area, pointed out primarily by the developed countries. It has been said that its studies were academic, repetitious, declamatory, proselytizing, too long, difficult to read, and even inferior in quality. The secretariat's resources were also strained by the great number of studies which it had to prepare for the Board, the committees and the Conference. Most of these criticisms were justified, but one can hardly escape the suspicion that at least some were related to the substance of the papers—i.e., if the secretariat had said something more agreeable to certain governments, its work would not have undergone such a critical scrutiny. Anyway, the UNCTAD secretariat's quality as a research unit was improving noticeably; its studies were beginning to find more general acceptance and their higher technical quality was increasingly recognized by all delegations.

the realm of principle to the firm ground of preparing for negotiations and practical elaboration of the system, the secretariat's study presented all sides of the problem, outlined the proposed schemes showing the advantages and disadvantages of each, and tried to take into account the interests of the various groups of countries. It did not offer a clear-cut or ideal solution in sharp terms of its original proposals, but presented a realistic picture of the situation about which negotiations were to be held.[26] The secretariat was beginning to appear in the role of a broker, as the sugar agreement negotiations were to prove later.

Certain measures on UNCTAD's agenda were slowly becoming ripe for negotiation and implementation, when, primarily for reasons of ill health, UNCTAD's first Secretary-General Raúl Prebisch resigned at the end of 1968. U Thant acted quickly in appointing Manuel Pérez-Guerrero of Venezuela as the new Secretary-General. Among the candidates whose names were submitted by Prebisch, he was the only one acceptable to "controlling" powers consulted by U Thant.[27]

The low-key, businesslike style of the new Secretary-General has deprived the UNCTAD secretariat of its controversial character, activism and new ideas common during the dynamic days of Prebisch.[28] It has cost it some of the developing countries' trust. It has given it a more bureaucratic image and decreased its role as a source of inspiration. The new approach, however, appears much more suitable for the flexible role of a mediator and broker. This is the role that the secretariat will be expected to play as various ideas and norms launched by Prebisch and the developing countries enter the negotiating and bargaining stage. Yet, the secretariat should continue also as the articulator of ideas and norms—a role which has suffered with the departure of the visionary and innovative Prebisch—especially so as many subjects that concern UNCTAD are still to be found in the controversial realm of principle and general policy.

26. TD/B/C.2/AC.1/7 (31 May, 1967). Although many developed and developing countries lauded the study, a few developing countries criticized it for having fallen into the trap of trying to accommodate every view and therefore ending up with the lowest common denominator.

27. He carefully avoided getting the matter ensnared in the group system, and the appointment came as a surprise in Geneva, both to most secretariat members and to delegates. The Latin American group in particular was angry at Prebisch for not having consulted it on the choice of his successor. Although Pérez-Guerrero headed the Venezuela delegation to the New Delhi Conference, he was not deeply involved in UNCTAD affairs. This absence of close ties with the UNCTAD scene made it easier to get western states to support his nomination for the post.

28. Prebisch's presence and leadership are missed by many. On the other hand, the departure of an articulate and dynamic champion of the Third World cause must have come as a relief to many developed countries.

314

Apparently, the western countries are showing a greater degree of confidence toward the UNCTAD secretariat under the new leadership. The lack of pronounced controversy is more conducive to the secretariat's task expansion and a more active mediating role than previously.[29] And the less the Secretary-General is hero for one side, the more prepared the other side will be to have him vested with greater policy prerogatives.

There has been some improvement of the organizational set-up of the secretariat. Among other things, the Secretary-General spends more time in Geneva than his predecessor, and it has been finally possible to appoint a deputy for him—Stein Rossen of Norway (former Director, ECE General Economic Research Division).[30]

To assure a happier relationship between an international secretariat and all governments means that the former should assume solely the role of a traditional civil servant. The problem in UNCTAD, and elsewhere, is whether it is possible for an international secretariat to remain non-aligned in a situation where two antagonistic groups of states confront each other, and whether it can remain passive and neutral when dealing with a subject matter which requires an activist role? UNCTAD's organizational ideology and the fact that the Group of 77 is actually the power base of the secretariat, to a large extent predetermine its role. Yet the secretariat has to keep good relations with the developed and socialist countries if the entire organization is to be placed in a more realistic and favorable environment.

29. Pérez-Guerrero played a very constructive role in the negotiations on preferences, and won the confidence of both sides. Note that Pérez-Guerrero had taken part in the formation of the Organization of Petroleum Exporting Countries (OPEC), and had acquired a useful experience in negotiations with western oil companies.

30. Pérez-Guerrero spends more time with his staff and delegates stationed in Geneva. He has likewise instituted regular weekly directors' meetings in an effort to bring about a better teamwork, and somewhat reduce the previous concentration of power. The appointment of the deputy has helped the administrative functioning of the secretariat, and given more time to the Secretary-General to concentrate on substantive matters.

Chapter XIV

DECISION-MAKING IN UNCTAD

Voting

It may be recalled that at the Geneva Conference voting was the central issue in the institutional controversy. The developed countries negotiated for a conciliation mechanism, because they anticipated that the Group of 77 would continuously attempt to use its overwhelming voting strength. The fact of the matter is that voting has been virtually absent from the continuing machinery; in New Delhi—which was a situation basically similar to that in Geneva in 1964—it was used very sparingly. Whenever a matter was brought to a vote, it was related to proposals for studies, the establishment of subsidiary bodies and their competence, or symbolic issues.[1] In spite of the atmosphere of confrontation, the dominant motto in UNCTAD was "consensus and conciliation"; so when the 77 did use their voting power, it was in some instances intended only as a bargaining move in the continuing process of adjusting the overall views.[2] Tactically, they appeared to turn to voting only when they were certain to achieve a specific effect.

In all the cases where voting had taken place, conciliation was not permissible under the provisions of the General Assembly resolution 1995 (XIX). From this should one conclude that the conciliation

1. In New Delhi, for example, issues came to a vote in four instances: (1) to ask for a study on restrictive business practices; (2) to establish a working group on international shipping legislation; (3) to symbolically reaffirm the principles of the Final Act; and (4) to recommend that South Africa be barred from UNCTAD until it ends its racist policies.

2. For example, the vote on international shipping legislation in New Delhi *inter alia* had the purpose of speeding up the process. Also, Brazil and the UAR, the chief sponsors of the draft resolution, wanted to use this as a warning signal to show the B Group that there could be possible showdowns in other areas. The inflexibility of the B Group on the issue (caused primarily by the United Kingdom, the home of Lloyd's) was yet another contributing factor for the 77's attitude. In fact, as we have seen, bargaining over the nature of the working group and its terms of reference continued for another full year. When the group was finally established, it was by consensus.

procedure acted as a deterrent in cases where voting might have been contemplated? Some observers have argued that the mere existence of the conciliation procedure influences governments to compromise rather than to vote on disputed proposals, and that the possibility of *de jure* conciliation has promoted and institutionalized *de facto* conciliation.[3] The cause-effect relationship between the formal conciliation procedure and non-voting is in reality not so firm; at most, one can claim that *de jure* conciliation has been only one of the factors which have contributed to the behavior of the 77.

The 1964 Geneva experience demonstrated that UNCTAD was not a legislative body which could vote "yes" on a measure and then have its members comply. Using votes to reach a decision on the subject matters laid before UNCTAD would in most instances be meaningless and would indicate a breakdown in the dialogue. Also, the very unfavorable reaction of the western press and of public opinion to what was dubbed the "steam-roller" voting tactics of the 77 in 1964 and the negative image that UNCTAD acquired as a result in the minds of many, made the developing countries especially careful not to cause unnecessary irritation among the developed countries.[4] Finally, voting on almost every issue would have gone strictly along group lines; with the results so predetermined, it would have been of little value in most instances, even as a device to gauge the alignment of the delegations.

Voices have been heard among the 77 favoring a more frequent use of voting; they feel it would underscore the group position, particularly on the recommendations that are of a general character and do not call for specific action, and are therefore not subject to a possible conciliation procedure. However, the view prevails that group policy statements and memoranda are a preferable method of forcefully expressing the group attitude. Even in New Delhi, at the height of frustration, suggestions that the 77 resort to public confrontation and voting did not receive widespread support. The delegate from Brazil—who was at the same time chairman of the Group of 77 and leader of the militant faction—argued that a clear failure of the Conference and a clear identification of the major parties responsible for such a failure were preferable to a compromise which would betray the Algiers Charter, or to a compromise which would be so innocuous as to present no more than a friendly declaration of goodwill. He suggested that if negotiating

3. Gardner, in *The Global Partnership, op. cit.*, p. 119. Note that the author was one of the members of the committee which elaborated the conciliation procedure.

4. Antagonizing the developed countries could impair the progress toward consensus, many felt, and could give them an excuse for being uncooperative.

efforts failed, the proposals of the 77 should be carried to a vote.[5] However, the conciliatory forces within the group—principally the Asian and the Latin American states—prevailed and there was no recourse to voting, in spite of the overall militant mood.[6] Instead, negotiations continued until the end, and at least some modest advances were achieved. To many, it appeared preferable to put the areas of agreement, disagreement, and partial agreement on record, and to pass this on in a clear form to the continuing machinery rather than to vote through a number of resolutions unilaterally.

In view of the disadvantages of voting, and of the developing countries' tactics of protracted negotiations and informal conciliation continuing from one session to the next, one could wonder whether there is any value at all in voting on the substantive issues in UNCTAD. Seasoned participants argue that a decision adopted by a majority vote, which highlights the disagreements, may have a greater influence on the governments that find themselves in the minority than a watered-down, often meaningless, compromise decision.[7] Voting may not be the best way to tell the developed countries to do something, because it is not backed up by sanctions for non-implementation; however, it is a powerful tool and it remains a threat. In many cases it can embarrass the B Group countries, especially at home where they have to face that segment of public opinion which is sensitized to Third World problems, and both sides know this. Thus, even though it is not frequently used, it plays a role in the tacit bargaining. Voting can also be useful to formulate a principle or to initiate a policy or a study. As the rigidities of the polarized situation which set-in following the Geneva Conference gradually ease, voting may become more acceptable and increase in value for the 77. It may be useful in allowing the developing countries to exert greater pressure by forming a coalition with members from the "liberal" wing in the B Group for a specific vote.

There is another still unexplored value of voting in UNCTAD. The main purpose of conciliation when it was negotiated in 1964 was to enable the minority of developed countries to delay a vote on the proposals which the majority favored but which they found un-

5. Document 77/II/5 (18 Mar. 1968).

6. The word "compromise" was not very popular at the time in the Group of 77. For example, Prebisch was rebuked by the developing countries at their private meeting when he suggested a conciliatory approach rather than voting. "Developing 77 Urged not to Force Decision on Basis of Majority," *Times of India,* (New Delhi), 8 Mar. 1968. It was argued that compromise requires concessions by both sides, and defining as compromise meaningless declarations which marked no progress at all was nothing else but a surrender.

7. J. G. Hadwen and J. Kaufmann, *How United Nations Decisions Are Made* (Leyden: A. W. Sijthoff, 1960), p. 65.

acceptable: they could thus make certain that there would be a lengthy negotiation process. We have seen that the formal conciliation procedure has not thus far been put into operation.[8] It does, however, contain some possibilities which the Group of 77 could find helpful in its quest to improve UNCTAD's machinery and the process of decision-making. Resolution 1995 (XIX) provides that the conciliation committee be small in size and that its members include those countries especially interested in the matter over which such conciliation was initiated; the committee is to be selected on an equitable geographical basis. By pressing for a vote—and thus initiating the conciliation procedure—the 77 could in fact achieve the creation of small working groups to negotiate on a very narrow range of issues. As we recall, one of the proposals at the Seventh Board in September 1968 was aimed at "streamlining" UNCTAD's machinery precisely through the creation and greater use of such working groups. The conciliation committee could focus on a given matter over an extended period of time, in a genuine atmosphere of consultations without the distractions that plague conference diplomacy in UNCTAD. There is yet another value in the conciliation procedure. In spite of everything that is said, one must keep in mind that the developed countries do not especially cherish the idea of being outvoted. Once the conciliation procedure is initiated, voting looms on the horizon, in case no compromise formula is agreed to, and introduces a greater expediency and more political pressure than in a situation where informal conciliation alone is resorted to as is usually the case in UNCTAD.

The 77, bent upon avoiding the ire of the B Group, and convinced that voting, for the time being is not a winning proposition in most cases, refrain from exploiting their majority. However, as the period of total confrontation ebbs away, it is likely that the possibilities offered by the conciliation/voting mechanism will be used from time to time.

The Nature of Negotiations in UNCTAD and the Bargaining Power of Developing Countries

We have argued that one of the important components in the controversy over UNCTAD's negotiating function is the disparity between the traditional behavior of states in matters of international trade and

8. At the fourth session of the Committee on Shipping, held in spring 1970, the United States unsuccessfully invoked the conciliation procedure in an effort to delay a decision on assistance to shipping (TD/B/C.4/SR.70). The United States withdrew its proposal after legal opinion was given, and especially because no other country would join it. As we have seen in Chapter VI, the draft resolution was finally adopted by a vote.

finance and the new problems posed to the international community by the economic development of the Third World. "In order to receive, it is necessary to be able to give," and "those having greater obligations must have greater rights," [9] were the classical tenets of GATT. Needless to say, they clashed with the aims of UNCTAD, where it was advocated that the world is not homogeneous, that the rules of world trade cannot be based solely on the principles of reciprocity and non-discrimination, and that equality of treatment is equitable only among equals. GATT's "bargaining process leading to a balanced set of mutually equilibrated concessions" was suited neither to the situation in UNCTAD nor to its goals. The majority of proposals offered in UNCTAD are "innovative" or "redistributive" rather than *quid pro quo*,[10] they are aimed at changing the existing relationships in the world economy in favor of the developing countries. Although the proposed measures are intended to benefit all countries through the establishment of new relationships (e.g. implicit or indirect reciprocity obtained by improving developing countries' position as buyers), the advantages are generally not immediate for the developed countries and they perceive the majority of such proposals as being "redistributive". The difficulty, of course, is that in a normal "redistributive" situation, the demanding side couples its stand with a credible threat to cause more harm to the defensive side than would be the case if its demands were accepted. The developing countries are not in a position to act in this way. Thus we ask: what inducements are there to persuade the developed countries to abandon their *status quo* position—especially in those instances where it is costly and disturbing to their internal economic structures and interests and to their external economic relations to do so?

One of the delegates from the Group of 77 expressed the view that the developing countries did not see the New Delhi Conference as a confrontation, nor as two sets of negotiators making concessions to each other. According to him, this negotiating technique could not really be applied to economic development.[11] However, reciprocity has been the cardinal ingredient and the main lubricant of trade and finance negotiations on the international level. Even when reciprocity was

9. *Proceedings*, Vol. V, p. 420.

10. "Redistribution" refers to a negotiating context where the "offensive" side asks for a change in its favor, with the "defensive" side bearing the loss; "innovation" refers to the attempts to set up a new relationship or obligation between parties, with the change supposedly working to the advantage of all concerned, although not necessarily to their equal advantage. F. Iklé, *How Nations Negotiate* (New York: Harper & Row, 1964), pp. 27 ff.

11. K. B. Lall of India, at a press conference held in New Delhi on 1 March 1968.

explicitly waived for the developing countries that participated in the Kennedy Round, it was clearly demonstrated how difficult it is to get "something for nothing". A comment made by one developed country succinctly sums up the problem: "Obligations cannot be imposed upon, nor commitments demanded of some member countries while others remain entirely free to contribute or not to the common task." [12] Some sort of a reciprocal commitment would promote matters and at least partially alleviate the inherent instability of one-way relationships. This is why Prebisch spoke of converging measures, and of the need to discard the notion of strict reciprocity and payment for a concession; in its place he would substitute a new concept of "international reciprocity", whereby a combination of political and economic commitments of all states would be sought, all leading to the achievement of a goal generally agreed upon.[13] However, until such time when an elaborate program of mutual obligations is adopted for the common endeavor of promoting economic development, those concerned will have to rely on the traditional negotiating approach.

The interaction in UNCTAD brings about the alteration of issues and changes in governments' positions, and the bargaining power of the developing countries is one of the possible means of speeding up this process. In 1964, the newly emerged Group of 77 in its monolithic strength exerted a good dose of "influence" on the developed countries, who made greater concessions than they would otherwise have done— especially in the institutional sphere. The collective bargaining posture of the 77 had created a sort of "countervailing power" against the dominant position of the developed countries.[14] The psychological-propagandistic effect of the group's emergence, as well as the fact that the developing countries benefited from each other's experience, better understood the causes of common difficulties, and pooled their resources in elaborating common demands had a very important role to play in establishing the new relationship vis-à-vis the West. However, this countervailing power could not continue and be truly operative if limited simply to the identification of the common interest and shared opposition to the existing world economic order; rather, its effectiveness depended on the existence of a positive program of action, and on the

12. Comments by Belgium, TD/B/175/Add.2 (3 Sep. 1968), p. 3. Traditional type negotiators and trade ministries from developed countries, reared in a *quid pro quo* milieu, have an almost psychological block against giving something away without receiving a commensurate return.

13. TD/B/173 (31 Jul. 1968), p. 8.

14. Galbraith's term was used by the Yugoslav delegate in his speech to the Fifth Board on 21 August 1967. See also J. Stanovnik, "Trade-Union of the Poor," *Review of International Affairs* (Belgrade), 1-6 August 1967.

solution of the group's internal problems as they emerge.

At the time of the New Delhi Conference, the general consensus was that the bargaining power of the 77 was somewhat weaker than in 1964. In contrast to the Geneva Conference, the East-West detente had firmly set in. There was actually some friction between the Group of 77 and the D Group, primarily because of the ill-feelings of the socialist countries provoked by certain demands of the Algiers Charter addressed to them and which they felt were not relevant to their economic system. This, in turn, reduced the cooperative communications between the two groups and deprived the 77 of some valuable outside support. In addition, the Group of 77 itself no longer exhibited the "monolithic traits" of 1964—its weak links, suspicions and cleavages had been uncovered. The developed countries learned that nothing serious would happen if they demonstrated a lack of eagerness and little expediency in meeting the demands of the developing countries; the process of conciliation would continue anyway. As far as the B Group was concerned, by 1968 UNCTAD was a familiar battleground and the opponent—his intentions, strategy and weaknesses—was well-known.[15] Although the developing countries maintained a common front in UNCTAD, they failed to achieve the true behavior of a "trade union". The stronger bargaining posture for the 77 could not be attained for two basic reasons among others. First, individual developing countries were weak and susceptible to bilateral deals and the manipulation of the West, thus weakening the unity and thrust of their group. Secondly, the developing countries could not as yet agree to act as a group forcefully and systematically in other international organizations but UNCTAD. Assuming that these factors will continue to be valid for the time being, what, then, is the crucial ingredient in the bargaining stance of the 77? Apparently, it is the application of a skillful and persistent group pressure [16] on the developed countries, grounded in an elaborate

15. In 1964, the developed countries were taken aback by the behavior of the Group of 77 and by the fact that some of their staunch political allies were in its forefront. Some feared a bloc of developing nations, hostile and bellicose, that would have to be faced in various international forums.

16. The consequences of "non-group" action were quite evident during the Kennedy Round. This was the first time that the developing countries participated *en masse* in the tariff negotiations in GATT. According to the GATT secretariat members and other participants, the developing countries lacked the initiative that they show in UNCTAD which makes one feel that they are a force to be reckoned with. Actually, some criticized the developing countries for atomizing their efforts, failing to coordinate their demands, and not even thinking of walking out from this "gathering of the rich"—a threat which supposedly would have compelled the developed countries to take the newly adopted "non-reciprocity" principle more seriously. As a matter of fact, one of the reasons which prevented

program, plus solid and rational arguments which are difficult for the other side to refute. This approach imposes itself in a situation where there is no possibility for barter between the negotiating sides,[17] or where the demanding side cannot induce "fear" in the opponent. Here, differences are settled predominantly through the intellectual process of examination of facts, analysis, and argumentation. This, in fact, has been the approach that we described in the previous chapters: it produces no spectacular results, but consensus nevertheless does slowly emerge.

Possible Trends for the Future

It has been said that one of the weaknesses of the United Nations is its excess of formal parliamentarianism, and that the General Assembly and other majority organs are deliberative rather than "decision-making" bodies. Especially in the field of economic development, discussions on matters of substance do not move the participants or influence the voting of their governments. The delegates are merely instructed puppets, and their debates and discussions are reminiscent of "two parallel lines taking an extraordinarily long time about meeting."[18] Many a participant in UNCTAD's labors would concur with this description; in fact, it is quite an appropriate one if applied to any isolated decision-making situation—for example, the New Delhi Conference. However, what is involved here is a continuous process which gradually but permanently alters the positions of governments and the quality of the issues. The real decisions are taken or influenced

---

a fuller satisfaction for the demands of the developing countries was that the developed nations were preoccupied with their own problems and had no time to worry about them. (GATT doc. L/2912, Annex I, p. 14). The developing countries were even easier to ignore because as a group they were rather quiescent. As a result of this experience, they are beginning to act in a somewhat more cohesive manner in GATT. In international financial institutions the representatives of developing countries likewise find it very difficult to act in unison. Thus, often there is no follow-up pressure for demands and proposals generated in UNCTAD. It has been suggested that the work style of these organizations prevents the developing countries from exerting pressure as a group. Others have imputed that in those organizations where they can obtain some concrete pay-offs, the individual developing countries are careful to remain in the good graces of the rich countries.

17. On a particular commodity, a group of producing countries can mount a considerable bargaining power, provided that they stay together and iron out their differences. The 1971 negotiations between OPEC and western oil companies is the case in point. Not only did the producers obtain higher prices, but also provisions were adopted for taking care of deteriorating terms of trade.

18. Schonfeld, op. cit., pp. 101-103.

at various points along the circular path of an input-output scheme which includes all of the following: ministries and parliaments of the developed countries; regional groupings of the developed countries; the OECD; capitals of the developing countries; regional foci of the 77; the Group of 77 in Geneva; capitals of socialist countries and CMEA; the UNCTAD secretariat; other international organizations; *ad hoc* negotiating conferences; private interests and lobbies (especially on matters ripe for implementation), etc. UNCTAD serves as the focal point, where consensus on a given issue emerges after one or several tours through the various decision-making channels.

We now turn to the possible future developments which can be expected to promote the process of conciliation in UNCTAD. Three areas deserve special attention: the group system; the bargaining tactics of the two groups of countries; and the role that the secretariat plays.

The functioning of groups is not new in international organizations. Regional groups have long existed in the General Assembly, and some operational characteristics of the UNCTAD group system can be found in the UN Economic Commission for Europe (ECE).[19] In fact, in large international organizations, groups are a *sine qua non* for the effective conduct of business and negotiations.[20] What can be considered a new development, however, is the virtual institutionalization of the group negotiating style in UNCTAD.

A major UNCTAD meeting usually goes on at three parallel levels: the plenary meetings of the formal body, where statements are made and public debate takes place; group and subgroup sessions, which are in reality separate and complicated conferences trying to attain a unified group position with which to confront the other side; and inter-group negotiations in small contact groups, where a compromise is sought (usually after a public confrontation in plenary meetings) and the agreement is hammered out. Only then is the final decision approved by the formal body of the organization. No formal records are kept of intra-group and inter-group meetings; what appears in the recommendations adopted by UNCTAD is just the end product of a long and submerged process that is basic to the decision-making of this organization.

19. During the Cold War period, the socialist and the capitalist countries negotiated as two tightly knit blocs in ECE. A draft resolution cleared by one group was then sent to an inter-group meeting attended by only a few representatives. Resolutions acceptable to both groups were then adopted. Voting never really occurred. This informal rigidity was broken for the first time in 1967, when some small countries from both sides—to the dismay of the major powers—jointly presented several resolutions without previously clearing them with their respective caucuses.

20. Kaufmann, *op. cit.*, pp. 141-148, and Hovet, *op. cit.*, pp. 29-46.

Before a given policy matter goes to the inter-group contact or to the formal level, it is first discussed by each group, and, in the case of the 77, also by regional groups. A country may display as much individual initiative within its group as it wishes. In plenary meetings or in inter-group contacts, however, one or a few spokesmen or negotiators represent the group and, ideally, receive the support of its other members. A group discipline has emerged, so that any matter of substance is cleared within the group before any comment is made in the formal meetings, and it is generally understood that dissenting countries will refrain from undermining the group position.

The group system facilitates the decision-making process in a multi-member organization because it provides for regular prior consultation and coordination of positions, and because a large number of delegations express their position through one spokesman. It is actually a good method of collective negotiation, especially for the formulation of principles and general trade policies. The fact that every issue is filtered through layers of deliberations provides for an eventual meaningful exchange of views. Yet, the rigidities of the group system—which were the effect of the polarization prevalent in UNCTAD—often had a circumscribing effect on the negotiating process in the continuing machinery. The notion of group discipline curtailed and inhibited diplomatic intercourse among the groups and limited the maneuverability of the delegates.[21] The inter-group consultations usually did not begin until group positions were formed, but by then it was already more difficult to compromise and explore for possible solutions. The negotiators who arrived at the contact group meetings often assumed inflexible positions, since they had to take into account the delicately-balanced consensus previously achieved in their own group.[22] What the group's negotiators agreed to did not commit the group as a whole and had to be submitted to it for final approval. In fact, their freedom of bargaining was limited: they had to return to their respective groups for further instructions whenever a significant concession or change in position was planned. Thus occasionally, a compromise which could be

21. In the Group of 77, especially, initiatives by individual delegations were not approved unless a prior authorization was obtained from the group as a whole. The Indian delegate who had informally contacted some B Group countries during the New Delhi Conference in a search for points of compromise was censured by his colleague for this unauthorized act. "Bid to Resolve UNCTAD Deadlock Dubbed 'Treason'," *The Indian Express* (New Delhi), 7 March 1968.
22. It is no wonder, then, that a complaint was heard that the group system in UNCTAD "has played havoc with the traditional method of negotiations" (i.e., where the countries most directly involved strove to work out a compromise and then tried to convince the non-participants that the compromise was reasonable). Comments by the Netherlands, TD/B/175/Add.3 (3 Sep. 1968), p. 7.

achieved in a small negotiating circle was lost when the matter was brought back to the parent groups for consultation. Also, the maximum common denominator demands of the 77 and the minimum common denominator offers of the B Group, often resulted in the interruption of a dialogue. Finally, the increase in the number of meetings overburdened the delegates, and impinged upon the work of the formal organs, while the intra-group process of consensus achievement was often so involved that insufficient time was left for negotiating with the other groups.[23]

At the New Delhi Conference, which met over a relatively short period of time and was supposed to cope with a long and complex agenda, many delegations became aware of how paralyzing the group system can be, especially when pushed to the limit or used purposely to stall the entire process.[24] Inflexible group positions serve only to block or slow down the evolution of a general consensus. The inability of one group to attain internal consensus has a similar effect: it precludes any efforts on the inter-group level. Of course, this can place one country, or a group of countries, in a strategically advantageous position. It (or they) can prevent consensus from emerging, either by insisting on a rigid and uncompromising group stand when facing the other side, or by not allowing their own group's position to crystallize. In this sense, groups resemble convoys, which move only at the speed of the slowest ship.

We must assume that basically the group system is in UNCTAD to stay, because it reflects the divisions outside this organization. (We shall refrain from speculations as to what possible effects the entry of

23. For example, the number of registered meetings held during the New Delhi Conference totaled 976 (only 194 had summary records). Of the 976 meetings, 464 were plenary, committee, working group, or other official meetings; 500 were group meetings (not including those of the D Group); and 12 were miscellaneous registered meetings. The B Group met 166 times during the Conference. The Group of 77 met 163 times as a whole; the African group met 70 times, the Asian group met 43 times, and the Latin American group met 48 times.

24. B. Gosovic, "UNCTAD: North-South Encounter," *International Conciliation*, No. 568 (May 1968), pp. 67-75. The plenary, five committees, and three working groups operated during the Conference. Superimposed on this was the complex and elaborate structure of the groups. For example, the structure of the Group of 77 in New Delhi was as follows: the 77 as a whole; the African, Asian and Latin American groups; and the coordinating committee of the 77. This structure was paralleled in each committee and working group of the Conference. (Of course, such problems do not exist on the level of the Board or in the standing committees, where the group system coexists quite comfortably with the formal machinery. It is simply a matter of size of the meeting and the nature of its agenda and the number of items on it.)

326

China and the German Democratic Republic into UNCTAD, or the enlargement of the EEC, might have on the operation of the group system.) [25] The question, then, is: along what path is the group system going to evolve? Some suggestions have been made to improve its organizational aspects—for example, that the groups should not engage in debates on organizational or procedural matters; that they take less time in tabling their draft resolutions and negotiating papers; and that a joint sponsorship of resolutions be permitted on those matters which are not of particular significance to the general policy stand of a group. However, the more substantive changes will result precisely with the trends away from group monolithism, and polarization, as well as from the fact that the policy process on many issues has entered or is approaching the "rule-making" and "implementation" stage. Thus, for example, a more effective and flexible communication between the 77 and the B Group is gradually emerging, and a continuous diplomatic intercourse is taking place, unlike previously when the two groups confronted each other only at the meetings of formal bodies.[26] Or, as we have seen in the case of preferences, when all participants— particularly the major western nations—engage in a constructive effort to reach agreement many of the rigidities of the group system tend to disappear. As monolithism further weakens, it becomes easier to overcome group inertia caused by the opposition of one or a few countries to a given policy or action. Then the more negative countries in the B Group will no longer be able to rely on the rule of group unanimity to support their policy stand; finding themselves isolated, they may come around to a policy change more rapidly than would otherwise have been the case. Furthermore, although a "global" solution would not be attained in the sense that a group's full membership has adopted

25. It is to be expected that the entry of China would introduce greater dynamism on the level of issue articulation, bring about the reexamination of issues and pose problems in a new light, and agitate the *modus vivendi* that is emerging in UNCTAD. China's political and economic weight and the rivalry that it is engaged in with other major powers, may impose a greater political influence of UNCTAD upon the North.

26. Thus, for example, a contact group composed of senior delegates in Geneva met between the Eighth and the Ninth Board in an effort to negotiate a text on UNCTAD's contribution to the second Development Decade. This new use of the contact group, which previously was resorted to mainly in the final stages of negotiations, has apparently introduced a greater relaxation in the decision-making process. Consultations between delegates belonging to different groups (the Nordic countries especially are appearing in the role of bridge-builder) are more frequent, and different proposals are explored informally before being thrown into the meetings of formal bodies. For a discussion of the decision-making process in UNCTAD see Cordovez, "UNCTAD: From Confrontation to Strategy," *op. cit.,* Chapter VIII, pp. 192-219.

a given policy, a move toward implementation would nevertheless be recorded. Similarly, the possibility of forming coalitions between the 77 and some developed countries for a given vote could in some instances contribute to consensus formation, while the open lines of communication between the moderate wings of the two groups could help in a search for compromise solutions. This brings us to the related problems of the bargaining tactics in the UNCTAD context.

In view of the peculiar negotiating situation in UNCTAD, the claim has been made that one cannot rely wholly on the process of concessions and counter-concessions as a means of bringing the initial negotiating positions closer together. It is not sufficient for the 77 to present elaborate programs of how North-South trade and financial relations ought to be, or to rationally and analytically demonstrate that they have a good case. Requests which go far beyond what is "negotiable" and do not take sufficient account of the problems of developed countries do not inspire the B Group to offer compromise proposals, and they even give it an excuse not to do so. The B Group can either say "no" or give reasons why the "excessive" demands cannot be met. In other words, if the 77 cannot generate sufficient political pressure to have the developed countries seriously consider their maximum demands, then a more flexible tactic ought to be developed. In fact, during the New Delhi Conference, the argument was heard that the militant tactics of the 77 negotiators made the developed countries flock together around the minimum common denominator, and even offered the most negative of the B Group members an excuse to be passive.[27] After a heated in-group debate, the 77 decided to change their bargaining posture;[28] a thaw in the negotiating situation resulted, and although no breakthroughs were made, some limited advances did occur near the end of the Conference.

27. It has been argued that since the hard-line approach makes it easier for the developed countries to disregard the wishes of the 77, perhaps some developed countries encouraged certain developing countries to advocate a radical line. This obviously is impossible to prove. On the other hand, such unsubstantiated rumors can be used precisely for the purpose of undermining the influence of the more militant faction among the 77, and thus reducing the pressure vis-à-vis the B Group.

28. Silveira of Brazil, chairman of the Latin American group and chairman of the 77, was the principal exponent of the hard line. The Latin American countries, however, opposed his tactics. As a result, he resigned his post as chairman of the Latin American group. He remained chairman of the 77, in order to avoid any embarrassment at this late hour of the Conference. In this role, he had access to the top negotiating group, but he was supposedly limited to participating only on procedural matters.

Negotiating tactics for the Group of 77 are an important issue, especially since one has to assume that the developed countries generally are not eager to obtain an agreement, and will not come forth voluntarily to offer concessions and to initiate new and sweeping policies. In fact, the B Group finds itself in a rather comfortable position.[29] It generally opposes the proposals advanced in UNCTAD, and therefore has available a larger choice of tactical moves to achieve defeat and deferment. The systematic insight into the functioning of the Group of 77, the secretiveness of its own work, a much larger number of delegates highly trained and experienced in negotiating techniques than among the 77, the absence of the need to fight for the acceptance of new ideas are among the factors which endow the B Group with a tactical edge over the developing countries.

Militant tactics of the 77 are suitable on occasions, particularly when the entire group is firmly united behind a given demand; conciliatory and flexible tactics may be preferable when the group consensus is not so firm, when the issue of principle is not a stake, or when concrete negotiations with a view toward policy implementation are taking place. It is not difficult to present a maximum demand on an institutional matter, bargain a part of it away, and settle for a compromise which is often quite low on the scale of possible solutions. The developing countries can return soon thereafter with an upgraded proposal. Substantive matters, however, are different. Some group members may not agree to bargain away the provisions that are important to them, just for the sake of compromise. Besides, if the 77 trade a point away, it generally weakens their case for the future.[30] By making a "deal", do

29. An observer from the South has noted that the rich in UNCTAD are patient as only the rich can be, and that they attempt to defeat specific proposals by the 77 by the all-too-familiar technique of an endless discussion of details. ("UNCTAD II: Hopes and Snags," *Hindustan Times* (New Delhi), 1 Feb. 1968.) An observer from the West characterized the B Group behavior in New Delhi as "repetitive verbal gymnastics and delaying maneuvers which helped time run out even before a dialogue could be initiated." (R. Lusardi, Report to the Council of the International Chamber of Commerce on the New Delhi Conference, March 1968.)

30. Thus, for example, had the 77 in New Delhi agreed not to press for full product coverage in GSP, they would have weakened the pressure on the preferences giving countries to include as many products as possible from Chapters 1-24 BTN into their submission lists. One may wonder what would have happened had the 77 asked for an intermediate solution on preferences for agricultural goods—i.e., that the part of the duty which is destined to protect the industrial transformation process be eliminated, while that part which protects the agricultural output be maintained. Would this more "conciliatory" approach have contributed more toward a conciliation of views, and especially to practical actions?

they compromise and undermine their ultimate goals? Should they be satisfied only with "crumbs from the master's table"? Is "reasonableness" more profitable than "excessiveness" in the UNCTAD context? The "learning" experience that the developing 77 have had in UNCTAD has introduced a trend toward greater flexibility and a scaling down of their demands. The negotiating tactics vis-à-vis the B Group will be an important and permanent item on the agenda of the 77, especially as decision-making situations diversify and proliferate, and the developing countries gain greater negotiating sophistication.

We come finally to the role of the secretariat as a contributor to conflict resolution on the inter-group level. It is important to keep several factors in mind which affect the role of the international secretariat. These are, briefly: the statutory position of the executive head; the degree of confidence that member states have in this man; their special trust in his integrity and political judgement, etc. In the case of UNCTAD, as we have seen, the Secretary-General has a very circumscribed mandate for participating in negotiations or for undertaking the role of a mediator.[31] Moreover the UNCTAD secretariat did not enjoy the confidence of at least one group of states, while Prebisch's opting for the role of militant official, leader and man of ideas, and the nature of the negotiating process in UNCTAD put further constraints on the role the secretariat could play in mediating the conflict between the developed and developing countries.

The UNCTAD secretariat had been unfavorably compared by some to the secretariat of GATT with an active role in negotiations. When one compensates for the GATT secretariat's greater negotiating experience and competence, its special links of trust with the developed countries, and its wider (informal) mandate, we find that the chief reason for its performance lies in the fact that only those countries who by definition subscribe to the underlying principles of GATT participate in its central decision-making process. Most matters on GATT's agenda

31. The UN Under-Secretary for Economic and Social Affairs has similar statutory prerogatives as UNCTAD's Secretary-General. It has been said that he has only rarely offered positive suggestions on his own initiative for the adjustments of differences between governments, and he has had little impact on substantive decisions. (Sharp, *op. cit.*, p. 63.) The main functions of the traditional UN secretariat are confined to proposing items for the provisional agenda, keeping members informed of questions brought to their body for consideration and making oral and written statements. (Kaufmann, *op. cit.*, p. 105.) In contrast, the vague provision that "usual duties of the secretariat shall be performed by the Executive-Secretary on a reimbursable basis" was used as a basis with which to invest the leader of GATT with the power to suggest solutions to governments so as to reach successful conclusions in negotiations. The new type of tariff negotiations in GATT and the many-sided disputes between participants placed the Director-General in a crucial position. (*Ibid.*, p. 189.)

330

are not controversial from the point of view of principle; it is much easier for the secretariat to mediate between two tariff-cut offers than between two conflicting policy positions. In the first instance, one can perform the role of a broker; in the second instance, this is much more difficult even if the secretariat's participation were invited by the governments concerned.

In contrast to GATT, actors taking part in UNCTAD's decision-making process were not like-minded on some basic issues; thus, it was more difficult for anybody trying to mediate between them. And although Prebisch's institutional locus meant that delegations would congregate around him when trying to resolve a deadlock, he preferred not to intervene directly in their dialogue on matters of principle and policy issues, even though he made his views amply clear in his speeches and studies.[32] He did participate actively, however, in negotiations on institutional matters, or on substantive issues in those instances where a basic agreement on principle already existed and attempts were being made to work out concrete rules and provisions (e.g., cocoa and sugar negotiations). The rigid group positions on policy matters—like those in New Delhi—left little room for anybody to contribute to the search for consensus. The secretariat's intervention in instances of this type was usually unacceptable to the developed countries; were it to propose compromises, it could easily expose itself to the ire of the 77 and lose their support.

The evolution of many policies and proposals on UNCTAD's agenda toward concrete negotiations and implementation, plus the fact that the polarization and confrontation of the early years have diminished, introduce new possibilities for the UNCTAD secretariat to contribute to conflict resolution in this organization. While the secretariat basically remains on the side of the developing countries, it can increasingly strive to define the common interest, reconcile divergent points of view, and play a role in the search for formulae that can be generally agreed upon. The possibilities are expanding. Exactly how the secretariat will perform its role will depend to a great degree on the international civil servant in charge, his ability and personal courage, and his perception of his own role.

---

32. Regarding matters of principle and policy issues, Prebisch always volunteered to take positions in his speeches in the formal UNCTAD meetings, rather than in negotiations and consultations. These speeches were at times taken over by the 77 as their policy line. The B Group, on the other hand, resented this unorthodox behavior of an international civil servant.

The reputation of UNCTAD is that of a class organization with member states who are engaged in a class-struggle. This image is the result of the long fight preceding its creation, of the peculiar type of problem which occupies its attention, of the conflict and controversy which surround its labors and of the fact that it is within its conference halls that the rich and the poor nations are in constant confrontation. Yet the evolution of UNCTAD has been accompanied by a lessening of its original dynamism and militancy. Thus although its task remains unchanged and although the gap between developed and developing countries is greater every day, there are many who now believe that UNCTAD has joined the ranks of the traditional "sexless" and "antiseptic" international organizations.

The change in the image presented by UNCTAD is the result of many factors. On the secretariat level, an increased respect for the sensitivities of member states and continuous pressure from those governments which wish to emasculate any organization whose policy aims are not in complete accord with their own, combined with the need to play at times the role of mediator between developing and developed countries, a growing preoccupation with technical, operational and administrative tasks, an "aging" and bureaucratization of the staff and, quite simply, the dulling effect of the daily routine, have detracted from UNCTAD's original activism. Nor can one neglect the effect of the departure of Prebisch who had the courage and independence to speak openly and press controversial ideas even at the cost of incurring the wrath of certain governments. It must not be forgotten that in an organization like UNCTAD the secretariat has a vital role to play in constantly generating new ideas and highlighting problems, which obliges it to keep several steps ahead of governments in its thinking. Part of its role is also to offer leadership to member states and to help to maintain the vigor of the organization.

On the decision-making level, too, there is evidence of diminished dynamism. Consensus-seeking through long and arduous negotiations is by nature not a spectacular and dynamic process. Many subjects have to be treated in a highly specialized and technical manner, while negotiations on some issues have progressed beyond the stage of contention over principle toward a defining of the concrete modalities of a given measure or agreement. In both instances the marked controversy of the early UNCTAD debates is absent. Considerable emphasis is also being placed on unanimous resolutions, even in those instances where verbal unanimity serves but to conceal both conflicting views and the true nature of the problem. Furthermore, the policies and tactics of governments and groups have succeeded in tempering the attitudes of the early UNCTAD. The developed countries may be involved in the process of consensus building but they strive their utmost to minimize pressures upon themselves, to adopt the least costly alternatives and to make UNCTAD as quiescent as possible. Procrastination is their watchword. Nor do the developing countries seem to have preserved their original zeal. The realization that solutions are not easily or quickly arrived at and that for the time being the implementation of new policies for trade and development requires limited steps and actions, has lengthened their perspective. No longer expecting quick breakthroughs, they have resigned themselves to a slow and weary process of international conciliation, and occasionally seem quite content with the minor concessions that the developed countries make here and there.

This "taming" of UNCTAD should not find favor in the eyes of the Third World because it dulls the conflictual aspect of this organization. Conflict helps to define issues with clarity and creates the basis for accommodation. Impassioned clashes between developed and developing countries at one point in time have not precluded the reaching of an agreement subsequently. Nor has conflict over one point prevented constructive dialogue on others. Indeed, had it not been for violent conflict there would have been no UNCTAD and it would not have been possible to include certain issues on its agenda and seek international solutions for them. Conflict has been a critical ingredient in the bargaining process between the poor and the rich nations; it has generated greater political pressure on developed countries and made UNCTAD salient and politically relevant to their central decision-makers. The main element of this creative process is the unity of the developing countries and their concerted political action.[1] However, the impact of the developing countries has been weakened, among other reasons because of their internal wrangles over essentially marginal issues and the tendency of at least some among them to lose sight once in a while of the central aims of their group action.

1. Conflict and united group action by developing countries, not incidentally, are the two traits of UNCTAD that the developed countries find most bothersome.

UNCTAD, then, may be seen as requiring reinvigoration. There are two developments which are likely to provide it in the short run: the entry of China into the world organization and the serious deterioration of the chronic international monetary crisis. China's presence means that UNCTAD will become more representative of global forces, and it will have an effect on the bargaining set-up and the balance of power in this organization. China's participation and aspiring to a leadership role is likely to infuse UNCTAD with greater dynamism and to make it much more relevant politically than in the recent past. As for the international monetary crisis, and the attendant perturbances in international trade, they exemplify once more the traditional disregard of the rich nations for the effects their actions and decisions have on the poor and weak countries. These latter, then, gather in UNCTAD to express their views, to generate conflict and pressures in an effort to influence the decisions and actions of the developed countries, which prefer to decide these matters in their own small circle. The international monetary crisis not only underscores the significance of UNCTAD's role, but also implies a greater likelihood of policy advances in the field of trade and development. In other words, at a time when the monetary and commercial system of IMF and GATT is in a state of flux, it can be argued that there is a better opportunity for UNCTAD philosophy to have greater effect than in the past when the patterns and rules of this system appeared to be immovable.

Ultimately, UNCTAD, and its successes and failures, have to be viewed in relation to the unfolding of two global processes of systemic change which began only recently with the end of the colonial era. The first process is that of the gradual redefinition of economic and political relations between the poor and the rich parts of the globe, and the change in the international division of labor. The second process is that of international community building, which implies the emergence of a new international consciousness, the imposition of attitudinal changes on states and the modification of their selfish behavior and long-standing practices. Both processes call for and represent significant discontinuities in international relations, as well as in the nature of the inter-state system, and require important changes in political and economic patterns in many countries. This transformation is encountering strong and entrenched resistance, and this is why the journey toward an equitable world economic order will be a long one indeed. What is important, however, is that this journey has begun.

A complete guide to UNCTAD documentation (classified according to symbols) is to be found in TD/DOCS/1968 and its updated versions which appear annually. A detailed guide to the documentation for the New Delhi Conference is in TD/INF. 3 and TD/INF. 3/Add. 1. A list of main reports, studies and basic reference documents (classified under subject headings) that were published since UNCTAD was established in 1964 is reproduced in "Guide to UNCTAD Publications", and supplements, put out by the UNCTAD Information Service.

Key to frequently used symbols:

TD/B/..	General documents of the Trade and Development Board
TD/B/SR..	Summary records of the Board
TD/B/C.1...	Committee on Commodities
TD/B/C.2...	Committee on Manufactures
TD/B/C.3...	Committee on Invisibles and Financing related to Trade
TD/B/C.4...	Committee on Shipping
TD/...	General documents of the Conference
TD/II/...	General documents of the New Delhi Conference
TD/B/AC.5/..	Special Committee on Preferences

Articles, monographs and books cited in the text

Alger, Chadwick. "Systematic Research on International Organizations". Paper presented to the Seventh World Congress of IPSA, Brussels, September 1967.

Bernstein, Edward M. "The International Monetary Fund", in R. N. Gardner and M. F. Millikan, eds., *The Global Partnership* (New York: Praeger, 1968), pp. 131-151.

Berthoud, Paul. "The United Nations Development Programme",

Journal of World Trade Law, Vol. 4, No. 2, March/April 1970, pp. 155-191.

Chenery, H.B., Baade, F., Kaufmann, J., Little, I. M. D., Klassen, L. H. and Tinbergen, J. *Towards a Strategy for Development Cooperation* (Rotterdam: Rotterdam University Press, 1967).

Chossudovsky, Evgeny M. "UNCTAD and Co-existence: Part One— From Geneva to New Delhi", *Co-existence*, Vol. 6, pp. 97-118.

Claude, Inis L. Jr. *Swords into Plowshares* (New York: Random House, 1964).

Cordovez, Diego. "The Making of UNCTAD, Institutional Background and Legislative History", *Journal of World Trade Law* (May-June 1967), pp. 243-328.

Cordovez, Diego. "UNCTAD: From Confrontation to Strategy, Legislative History and Institutional Review", (mimeo).

Cox, R. W. and Jacobson, H. K. "Decision-Making in International Organizations: An Interim Report". Paper presented at the Sixty-Fifth Annual Meeting of APSA, September 1969.

Curzon, Gerard. "The GATT: Pressures and Strategies of Task Expansion", in Robert W. Cox *International Organisation: World Politics* (London: Macmillan, 1969), pp. 248-257.

Dell, Sidney. "UNCTAD—Retrospect and Prospect", in *Annual Review of United Nations Affairs: 1964-1965* (Dobbs Ferry, N. Y.: Oceana Publications, 1966), pp. 52-85.

Erb, G. F. and Schiavo-Campo, S. "Export Instability, Level of Development, and Economic Size of Less Developed Countries", *Bulletin* (Oxford University Institute of Economics and Statistics), Vol. 31, No. 4, 1969, pp. 263-283.

Evans, John W. "The General Agreement on Tariffs and Trade", in *The Global Partnership*, op. cit., pp. 72-98.

Frank, Isaiah. "New Perspectives on Trade and Development", *Foreign Affairs*, April 1967.

Frank, Isaiah. "The Role of Trade in Economic Development", in *The Global Partnership*, op. cit., pp. 44-71.

Gardner, Richard. *In Pursuit of World Order* (New York: Praeger, 1966).

Gardner, Richard, "The United Nations Conference on Trade and Development", in *The Global Partnership*, op. cit., pp. 99-130.

Gardner, Richard. "Trade and Development in the UN: A Challenge to U.S. Policy" (Council on Foreign Relations, March 31, 1966).

Gardner, Richard N. and Millikan, Max F. (eds.) *The Global Partnership* (New York: Praeger, 1968).

Goodwin, G. L. "The United Nations Conference on Trade and Development: Beginning of a New Era?" in *The Year Book of World*

Affairs: 1965 (London: Stevens and Sons Ltd., 1966), pp. 1-25.

Gosovic, Branislav. "UNCTAD: North-South Encounter", *International Conciliation*, No. 568, May 1968.

Gregg, Robert W. "Program Decentralization Through the Regional Economic Commissions" in Mangone, *op. cit.*, pp. 231-284.

Haas, Ernst B. *Beyond the Nation-State* (Stanford, Cal.: Stanford University Press, 1964).

Haas, Ernst B. "International Integration, the European and the Universal Process", *International Organization*, Vol. XV, No. 4 (Autumn 1961).

Haas, Ernst B. *Tangle of Hopes* (Englewood Cliffs, N.J.: Prentice-Hall Inc. 1969).

Hadwen, John G. and Kaufmann, Johan. *How United Nations Decisions Are Made* (Leyden: A. W. Sijthoff, 1960).

Hagras, Kamal. *UNCTAD: A Case Study in UN Diplomacy* (New York: Praeger, 1965).

Hovet, T. Jr. *Bloc Politics in the United Nations* (Cambridge, Mass.: Harvard University Press, 1960).

Iklé, Fred Charles. *How Nations Negotiate* (New York: Harper & Row, 1964).

Johnson, Harry G. *Economic Policies Toward Less Developed Countries* (Washington, D.C.: The Brookings Institution, 1967).

Kaufmann, Johan. *Conference Diplomacy* (Leyden: A. W. Sijthoff, 1968).

Kotschnig, Walter M. "The United Nations as an Instrument of Economic and Social Development", *The Global Partnership, op. cit.*, pp. 16-43.

Krishnamurti, R. and Cordovez, Diego. "Conciliation Procedures in UNCTAD", *Journal of World Trade Law*, Vol. 2, No. 4, July/August 1968, pp. 445-466.

La Charrière, Guy de. "La Conference des Nations Unies sur le Commerce et Développement, Bilans et Perspectives", *Revue du Marché Commun* (October 1964), No. 73, pp. 438-443.

Little, I. M. D. and Clifford, J. M. *International Aid* (London: Allen and Unwin, 1965).

Malinowski, W. R. "Centralization and Decentralization in the United Nations Economic and Social Activities", *International Organization* (1962), Vol. XVI, No. 3.

Mangone, Gerard J. (ed.) *UN Administration of Economic and Social Programs* (New York: Columbia University Press, 1966).

Mates, Leo. "Non-Alignment After Lusaka", *Review of International Affairs* (Belgrade), December 5, 1970.

Meier, G. M. and Baldwin, R. E. *Economic Development-Theory,*

History, Policy (New York: J. Wiley and Sons, 1957).

Meron, Theodor. "Administrative and Budgetary Coordination by the General Assembly" in Mangone, *op. cit.*, pp. 37-101.

Metzger, Stanley D. *Law and Policy Making for Trade Among "Have" and "Have-Not" Nations* (Dobbs Ferry, N.Y.: Oceana Publications, 1968).

Millikan, Max F. "An Introductory Essay", in *The Global Partnership*, *op. cit.*, pp. 1-15.

Narasimhan, S. "International Commodity Problems", *Foreign Trade Review* (New Delhi), Oct.-Dec. 1970.

Nelson, Joan M. *Aid, Influence, and Foreign Policy* (New York: Macmillan, 1968).

Nye, Joseph S. "UNCTAD: Populist Pressure Group", (mimeo).

Ohlin, Goran. *Foreign Aid Policies Reconsidered* (Paris: OECD, 1966).

Ohlin, Goran. "The Organization for Economic Cooperation and Development", in *The Global Partnership, op. cit.*, pp. 231-244.

Pearson, Lester B. *Partners in Development, Report of the Commission on International Development* (New York: Praeger, 1969).

Pincus, John. *Trade, Aid and Development* (New York, N.Y.: McGraw Hill, 1967).

Pincus, John. "What Policy for Commodities?" *Foreign Affairs* (January 1964).

Pollock, David H. "Pearson and UNCTAD: A Comparison", *International Development Review*, 1970/4, pp. 14-21.

Prebisch, Raúl. *Towards a Global Strategy of Development* (UN Publication Sales No. 68.II.D.4).

Prebisch, Raúl. *Towards a New Trade Policy for Development* (UN Publication Sales No. 65.II.B.4).

Reston, James. *"Punta del Este: Least-Favored Nation Doctrine", The New York Times* (international edition), April 15-16, 1967.

Robertson, Charles O. "The Creation of UNCTAD" in Robert W. Cox, *International Organisation: World Politics* (London: Macmillan, 1969), pp. 258-274.

Rubin, Seymour J. *The Conscience of the Rich Nations* (New York: Harper & Row, 1966).

Schonfeld, Andrew. *The Attack on World Poverty* (New York: Random House, 1960).

Sharp, Walter R. *The United Nations Economic and Social Council* (New York: Columbia University Press, 1969).

Siotis, Jean. "ECE and the Emerging European System", *International Conciliation*, No. 561, January 1967.

Siotis, Jean. "Les Missions Permanentes à Genève et la CNUCED: Rapport préliminaire", (Genève: Dotation Carnegie, 1968).

338

Singer, J. D. *Financing International Organization* (the Hague: Martinus Nijhoff, 1961).

Stanovnik, Janez. "Trade-Union of the Poor", *Review of International Affairs* (Belgrade), 1-16 August, 1967, pp. 1-2.

Townley, Ralph. *The United Nations, A View From Within* (New York: Scribner's, 1968).

Walters, Robert S. "International Organizations and Political Communication: The Use of UNCTAD by Less Developed Countries", *International Organization* (forthcoming).

Weintraub, Sidney. "After the UN Trade Conference: Lessons and Portents", *Foreign Affairs* (Oct. 1964), Vol. 143, No. 1, pp. 37-50.

Weintraub, Sidney. *Trade Preferences for Less Developed Countries* (New York: Praeger, 1966).

Wilcox, Clair. *A Charter for World Trade* (New York: MacMillan, 1949).

Adebanjo, M., 278n
Administrative Committee on Coordination (ACC), 186, 210
Advisory Committee on Administrative and Budgetary Questions (ACABQ), 184
Advisory Committee on the Application of Science and Technology to Development (ACAST), 225
African countries, 16-17, 79, 83, 88n, 160, 274, 281
aid flow, 25-26, 33-34, 115-121, 124-125, 297
    DAC average, 120
    official aid sub-target, 118-119
    one percent target, 24, 24n, 116-121, 124, 297
    outflow of capital from developing countries, 120-121
    private capital flow, 118
    See also aid tying, gross national product, national income, terms of aid, supplementary financing
aid tying, 125-127
    direct cost, 125
    second Development Decade, 126
    untying, 126-127
Alger, C., 270n
Algiers Charter, 77, 79, 105, 108, 110, 122, 128, 130, 144, 148, 155, 159-160, 166-168, 211, 231-232, 251, 317, 322
Algiers Conference, 159-160, 272, 279-280, 286, 292, 311
Alliance of Cocoa Producing Countries, 96n, 285
Alliance for Progress, 101, 131n
Alta Gracia Charter, 30, 35n, 49

B Group, X, 46n, 195, 250-251, 269-270, 293-301, 322
    bargaining tactics, 259, 284-286, 328-329
    big four, 70, 195-196, 295n, 298n
    burden sharing, 136, 297n
    decision-making, 294, 298-300
    differences and cleavages, 109, 143, 149n, 193n, 196, 244, 249n, 263n, 296, 300-301
    institutional advantages, 295
    internal balances, 299-301
    leaders, 295-298
    membership, 293n
    minimum common denominator, 299-301
    OECD, 293-296
    political desire and will, 297n
    rigid collective positions, 293
    solidarity, 301
    spiritual leadership, 296
    veto powers, 295
    See also developed countries
Baldwin, R. E., 6n
Belgrade Conference, 16
Bernstein, E. M., 32n
Berthoud, P., 309n
Brasseur Plan, 31n, 67n
Brillantes, H., 278n, 284n
Brussels Tariff Nomenclature (BTN), 73, 82, 84-86, 89
buffer stock, 31, 97, 105-107
    financing, 105-106
    international financing institutions, 106-107
    jute, 104
    tin, 105
Burma draft resolution, 39, 49, 308n

Cairo Conference, 17-18
Chossudovsky, E. M., 260n
Claude, I. L. jr., 307n
Clifford, J. M., 121n
cocoa, 96-99
  cocoa traders, 97
  New Delhi Conference, 98
  1967 memorandum of agreement,
    97
  Prebisch, 97n
  special preferences, 98-99
  US Senate, 97
coffee, 101-103, 229
  diversification fund, 102
  soluble coffee, 98n, 102
Committee for Development Planning,
  191
Committee of the European National
  Shipowners' Association (CENSA),
  145n
commodities, 6-7, 11, 29-32, 93-114
  classification, 94
  commodity-by-commodity strategy,
    95
  commodity councils, 229n
  diversification, 102, 114
  fluctuations of prices, 31
  free play of market forces, 93
  general agreement on commodity
    arrangements, 95
  hard fibers, 104
  informal commodity agreements,
    104
  New Delhi Conference, 104
  oilseeds, oils, fats, 104
  pricing policy, 95, 110
  remunerative prices, 31, 103-104
  special preferences, 110-111
  stabilization of prices, 31
  standstill, 30, 107, 110
  trade liberalization, 107-111
  See also buffer stock, cocoa, coffee,
    sugar, synthetics and substitutes,
    wheat
compensatory financing, 14, 32, 127
  liberalized, 127
  See also supplementary financing
conciliation, see decision-making
consensus, 63n
consensus evolution, 63-172, 91-92,
  114, 152, 171-172, 232, 234, 262,
  292, 298-299
  See also problem recognition, re-

commendation
Convention on Transit Trade of Land-
  Locked Countries, 227n
convergent measures, 224, 321
coordination, 15, 41, 46, 179-180, 185-
  197, 251, 255-259, 263
  commodity councils, 228
  duplication, 251, 256n
  duplication/coordination, 185-197
  ECOSOC, 186
  UNCTAD and Department for
    Economic and Social Affairs, 187n
  See also GATT, UNCTAD-GATT
    relations
Cordovez, D., 15n, 17n, 18n, 19n, 21n,
  28n, 38n, 40n, 44n, 47n, 177n,
  181n, 190n, 194n, 195n, 198n, 225n,
  236n, 309n, 327n
Council for Mutual Economic Assistance (CMEA), 276, 301-302, 324
Cox, R. W., 5n, 22n, 277n
Crawford, Sir J., 20n
Cuba clause, 80n
Curzon, G., 22n, 204n
cyclamates, 113n

D Group, X, 46n, 233n, 257-258. 269,
  301-303, 322
  disillusionment with Group of 77,
    303n
  See also socialist countries
decision-making in UNCTAD, 63n,
  151, 223, 269, 316-331
  actors, 269
  bargaining, 155, 316n
  bargaining in GATT, 320
  conciliation mechanism, 43, 47-48,
    56-57
  conciliation process, 317-319
  innovation, 320
  nature of negotiations, 319-323, 328
  reciprocity, 131, 320-321
  redistribution, 320
  See also B Group, D Group, Group
    of 77, group system, voting
Dell, S., 30n, 309n
Department of Economic and Social
  Affairs, 20, 38, 178n, 180, 191, 194,
  241, 243, 245, 256n, 304, 308n
De Seynes, P., 20n, 43n, 182n, 186n,
  188n, 243n, 308n
developed countries, X
  inertia, 26

institutional issue at Geneva Conference, 35-44, 52-57
public opinion, 26
view of UNCTAD, 175-176
See also B Group
developing countries, X, 28
definition, 77
difficulties in 1950s, 6-8
economic characteristics, 6
exports, 7, 76n
at Geneva Conference, 46-52, 291-292
institutional issue at Geneva Conference, 35-44, 48-57
joint actions, 16-21
Joint Declaration of 1963, 26-27, 48
joint proposal on preferences, 68
political mobilization, 49
ratio of public dept service to export earnings, 121
share in world fleet, 138
terms of trade, 6-7
unity at Geneva Conference, 49
view of UNCTAD, 175-176
See also Group of 75, Group of 77, LDDCs, voting
Development Assistance Committee (DAC), 115, 119, 122-127, 137, 293
See also aid flow, aid tying, terms of aid
Development Decade first, 24-26
Development Decade second, 87, 113, 119, 124, 127, 136, 189-197, 224
donors, national motives, 25
Drummond, E., 307n
duplication (see coordination)

East-South trade, 165-167
East-West trade, 15, 19, 35, 166-168, 259-261
consultations, 261
Geneva Conference, 259
New Delhi Conference, 167-168
UNCTAD role, 259-261, 265
Eckenstein, C., 309n
Economic Commission for Africa (ECA), 178, 274
Economic Commission for Asia and the Far East (ECAFE), 5, 178, 275
Economic Commission for Europe (ECE), 178, 260-262, 324
Economic Commission for Latin America (ECLA), 5, 16, 178, 187n, 203,

273, 308, 311
economic development planning, 24
Economic and Social Council (ECOSOC), 4, 15, 19, 39-46, 56, 177, 178-180, 185-197, 225, 312
relations with UNCTAD, 177-197
effective tariff, 67n
equivalent advantages, 68n, 110
Erb, G. F., 132n
escape clause, 74
European Economic Community (EEC), 23
African Associates, 67, 71, 83n
Evans, J. W., 12n

Final Act, 28-29, 34-35, 43, 59, 96, 101, 107-108, 165, 219
Food Aid Convention, 103n, 104n
Forthomme, P., 298n
Frank, I., 7n, 12n, 29n

Gal-Edd, I., 22n
Gardner, R. N., 3n, 4n, 5n, 22n, 29n, 43n, 50n, 54n, 56n, 134n, 135n, 186n, 310n, 317n
General Agreement on Tariffs and Trade (GATT), 3, 9-14, 16, 21-23, 37-39, 41n, 44, 57-58, 198-217, 244-246
and ACC, 210
agricultural protectionism, 201
Article XVIII, 11-12
changes, 21
Committee III, 22
Committee on Trade and Development, 58, 204n
commodities, 11-12, 13n, 206-207
developing countries, 12-14, 198, 201-205
Director-General, 58n
Final Act, 57
Geneva Conference, 38, 57
Haberler Report, 13, 22
ICITO, 11, 198
membership, 10-11, 14, 23n, 42
non-tariff barriers, 201
Part IV, 23, 57-58, 198-199, 213, 217
patching operation, 23
program of action, 23, 107
protection of competence, 37
reciprocity, 12-13, 22-23
relations with UNCTAD, 198-217

rich men's club, 14
search for role, 200
secretariat, 22, 203-217
trade expansion program, 22
Trade Information Center, 23-24,
    204n, 209-212, 244-246
Trade Negotiations Committee
    (TNC), 207-208
Working Party on Preferences, 23
See also UNCTAD-GATT relations
General Assembly, 4, 15-17, 19, 24,
    41, 44-48, 54-55, 177-180, 183-184,
    190-191, 194-197, 212, 236, 244,
    248, 273, 280, 313
General Assembly resolution 1995
    (XIX), 44-48, 176, 179-180, 219,
    225, 237, 239, 319
Geneva Conference, 28-64
    composition of standing committee,
        41-42, 50
    decision to convene, 18-19
    developed countries, 49
    developing countries, 48-52
    institutional matters, 15-21, 29, 35-
        48, 175, 190
    Final Act, 28-29, 34-35, 43, 107, 219
    legacies, 59
    Prebisch's leadership, 20n, 43
    Preparatory Committee, 20
    problems leading to, 5-14
    situation prior to, 21
    substantive results, 29-35
    voting controversy, 52-57
global strategy, 254
Golt, S., 298n
Goodwin, G. L., 30n
Gosovic, B., 326n
Gregg, R. W., 178n, 241n
gross national product at market prices,
    116n
Group of 75, 18-19, 40, 49n
    conciliation, 43
    incipient solidarity, 49
    radical wing, 42-43, 50-51
    splitting up, 51
    See also developing countries, Group
        of 77
Group of 77, X, 48, 52-57, 269, 271-
    293, 316-330
    A list, 46n, 269
    African Associates, 79, 285
    African group, 274
    African states, 79, 83, 88n, 160, 281

Asian group, 274, 287n
bargaining tactics, 19, 81-83, 130,
    239, 241, 262, 290, 316-323, 328-
    330
bargaining power, 300, 319, 322
bilateral advantages, 285
class struggle, 50
cleavages and conflicts, 70, 82, 110-
    111, 159, 279-286, 287n, 293
collective bargaining, 289
conciliatory approach, 196n, 290
consequences of non-group action in
    GATT, 322n
cross-regional alliance, 159
countervailing power, 321
decision-making, 110-111, 255-256,
    285-291
discipline, 202
divisive trends, 285
egalitarianism and pluralism, 278
equivalent advantages, 288
flexibility, 130, 290, 330
Group of 31, 273
inefficiency of in-group decision-
    making, 287
in other international organizations,
    322n
Joint Declaration of 1964, 52, 271
Latin American group, 160, 273-274,
    281, 287n
leadership, 272, 276-279
learning, 330
least developed (LDDCs), 159, 280,
    288
machinery, 275
maximum common denominator,
    289-290, 299
minimum common denominator, 289
New York-Geneva dichotomy, 272-
    273
over-stating the claim, 290
package deals, 288-289
parliamentary norms, 287
physiognomy, 272-276
radicals, 50-51, 280
solidarity, 49, 292
splitting the differences, 289
stratification, 281
trade-union, 322
UNCTAD secretariat, 275
unity, 82, 89, 158, 160, 271, 284,
    291-293
vulnerability, 285

See also decision-making, developing
countries, group system, LDDCs,
special preferences
group system in UNCTAD, 40, 269-
270, 289-291, 300, 324-328
contact groups, 327n
discipline, 325
disparity of bargaining power, 269
gentlemen's agreement, 270n
maximum common denominator demands, 81, 289-290, 293, 326
minimum common denominator offers, 299-301, 326, 328
negotiation, 269
New Delhi Conference, 326
rigidities, 300n, 325, 327
solidarity, 255n
See also B Group, D Group,
decision-making, Group of 77,
UNCTAD secretariat
Group of Ten, 133-134
Guevara, E. S., 28

Haas, E. B., 115n, 177n, 221n, 289n
Hadwen, J. G., 185n, 188n, 318n
Hakim, G., 272n, 278n
Havana Charter
Article XV, 65
Chapter VI, 10-11, 134
economic development, 8-10
weighted voting, 53n
Heath, E., 50n
Horowitz proposal, 122n
Hovet, T., jr., 301n, 324n

Iklé, F. C., 320n
implementation, 64, 172, 219-225, 236,
263, 327
DAC procedure, 221
formalized reporting, 220, 224-225
GATT Part IV reporting, 220-221
implementation crisis, 220, 263
implementing function, 236
obstacles, 223-224
report by UNCTAD secretariat, 221
second Development Decade, 224,
225n
unofficial sources of information,
222
See also negotiations, UNCTAD
import substitution, 7
institutionalization, 176
Inter-Agency Consultative Board

(IACB), 242
Inter-American Committee on the
Alliance for Progress (CIAP), 71n
Intergovernmental Group on Trade
Expansion, Economic Cooperation
and Regional Integration among De-
veloping Countries, 157
Intergovernmental Group on the
Transfer of Technology, 258, 270n
Interim Commission of ITO (ICITO),
11, 198
Interim Coordinating Committee for
International Commodity Agree-
ments (ICCICA), 14, 206n, 207n
International Bank for Reconstruction
and Development (IBRD), 3, 9, 103,
113, 114n, 122, 128-132, 136, 230-
231
International Coffee Council (ICC),
229
International Development Agency
(IDA), 14, 122, 125n, 131
International Grains Arrangement,
103n
International Maritime Committee,
248
International Maritime Consultative
Organization (IMCO), 248
International Monetary Fund (IMF),
3, 9, 14, 32, 53n, 114n, 127, 133
IMF/IBRD study, 106
integration tranche, 157
multilateral payments arrangements
of developing countries, 157
buffer stock financing, 106-107
international monetary reform, 133-
136
See also compensatory financing
international monetary reform, 133-136
opposition to discussion, 133-134
link, 134-135
Special Drawing Rights, 134-135
international shipping legislation, 151n,
247-251
International Sugar Council, 99
International Trade Center (ITC)
see GATT, technical assistance,
UNCTAD-GATT relations
International Trade Organization
(ITO), 8-10, 21, 35-36, 41, 46n, 49,
53, 261
See also Havana Charter
International Wheat Council, 230n

344

Jacobson, H. K., 277n
Jeanneney Report, 25n
Johnson, H. G., 9n, 12n, 25n, 29n, 31n, 66n, 133n
Jolles, P., 43n, 298n

Kaufmann, J., 185n, 188n, 200n, 219n, 226n, 307n, 311n, 318n, 324n, 330n
Kennedy Round, 23, 66, 216, 321-322
  evaluation of, 205
  package, 103
  unsatisfactory for developing countries, 71, 205n
Kojève, A., 298n
Kotschnig, W. M., 3n, 180n, 198n, 226n, 190n
Krishnamurti, R., 47n, 309n

La Charrière, G. de, 29n
Lacarte, J. A., 43n
Lagos Convention, 75n
Lall, K. B., 278n, 310n, 320n
Latin American countries, 16-17, 39
Latin American Free Trade Association (LAFTA), 14, 68n, 203
learning process, 241, 330
least developed among developing countries (LDDCs), 68, 76-77, 79, 83, 158-164, 282-283
  African countries, 160, 161n
  Algiers Charter, 159-160
  Committee for Development Planning, 163
  hard-core, 163-164
  identification, 158, 163
  landlocking, 162
  Latin American countries, 159n, 160
  level-of-development index, 162n
  New Delhi Conference, 161
  second Development Decade, 163
  UNCTAD secretariat, 162
Linder, S. B., 22n
link, 134-136
  experts, 135
  second Development Decade, 136
  SDRs and development finance, 134-136
Little, I. M. D., 121n
Long Term Arrangement on Cotton Textiles, 74
Lusardi, R., 329n

Mahmood, A., 278n
Malinowski, W. R., 43n, 178, 308, 308n, 309
Mangone, G. J., 178n, 186n
manufactures and semi-manufactures
  definition, 82
market sharing, 109
Mates, L., 43n, 276n
maximum common denominator demands, 326
Meier, G. M., 6n
Meron, T., 186n, 188n
Millikan, M. F., 3n, 25n, 192n, 193n
minimum common denominator offers, 326
most favored nation (MFN) principle, 33, 66-67, 69, 89
  philosophical amendment, 78
multilateral interest equalization fund, 122-124

Narasimhan, C. V., 188n
Narasimhan, S., 114n
national income, 116, 117n
negotiations, 41, 46, 199-200, 206-209, 225-234, 236, 263, 265, 319-323
  B Group position, 225-226
  commodities, 206-207, 227-230
  consultations, 231, 237-238
  Convention on Transit Trade of Land-Locked Countries, 227n
  de facto, 227, 232
  nature of, 319-323
  New Delhi Conference, 226
  preferences, 80, 231-233, 265
  quid pro quo, 226
  role of UNCTAD, 227
  Special Committee on Preferences, 233
  sugar agreement, 228n, 265
  See also implementation, UNCTAD
Nelson, J. M., 297n
New Delhi Conference, 77, 80-83, 95, 98, 101, 104-105, 108-109, 117, 122, 126, 140, 144, 146, 155, 167-168, 226, 235, 238, 249, 254, 256, 261, 264, 278, 287n, 290, 299n, 316, 320, 323, 326-329
Niamey resolution, 35n, 49
nominal tariff, 67n
Nye, J. S., 297n, 307n

Office of Technical Cooperation, 243
official export credits, 124
Ohlin, G., 123n, 225n
Organization of African Unity (OAU), 274
Organization for Economic Cooperation and Development (OECD), 3, 36-37, 72, 78-80, 87, 91, 149, 225n, 276, 293-295, 298, 301, 324
Organization for European Economic Cooperation (OEEC), 3
Organization of Petroleum Producers (OPEC), 315n, 323n
Organization for Trade Cooperation (OTC), 11, 15, 53

Pearson Commission, 119n, 120, 124n, 127n, 171n
Pérez-Guerrero, M., 314-315
Pincus, J., 3n, 6n, 7n, 29n, 30n, 31n, 32n, 66n, 84n
Piñera, J., 272n
Pollock, D. H., 171n
Populorum Progressio, 26
Prebisch, R., IX, 36, 43n, 187n, 188n, 212, 217, 226, 235n, 238n, 245, 263, 304-314, 321, 330-331
  Cairo Conference, 17n
  convergent measures, 224
  Executive Secretary ECLA, 5
  leadership role, 307, 309, 314n, 331n
  mediator, 43, 160n, 227n, 330-331
  militant official, 330
  Prebisch paper, 51
  proposal on joint UNCTAD/GATT Trade Center, 210
  retirement, 265, 314
  second Development Decade, 191-193, 195n
  Secretary-General of Geneva Conference, 20
  Secretary-General of UNCTAD, 48
  sugar negotiations, 99
  and UNCTAD secretariat, 304-315
  and UN Secretary General, 182, 182n
  view of duplication with GATT, 213
  writings, 272
  Wyndham White comparison, 203, 309, 330-331
  See also UNCTAD secretariat
preferences, 33, 65-92, 231-233
  ab initio exclusion, 80n

African countries, 79, 83, 88n
Algiers Charter, 77, 79
  comparison with OECD report, 79
beneficiaries, 77
between Geneva and New Delhi, 69-80
duration, 80, 89
equitable burden sharing, 77-78
equivalent advantages, 75
escape clause, 73, 78
Latin American countries, 70, 79, 81
LDDCs, 68, 90, 161n
main issues, 72
market disruption, 74n
New Delhi Conference, 77, 80-83
New Delhi aftermath, 83-92
OECD platform, 77-78
offers by donors, 89
product coverage, 67, 72-73, 82, 84, 87-89, 329n
reverse preferences, 76, 78, 81, 89, 222n
review and implementation, 91, 232-233
rules of origin, 86, 90
safeguards, 73, 85, 89
second Development Decade, 87
selective preferences, 66
self-election method, 80, 89
socialist countries, 90
Special Committee on Preferences, 83, 91, 232-233
special preferences, 71, 74, 79, 81
take-it-or-leave-it, 87n
tariff quota, 74, 78
See also special preferences
Preparatory Committee for the Second Development Decade, 194-197
problem recognition, 64, 151, 292, 298
processed and semi-processed agricultural products (1-24 BTN), 82
public opinion, 263n

reciprocity, see decision-making, GATT, negotiations
recommendation, 64, 292
Reed, M., 298n
Reston, J., 70n
reverse preferences, 76, 78, 81, 89, 222n
Robertson, C. O., 5n, 14n, 18n, 20n, 51n, 66n
Rossen, S., 315

346

Royer, J., 200n
Rubin, S. J., 115n, 221n
rule-making, 64, 327

Santa-Cruz, H., 278n
Schiavo-Campo, S., 132n
Schonfeld, A., 186n, 323n
Sharp, W., 179n, 330n
shipping, 34-35, 138-152, 247-251
  assistance to, 147-149
  boycott of UNCTAD probe, 145
  code of good conduct for shipowners,
    151
  common measure of understanding,
    34
  conference practices, 139, 142, 145,
    149, 151n
  consultation machinery, 34, 139-142
  Consultative Shipping Group, 151n
  developing countries' merchant
    fleets, 34, 139, 146
  freight rates, 139, 141-144
  institutional obstructionism, 151
  international shipping legislation,
    150-151, 247-251
  OECD understanding on export
    credits for ships, 147-148
  route studies, 143
  ship finance, 147
  terms of shipping, 148
Silveira, A., 278n, 287n, 328n
Singer, H., 24n
Singer, J. D., 183n
Siotis, J., 181n, 260n, 272n
socialist countries, 5, 15, 17, 40, 44,
  164-170, 195, 215, 261, 301-303
  Algiers Charter, 166-167
  birth of UNCTAD, 169
  financing targets, 165
  Geneva Conference, 164
  ITO, 35
  marginal actors, 165
  New Delhi Conference, 167-168
  preferences, 90-91
  in UNCTAD, 169
  See also D Group, East-West trade
Solomon, A. M., 71n
Special Committee on Latin American
  Coordination (CECLA), 273
Special Committee on Preferences, 83,
  91, 232-233
Special Drawing Rights (SDRs), 134
special preferences, 30, 66n, 67, 70-71,

74-76, 78, 88, 98, 110-111, 285n,
  289
  See also reverse preferences
Special UN Fund for Economic Development (SUNFED), 4, 56
Stanovnik, J., 278n, 309n, 310n, 321n
Stevenson, A., 18n
sugar, 99-101
  access guarantees, 100
  hardship fund, 100
supplementary financing, 32, 128-133,
  231
  Algiers Charter, 130
  alternative scheme, 128-129
  basic development finance, 131
  comparison with compensatory
    financing, 128n
  compromise, 130
  cost, 128
  Group of 77 flexibility, 130
  IBRD, 128-132, 231
  Intergovernmental Group of Supple-
    mentary Financing, 128, 130
  New Delhi Conference, 129
synthetics and substitutes, 111-113

task expansion, 240-262
  causes, 241
  cross-fertilization, 251
  definition, 240
  East-West trade, 259-262
  in GATT, 198-203
  indirect, 251
  international shipping legislation,
    247-251
  pattern of, 258-259
  significance of, 262
  technical assistance, 241-247
  trade expansion among developing
    countries, 251-254
  transfer of technology, 255-259
technical assistance, 241-247
  agency salesmanship, 246
  Chapter V UN budget, 245-247
  GATT, 209-213
  operational role, 236, 241-247, 264
  participating agency in UNDP, 236,
    238, 242-245
  technical assistance projects, 246
  See also International Trade Center,
    UNCTAD-GATT relations
Teheran resolution, 35n, 49
terms of aid, 34, 121-125

Algiers Charter, 122
concessional element, 123n
DAC targets, 122-123
debt burden, 8n, 121
Geneva Conference, 121
New Delhi Conference, 123
terms of trade, 6
Thomas, A., 307n
Townley, R., 53n, 177n
Trade and Development Board
composition, 46n
decisions, 47
functions, 46
trade and development link, 5, 14-15
trade expansion, economic cooperation
and regional integration among developing countries, 153-158, 251-254
Algiers Charter, 155
intergovernmental group, 253
inter-regional cooperation, 156
multilateral payments arrangements,
156n, 157
New Delhi Conference, 155-156, 252
special difficulties, 153-154
UNCTAD secretariat research, 154
transfer of technology, 202n, 255-259
B Group, 258
Intergovernmental Group on the
Transfer of Technology, 258
UNCTAD role, 256-258

U Thant, 20, 182, 188, 188n, 314
United Nations
activities on trade and development,
5, 15-21
Charter, 3-4, 41, 44, 179
Commission on International Com-
modity Trade (CICT), 14, 38,
206n, 207n
Commission on International Trade
Law (UNCITRAL), 150, 248, 250
Development Program (UNDP),
209-211, 242-247
export promotion program, 210
Industrial Development Organization
(UNIDO), 182, 242-247
membership transformation, 16
Regular Program of Technical Co-
operation, 245
Secretariat, 40
United Nations Conference on Trade
and Development (UNCTAD), X, 44
achievements, 171

aims, X, 63
birth, 35-48
budget, 183-185
Conference functions of, 44
coordinating powers, 46, 194
and ECOSOC, 44, 177, 179-180,
192
evolution, 265
forum, 214, 234
and General Assembly, 177
historical background, 3-28
independence, 264
influence on other organizations,
114n, 172
institutional growth, 175-266
institutionalization, 176, 239
location of headquarters, 180
machinery sketch of, 44-48
machinery streamlining of, 234-239
membership, 44
milestones in history, 264-265
and multilateral financial institutions,
137
role, 137, 199-200, 218-239, 247,
252
in reform of international monetary system, 134
in second Development Decade,
189-197
secretariat, 48, 182, 304-315
within United Nations, 177-197
viewed with scepticism, 263
See also implementation, negotiation,
task expansion, technical assistance
UNCTAD-GATT relations, 189, 198-
217, 220, 244-246, 305n, 306n, 311-
312, 330-331
committee on coexistence, 214
developing countries, 201-203
differences, 199
duality, 216
duplication, 199, 206-213
emulating each other, 216
evolution of relations, 213-217
GATT Trade Negotiations Committee (TNC), 207-208, 252n
International Trade Center (ITC),
204n, 210-217, 241-247, 264
Kennedy Round evaluation, 205
preferences, 212-213, 232n
secretariats' relations, 203-205, 213-
217

technical assistance and export promotion, 209-213
trade expansion among developing countries, 207
wheat, 206
See also, GATT, Prebisch, Wyndham White
UNCTAD secretariat, 180-185, 237-239, 246, 253n, 254, 255n, 263n, 275, 288, 304-315, 330-331
B Group, 310-312
broker, 314
budget, 183-185
deputy to Secretary-General, 308, 310
Group of 77, 275, 288, 311
LDDCs, 161-162
leadership, 307
operational autonomy, 180-185
partiality, 310
Prebisch organizer and administrator, 308
role in negotiations, 237, 330
Secretary-General, 238, 253-254
servicing meetings, 312
shortcomings, 313n
staffing, 304-305
studies and research, 151-154, 313-314

task expansion, 254
See also Prebisch
Unwin, K., 43n

vertical preferences, see reverse preferences, special preferences
Viaud, M., 43n, 298n
Viteri, J., 309n
voting, 41-43, 50, 52-57, 134, 143, 149, 193, 195n, 196, 205n, 229, 249n, 257, 316-323
dual voting, 54-55
Geneva Conference, 41-43, 47, 50, 52-57
Group of 77, 317
Havana Charter, 53n

Walters, R. S., 171n
Weintraub, S., 29n, 66n, 71n, 111n
wheat, 103-104, 206-207, 229-230
Wilcox, C., 10n, 53n
Wyndham White, E., 22, 58n, 199n, 200n, 203, 204n, 207n, 208-210, 212n, 213, 309

Yaoundé Convention, 70, 75n, 83n, 110n

zonk, 13